MW00576227

Gospel-Centered Hermeneutics

FOUNDATIONS AND PRINCIPLES OF EVANGELICAL BIBLICAL INTERPRETATION

Graeme Goldsworthy

An imprint of InterVarsity Press
Downers Grove, Illinois

InterVarsity Press
P.O. Box 1400, Downers Grove, IL 60515-1426
World Wide Web: www.ivpress.com
E-mail: email@ivpress.com

Published in the United States of America by InterVarsity Press, Downers Grove, Illinois, with permission from Inter-Varsity Press, Nottingham, U.K.

InterVarsity Press® is the book-publishing division of InterVarsity Christian Fellowship/USA®, a movement of students and faculty active on campus at hundreds of universities, colleges and schools of nursing in the United States of America, and a member movement of the International Fellowship of Evangelical Students. For information about local and regional activities, write Public Relations Dept., InterVarsity Christian Fellowship/USA, 6400 Schroeder Rd., P.O. Box 7895, Madison, WI 53707-7895, or visit the IVCF website at <www.intervarsity.org>.

Design: Cindy Kiple
Images: Chris Thomaidis/Getty Images

ISBN 978-0-8308-3869-1

Printed in the United States of America ∞

InterVarsity Press is committed to protecting the environment and to the responsible use of natural resources. As a member of Green Press Initiative we use recycled paper whenever possible. To learn more about the Green Press Initiative, visit <www.greenpressinitiative.org>.

Library of Congress Cataloging-in-Publication Data

Goldsworthy, Graeme.
Gospel-centered hermeneutics: foundations and principles of evangelical biblical interpretation/Graeme Goldsworthy.
p. cm.
Includes bibliographical references (p.).
ISBN 978-0-8308-2839-5 (cloth: alk. paper)
1. Bible—Hermeneutics. 2. Evangelicalism I. Title.
BS476.G655 2007
220.601—dc22

2006101623

P 21 20 19 18 17 16 15 14 13 12 11 10 9 8 7 6 5 4 3 2
Y 28 27 26 25 24 23 22 21 20 19 18 17 16 15 14 13

In memoriam
Robert Alan Cole
1923–2003

CONTENTS

ABBREVIATIONS

BBR	*Bulletin for Biblical Research*
CBQ	*Catholic Biblical Quarterly*
CJ	*Concordia Journal*
CSR	*Christian Scholars Review*
EQ	*Evangelical Quarterly*
ERT	*Evangelical Review of Theology*
ESV	English Standard Version
JETS	*Journal of the Evangelical Theological Society*
JSNT	*Journal for the Study of the New Testament*
KJV	King James Version
NDBT	*New Dictionary of Biblical Theology*
NEB	New English Bible
NIV	New International Version
NKJV	New King James Version
NRSV	New Revised Standard Version
RTR	*Reformed Theological Review*
SBET	*Scottish Bulletin of Evangelical Theology*
SHS	Scripture and Hermeneutics Series
SJT	*Scottish Journal of Theology*
TB	*Tyndale Bulletin*
TJ	*Trinity Journal*
TT	*Theology Today*
WTJ	*Westminster Theological Journal*

PREFACE

Since 1995 I have taught a fourth-year BD elective in hermeneutics at Moore Theological College. After a couple of years the college agreed to my request to a change in the course from a general study of hermeneutics to one designated as 'Principles of Evangelical Hermeneutics'. My main motivation in seeking the change was a pastoral one. I was concerned that the possession of the Bible by the people of God, the so-called people in the pews, was being eroded by the tremendous upsurge of interest in hermeneutics at the academic level. Not that the subject itself is illegitimate, but the regressive nature of much modern hermeneutics under the influence of the latest philosophical moods has contributed to the eclipse of the gospel in biblical interpretation. Sooner or later, the concerns of academia begin to affect the pastors and teachers exposed to them during their time as students, and are passed on through sermons and Christian education to the laity.

Although I am now retired from full-time teaching and ministry, I am glad to comply with the request of Moore College to continue in a visiting capacity to teach the same course. Because I now live some distance from Sydney, the course is taught by intensive mode in two blocks, about six weeks apart. This necessitated the preparation of a comprehensive student reader for the class of 2000, which I have revised heavily in subsequent years. After ten years of development the course has taken on some semblance of shape, and I submitted the class reader (revised edition) to Dr Philip Duce, Theological Books Editor at Inter-Varsity Press (UK). He has encouraged me to work on revising and reworking the reader again, this time into a publishable form. I am grateful to Dr Duce for his valuable advice and encouragement, and to IVP for being willing to publish this work. Given the broad scope of hermeneutics, it is with some trepidation that I have undertaken to prepare this book for publication. If the endeavour succeeds in encouraging pastors, preachers and Bible teachers to press on with confidence in the supreme authority of the Bible as the word of God, it will not have been in vain. Writing this book would not have been possible without the opportunity to teach hermeneutics at Moore College, the encouragement of colleagues on the faculty, and the contributions of my students in class discussions and essays. Nor would it have been possible without the patient support of my wife Miriam, who has continued to encourage me while quietly enduring my long hours in the study and my absences in Sydney.

I dedicate this book to the memory of Alan Cole (1923–2003). To me he epitomized everything that I believe hermeneutics to be about: making Christ known. He was to me a teacher, mentor and friend. His brilliance as a biblical scholar and linguist was matched by his deep devotion to Christ and the gospel. He left his native Ireland and ministered in the UK, in Australia, and in missionary service in several locations in South-east Asia. He was a caring pastor, and a godly man of prayer. And he constantly sparkled with irrepressible Irish humour.

Graeme Goldsworthy

INTRODUCTION: CAN HERMENEUTICS BE SAVED?

In this book I aim to achieve three main goals. In Part I, I consider the foundations and presuppositions of evangelical belief, particularly as it applies to the interpretation of the biblical text. In Part II, I take a selective overview of important hermeneutical developments from the sub-apostolic age to the present. This is not intended to be a comprehensive history of hermeneutics or an exhaustive exposition of hermeneutical theory, but rather a means of identifying some key influences that are alien to the gospel in hermeneutic thought. In Part III, my goal is to evaluate ways and means of reconstructing a truly evangelical, gospel-centred hermeneutics. This section will build on the foundations that I seek to lay in Part I. It will do this with an eye to the kind of alien influences on hermeneutics exposed in Part II. If there is a fourth main aim, it is this: I want to commend the much neglected role of biblical theology in hermeneutical practice. To that end I try to show how the method of biblical theology provides a basic tool in any biblical research, and how it functions as the matrix for understanding the relatedness of the whole Bible to the person and work of Jesus. In all these aims, the pastoral concerns remain uppermost.

For the ordinary reader who has some acquaintance with the seemingly endless production of books and articles on hermeneutics, the answer to the question in the title above may well be a sceptical shake of the head. The evangelical Christian in particular could be excused for thinking that theorizing about hermeneutics has long since lost its way. After all, well before names like Schleiermacher, Bultmann, Troeltsch, Ricoeur, Gadamer and Derrida were heard of, Christians had read the Bible with real comprehension, if not with impeccable understanding, and had lived, as they continue to live, lives of dedicated service to Christ and his gospel. For evangelicals, the main purpose of reading and understanding the Bible is to know God and his will for our lives. We believe that only as we know God can we really know ourselves and the true meaning of life. Evangelical Christianity stands firmly on the conviction that we know God through his Son, Jesus Christ, whom, in turn, we know only through Scripture. Our knowing God centres on Jesus, the Word of God who has come in the flesh, and on the Bible, the Spirit-inspired, written word of God that is the true testimony to this incarnate Word. God has spoken his word into a world darkened by human rebellion against him. It is a word of grace as well as a word of judgment. If to know God is to know him through his Word/word, then we must read, hear and understand that word in the Bible. Faith must rest on the reality of God's true word and, thus, on a reliable understanding of that word.

This is where the study of hermeneutics comes in. From an evangelical point of view, the goal of hermeneutics is, or should be, a right understanding of what God says to us in his word. We want preachers and teachers to become better at communicating the word of God, and Christians to live more godly lives. I would add that any sense of individual understanding must go hand in hand with the understanding of our Christian existence within the church as a communal experience. What God says to me individually and what he says to all his people may at times be distinguishable, but they are never separable. Hermeneutics focuses on the gospel as it has its outworking in the realm of our understanding of the Scriptures. Thus it is an aspect of our ongoing sanctification. We need to be reminded of this central fact in view of the proliferation over the last few decades of publications relating to hermeneutics. But if hermeneutics is an aspect of our sanctification, it must rest on and be driven by our justification in Christ. Theologically, the priority of justification to sanctification means that the action of God in Christ, the grace of God acting *for* us, is prior to, and is the source of, the action of God *in* us. In simple terms this means that God puts us into a right relationship with himself as the prerequisite for the ongoing change in our lives. This theological perspective also applies to hermeneutics. Our ability to interpret Scripture must be saved, justified and sanctified through the gospel.

One could easily gain the impression from the recent developments in hermeneutical research and discussion that, once again, it is only the skilled specialist who can venture into the minefields of the biblical text to propose an interpretation of its meaning. Yet it is one of the givens of Protestant and Reformed Christianity – of evangelicalism – that the Scriptures are essentially clear. This means that, despite the many and varied interpretations of certain details, and despite the many difficult texts, the humble believer will not be led astray in the reading of the Bible's essential message, and spiritual sustenance will be delivered to young and old, to the uneducated and the sophisticated alike.

All of our cognition involves interpretation of what is seen, heard or felt. In reading the Bible we are interpreting the words and sentences according to our whole life's experience of learning what such words can mean and how their meaning can be altered or qualified by the wider context of sentence, paragraph and corpus in which they occur. The complexity of this process is usually in the background of our thinking and almost totally unreflected upon by most readers or hearers. Only when an apparent obscurity or a clash of ideas emerges does the concept of *interpretation* surface. Thus, as Nicholas Wolterstorff reminds us, we can distinguish interpretation, which we all practise all the time, from the theory of interpretation, or hermeneutical theory.[1] However, for the purposes of this study I shall use the term *hermeneutics* to cover both the theory and practice of interpretation.

Hermeneutics, then, is an aspect of the renewing of the mind or its sanctification. Paul refers to it in Romans 12:1–2 thus:

> I appeal to you therefore, brothers, by the mercies of God, to present your bodies as a living sacrifice, holy and acceptable to God, which is your spiritual worship. Do not be conformed to this world, but be transformed by the renewal of your mind, that by testing you may discern what is the will of God, what is good and acceptable and perfect.

Here he ties Christian transformation to the radical change in mindset that the Christian undergoes. Evangelical hermeneutics will often overlap with non-evangelical, even non-Christian, hermeneutics in something the same way that evangelical ethics, as an aspect of our sanctification, overlaps with general ethics. There is a theological reason for this that we refer to as *common grace*. In other words, non-Christians have an understanding of meaning and a sense of right and wrong which is the result of the goodness of God and of

1. Nicholas Wolterstorff, 'The Importance of Hermeneutics for a Christian Worldview', in Roger Lundin (ed.), *Disciplining Hermeneutics* (Grand Rapids: Eerdmans; Leicester: Apollos, 1997), p. 27.

being created in his image. The fact that the non-Christian repudiates such a notion is not the point. But evangelical ethics and hermeneutics need careful delineation so that we do not allow the common ground we share with the non-Christian to lure us into the mindset of the world. Paul urges believers not to be conformed to the world, but to be transformed by the renewing of their minds. To that end I endeavour in this study to tease out the implications of evangelical faith for the renewal of our minds and their application to the interpretation of the Bible. At the same time I try to identify those alien elements that occur in hermeneutical theory to which we should not conform.

If hermeneutics is an aspect of our minds being conformed to the mind of Christ, it must be engaged through the gospel. Any aspect of sanctification, or growth in holiness, is clouded by our ongoing sinfulness and ignorance of the truth, yet we remain secure in the knowledge of our free justification on the grounds of Christ's righteousness for us. This justification does not, as it is sometimes represented, relieve us of the motive or responsibility to strive for holiness. Indeed, our free justification provides the only legitimate grounds and the most powerful motive for such striving. Likewise, the gospel presents us with the righteousness of Jesus Christ, who, in his earthly life, perfectly interpreted the word of his Father. In so doing he justified the fallible attempts of his people to interpret the word. The justification of our hermeneutics by the perfect hermeneutics of Christ is the motivation for us to strive for hermeneutical sanctification. We are not saved by good works, but we will not be saved without good works (Eph. 2:8–10). In the same way, we are not saved by the purity of our hermeneutics, but we will not be saved without some measure of hermeneutical sanctification taking place. The ordinary Bible-reader may be completely unreflective about this, but every effort to understand the Bible aright is a striving for hermeneutical sanctification. At the grass roots, hermeneutical conversion takes place when one becomes a believer. The Bible will never be the same again to us because we, as believers, have made a quantum shift from unbelief and rejection of God's word to faith and trust in that word, and submission to it. There are clear biblical grounds for the importance of exposing false teachings and behaviour patterns that are inconsistent with the gospel. That fact alone is reason enough for devoting the second section of this book to the study of the ways in which the gospel has been eclipsed in biblical interpretation.

Nevertheless, my main concern is to set out in a positive fashion the foundational principles of evangelical Christianity, and the outworking of these in the matter of biblical interpretation. The need to specify a gospel-centred, evangelical approach to hermeneutics arises from the distinctive beliefs of evangelicalism. As difficult as these may be to pin down, we must endeavour to understand them and to test them for their consistency and validity. If Christ truly is our Lord and Saviour, then he is the Lord and Saviour of our hermeneutics.

PART I

EVANGELICAL PROLEGOMENA TO HERMENEUTICS

Introduction

The purpose of Part I is to consider the grounds and basic assumptions, along with their justification, of evangelical belief and biblical interpretation. Evangelicals have always believed that, although there is great diversity in the Bible, there is a discernible and essential unity to its message. At the heart of evangelicalism is the belief that the gospel of Jesus Christ is the definitive revelation to mankind of God's mind, and the defining fact of human history. The person and work of Jesus provide us with a single focal point for understanding reality. The Bible also makes it clear that we are either for Jesus or against him, we either have the Son or we do not. In other words, there is no neutral position, no objective starting point, which is common to believers and unbelievers, for judging what is ultimately real and what is true.

Neutrality and complete objectivity are the presuppositional myths of the modern secular outlook, and they are also the assumptions, sometimes unexamined, of many Christian thinkers. On occasions we have to struggle to discern the basic assumptions of someone's position. I prefer to declare my position from the outset, and then to give my reasons for it. Broadly speaking, I write from the perspective of the orthodox Christian theism that undergirds what we understand by the labels of evangelical and Reformed Christianity. In Part I of this study I will examine the foundations of evangelical faith as the basis of our reconstructive endeavours in Part III. These will also provide the norms that bring alien philosophical influences under scrutiny in Part II. This requires some definition of the terms 'evangelical' and 'gospel'. We will be concerned with authority and meaning as we enquire into the function of the Bible in God's outworking of our salvation. We either stand by the supreme authority of God, or we adopt the assumption of human autonomy. The one is the classical position of Christian theism,[1] and the other is the position of humanistic rationalism[2] in all its varieties. That is why chapters 1–4 will deal with such things as the basic and doctrinal presuppositions of the evangelical position. In Part III we will apply these to the practicalities of interpretation.

If our presuppositions are unsustainable, then our whole system fails. Evangelical presuppositions must be shown to be preferable to those of modern philosophical hermeneutics. The question of the contribution of philosophical hermeneutics cannot be ignored, but neither can the implications of Christian theism for a biblical philosophy. If the Bible does indeed provide the data for assessing the nature of reality (metaphysics), the validity of knowledge (epistemology), and the criteria of right and wrong behaviour (ethics), then it contains the basis of a Christian philosophy. It also means that the principles of hermeneutics are to be found within the Scriptures themselves. In Part I, then, we examine the presuppositions and main tenets of Christian theism as the basis for an evangelical approach to hermeneutics.

---

1. Theism is the name given to those systems of belief that centre on a supreme deity, god or God. Christian theism is the specific form of this that centres on the one and only supremely authoritative God, who is the God and Father of our Lord Jesus Christ.
2. I use the term 'rationalism' here loosely to describe non-theistic thinking that places autonomous human reason above any idea of divine revelation. A more accurate philosophical account of such thought would at least include empiricism.

1. THE NECESSITY FOR HERMENEUTICS

Much ado about nothing?

> 'Surely it's a matter of common sense!'
>
> 'I've been reading the Bible for thirty-five years, and I don't need a lot of intellectual theories to tell me what it's all about.'
>
> 'The Bible is quite clear and understandable. And while we're talking about it, what do you think Isaiah meant in this difficult passage?'

We have all heard similar expressions from time to time. On the one hand, the Bible is read by millions and largely understood. On the other hand, any thoughtful reader knows there are passages that are less clear than others. We also know that Christians who express the same essential understanding of the inspiration and authority of Scripture can disagree about important issues such as the interpretation of prophecy, the meaning of baptism, the normative nature of Acts 2, or the structure of the second coming of Christ. Of course, when a common enemy such as secularism or liberalism threatens evangelicals, then there is neither Baptist nor paedobaptist, amillennialist nor premillennialist, dispensationalist nor covenant theologian, Anglican nor Presbyterian, for all are one in Christ! Christians with a diversity of views will come together under the common umbrella of evangelicalism if they think they have sufficient reason. In less challenging times, however, differences can become matters of potential and real division, and even hostility, being expressed under that broad evangelical umbrella. Suddenly the clarity of Scripture seems to mean, 'It's quite clear to me: why can't you see what is obvious?' Throwing proof texts at each other like so many grenades only results in unseemly shrapnel and much suspicion and hurt. But if I as an Anglican am to understand my Baptist brethren; if I as a Calvinist am to understand my Arminian brethren; if I as an amillennialist am to understand my premillennialist brethren; and if they are to understand me, then we must try to understand each other's starting points and theological assumptions. This is where hermeneutics should play an important part. Even more basic is the desire of all of us simply to know and understand what God says to us in his word. We are concerned to be Christians in an alienated world, and we desire to see Christ glorified in this world. We want to hear and know God through his word.

Hermeneutics as a recognized discipline originally was mainly concerned to deal with problem texts in the Bible. The ordinary reader can easily skate over difficult readings with perhaps the intention to come back another time to try to figure them out. But what, after all, *is* a problem text? We conclude there is a problem when we cannot make sense of a passage. Mostly we recognize that problems arise because we, the readers, lack understanding of the theological, historical or cultural context of particular texts. Occasionally we may discover that there are real textual or linguistic problems. These show up where the Bible translators have provided their considered rendition while adding marginal notes such as 'Hebrew uncertain'. But otherwise, we tend to regard the problem as being in the readers rather than inherent in the text. When we differ from other evangelicals on doctrinal matters, our inclination is to see the problem as lying in those who differ from us about something we regard as clear. Our confidence in the overall clarity of Scripture remains unshaken.

What is/are hermeneutics?

Hermeneutics is about communication, meaning and understanding. 'Hermeneutics', according to the *Concise Oxford Dictionary*, is a plural noun. Common usage applies the plural word to the process of interpretation. So we will frequently use 'hermeneutics' as meaning the formal (academic) discipline, and treat it as a singular noun with a singular verb. Definitions of hermeneutics that are found in the recent literature include the following:

> The study of the locus of meaning and the principles of interpretation.[1]
>
> The science of reflecting on how a word or an event in the past time and culture may be understood and become existentially meaningful in our present situation.[2]
>
> The task of finding out the meaning of a statement for the author and for the first hearers or readers, and thereupon to transmit that meaning to modern readers.[3]
>
> Defining the rules one uses when seeking out the meaning of Scripture.[4]

Other authors imply the definition in their description of the goal or problems of hermeneutics, for example:

> The goal of biblical hermeneutics is to bring about an active and meaningful engagement between the interpreter and text, in such a way that the interpreter's own horizon is re-shaped and enlarged.[5]
>
> The goal of interpretation . . . is 'to know the Author's/author's intended meaning as it is expressed in the text'.[6]
>
> The central problem of biblical hermeneutics [is] 'How can the human word of a time long since vanished be understood as God's word to the present?'[7]

These are fairly typical definitions, and it can be seen that simply to refer to interpretation is to raise a number of questions. These definitions are drawn from authors of differing theological stances, a fact that becomes more obvious when we investigate further the way these definitions are followed through. The reason for such differences is that the seemingly innocuous definitions carry a great variety of presuppositional baggage. Since we are dealing with the written documents of the Bible, different assumptions can be made about how meaning is related to the documents themselves. The definitions vary in their focus on the author/s, the text and the readers. Each of these dimensions will need some clarification if we are to make sense of the task.

---

1. W. Randolph Tate, *Biblical Interpretation* (Peabody: Hendrickson, 1991), p. xv.
2. Carl Braaten, *History and Hermeneutics* (Philadelphia: Fortress, 1966), p. 131.
3. A. B. Mickelsen, *Interpreting the Bible* (Grand Rapids: Eerdmans, 1963), p. 5.
4. Donald McKim (ed.), *A Guide to Contemporary Hermeneutics* (Grand Rapids: Eerdmans, 1986), p. xiii.
5. Anthony Thiselton, *The Two Horizons* (Exeter: Paternoster, 1980), p. xix.
6. Elliott E. Johnson, *Expository Hermeneutics: An Introduction* (Grand Rapids: Acadamie, 1990), p. 15.
7. A. Oepke, quoted in Gerhard Maier, *Biblical Hermeneutics*, trans. Robert Yarborough (Wheaton: Crossway, 1994), p. 19.

The necessity for hermeneutics

The 'ordinary, Bible-believing Christian' may well question the need for such an enquiry and discipline as hermeneutics. After all, does it not make a simple, straightforward matter of reading the Bible unnecessarily complicated? Protestantism has always held to the notion of the clarity of Scripture. The rejection of priestcraft, of a supreme ecclesiastical authority that displaced the Bible, was a mark of the Reformation for the ordinary Christian. The medieval church did not use the Bible in either the original or the vernacular languages, but had recourse mainly to the Latin version. Church authority had resisted translations into the common language so that the Scriptures were not accessible to any but the clergy, and not always to them. The Reformers worked with a view to every man and woman having direct access to the Scriptures. Yet anyone who has attempted the task of translation will know that it is not a simple and straightforward process.

It is not only the fact that the biblical texts were originally written in languages foreign to our own, and within cultural contexts very different from our own, that necessitates hermeneutics. Translation, reading and proclamation all include varying degrees of adaptation to the readers' and hearers' culture, a process we call contextualization.[8] Neither can be achieved without consideration of meaning. Translation involves recasting a text in a different language from its original. Contextualization involves the restating of the meaning of the text in a way that is understandable to the intended receivers. We also recognize that interpretation is not solely required by our remoteness from the time and culture of the texts. Cognition of words spoken to us by our immediate contemporaries requires some measure of interpretation. There is also the fact of our sinfulness and consequent inconsistency with our accepted principles of the inspiration and authority of the Bible as God's word written.

All human communication is done using symbols, either visual or auditory.[9] The question we face in the process of interpretation is what relationship the symbol has to its referent – that is, to the thing it symbolizes. For example, the same word-symbol may occur in two different languages and mean totally different things. Again, the same sentence in a range of different contexts may mean something different in each context. The same symbol, for example the

8. See ch. 18.
9. Communication can, of course, be tactile, such as in the use of Braille texts for the visually impaired. Touch can also be used to communicate in a multitude of other ways.

number 60 inside a red circle, on a sign by the roadside, can mean different things in different countries.[10] The context of a given word, sentence or paragraph may be so far removed from the world of the reader or hearer as to be open to misunderstanding or incomprehension. The function of hermeneutics could be stated as the attempt to bridge the gap between the text inside its world and the readers/hearers inside their world. We attempt this bridging because we are engaging in the quest for the application of the significance of the biblical text to ourselves in this twenty-first century.

As already noted, we take our stand on certain presuppositions or assumptions when we are involved in this process. A lot of confusion could be avoided if interpreters recognized and owned the assumptions they make in seeking the meaning of any act of communication. One key assumption that most Christians make about the Bible is that the meaning of the text has significance, not only for the original hearers or readers, but also for others, including us. Thus we recognize a process of moving from what it meant then to what it means now. This may be thought of as beginning with a process of exegesis of the text in order to understand what it originally meant. This is followed by relevant hermeneutical procedures to bridge the gap between the text and us. Finally, there is the application of this meaning to us and the relaying of it, perhaps across a further gap, to others.[11] In other words, the divine revelation of Scripture has validity for all time even if the significance of certain texts undergoes some kind of transformation. Thus, for example, the word of the Lord through Moses the prophet to the Israelites in the wilderness, about the ritual requirements of the service of the tabernacle, has meaning and significance for us, but it is not the same meaning and significance it had for the Israelites. The historical, geographical and theological contexts have all changed.

We acknowledge the hermeneutical task when reading the Bible. We are aware of at least some of the possibilities for the way words and language can be used. We recognize the language gap between the ancient writer and ourselves. We also have to account for the historical and cultural gaps between the ancient text and ourselves. With the Bible we also start with

---

10. Miles per hour in some and kilometres per hour in others.

11. This is the simple view I expressed in my earlier work, *Gospel and Kingdom: A Christian Interpretation of the Old Testament* (Exeter: Paternoster, 1981), p. 43. I still believe this to be fundamentally accurate, but I would want to add that there is more than a simple progression from one stage to the next. The bridge is always open to two-way traffic, as I hope to make clear in these introductory chapters.

certain assumptions about the ultimate responsibility for its authorship and its authority. While acknowledging the divine authorship, we also take account of the human authors and their languages. We recognize the difficulties of translating from Hebrew, Aramaic and Greek into our own language. We know that our language is constantly changing and that our contemporary English can be quite distant from older translations.[12] We might summarize some of the driving forces for a discipline of hermeneutics in terms of what separates the receiver of a communication from the message and the sender. Thus various kinds of gap exist between the text and us. These all relate to each other and often overlap quite a lot. They include the following.

The language gap

This suggests that the matter can be dealt with by the simple act of having specialists in the biblical languages and our own language to translate the text. We will consider some of the complications of translation in chapter 18. You need only think of the differences between various Bible translations into English to be able to anticipate some of the problems involved. At its base, this gap concerns the need to obtain an accurate translation from the Hebrew, Aramaic and Greek texts of the Bible into our own language. That is not as simple as it sounds, for there are many significant regional and national differences between English-speaking peoples of the world.[13]

The culture gap

This can involve a host of matters relating to the world of the Bible, and the many differences between it and our own world. An educated Westerner would presumably have only moderate difficulty in bridging such gaps,

---

12. For example, in 1960 one of the translators of the New English Bible expressed the opinion that there would need to be a new translation done about every ten years for the language of the NEB to keep pace with the changes in colloquial English as spoken in England.
13. As a student in Cambridge in 1960, I was tutored in Greek by Professor C. F. D. Moule. He was in the habit of comparing my bumbling translations of New Testament texts to 'what the New English Bible is going to say'. The NEB was at that time yet to be published and Professor Moule would refer to a bulky manuscript in his possession. On several occasions I expressed to him my incomprehension of the proposed NEB translation because of the differences between my own colloquial Australian English and the NEB's very colloquial British English.

particularly if there were background resources available. We can learn to appreciate and make allowances for such gaps that exist between Ancient Near Eastern culture and modern Western culture. Even children at Sunday school soon learn to recognize the basics of the culture in the biblical world. They expect differences in dress, food and methods of transport. They know that they are dealing with a pre-industrial age that has only the rudiments of technology. It is a world of swords, spears and arrows; a world devoid of public transport and hospitals; a world without explosives and computers. The cultures of the various world-views and religions of the biblical world are different from our modern culture. In short, it is a world that is vastly different from ours, and yet it is similar enough not to be totally alien.

The history gap

This relates very closely to the culture gap, but also includes the problem of understanding the events recorded in biblical narrative for their historical value. Since the significance of the Christian faith rests upon key events in history, we must be concerned to understand the kind of history writing of the biblical narratives and how they give a coherent account of these events.[14] Reconstructing the historical events and understanding how they fit into the larger picture of world history becomes important. The Bible places great importance on certain events that modern historians either discount or regard as unimportant.

The literature gap

As we are dealing with ancient documents, the question of how ancient authors wrote is a key matter for hermeneutics. This means that types, or genres, of literature, as well as the multitude of idioms and literary devices, will affect the way we interpret the literature. For example, it is obvious that the biblical historians did not set out only to report historical events in a clinical, factual way.[15] Like all historians, they were selective and presented a point of

---

14. For example, arguments will probably always continue, even between evangelical Christians, as to how the narratives in the early chapters of Genesis relate to what actually happened.

15. Even modern historians are selective, interpretative and at times argumentative. The most clinically objective chronicles, for example verbatim court or parliamentary transcripts, cannot reproduce body language or tone of voice, and tend to be devoid of colour and emotion.

view. Nor can we assume that chronological order is the only way a string of events can be recorded. Once we get into the realm of genre and literary device we can see how easy it is to misunderstand, and thus to misinterpret, a given text.

The textual gap

One area of scholastic endeavour that is foundational for hermeneutics is textual criticism. Because we do not possess any of the original biblical documents (autographs), we are thus reliant on the transmission of the text by handwritten texts until the invention of the printing press. Even the non-technically trained Bible reader will recognize this problem from the occasional footnotes that occur in most standard translations, which draw attention to textual variants or uncertainties of translation because of obscurities in the accepted text. Only those instructed in textual matters would appreciate the differences in the New Testament text behind the KJV (and NKJV) from the text used for many other standard versions.

The intended reader/hearer gap

Humanly speaking, we are not the intended readers or hearers of a biblical text. If God gave the law to Moses to relay to the Israelites in the wilderness, in what sense is he giving that law to us today? And in what sense was he giving it to later generations of Israelites? If a Hebrew prophet utters an oracle specifically aimed at either Judah or Israel, what can such an oracle say to us? If Paul addresses a synagogue in Asia Minor, or writes a letter to Christians in the ancient city of Corinth, in what sense is he addressing us? In dealing with this as an aspect of the history gap, we must also take account of the continuing relevance of the Bible to us as the word of God. God is lord of history, so that his word spoken in and to a given ancient historical situation can still be intended to speak as his word to all generations. How the ancient text of the Bible is relevant to us is a concern of hermeneutics.

Communication and its principles

One of the most basic assumptions in evangelical hermeneutics is that God has communicated by his word and that he is certainly capable of doing this in the way that meets his purpose of effective communication. At the quite basic and purely secular level, we observe that effective communication can be viewed in terms of a sender and a receiver, the signal sent and received, and a level of common understanding.[16] The assumption is that there is a meaningful link between what the communicator sends and what is received. In communication we thus identify certain basic dimensions:

- the communicator (behind the text: the author and his/her intentions);
- the communicated message (inside the text: the meaning of the text as text);
- the receiver (in front of the text: the reader's presuppositions, culture and role in giving meaning).

Our assumptions about the Bible require us to define these dimensions more closely.

The communicator

The first question arises as to who the sender or communicator is. Is it God, whose word we believe the Bible to be? Or is it a number of different human beings whom we believe actually wrote or compiled the documents as we have them in the Bible? If we assume, on the basis of the Bible's own testimony about itself, that God effectively revealed his word to the human authors, we need to clarify what we understand about those involved in this double authorship, and the relationship between them. While accepting the notion of divine inspiration, I do not intend to get into the area of the psychology of inspiration – that is, the subjective experience of the human authors. Some biblical documents, for example prophetic oracles, express the authors' conviction of having 'the word of the Lord' coming to them, but rarely the subjective experience of this reception. Other documents, for example some New Testament epistles, may well have been penned without any sense on the part of the author that these were destined to be canonized as inspired Scripture.[17]

The communication

The second dimension is the message itself and the medium through which it is communicated. It should be noted that even basic theories of

---

16. This, in essence, is the definition provided by E. C. Eyre, *Effective Communication*, in the Made Simple series (London: W. H. Allen, 1979), p. 1.
17. For example, the overwhelming sense in the Psalms is that, for the most part, they are human addresses to God and not divine addresses to us. The genre of proverbial sentence majors on the crystallizing of human observation and experience.

communication would recognize that attempts to communicate can have varying degrees of success. For that reason some have suggested that it is more appropriate to refer to 'address' rather than communication. Hermeneutic theorists have emphasized the need to distinguish not only various kinds of address, but also the role of those addressed in the interpretative process.

Double authorship implies double receivership, for the human author presumably must receive the word that he will in turn address to others. Furthermore, once we allow the possibility of double authorship, we face many questions about the message. Not least of these is the form of the message and how that might relate to the intention of the author/s to communicate something. To what extent does the human manner of communication, and the human situations which constitute its context, affect the divine author's intent? At the centre of much hermeneutic debate lie the questions of revelation and the sufficiency of human language and thought forms to reveal the truth of God. This goes to the heart of the question of the identity of the Bible as the word of God. Evangelicalism differs radically from neo-orthodoxy on this matter.

The receiver

Third, there is the dimension of the receiver and what characteristics of the receiver must be accounted for in the matter of interpretation of meaning. What common understanding exists between the sender (God) and the receiver (human beings) that enables effective communication to take place? After all, we are quite aware of the fact that many people hear or read the biblical text but remain uncomprehending of its significance. According to the Bible itself, it is not only the cultural context of the reader/hearer that affects understanding, but also the opening of one's mind through regeneration and faith.

Divine communication

We can see that there are common concerns in the study of communication in a purely secular manner and the study of what purports to be divine communication. There are also some significant differences which have to do with the presuppositions and assumptions we make about all three dimensions (sender, message and receiver). An evangelical reading of the Bible proceeds on a number of assumptions concerning God, his word and us as receivers. How, then, do we arrive at such assumptions, and what confidence can we have in them? The usual evangelical assertion on biblical authority should be understood for what it is. We can state it thus: *We believe the Bible to be the infallible word of God because the Bible itself tells us that this is the case.* The immediate objection is that this is a circular argument – which of course it is! But is it really different from saying we know that God is God because he says he is? Can circularity be avoided and, if so, how? There are those who suggest it can be avoided merely by refusing to make assumptions, and by allowing the evidence to speak for itself. But this is to make another set of assumptions about what constitutes evidence and how it does speak for itself. If we refuse to start with the assumption that the Bible tells the truth in claiming to be God's word, we must start with another assumption: that it does not or may not tell the truth and, therefore, it is not or may not be God's word. If we seek to avoid the obvious circularity of this latter approach by saying that we must test the Bible by certain objectively neutral facts, then who determines what is neutral and which facts are applicable? In the end, it becomes human reason that judges what is reasonable evidence about the nature of the Bible. As soon as we admit this, then we see that it is a choice of two opposing circular arguments: one that assumes the ultimate authority of God and his word, and the other that assumes the ultimate authority of unaided human reason. We must examine these two positions more closely in pursuing the basis of valid interpretation of the Bible. Perhaps it will emerge that one position is really an exercise in futility in that it undermines itself by its own assumptions.

The concept of the hermeneutical spiral can assist us to make a start in dealing with the Bible as God's communication to mankind. We must make an assumption about the Bible and its significance and, on that basis, make a determined move to discover the dimensions of hermeneutics. As evangelicals we stand by a theology of the Word/word as central to our approach to the Bible. The Bible says such things as the following:

> In the beginning was the Word. (John 1:1)
> And the Word became flesh and lived among us . . . full of grace and truth. (John 1:14)
> My sheep hear my voice, and I know them, and they follow me. (John 10:27)

Evangelical hermeneutics can at least be described as gospel-driven. God has spoken by his Word, the Word who became a man for us. He knows us and we know his voice so that we follow him. Any hermeneutics that loses this plot has ceased to be evangelical and is out of touch with biblical truth. The evangelical interpreter must decide what assumptions are brought to bear on the subject of understanding the Bible, and to what degree we can apply non-biblical categories to our study without compromising our principles. The concept of communication involving the communicator, the message and the receiver suggests the following formal dimensions to the study of biblical hermeneutics.

Diagram 1: The dimensions of divine communication to humans

COMMUNICATOR: GOD	**THEOLOGICAL DIMENSION**
COMMUNICATION: GOD'S WORD Incarnate and inscripturate	**CHRISTOLOGICAL 'SALVATION HISTORY' DIMENSION** **LITERARY DIMENSION**
RECEIVERS and PROCLAIMERS	**ANTHROPOLOGICAL DIMENSION** **HISTORY OF INTERPRETATION**

This analysis does not pre-empt the kind of synthesis we may come up with in the end, but it at least suggests a way of itemizing the individual areas of study that go to make up a comprehensive study of hermeneutics. The categories designated are not watertight and will, because of the nature of things, often overlap or interact. Thus Christology can be shown to be also at the heart of understanding the receivers of God's word, in that Christ was the true receiver and interpreter of his Father's word. Our true receiving of the word relates to our union with Christ the receiver. History writing and literature are both human activities, so the divine-human relationship is central to God's word.

The communicator: God

Christian theistic presuppositions include the acceptance that God is there, that he communicates with us through the Bible, and that, therefore, he is involved in the authorship of the Bible in such a way that it really does say what he intends. To this we must add the fact of our being created in the image of God, so that we are made to be able to receive and understand God's communication. Consequently, our approach to interpretation will take account of these presuppositions. To ignore them is to repudiate them.

This brings us to the theological question: what kind of God is it who communicates with us? Some theological liberals would appear to assume the unwillingness or the inability of God to make a good job of getting his message across to mere mortals! They assert that finite human language is incapable of expressing the infinite. Yet we have reason to suggest a correlation between the refusal to allow that Jesus was truly God as well as the clearest word of God to humanity, and the refusal to allow that the human words of an inspired Bible are able to communicate divine truth.

The communication: God's word

When we talk about God's word we have something of a dilemma. There are two distinct, if related, ways of identifying God's word. We speak of both Jesus Christ and the Bible as God's word. Putting an upper-case W on Word when we speak about Jesus as the Divine Word may remove some ambiguity, but we need to understand the relationship between the two. Jesus is the Word of God incarnate. He is the revealer, communicator and saviour. How we understand Jesus will affect the way we understand the communication of God in the Bible, but we only understand Jesus as the Word through the Bible.

The Bible is a book and as such must be treated as a book. How does this reflect the nature of Jesus? Our presuppositions about Jesus and the Bible are crucial. Again we face the question of circularity. If the Bible is God's book, how do the dimensions of human authorship and the cultural and historical contexts of the Bible affect its meaning and our understanding? We may propose that the relationship of the divine and human natures in the person of Jesus provide a paradigm for understanding the relationship of the divine and human words in the Bible. That is, we go to the Bible to find the necessary data for understanding the Bible.

We will need to revisit later the question of the relationship of God's word to human words. To assert that no human language is adequate to express the truth about God can be an exercise in evasion. Of course we accept that human minds, human thought forms and human language can never plumb the depths and the mysteries of infinite divine Being. But we also recognize that our personhood, our thought forms and our language have their origins in God, as he created us in his image. We are finite and limited by our humanness, but we reflect the image of God nevertheless. Thus we can make a distinction between absolute and exhaustive knowledge of the truth, which only God has, and true though finite knowledge, which we are created to have.

The receivers: God's people

Our presuppositions about humanness and the relationship of humanity to God will affect the way we understand ourselves as interpreters of the Bible. We cannot avoid the question of human sin and its effects on our ability to receive and to know the truth. Biblical assertions about the effect of sin on our minds are not our only concern. What the Bible says about the effect of salvation on our minds is integral to hermeneutics. Hearing and understanding the address of God to us is part of the saving process. The relevance of the ministry of the Holy Spirit to hermeneutics then becomes an issue. What, then, can we say about receivers who do not acknowledge the truth and authority of the Bible? Can they in any sense understand it truly? Some would say that the difference between believer and unbeliever is in submission to the authority of the word. Others argue that submission brings enlightenment and understanding that rebellion forgoes.

How can we know what the Bible means, and how can we communicate this meaning to others? We believe a rational, communicating God has made us in his image as rational, communicating people. But what processes are involved in our communicating? If the Bible is the divine word using human words and thought forms, how do we penetrate to the human authors' meaning and, through it, to the divine author's meaning? We will examine various approaches to this basic question and attempt to express the role of the gospel in this process.

The dimensions of hermeneutics

Given that the dimensions of communication at the very least involve the sender, the message and the receiver, what, if any, are the particular concerns of the evangelical interpreter of the Bible? Starting with the analysis set out in Diagram 1 (above), we may propose as a working hypothesis a range of dimensions that attach to each main category. These will not all have the same significance for the interpretative task, but it is well to err on the side of detail simply to show the interconnectedness of the matters that relate to the main dimensions. Diagram 2 (below), then, is suggestive rather than definitive. We must enquire in more detail into some of the main aspects of the presuppositional basis of hermeneutics in the next chapter. It will be apparent that hermeneutics is an integrative subject that embraces almost all areas of theological study.[18]

18. Those of my readers who have engaged in formal theological study will appreciate that they have been concerned with hermeneutics from the start. Hopefully this study with assist them in integrating a range of subjects.

Diagram 2: The theological dimensions of hermeneutics

COMMUNICATOR: GOD Question of the divine Author's intended meaning	GOD 1. His existence 2. What is his nature? – ontological Trinity 3. How does he manifest himself? – economic Trinity • Creator • Controller of history • Author of true rationality • Revealer to people • Judge and Saviour • Author of truth and meaning

COMMUNICATION: GOD'S WORD which includes interpretation of GOD'S ACTS (God's speech-acts) (The Word incarnate and the word inscripturate) Question of the meaning of the text	JESUS CHRIST 1. Who and what is Jesus? • God-Man • Redemptive revelation of the whole Bible • Word of God in the flesh • Mediator of salvation • Embodiment of truth and all meaning 2. What did he achieve? 3. How does he relate to the Bible? THE BIBLE 1. What is the Bible? 2. How was it produced? • relationship to history and culture 3. How does it relate to God and his truth? • infallibility, inerrancy, inspiration 4. What is authority? 5. How does human language work? 6. How can it be understood and applied? 7. What is its unity and central message? 8. What is its diversity? 9. What are its canonical limits? 10. Meaning: is it in the author, the text, the reader, or in all three?

RECEIVERS and PROCLAIMERS **Question of the reader's understanding of the text**	**PEOPLE** **1. What is it to be created in the image of God?** **2. What are the noetic effects of sin?** **3. What are the noetic effects of regeneration?** **4. How can we know something truly?** **5. How can we know what the Bible means?** **6. What is our ultimate reference point for truth?** **7. How can we communicate the truth of the Bible?** **8. Contextualization of the proclamation.** **9. How does the reader affect perceived meaning?**

2. PRESUPPOSITIONS IN READING AND UNDERSTANDING

The historical shift in presuppositions

For the purposes of this discussion I will use the term 'presupposition' as defined by John Frame:

> A presupposition is a belief that takes precedence over another and therefore serves as a criterion for another. An ultimate presupposition is a belief over which no other takes precedence.[1]

Every thinker and observer makes unprovable assumptions about reality. It is the claim of Christian theism that non-Christian world-views make unsustainable assumptions. Empiricism, for example, depends on certain presuppositions that are not arrived at empirically. Thus it can never get to ultimate truth by purely empirical means. There was a time when Western thought was not totally driven by rationalist empiricism, but accepted divine revelation in Scripture as the absolute norm. There were various distortions of this, but it remained the foundational belief in the understanding

---

1. John Frame, *The Doctrine of the Knowledge of God* (Phillipsburg: Presbyterian and Reformed, 1987), p. 45.

of reality. The divine Author was the defining point both as to the nature of the communication and as to the ability of author and reader/hearer to make sense of the communication. Historic Christianity made assumptions based on the conviction that Scripture conveyed the truth about God, mankind and the world. In other words, the biblical doctrines of creation and the lordship of God over time and space meant that he who created all things, and who governs all things, alone could interpret all things.

The Enlightenment led to different assumptions. Over a period of time, the natural universe came to be seen as the ultimate reality; God came to be viewed as part of this general reality and as thoroughly immanent. It was, then, a short step to regarding God as irrelevant or even non-existent. Human beings were the summit of natural processes, and human reason autonomous. Thus the theological dimension in hermeneutics, even when dealing with theological texts, was eventually either ignored or ruled out as impossible and irrelevant. The modern result of this change is the set of presuppositions that include:

- the supremacy of humanity and the autonomy of human reason;
- scientific method (reason plus empirical input from our senses) as the only valid way to the truth.

Modernism continued to acknowledge the author, but only the human author, as having a major role in the creation of meaning in the biblical text. In time, the emphasis shifted from the communicator (the emphasis of historical-critical method) to the communication itself (the emphasis of the new literary critical methods). Postmodernism is generally seen as having moved beyond the presuppositions of modernism, although there is still much discussion whether or not this is really so. There are some significant changes of perspective, however, which affect the way people perceive reality. Postmodernism presses further with the autonomy of the individual to the point where it is the receiver who creates meaning. Confidence in rationality is gone and the metanarrative (the big picture of a unified reality) is rejected. Modernism's claim to objectivity is rejected. The author and the text cease to be the creators of meaning and it is left to the reader to create the meaning in the text.

Alternative presuppositional stances in theological study

Theologians have suggested three main historical positions in theological study and, therefore, in the understanding of the Bible.[2] The study of apologetics, the rational defence of the Christian faith, is useful for showing up the presuppositions that theologians use. Thus Bernard Ramm highlights the emphasis on subjectivism, or empiricism, or revelation.[3] The three positions are exemplified by the following figures.

(i) Tertullian (born c. 160), who wrote at the beginning of the third century, was sceptical about the use of philosophical reasoning. 'I believe what is absurd' is said to characterize his approach.[4] As Avery Dulles notes, 'He wishes to bring out the distinctiveness of faith as it towers above all human reasoning and leaves man's intellect prostrate in adoration before the unfathomable mystery of God.'[5] It is in essence the rejection of pure rationality in assessing objective realities. Tertullian anticipates existentialism, which focuses on self-understanding and plays down the importance of objectivity. Fideism is similar in its subjectivity and involves a 'leap of faith' approach to reality. It leaves little place for rationality or evidences in assessing truth.

(ii) Thomas Aquinas (1225–74) represents the position, 'I understand in order to believe.' Human rationality assesses the evidences upon which faith is based. This leads to natural theology, empiricism and evidentialism. Thomas Aquinas 'baptized' Aristotelian empiricism and accepted that rational thought and empirical evidences provide the framework within which revelation is to be understood. Evidentialism is an apologetic approach that places great importance on historical and empirical evidences for the establishment of the truth.[6] Like Thomism, it assumes some common neutral ground upon which believers and unbelievers can agree about ultimate reality.

(iii) Augustine (354–430) is, according to Carl Henry, characterized by the phrase 'I believe in order to understand.' This recognition of the interpretative

---

2. See C. F. H. Henry, *Toward a Recovery of Christian Belief* (Wheaton: Crossway, 1990) and Gordon H. Clark, *Three Types of Religious Philosophy* (Nutley, NJ: Presbyterian and Reformed, 1973).
3. Bernard Ramm, *Varieties of Christian Apologetics* (Grand Rapids: Baker, 1962).
4. Henry, *Toward a Recovery of Christian Belief*, p. 40.
5. Avery Dulles, *A History of Apologetics* (New York: Corpus Instrumentorum, 1971), p. 43.
6. This is not what Calvin is doing in providing proofs for the credibility of Scripture: *Institutes of the Christian Religion*, 1.8. For him such rational proofs will be acceptable only to those who are enlightened by the Holy Spirit.

lordship of the Creator characterizes presuppositionalism in Christian theism. This is the consistent epistemological position of Reformed Christianity, although many evangelicals repudiate it. Presuppositionalism, unlike fideism, does not dispense with evidences and, we should note, evidentialism does not dispense with presuppositions. The point at issue is not presuppositions and evidences, but rather what constitutes a sound and consistent set of presuppositions and, consequently, by what criteria we can judge evidences.

These three positions are useful for our purposes to illustrate basic stances with regard to how our humanity relates to God in the matter of truth and understanding. It is thus not my purpose to critically examine the positions of the three theologians mentioned. Nor will I ask whether or not these men would really own these slogans and the apparent logical extensions of them, or were consistent with them in their theologizing. What is important for us is that these three basic stances help us to get to the heart of the presuppositional choices facing the evangelical interpreter. The first (Tertullian) expresses the virtual eradication of human reason as having any authority. The second (Thomas Aquinas) indicates the subordination of divine revelation to an epistemological framework established by autonomous human reason that assesses empirical evidences. The third (Augustine) expresses the importance of human reason and understanding, but only as they are subordinated to divine truth and revelation.

In both apologetics and hermeneutics we have at some point to deal with the universality of presuppositions and the significance of different presuppositional starting points. Then we must try to show why the presuppositions of Christian theism are more sustainable than those of the non-Christian as the basis for understanding truth. Non-Christian presuppositions must be shown to be self-referentially incoherent – that is, as failing to meet their own requirements for distinguishing the truth. This is essentially the method of the Reformed presuppositional apologetics expounded by Cornelius Van Til and largely adopted by Francis Schaeffer and John Frame.[7] Although we may classify various presuppositional stances in the way we have, the matter is by no means simple. Anthony Thiselton acknowledges this in his treatment of

---

7. C. Van Til, *The Defense of the Faith* (Philadelphia: Presbyterian and Reformed, 1975); *The Reformed Pastor and Modern Thought* (Nutley, NJ: Presbyterian and Reformed, 1971); Francis Schaeffer, *He is There and He is Not Silent* (London: Hodder and Stoughton, 1972); and more recently, John M. Frame, *Apologetics to the Glory of God* (Phillipsburg: Presbyterian and Reformed, 1994).

horizons of understanding or expectation.[8] The main difference between these terms and the more general idea of presupposition is the recognition of their impermanence and potential to be transformed. Presuppositions, on the other hand, 'can only be changed and revised with pain or at least with difficulty'.[9]

The unavoidability of presuppositions

Can there ever be neutral objectivity? Can we ever observe, reason and make judgments about objects and events without taking into account ourselves and our whole pre-existing mental baggage? Many scholars, particularly those following the thinking of the Enlightenment, seem to have assumed so, though one wonders if they really did think such a thing possible. If we take our basic dimensions of communication – sender, message and receiver – we soon see that what we understand each of these to be is really important for the way we perceive the viability of communication. If the sender is a humpback whale, the message a series of subsonic emissions and the receiver a deaf man paddling in the surf, there probably will be no communication. Even if the message is sonic and the receiver a human scientist equipped with a hydrophone, the sound may be picked up, but will any message be received?

Thus in dealing with the biblical text, the assumptions we make about the sender, both divine and human, about the nature of the message as part of the Bible and about us will all be relevant to the interpretation of the text. These assumptions either directly or indirectly deal with the question of God. We assume that either he is or he is not the sender of the message. We assume that the text of the Bible is a word from God or it is not. We assume that we as receivers are subject to God and created in his image or we are not. A. B. Mickelsen, in his enquiry into the source of the interpreter's principles, expresses the significance of our assumptions about God thus:

> There is no neutral ground in this controversy. If God did break through into history as the Bible records, then he is not only active in history, but he acts freely and purposefully above and beyond history.[10]

---

8. Anthony Thiselton, *New Horizons in Hermeneutics* (Grand Rapids: Zondervan, 1992). See his preliminary discussion on pp. 44–46.
9. ibid., p. 45.
10. A. B. Mickelsen, *Interpreting the Bible* (Grand Rapids: Eerdmans, 1963), p. 8.

Many scholars would say that this supposition of God in history involves a pretty big 'if'. Thus Ernst Troeltsch crystallized the historical-critical method in principles that were grounded on wholly different presuppositions.[11] For him the universe is a closed system of cause and effect, and consequently there can be no such thing as divine intervention – such as miracles – and certainly no word-revelation from God. With that key assumption alone he ruled out the whole supernatural realm of which the Bible speaks. Miracles do not happen in a closed universe, so events like the resurrection clearly cannot happen. Troeltsch was, of course, giving expression to the assumption that the only truth is empirical truth, that which is discoverable by our senses. This is the non-empirical assumption that cannot be demonstrated empirically and therefore by its own standards cannot be affirmed. At best it can only be a possibility that is yet to be proved when *all* the data of *all* reality are in. It implies an exhaustive knowledge that it knows it does not have.

To summarize, taking the approach to communication that is set out in the previous chapter, evangelicals make assumptions about each element involved:

- the sender/author: the God and Father of our Lord Jesus Christ;
- the message: Scripture as the reliable word of God;
- the receiver: human beings created in the image of God.

These assumptions or presuppositions are bound up with one another. If we accept that the Bible is God's word, then he is the sender by whatever human medium. The receivers can be differentiated as original receivers – human authors used by God to speak and write his word; modern receivers – people of God/believers; unbelievers; and inconsistent believers who accept some of the presuppositions of unbelievers. In each case we are making assumptions in the realm of ontology, which deals with what things are in themselves.[12] Part of this ontology concerns epistemology, which focuses on us as knowing beings.

---

11. See the critique of Troeltsch in Sidney Greidanus, *The Modern Preacher and the Ancient Text* (Grand Rapids: Eerdmans; Leicester: IVP, 1988), pp. 24–47.
12. Ontology is a word derived from a form of the Greek verb *to be*. We can have ontological concerns for any aspect of reality. Thus ontology may be conceived of as another name for metaphysics, which is the branch of philosophy that is concerned with what is real.

Basic evangelical presuppositions

An examination of some evangelical introductory texts on hermeneutics might suggest that evangelical hermeneutical method produces an uncertain sound. Where should an evangelical begin in the business of formulating valid principles of hermeneutics? It is interesting to note how some evangelical texts have been organized, what is included and, more to the point, what has not been included. In some of the titles footnoted[13] there is an apparent tendency, though not uniform, to concentrate on the history of hermeneutics and the literary dimensions of the biblical text. Berkhof gives a theological introduction in traditional terms of the nature of the Bible. McCartney and Clayton begin with a discussion of presuppositions. Mickelsen's introductory section on principles contains little theology. It is understandable that evangelicals will tend to write such books with a view to apologetic needs, but this can tend to be reactionary. Thus, in the face of postmodernism, Millard Erickson proposes a new paradigm for a postmodern evangelical hermeneutic.[14] My response to his proposal is that perhaps we also need to reaffirm a biblical hermeneutic.

It is unlikely that Christians in general begin their spiritual journey by laboriously working through their basic assumptions and beliefs until some coherent structure is reached. But, however we arrive at it, the belief system that forms the assumptions we make as we read the Bible is a system that is always open to adjustments and fine-tuning as we understand more and more of the teaching of the Bible. We may indulge in nostalgic reflection on our experience of coming to faith, but in the end we are thrown back to the biblical analysis of everything involved. If we neglect to search the Scriptures for the truths relating to our conversion, we easily end up with an experience-based account that may be quite erratic and erroneous. Thus evangelical presuppositions may start with basic assumptions about the existence of God and the reality of an objective world that we are in touch with by our senses. In the apologetics of pre-evangelism we may try to lead someone through such basic beliefs. But as evangelical readers

---

13. L. Berkhof, *Principles of Biblical Interpretation* (Grand Rapids: Baker, 1950); A. B. Mickelsen, *Interpreting the Bible* (Grand Rapids: Eerdmans, 1963); E. E. Johnson, *Expository Hermeneutics: An Introduction* (Grand Rapids: Academie, 1990); W. Klein, C. Blomberg, and R. Hubbard, *Introduction to Biblical Interpretation* (Dallas: Word, 1993); W. Kaiser and M. Silva, *An Introduction to Biblical Hermeneutics* (Grand Rapids: Zondervan, 1994); Dan McCartney and Charles Clayton, *Let the Reader Understand* (Wheaton: Bridgepoint, 1994).
14. Millard Erickson, *Evangelical Interpretation* (Grand Rapids: Baker, 1993), pp. 114–125.

of the Bible we have arrived at a belief structure that we accept as valid, though we are always open to some adjustments in the light of Scripture.

Evangelicals repudiate the notion that the Bible is merely a human document. We thus reject at least some of the presuppositions of those who do regard the Bible in this humanistic way. This is not, of course, to reject the human dimensions of the Bible in its human authorship, its use of human language, and the human cultural and historical contexts of the various documents. In the previous chapter we looked at the dimensions involved in the consideration of the basic assumption that the Bible really is the divinely inspired word of God, written down by the agency of human authors, conveying in a variety of literary genres the revelation of God to human hearers and readers. This is not the place to try to defend this set of assumptions, but rather to state them, recognize them and enquire into their implications. The defence of them will come about both directly and indirectly as we build a picture of how these assumptions or presuppositions function.

Modern evangelicals are usually fairly comfortable with the notion that their position is not novel but has roots in the Protestant Reformation of the sixteenth century. This, in turn, implies identification with the Reformers' claim to be recovering the pure doctrines of the apostolic gospel. In the course of the Reformation the four 'alones' emerge that express the heart of the matter theologically: *grace alone*, *Christ alone*, *Scripture alone* and *faith alone*. The question then arises as to how there can be four 'alones' that relate. A further question for this study is, in what way do the 'alones' help us understand the heart of evangelical hermeneutics?

In the historical context of the Reformation, each one of the 'alones' is both a positive assertion of a key theological principle and the definite rejection of a perceived theological error of the medieval Catholic Church. While the focus of each may be distinguished, they all represent a certain perspective on the biblical way of salvation. There can be four 'alones' because they are distinct emphases on the one essential truth of the gospel. Because there are four of them (some would add a fifth: *the glory of God alone*), the question of priority arises. Is there logically a priority that must be given to one of these dimensions, a priority among equals, that in no way compromises the others?[15]

Modern hermeneutical enquiry has done much to formalize, categorize and analyse the issues that relate to reading and understanding the Bible. A brief

---

15. Obviously the equality is between the use and application of the theological concepts and not between the things in themselves. No one could for a moment suggest that the Bible, or our faith, is equal to God or Christ.

survey of the history of biblical interpretation, however, reveals that many of the issues of modern hermeneutics have been discussed and studied from the earliest times of Christian exposition of Scripture. Since evangelical theology stands firmly on the shoulders of the Reformation, we might enquire how some of these modern hermeneutical concerns were expressed then. One of the most important areas to investigate, in my opinion, involves the theological foundations of evangelical biblical interpretation. Let us, then, examine some of the implications of the characteristic 'alones'.

Grace alone

Grace alone is understood first of all in relation to the way salvation comes to us, and how we receive it. It is a principle that applies the notion of grace as the totally unmerited gift of God, whereby he acts for the good of those who deserve only his condemnation. It therefore rules out any sense that we can merit our salvation or contribute to it. Christ died for us while we were still helpless sinners. *Grace alone* stems from the reality of creation and the fall of the human race. The narrative of Genesis 1 – 3 leaves room only for a total end there and then, or for the grace of God to operate in the whole process that leads eventually to the new creation and the glorious kingdom of God. The mediator of the process is ultimately and exclusively Jesus Christ. All of this happens because God is who he is. The nature and attributes of God are either a fiction, or they are essential to our being, knowing and interpretation of any communication. Grace is a doctrinal way of saying something about the essential being of God: what he is and what characteristics of his being he reveals. Grace speaks of the priority of God's being as the source of all things and the measure of all things. In philosophical terms this is a matter of ontology. That God shows grace also demonstrates that the recipients are in need of it. *Grace alone* was thus the Reformation repudiation of the Roman Catholic notion of nature plus grace.[16]

The principle of 'grace alone' points us to the ontological priority of God.

Christ alone

Christ alone means that salvation is found nowhere else but in the person and

16. See below, ch. 7.

work of Jesus Christ. This exclusivist conviction is based on the evidence of Scripture. Such evidence includes the specifically exclusivist claims concerning Jesus, and also the coherence of the biblical story. This story tells of events from creation to new creation in a narrative that takes us through the fall, the call of Abraham, the redemption of Israel, the fortunes of the nation and the prophetic promises and expectations for the fulfilment of the original covenant promises. At the climax of the story is the event of the incarnation of the Christ, his life, death, resurrection and ascension to glory. The purposes of God in this story are expressed in such a way as to show that the destiny of all the peoples of the world and of the whole universe is tied to the work of God in Christ. The cross of Christ is the redemptive event that has ramifications for the redemption of the whole created order.

If the biblical story is true, Christ is the only saviour for humankind and there is room for no other way to God. If the story is true, Jesus Christ is the interpretative key to every fact in the universe and, of course, the Bible is one such fact. He is thus the hermeneutic principle that applies first to the Bible as the ground for understanding, and also to the whole of reality. Interpreting reality correctly is a by-product of salvation. Thus we must assert that the person and work of Jesus Christ are foundational for evangelical hermeneutics. As we shall examine in more detail, Christ interprets all facts, since all things were created in him, through him and for him (Col. 1:16). As the one mediator between God and man (1 Tim. 2:5), Christ mediates the ultimate truth of God about all things and thus about the meaning of the Bible.

The principle of 'Christ alone' points us to the soteriological and hermeneutical priority of the gospel of Christ.

Scripture alone

Nothing exists except by the decree of God. We know this fact, and we know God, only because he has revealed himself through his Son, Jesus Christ. Furthermore, we know this fact, and we know Jesus Christ, only because he is revealed to us in Scripture. When the Reformers enunciated the principle of *Scripture alone* they asserted that there is no other source of truth available to us by which we can know Christ and, through him, God. Negatively, they repudiated the notion of a living tradition of the church as a separate source of truth that enjoys a similar authority to that of the Bible. They were not repudiating the role of tradition as such, but only seeking to subordinate it to the final authority of Scripture. It was not tradition that was the concern, but tradition that contradicted Scripture.[17] They rejected the doctrine of a teaching magisterium that alone could provide the true interpretation of Scripture. Instead of the Roman Catholic assertion that, since the church gave us the Bible, the church alone could interpret the Bible, the Reformers rightly said that God, by his word, creates the church, which must therefore submit to biblical authority. For the ordinary Christian *Scripture alone* simply means that we must read the Bible or hear the message of the Bible if we are to know God. The relationship of the God of the Bible to the whole of reality is such that no empirical facts are ultimately understood until they are understood as facts of the Creator. To know God and his creation, we have to take account of the nature of Scripture and of the phenomena that present themselves in Scripture. Hermeneutics is concerned with the practical application of *Scripture alone.*

The principle of 'Scripture alone' points us to the phenomenological and material priority of Scripture.

Faith alone

Faith alone was the implication that Luther saw in the biblical teaching that 'the righteous shall live by faith' (Rom. 1:17, quoting Hab. 2:4). It is the truth expressed by Paul in Ephesians 2:8–9 that no human effort or good work can contribute to our salvation. Negatively, *faith alone* was a rejection of the whole Roman Catholic system of merits. It was a reversal of the upside-down gospel of Rome that put our subjective sanctification as the basis of justification. This had in effect opened the door to our works of sanctification being made the grounds of salvation. But the question of faith also raises several vital questions – for example, what is faith and how do we come to have it? The simple answer is that faith is a gift of God's grace. It is an attitude, born in us by the Holy Spirit, of trust in the promises of God relating to the efficacy of Christ's life, death and resurrection on our behalf. It is a gift in that we cannot, by our unaided will, exercise it. Yet it is a subjective thing, for we do exercise it and are fully conscious of doing so. The Bible says much about unbelief or lack of faith. It also says and implies much about the bondage of the human will when in rebellion against God. It thus

---

17. Craig D. Allert, 'What Are We Trying to Conserve? Evangelicalism and *Sola Scriptura*', *EQ* 76/4 (2004), pp. 327–348.

points to two things with regard to faith: the inability of the sinner, and the need for the regeneration of the Holy Spirit if the sinner is to be made able to have faith. Faith is always defined by its object: the person and work of Christ.

The principle of 'faith alone' points us to the ontological inability of the sinner and the epistemological priority of the Holy Spirit.

The four 'alones' and the Trinity

In outlining these four 'alones' of the Reformation I have tried to demonstrate that the consideration of presuppositions, which we may now investigate in more philosophical terms, were at the heart of Reformation theology and understanding of the Bible. We do not seek to subvert *Scripture alone* by slavishly following a tradition handed down from the Reformers. But we do not want to reinvent the wheel and so are not afraid (to mix the metaphors) to climb on the shoulders of the great ones who have gone before us.

It is important to grasp that the four 'alones' really take their essential characteristics from God as Trinity. Consequently, none of the 'alones' can exist without the others. Nor can the evangelical assumption that the Bible is the word of God remain at the level of undefined generality. What kind of God speaks his word to us? How does he reveal himself to us? If we answer that he is the God of the gospel, we only point to the need to deepen our understanding of the gospel beyond the level of superficiality to take account of what the Bible reveals the gospel to be. The gospel of our salvation through faith alone, in Christ alone, by grace alone, as revealed in the Bible alone, is what it is only because God is the kind of God he is. Those groups who claim to be Christian while rejecting the historic Christian faith in the divine and human natures of Christ, and in the Trinity, usually end up with a gospel that is denuded of grace and that amounts to salvation by faith in a diminished Christ who is then augmented by our works of obedience. It would not be an exaggeration to say that 'grace alone' is unique to biblical Christianity.

Because these dimensions stem from the ontological nature of God as Trinity, we can see that their relationships are derivative of the relationships within the Trinity. The doctrine of the Trinity is essentially ontological, not manifestational (economic). That is, the three-ness of the unity of God is not just a way of talking about three different roles that the one God assumes:

Creator, Saviour and Indweller.[18] We recognize that the Bible presents different kinds of clues to this nature of God, not least of which is the incarnation. If Jesus is God and yet speaks about God the Father and the Spirit of God in the third person, he is clearly mistaken, or else God *is* Trinity. But because God is also perfect unity, it is impossible to consider any one person of the Trinity without also considering the other two. The other side of that coin is that the three persons are not interchangeable in their functions. The Father sends the Son, the Son suffers and dies, the Father and the Son send the Holy Spirit among the people of God, and so on. Another way of stating this co-dependence of the persons of the Trinity is to say that there is unity of the persons without fusion; there is distinction without separation.

The kind of God we presuppose to be in control of creation and salvation is Trinity. If the world had been made by a different kind of God, for example the undifferentiated Allah of Islam, or the monistic God of modern Judaism,[19] Watchtower (Jehovah's Witnesses) or Christadelphianism, of necessity it would be a different kind of world. It is significant that each of these non-Trinitarian religions has its own particular doctrine of salvation by works.

To summarize, the basic evangelical presuppositions are those that relate to the existence, not of a god or divine being, but of the God and Father of our Lord Jesus Christ. Since he is the Creator and Lord of all things, then this basic presupposition affects the way we think about every other fact available to us. The basic presupposition is thus an ontological one concerning the being of God that establishes the ontology of the universe and every creature in it. This then leads us to derivative presuppositions that will be expressed largely in terms of dogmatics or systematic theology. There is a hierarchy of presuppositions in that we do not start every new theological or hermeneutical endeavour by going back to the absolute basics. We will come each time to the biblical text with an

18. The technical term for this emphasis on the roles of God as the essence of Trinity is *modalism*, or the *economic Trinity*.

19. Christians believe that the Trinity, while not *fully* revealed as such in the Old Testament Scriptures, is the outcome of that which is revealed of God in the Old Testament. Judaism, then, in so far as it rejects the Trinity, is inconsistent with its own Scriptures. Gordon Jessop, *No Strange God* (London: Olive Press, 1976), pp. 103–104, refers to a suggestion that by the time of Moses Maimonides (b. 1135) Judaism had hardened its attitude to Trinitarianism because of Christian persecution of Jews. Maimonides describes the unity of God as *yāḥîd*, whereas the usual biblical word is *'eḥād*, used in the *shema* in Deut. 6:4f., which can express diversity in unity; see also Gen. 2:24; Judg. 20:1; Ezek. 37:17.

already formed and, for some, elaborate theological framework. As we build our systematic theology as an interpretative presupposition it is important that it does not become set in concrete. Doctrinal confessions or subordinate authorities must not become ultimate authorities. Thus, although we do not re-establish our basic assumptions every time we come to the text, it is still an ongoing concern that we constantly check them to see that they are true to Scripture. The hermeneutical spiral is always present in the interpretation of Scripture. This spiral is the ongoing process that seeks to maintain the integrity of our method.

The function of evangelical doctrine

As Carl Henry states:

> Each world view has its distinctive starting point or touchstone thesis through which it attempts to unify and explain human experience. The Christian philosopher is under no intellectual compulsion, therefore, to accept rival premises, however fashionable, as the starting point for advancing his or her theistic world view.[20]

Francis Schaeffer makes this observation:

> Many people catch the presuppositions like some children catch measles. They have no idea where they come from. But that is not the way the thinker chooses his presuppositions. His presuppositions are selected on the basis of which presuppositions fit what is; that is, what presuppositions give solid answers concerning what is. It is only the Christian presuppositions which explain what is – in regard to the universe and in regard to man.[21]

The non-Christian's axioms are just as much assumed as are the Christian's. Let the reader understand! We do not have to allow the Enlightenment agenda to determine ours. Only in a relative way can it be permitted to dictate our concerns as we try to understand modernism and postmodernism and determine our response to them. We may test all presuppositions for explanatory power and logical consistency. Tests of rational consistency are important.

---

20. Henry, *Toward a Recovery of Christian Belief*, p. 65.
21. Francis Schaeffer, *The Church at the End of the Twentieth Century* (London: Norfolk Press, 1970), p. 31.

Presuppositions about God include the fact that he is a rational being who has created us in his image as rational beings. This rationality is never to be confused with philosophical rationalism, however much they may overlap.

Presuppositions will decisively influence the interpretation of data. Christian theism affirms God in his revelation as the basis of experience. If the biblical picture is true, then this is the only way it can be. Thus we reckon on Christian theistic presuppositions because they are consistent with what the Bible says about God, sin, our world and us. What is more, they lead to a coherent view of reality that is capable of explaining our experience of reality. We believe that we can live, and account for our experience, consistently with our presuppositions in a way that non-theistic systems cannot. Basic Christian doctrine, then, becomes the presupposed basis for the evangelical interpretation of Scripture. This raises again the question of how we arrive at this doctrine, if not by interpreting the Scriptures. Only some kind of hermeneutical spiral can cope with this circularity. The derived presuppositions of Christian theism will include the following.

- God has revealed himself as rational, and as communicator, as well as sovereign Lord and Creator.
- Human beings are rational receivers of God's communication, because that is how he has made us.
- Sin consists in, among other things, a wilful refusal of truth and the substitution of human reason as autonomous in the place of God's self-attesting revelation.[22]
- Redemptive revelation and the work of the Holy Spirit are necessary to restore humans to a state where they can receive ultimate, but not exhaustive, truth.
- The mediatorial role of Jesus of Nazareth is the guarantee of real communication between God and people. The gospel of Jesus Christ reveals him as the Word of God who is the truth. Jesus as the divine communicator, the saving message and the human receiver demonstrates where the heart of true hermeneutics lies. The gospel is the power of God for salvation, which includes hermeneutical salvation.

---

22. Kevin Vanhoozer, *Is There a Meaning in This Text?* (Grand Rapids: Zondervan; Leicester: Apollos, 1998), ch. 2. All hermeneutic theories which play down the nature of God as communicator, and which move the focus to either the autonomous text or the autonomous reader, are expressions of hermeneutical atheism.

These points involve us in a theology of the Word that is inseparable from the big picture of Christian theism. A biblical theology of the Word of God and of interpretation will be our concern in chapter 4. For the moment, however, let us note the contrast between the two presuppositional stances of Christian theism and humanism. The one asserts the impossibility of knowledge of the truth apart from the source of truth, which is God. The other places autonomous human reason above the claims of the Creator to be the source and the communicator of truth. The implication of theism for hermeneutics is that we must resist all attempts to remove the sovereignty of the Creator-Word from our thinking about meaning and communication. Consistent evangelical hermeneutics must begin with God as he has revealed himself in Jesus Christ.

A case must be established for the essentially Christological nature of authentic hermeneutics, biblical and general. We assume either that God is there and that he has communicated with us, or that there is no one there and thus no communication has come from without. If we assume the former, then we must allow that the transcendent and sovereign God has made the ground rules for the communication. What, then, are those ground rules?

Ontology

We have considered something of the importance of understanding the Trinity both in economic and ontological terms. We make ontological assumptions about the kind of God who has spoken, about the kind of word he speaks, and about the kind of people we are who receive the word. Every Christian builds up a concept of God over time through reading the Bible, hearing sermons and talking to other Christians. In doing this we will be somewhere on a continuum between inconsistency and consistency with the four 'alones'. An evangelical tries to be biblical and thus to be as consistent as possible with these biblical dimensions. One way of stating this is that we begin with a basic assumption about the existence of God. We further assume that this God is behind the form and the content of the Bible. As we read the Bible we build on our understanding of God, while at the same time eliminating previously held misunderstandings or erroneously formed concepts of God. This in turn affects the way we conceive of the Bible and of ourselves as the readers of the Bible.

By this process we develop, by whatever name, a doctrine of God and his word. Because we are not isolated from our Christian peers, or from those who have gone before, we can build an understanding that is to a greater or lesser degree dependent on the community of understanding in the Christian church that spans the centuries. Some, unfortunately, will care little for this process and will be content to live with an immature understanding and a stunted faith. Others will be attracted to Christian communities that major on 'experience' and on being 'Spirit-driven'. They will develop a hermeneutic that understands the Bible in the light of experience rather than interpreting experience by the Bible.

When we speak of the ontological priority of God, we mean that nothing exists except for the prior existence of God who is the Creator of all things. Once we accept that principle, it is impossible simply to shove it away in a pigeonhole for safe keeping. Its ramifications cover everything else that exists and everything that happens. This, of course, includes the Bible and all that it speaks about, including us as God's creatures. It means that the ontological considerations of everything that is not God must include the property of being created by God and, thus, being interpreted by him.

Epistemology

After ontology, the philosophical category that most affects our pursuit for understanding is epistemology. This concerns the questions of what we know and how we know that we know it. At a common-sense level we assume that there is some real link between what we perceive with our senses and what is really there. The philosophical discussions about epistemology began in earnest with the ancient Greeks.[23] It may suffice as a common-sense Christian approach to say that God made and knows all things, and he has made us in his image to know things truly, if not exhaustively. We shall pursue this line in chapter 4. As we try to pin down a biblical epistemology, we should at the same time be aware of the challenges to any such thing from modern hermeneutical theory. Modernism in the scientific age moved beyond Kant to express the ultimate confidence in objectivity that is philosophically neutral. Postmodernism has swung to the other extreme in subjectivity. Yet both are

---

23. W. Andrew Hoffecker and Gary Scott Smith (eds.), *Building a Christian World View*, vol. 1 (Phillipsburg: Presbyterian and Reformed, 1986); Cornelius Van Til, *A Survey of Christian Epistemology* (n.p.: den Dulk Christian Foundation, 1969). I refer here to the conscious consideration of knowledge. To be accurate we would need to point out that concerns about human thought and understanding are probably as old as humankind itself. The ancient Babylonians wrote about wisdom in the third millennium BC, and we know of Egyptian and Hebrew wisdom writings pre-dating the Greek philosophers.

expressions of a view of human autonomy and complete independence of any God or gods.

The biblical view of things provides us with a perspective that values both objectivity and subjectivity together. At its most basic level, it is summed up in the view that the God of the Bible made us in his image as reasoning, perceiving and responsible beings. God thus addresses us as responsible beings who have some contact with reality, even when our repudiation of our nature as being made in God's image renders our perceptions faulty and even fatal. Thus Christian theism involves us in an epistemology that accepts the following biblical notions:

- the exhaustive and infallible knowledge that God has of all things;
- the creation of human beings to be able to truly know God and his creation;
- the fallenness of our thinking and reasoning so that truth is suppressed;
- the redemptive renewing of our minds through the gospel of Christ;
- the redemptive revelation of God's truth as objective reality;
- the regeneration by the Spirit enabling subjective apprehension of God's truth.

Christology and hermeneutics

How can we unpack the notion that the gospel is the power of God for hermeneutical salvation? What are the hermeneutics of Christ?[24] The question might be stated as the relationship of the three major dimensions of communication to Jesus Christ. According to the gospel the real link between the communicator, the message and the receivers is the incarnated God/Man, thus:

- Jesus is God, the infallible communicator;
- Jesus is the Word, the infallible message;
- Jesus is the God/Man, the infallible receiver.

We can go further than this to assert, on the basis of the gospel, that because Jesus is the ideal and true receiver of the word of God, he is also the true and faithful human responder to the word and proclaimer of that word.

---

24. This is to anticipate the conclusions in ch. 19.

According to the gospel, everything he is in his perfect humanity, he is on our behalf as our representative and substitute. He justifies us as receivers and responders to the word of God. Our hermeneutical endeavour is ideally the sanctificational process that is the fruit of our Saviour's perfect hermeneutics and response to the word of God. It will be this only if our hermeneutics is gospel-centred. In what follows I aim to work through some of the implications of a gospel-centred approach.

3. GOSPEL-CENTRED HERMENEUTICS

The presuppositions of the gospel

For hermeneutics to be gospel-centred, it must be based on the person of Jesus Christ. That is, the person and work of Christ are at the heart of our hermeneutics. The final outcome of this study will be a consideration of the hermeneutics of Christ. Let us now try to crystallize the implications of the matters dealt with in the previous chapters for gospel-centred hermeneutics. For the purposes of this study I propose the following delineation of the gospel:

> The gospel is the event (or the proclamation of that event) of Jesus Christ that begins with his incarnation and earthly life, and concludes with his death, resurrection and ascension to the right hand of the Father.[1] This historical event is interpreted by God as his preordained programme for the salvation of the world.

The gospel centres on what God did for us in the incarnate Christ in order to save us from sin, the devil and death. Its goal is the new creation where

1. The event and the proclamation of the event are distinguishable, if not separable. Simply to describe the event is in one sense to proclaim it, provided the event is not left without interpretation.

the people of God redeemed by Christ will enjoy the presence of God for eternity. The gospel is what we must believe in order to be saved. To believe the gospel is to put one's trust and confidence in the person and work of Jesus Christ as Saviour and Lord. To preach the gospel is faithfully to proclaim that historical event, along with the God-given interpretation of that event. It cannot be stressed too much that to confuse the gospel with certain important things that go hand in hand with it is to invite theological, hermeneutical and spiritual confusion. Such ingredients of preaching and teaching that we might want to link with the gospel would include the need for the gospel (sin and judgment), the means of receiving the benefits of the gospel (faith and repentance), the results or fruit of the gospel (regeneration,[2] conversion, sanctification, glorification) and the results of rejecting it (wrath, judgment, hell). These, however we define and proclaim them, are not in themselves the gospel. If something is not what God did in and through the historical Jesus two thousand years ago, it is not the gospel. Thus Christians cannot 'live the gospel', as they are often exhorted to do. They can only believe it, proclaim it and seek to live consistently with it. Only Jesus lived (and died) the gospel. It is a once-for-all finished and perfect event done *for us* by another.

When we confuse the fruit of the gospel in the Christian life for the gospel itself, hermeneutical confusion is introduced. The focus easily turns to the life of the believer and the experience of the Christian life. These can then become the norms by which Scripture is interpreted. Instead of interpreting our experience by the word, we start to interpret the word by our experience. Such reversal of perspective from Christ to self really begins the movement towards the autonomy of human reason in hermeneutical theory.

The presuppositions of the gospel are the prior truths without which the gospel could not be the gospel. These are the presuppositions of Christian theism that I discussed in chapter 2. The material priority of the Scriptures, as they witness to Christ's soteriological priority, necessitates gospel-centred hermeneutics. The presuppositions that we have already considered can now be expressed in terms relating specifically to hermeneutics:

- The God who is there is the God of the Bible, who is (among other things) Creator, Saviour and Communicator.

2. Regeneration is a result of the gospel in that it is possible only because of the historic work of Christ. This is not the same as saying that it is the result of a person's decision to receive the gospel.

- Human beings were created in his image, which involves us as those with whom God communicates.
- The truth of God is evident in all creation.
- Sin means the human declaration of independence from God, and the suppression of his truth.
- Grace means that God mercifully provides special revelation that informs, redeems and makes God present to us.
- This redemptive revelation, the word of God, is focused on Jesus Christ.

From the evangelical perspective we say that God not only exists, but he has spoken to us through his Son. It is also clear that this speaking through the Son implies that the receivers are in a position to know what the intention of the author is. The word is never simply word; it is always the word from the sovereign Lord God addressed to those created in his image. While this revelation is confused by our sinful rejection of the truth, the truth is there nevertheless. The whole biblical expression of revelation implies that the three aspects of communication are involved: the communicator, the communicating word and the receiver. Christian theism maintains that these presuppositions of the gospel are foundational truths that stand the tests of having explanatory power for all human experience and having rational consistency.

The gospel and noetic salvation[3]

The gospel is the power of God for salvation (Rom. 1:16), but this salvation includes the renewal of the mind (Rom. 12:2). It stands to reason that, if the fall involved an epistemological disaster, then salvation must include epistemological redemption. But what is the manner of epistemological salvation? Is it a process? The answer is surely in the affirmative, for there is no perfection yet. We have to work at our epistemological sanctification.

Sinful thinking is 'snake-think', the kind of noetic rebellion proposed by the serpent in Eden. It is diametrically opposed to the mind renewed by the gospel. We will pursue this idea in chapter 4. At this point we can say that the godless

---

3. The term 'noetic' includes all aspects of the working of the mind, including the will, and is therefore wider than 'epistemology', which focuses on knowledge.

presuppositions underlying the temptation and fall in Genesis 3 include the following.

- If God is there, he does not communicate the truth.
- We do not need God to reveal the rational framework for understanding reality.
- Human reason is autonomous, and the ultimate arbiter of truth and falsity, right and wrong.

In essence, these presuppositions are those of the secular mind that were given such sophisticated expression in the philosophies of the Enlightenment.

Genesis 3, then, shows us that the mind is 'fallen' because Adam and Eve gave in to the snake's suggestions. This noetic fall, therefore, must be addressed by the gospel if the salvation of fallen humans is to be complete. The gospel achieves noetic salvation for us through the perfect mind of Christ our Saviour. This is part of his righteous make-up as the perfect human being. His is the human mind in perfect relationship with the mind of God. To be justified includes our noetic justification. In this sense all believers have the mind of Christ (1 Cor. 2:16). Our noetic sanctification is the fruit of our justification in Christ. It is the gradual formation within us of what we have in Christ through faith. The renewal of the mind is an ongoing process by which our thinking is conformed more and more to the truth as it is in Jesus.

Two reality-views are clearly contrasted in Paul's treatment of wisdom in 1 Corinthians 1 – 2. There is little doubt that Paul, along with Jesus and the Gospel writers, moves in the framework that includes Old Testament wisdom. Christ is designated 'the wisdom of God' (1:24) and also 'our wisdom' (1:30). He is the difference between the world's wisdom, which in reality is foolishness, and the wisdom of God, which the world perversely assesses as foolishness. The epistemological framework that corresponds with reality is the gospel itself. What Paul states in 1 Corinthians is in line with the epistemology of the Old Testament wisdom, and specifically that of Proverbs 1:7 and 9:10 where the fear of the Lord as the basis of rational understanding is a faith response to God's revelation.

The biblical doctrine of interpretation, then, includes the epistemological dimension and the significance of the noetic effects of human sin (e.g., Rom. 1:18–32). Natural revelation (as distinct from natural theology) is everywhere. What sinners, who are in angry revolt against the Creator-revealer, do with this revelation is an important issue. We see an aspect of this in the eclipse of Christ in hermeneutics. The ultimate expression is Nietzsche's assertion that God is dead. This epistemological atheism is the foundation of postmodernism.[4]

The word of God spoken by the Old Testament prophets points forward to the Word incarnate (Heb. 1:1–2). Christian theism maintains that what we think of the one will affect what we think of the other. In other words, the hermeneutical question about the whole Bible correlates with the question, 'What do you think of Christ?' The authority of Christ appropriates the spoken/written word in the Bible. The hermeneutic centre of the Bible is therefore Jesus in his being and in his saving acts – the Jesus of the gospel. This appears to beg the question as a circular argument. Once again we note the hermeneutic spiral as unavoidable. We proceed to test our presuppositions and to adjust our conclusions if necessary. One way to proceed is to investigate the consistency of a biblical view of interpretation using the method of biblical theology, and I shall outline such an approach in chapter 4.

Christ as mediator means the gospel is the hermeneutic norm of Scripture

The fact that Jesus is the one mediator between God and people has enormous hermeneutical implications (1 Tim. 2:5).[5] The Christology of mediation brings the major dimensions of communication into contact so that they operate in a way that human sin had rendered inoperable. Thus the communicator (God), the message (God's word) and the receiver (humanity) are all united in the God/Man who is himself the message. If we are united to Christ we are true receivers of the message. To receive a message so that it is not garbled or meaningless or misleading, we must at the same time interpret it aright. Our confusion and our sinfulness conspire to lead us always towards a Christless interpretation. As living a faithful Christian life involves a conscious decision to work at it, so also interpreting the Bible by the gospel involves the conscious decision to work at the relationships of all parts of the Bible to the gospel.

If Jesus is the one mediator between God and man, then he must mediate the meaning of the whole of God's communication to us. Our

---

4. See Kevin Vanhoozer, *Is There a Meaning in This Text?* (Grand Rapids: Zondervan; Leicester: Apollos, 1998), pp. 66–73.
5. Although Paul makes this point in reference to another matter, the important thing is the principle which is valid in all considerations of our relationship to God.

understanding of this mediatorial role comes from the unpacking by the New Testament writers of the gospel event and how it works for our salvation. This raises the question of the significance of all the parts of Scripture that are not explicitly expositions of the gospel. We can say that, while not all Scripture is the gospel, all Scripture is related to the gospel that is its centre. I will deal with this in greater detail in Part III, particularly in the question of the relationship of the two Testaments, and the unifying element or centre of biblical theology.

The Bible makes a very radical idea inescapable: not only is the gospel the interpretative norm for the whole Bible, but there is an important sense in which Jesus Christ is the mediator of the meaning of everything that exists. In other words, *the gospel is the hermeneutical norm for the whole of reality*. All reality was created by Christ, through Christ and for Christ (Col. 1:15–16). God's plan is to sum up all things in Christ (Eph. 1:9–10). In him are all the treasures of wisdom and understanding (Col. 2:2–3).[6] As a consequence, the ultimate significance of all non-biblical literature can be summed up in biblical-gospel terms.[7] Only through the gospel can we know what it means for humans to be sinful and for cultures to be godless. The atoning work of Christ has redemptive ramifications for the whole universe. It is God's means of renewing the universe to be the perfect new creation that was foreshadowed by the perfection of creation before the fall. Hence the ultimate interpretation of the meaning of everything is found only in Christ. This includes every text of the Bible. Eschatology (the doctrine of the end times) and hermeneutics are inseparable.

For the student of the Bible, the gospel becomes the norm by which the whole Old Testament and all the exhortations and other non-gospel aspects of the New Testament are to be understood. To put it another way, Christian conversion should lead to sanctified thinking about reality. While alien philosophies may seek to seduce us into thinking otherwise, we should reckon every fact and event in the universe to be what they in truth are: eloquent of the living God and interpreted by him.

---

6. This matter is developed in ch. 16.
7. Whereas the Enlightenment philosophers began to claim that the Bible was a purely human book like any other book, the only thing that enables anyone to read and understand other books are the realities expressed in Christian theism. Thus we should read all other books as we read the Bible in the sense that the ultimate interpretation of all literature, of every spoken or written word, can only be achieved in the light of Christ.

The resurrection and hermeneutics

When we speak of the risen Christ, we are referring not only to the historical event of the resurrection of Jesus of Nazareth but also to its theological interpretation. The resurrection is the ultimate demonstration of Christology and of God's hermeneutical reference point. Thus the resurrection of Christ confronted his disciples with a radical change of perspective and challenge to their hermeneutics. Although this new perspective had already been foreshadowed in the prophets and declared by Jesus, the disciples proved to be rather impervious to the truths involved. Partly this was due to their inability to grasp that the Messiah should suffer before entering his glory (Matt. 16:21–23; Luke 24:26). They needed instruction in how the Old Testament is about the Christ (Luke 24:27, 44–45).

Jesus pressed this resurrection hermeneutic home in response to the question about the restoration of the kingdom (Acts 1:6–8). His resurrection and impending ascension would change the relationship between himself and the world. The disciples' expectations of a present, political kingdom needed revising. Christ's kingdom would come through the preaching of the gospel in the entire world. This view of reality, based as it is on the events of Christ culminating in his resurrection and ascension, affects all the dimensions of hermeneutics. What, then, did happen in this climax to the earthly presence of Jesus? The New Testament testifies to the great importance placed on the bodily resurrection and ascension of Jesus. Among the perspectives of the various New Testament documents, we note the following.

- Jesus' human life is shown by the resurrection to be completely acceptable to God, and he is justified by his life of perfect obedience.[8]
- The union in Christ of his divine and human natures is shown to endure, not only through death, but also as an indissoluble union for ever.
- In Christ believers now have their representative in the heavenly sanctuary and, because of their faith union with him, they are accounted as already having reached that goal.
- The resurrection of Jesus is the means of our new birth in him.[9]

---

8. The resurrection as the justification of Jesus is emphasized by Richard Gaffin, *The Centrality of the Resurrection* (Grand Rapids: Baker, 1978).
9. 1 Pet. 1:3 puts the objective slant on our regeneration focusing on Christ's resurrection, while v. 23 gives the subjective perspective focusing on the word of the gospel coming to us.

- Christ in heaven has not only reached the goal, he is himself the goal, the *eschatos*, the last one. As such, he gives meaning to all that has transpired or will transpire in human history and, therefore, he interprets all the words and deeds of God.
- The union of God and humanity is the union of God and the created order, of which humans are the pinnacle. The resurrection shows that Jesus is the first expression of the new creation.
- The perfect and enduring union of the two natures of Christ provides the paradigm for relationships that reflect the creative hand of the triune God. The relationship of the one to the many – that is, of singularity to plurality, of the particular to the general – is established as one of both unity and distinction. This perspective is essential to Christ-centred hermeneutics.

Christocentricity is not Christomonism

Christomonism is a term that has been used to describe the virtual separation of the person and work of Jesus of Nazareth from God the Father and God the Holy Spirit. G. E. Wright quotes a modern theologian as saying, 'We cannot talk about God any more; but we can talk about Jesus.'[10] The problem with this focus on Jesus is that it ignores the fact that he talked about God the Father and the Holy Spirit, and that the Christocentricity preached by his apostles was in fact an assertion of the distinct role of Jesus in the Trinity. In some expressions of evangelical piety the focus on Jesus can become almost total. Wright refers to this tendency in the Lutheran pietism that found expression in the great choral works of J. S. Bach, and also in many of the popular hymns of the nineteenth century. He also criticizes the Christomonism of both Barth and Bultmann. The 'Jesus-ology' of evangelical pietism may have a number of causes. Early pietism reacted against what it perceived as a sterile systematic theology. The Christomonism of modern theologians would appear to be more obviously linked with the philosophical influences of the time, especially the subjective emphasis of existentialism.

I suspect, then, that modern evangelical tendencies to Christomonism are the outworking of inclinations that have worrying similarities with alien

10. G. E. Wright, *The Old Testament and Theology* (New York: Harper & Row, 1969), ch. 1, 'Theology and Christomonism', p. 19.

philosophies.[11] These tendencies produce hermeneutical stances that do not really stand up under careful exegesis of the relevant texts, or in the light of Trinitarian theology. Bultmann's existentialism leads him to reject the Old Testament as being relevant to the Christian in any positive way. Similarly, evangelical neglect of the Old Testament often springs from the focus on Jesus which links him more with present subjective experience than with the revelation of God throughout salvation history. A hermeneutical framework that has shifted away from God's activity in human history can lead us to a Jesus whose saving work is no longer the climax of salvation history two thousand years ago in Israel, but is primarily an experience in the believer now. Gospel-centred interpretation will not follow this false trail.

---

11. I discuss some of these tendencies in ch. 12.

4. TOWARDS A BIBLICAL THEOLOGY OF INTERPRETATION

The method of biblical theology

The modern study of hermeneutics demonstrates the concern for hermeneutical models detailing how scholars understand the dynamics of interpreting texts. Mostly, as we shall see in the second section of this work, not only Enlightenment and post-Enlightenment theories, but many from earlier times, are heavily influenced by philosophical presuppositions that are often many stages removed from biblical presuppositions.[1] An evangelical hermeneutic needs to be more than merely reactive to anti-theistic or inconsistently theistic theories. A proactive approach is also needed. Since we are concerned with the interpretation of texts, there is also the matter of defining what is meant by a text. What is the basic unit of communication? Can we assume that verbal communication requires the same approach as written texts? This is obviously important for the consideration of the biblical texts, since many parts of Scripture are reports of what someone has allegedly said. This is especially

1. The chapter headings that Thiselton gives in his *New Horizons in Hermeneutics* (Grand Rapids: Zondervan, 1992) illustrates the point: there are hermeneutics of tradition leading to hermeneutics of understanding, self-involvement, metacriticism, suspicion and retrieval, and so on.

significant when we approach the 'Thus says the Lord' kind of report. Here we have the following possible process: God says – the prophet says – perhaps others say – until eventually someone writes it down.

If we accept the main presuppositions of Christian theism, then we accept that God is in the business of communicating the truth to us in such a way that we can know and understand the truth aright, even if not exhaustively.[2] This relates to our understanding of Scripture as the ultimately authoritative communication from God to the world for all time. The Bible says much about God's word-communication. Thiselton rightly reminds us that 'address' is a better term to use than 'communication', in order to avoid the notion that we are dealing simply with the transfer of information. It also enables us to accommodate better the role of sin and ignorance in hindering communication. Provided we keep in mind that God's address comes in various ways and may or may not communicate to hearers, the word 'communication' is useful. A complicating factor in this discussion is one that is unique to Christian theology. Does revelation equate with God's communication?[3] If it does, the distinction between oral and written address must be broadened to include the non-verbal address. I am not thinking here of the notion, made popular by some biblical theologians, that historical events in themselves are revelation. Rather we need to consider the role of what theologians refer to as general revelation: that which occurs in the created order. It cannot be ignored, for Paul tells us that it renders all people 'without excuse' because, though it is available to all, they suppress it in wickedness (Rom. 1:18–23).

The Christian theistic assumptions about interpretation are self-consciously drawn from the Bible itself. Consequently, biblical theology is uniquely appropriate for the task of understanding what kind of hermeneutical model fits the world-view of Christian theism. This is because biblical theology is essentially the examination of the individual parts to see how they fit into the big picture. As to the method, I prefer a biblical theological investigation of any theme or subject to begin with the gospel, because it is through Jesus, who is the way, the truth and the life, that we are put in touch with truth and ultimate reality.

---

2. Cornelius Van Til points out in a number of his works that for non-theists to claim true knowledge they must claim exhaustive knowledge. This is because things are not known truly and exhaustively except in relation to all other things. The Christian theist claims true but not exhaustive knowledge on the basis of revelation from the One who has exhaustive knowledge.
3. Nicholas Wolterstorff, in *Divine Discourse* (Cambridge: Cambridge University Press, 1995), argues that divine speaking does not equate with divine revelation.

In Jesus, who is God come in the flesh, we have the perfect juncture of all the concerns of hermeneutical theorizing. We can summarize the hermeneutics of the person of Jesus Christ in the following way.

- Jesus Christ, the God/Man, is the eternally communicating God, the creator of all speech and understanding.
- He is God, the author of special revelation.
- As the incarnate Word of God, he is the ultimate divine message and sums up the meaning of all revelation, both natural and special.
- As a perfect human being, he is the compliant listener who receives the address of God to man with perfect interpretation, understanding and acceptance.
- Jesus' relationship to the Father includes his making the only sinless human response to the word of God to man.

It is of practical importance, then, to ask how the questions related to interpretation are raised in Scripture. Is there, for example, a biblical theology of contextualization?[4] And, since we are concerned with interpretation, we are also involved in the quest for a biblical theology of the word of God.[5] It is not possible to go into this in detail here, but we should at least be aware of the potential for such study to provide us with the confidence that traditional biblical interpretation has expressed when speaking of the clarity of Scripture. Furthermore, it is clear from the biblical texts that the notion of the word of God is never an abstraction, but is always tied to historical events. When a prophet declares, 'The word of the Lord came to me', this is always within the historical circumstances of the prophet. Any attempt to pin down a biblical theology of the word and its interpretation will involve us in the search for a biblical theology of history. In Part III we will also examine the nature and role of history in evangelical interpretation.

Just how does one pursue this topic of interpretation using some form of biblical theological method? A study of biblical occurrences of the word 'interpret' and its cognates is not likely to reveal much. Taking a more indirect approach by first trying to understand the dimensions involved in interpretation, and then pursuing these through the progress of biblical revelation, is more promising. But, as diagram 2 in chapter 1 seeks to show, there is hardly

---

4. See ch. 18.
5. We will examine the role of a comprehensive biblical theology in the reconstructive Part III of this book.

anything that is not involved. Are we therefore frustrated by the sheer weight of material? Perhaps not, for if we concentrate on the major factors of the nature of the author, the communication and the receivers, we may find some help in addressing the key issues raised in modern hermeneutic theory. As I indicated above, there is a sense in which any biblical theological enquiry properly begins with the gospel. Jesus Christ as the Word who has come in the flesh, as God's final and definitive word to mankind, establishes the essential framework. However, provided that we acknowledge our Christian presuppositions, which stem from the gospel, we can also proceed from the beginning of the biblical story. Thus the questions of starting point and priorities that I briefly alluded to in chapter 2 are once again before us. In hermeneutical terms, do we start with the authors, divine and human, or with the text, or with the hearers and readers of the communications? There can be little argument about beginning with the Creator as divine Author. In what follows we will examine some key biblical areas relating to interpretation. We have already touched on some aspects in the previous chapter, and will need to gather up the threads in Part III.

Creation and fall

The biblical view of creation impinges on every hermeneutical issue that has been raised in both ancient and modern concerns for interpretation and understanding. Furthermore, the narratives concerning creation in Genesis 1 and 2 contain, either implicitly or explicitly, the foundations for the fuller Christian doctrine of creation. The declarations that the creation is very good, along with the implications of the sovereign purpose of God, prepare the way for the post-fall broadening of the view of creation to find its redemptive consummation in the new creation. The creation narratives of Genesis, along with other notable passages such as Psalms 8, 19, 104, and Job 38 – 42, are essential to the Christian world-view that maintains the distinction between God and the creation. This distinction, in turn, is basic for the understanding of the authority of the divine Author, which is from a Christian point of view tautological, but which has been largely rejected in modern thinking.[6] The modern hermeneutical dismissal of the author and his intention simply could not happen within a framework of Christian theism.

---

6. *Author* implies *author-ity*.

It is significant that God creates by his word, for it establishes the authority and effectiveness of the divine speech-act that infallibly achieves its purpose.[7] God's word, 'Let there be . . .', produces what God intended. Nothing can go wrong; his meaning is clear and results in something that he loves and approves. The fact that, at this juncture, God is not addressing other rational beings does not alter the infallibility of the author's intention and word. The fact that the divine word brings creation from nothing means that God's word is clear as to meaning, sovereign as to power, incontrovertible and inerrant. The creative word is both self-authenticating and self-interpreting. What God commands is exactly what happens. Then God, by his word, creates humans in his image and addresses them. This word from God provides the framework of meaning within which they have understanding of reality. The 'I – Thou' address establishes the existence of the true subjectivity-objectivity relationship. Objective reality is the creation of all things by an omnipotent God. The whole of creation is objective reality to God. He creates humans as the pinnacle of this created reality and gives them the subjective reasoning and self-consciousness that reflect his own, including knowledge of the real objectivity. This imaging and the divine address that defines the derived dominion of humans over the rest of creation validate the subjectivity of the human interpreter by its relationship to the objectivity of God, his word and his work.

The divine word and the human understanding of the meaning of that word, then, are first seen in the age of human innocence. The word of God to humans is the interpretative framework for the task of discovering truth (Gen. 1:28–30; 2:16–17). Adam did not need evidences to prove that it was God speaking to him. Things and events that depend for their existence on the word of God cannot be used as higher authorities than that word in order to critique it. It should be recognized that these words to Adam and Eve are imperatives. The commands to 'be fruitful and multiply and fill the earth and subdue it and have dominion' (Gen. 1:28) by their very nature must be self-authenticating. Commands cannot be tested by evidences; they can only be obeyed or disobeyed. We either recognize the authority of the commander, or we do not. It is in the nature of those created in God's image to recognize that authority.

The account of the fall in Genesis 3 involves the rejection of the true hermeneutical framework of God's authoritative and self-authenticating

---

7. The application of speech-act theory will be considered in ch. 14. The term is now widely used to describe the view that speakers can perform a range of acts by speaking.

word. The probation that is based on the assertion 'in the day that you eat of it you shall surely die' (Gen. 2:17) contains the strongest possible sanction of death, and this was clearly meant to be understood and received as spoken with the full authority of its author. That the hermeneutical failure is linked here not with finitude, ignorance, or lack of experience, but with moral revolt against the word of the Creator, is important. It indicates that there is an ethical dimension to interpretation. In Genesis 3 the essence of 'snake-think' is the assumption that God's word is not self-authenticating, and that it can and must be assessed as to its truth claims by a supposedly autonomous human reason. The assumption of autonomy is a false assumption and so can only be adopted by suppressing the truth in wickedness (Rom. 1:18). This new condition is described as death and alienation from the source of truth, a separation from God. Philip Hughes states it thus:

> But the epistemological situation becomes one of disastrous upheaval, for sinful man, by making himself instead of God the center and key to the understanding of the reality both of himself and of the universe, severs the life line of the Creator-creature relationship *so essential to the right knowledge of things* and drifts off in to the ocean of alienation, where the fulfilment he desperately seeks will always elude him.[8]

Hermeneutics, then, must address the spiritual problem and not simply be part of it. Only gospel-centred hermeneutics can do this. The opposite of the deadly revolt is that those addressed by God give their personal and willing commitment to his authority as expressed in his word. Redemptive revelation begins with the assumption that God can and will communicate such truth about himself and his gracious purpose, and in such a way that the intended recipients can and will understand it. The biblical account points to the universality of revolt. The fact that a hermeneutics of suspicion[9] now characterizes rebellious humanity requires that any word of God spoken into the fallen world must be more than merely informative; it needs also to be powerfully redemptive.

Leaving aside for the moment the questions of ancient styles and strategies in the writing of history, we see that the narratives of Genesis 1 – 11 are

---

8. Philip Edgcumbe Hughes, 'Crucial Biblical Passages for Christian Apologetics', in E. R. Geehan (ed.), *Jerusalem and Athens: Critical Discussions on the Philosophy and Apologetics of Cornelius Van Til* (Phillipsburg: Presbyterian and Reformed, 1980), p. 133. Italics mine.
9. 'Hermeneutics of suspicion' is a term used with approval by many modern hermeneutic theorists. See Thiselton, *New Horizons in Hermeneutics*, ch. 10.

presented as the commencement of a straight-line historical progression that eventually brings us into the world of verifiable historical events. All human history after Genesis 3 is history under both judgment and the redemptive covenant of the Creator. All human history is thus given its ultimate and true interpretation only when viewed within this framework of covenant and redemption. The hermeneutical disaster of Babel (Gen. 11) again shows the dimension of divine judgment in the confusion of linguistic understanding. This clash between God and the tower-builders, presumably representing the whole of humanity, is a clash of authority in the interpretation of reality. Self-definition and self-interpretation without the word of God can only lead to greater disasters. Long before Descartes and the Enlightenment, humanity began its search for reality starting from within rather than from without. That which began as the hermeneutical suicide pact of our first parents is now shown to be a universal phenomenon. The confusion of languages is a hermeneutical confusion.

Torah (the Pentateuch)

The account of the patriarchs (Abraham, Isaac, Jacob and the sons of Jacob) in Genesis develops the themes of grace and covenant that first emerged in the Noah narrative.[10] It assumes that special revelation is perspicuous and that, when it comes in a more indirect way (e.g. Jacob's dream in Gen. 28; Pharaoh's dreams in Gen. 41), the meaning is made clear by verbal interpretation. Whatever weight modern historians might place on the patriarchal narratives of Genesis 12 – 50, there can be little doubt that they were intended to be read as history that is interpreted by the covenant promises of God.

In Exodus to Deuteronomy Moses is the minister par excellence of God's word and, as such, the mediator of salvation to Israel. The conflict with Pharaoh shows that a hardened heart prevents true understanding by a wicked refusal of the truth, even when that truth is born out by evidences that should compel the most sceptical secular mind. When the people of God do act by faith in the truth of God's word, they receive abundant evidence of God's faithfulness to his word. The redemptive word is not exhausted by the word

10. The Hebrew words for covenant (*bĕrît*) and grace (*ḥen*) both appear for the first time in the Noah narrative. However, William Dumbrell, in *Covenant and Creation* (Exeter: Paternoster, 1984), has argued, correctly I think, that the covenant idea is implicit in the creation and that the covenant with Noah formalizes it.

of God concerning the Exodus redemption, for this is but the start of the prophetic word to Israel. The words of the Sinai law are unequivocal, and the law itself functions as a secondary hermeneutical norm by being a framework for the understanding of reality. The primary norm is the word of grace interpreting the saving acts of God. Grace precedes and interprets the law, and these together interpret reality for the people of God. Thus 'I am the LORD your God, who brought you out of the land of Egypt, out of the house of slavery' is the preface to, and the primary hermeneutic framework to, 'You shall have no other gods before me' (Exod. 20:2–3).

A further hermeneutical significance of the law, as the word from God that he fully intended his people to understand, is that it could never function in the abstract. The opening words that preface the Decalogue remind us that the author is Yahweh, 'the LORD', and that he is the covenant God who has saved his chosen people out of the Egyptian bondage. The framework of grace governs the understanding of the text of the law. Furthermore, the law itself is historically conditioned so that it cannot be extrapolated from the specific context of the acts of God and the experiences of Israel. This may seem to imply that, as historical circumstances change, further expressions of law would be appropriate to apply to the new contexts. This is partly true, but at least two things prevent this historically bound nature of things from becoming relativistic. The first is the unchanging nature of God, who binds a people to himself with promises that have eschatological and eternal significance. The second is that God himself provides the definitive word on just what is appropriate to the specific situation. The ultimate historical context enabling the word of God to be understood is that created by the coming of Jesus Christ. How, for example, the moral law of Israel applies today must be determined from within revelation, not by the ethical standards of modern secular society.

The Torah material was a living tradition in that what Moses relayed to the Israelites was to be passed on to later generations. This is particularly clear in Deuteronomy:

> And these words that I command you today shall be on your heart. You shall teach them diligently to your children, and shall talk of them when you sit in your house, and when you walk by the way, and when you lie down, and when you rise. (Deut. 6:6–7)
>
> When your son asks you in time to come, 'What is the meaning of the testimonies and the statutes and the rules that the LORD our God has commanded you?' then you shall say to your son, 'We were Pharaoh's slaves in Egypt. And the LORD brought us out of Egypt with a mighty hand.' (Deut. 6:20–21)

Thus the ethical and social framework of Israel's reality was interpreted by the 'gospel' of their redemption from slavery. Redemptive grace in the Old Testament foreshadows the Christ as the hermeneutic key to reality.

Wisdom

Wisdom teaching is important for its epistemology. Biblical wisdom formulated from human experience expresses the common ground with all humanity as it engages in the cultural mandate to have dominion. But Israel's wisdom has the vital distinctive that 'the fear of the LORD is the beginning of wisdom'.[11] Thus Israel's empirical wisdom always stands within the framework of revealed wisdom for its ultimate validity.[12] Biblical theologians have frequently viewed the relative silence of the wisdom corpora about the covenant and salvation history as a problem for the integration of wisdom into the mainly covenantal theology of the Old Testament. The tendency to view wisdom literature as focusing more on creation than on salvation history is helpful, provided we do not thereby assume that these are anything other than two perspectives within the one great reality.[13] The sages of Israel were not founders of an eccentric sect. They were truly men and women of the covenant. The focus on wisdom as the handmaid of Yahweh in creation (Prov. 8:22–31) shows the divine wisdom as the source of all true understanding. In Proverbs 10 – 15 righteousness and wisdom are synonymous. We conclude that righteousness, at least in the wisdom tradition, is much more than ethical. It includes the entirety of God-ordained relationships in creation. It is 'world order', as Hans Heinrich Schmid has so aptly expressed it.[14]

Nothing could be more oriented to salvation history than the traditions of Solomon and his wisdom in 1 Kings 3 – 10, a tradition specifically linked with

11. 'Wisdom' and 'knowledge' in the wisdom literature of the Old Testament are usually synonymous terms: Prov. 1:7; 9:10; 15:3; Ps. 111:10.
12. The term 'empirical wisdom' is used to designate those wisdom sayings and literary constructions based on human observation and experience. See Graeme Goldsworthy, *Gospel and Wisdom* (Exeter: Paternoster, 1987), now published as part of *The Goldsworthy Trilogy* (Carlisle: Paternoster, 2000).
13. See, for example, Leo G. Perdue, *Wisdom and Creation* (Nashville: Abingdon, 1994). I discuss this matter in *Gospel and Wisdom.*
14. Hans Heinrich Schmid, *Gerechtigkeit als Weltordnung* (Tübingen: J. C. B. Mohr, 1968).

the book of Proverbs.[15] Here wisdom is seen to embrace the covenant, and to be the hallmark of the glory of Solomon's reign. This, significantly, includes the building and dedication of the temple as the symbolic climax of the whole covenant-based salvation history process from Abraham to David and Solomon. Thus the interpretative benchmark in Proverbs 1:7 and 9:10, 'The fear of the LORD is the beginning of knowledge/wisdom', reminds us that the sages of Israel, including Solomon, were caught up in salvation history as much as the prophets. The fear of the Lord is the Old Testament equivalent of a gospel-centred hermeneutic.

The epistemology of wisdom is important for helping us to come to terms with the cultural commonality of human beings.[16] That Moses was schooled in all the wisdom of Egypt is reported by Stephen with obvious approval, for he goes on to say, 'and he was mighty in his words and deeds' (Acts 7:22). Few scholars would deny that Proverbs 22:17 – 23:11 draws heavily on the pagan Egyptian wisdom of Amen-em-ope. But the 'baptism' of this passage into Israel's Yahwistic wisdom was not achieved by simply inserting the name of Yahweh throughout, for this name occurs but twice. Our Israelite editor placed it, along with everything else in Proverbs, under the general rubric of *the fear of the Lord.* As an intellectual activity, empirical wisdom is something shared by all peoples and cultures. In the book of Proverbs there is minimal God-talk, and virtually no references to the covenant and Israel's salvation history. It is this that makes Proverbs so immediately appealing to Christians today: it is simply about being human. Of course there are culture-specific aspects to empirical wisdom in the Bible, and it is certainly coloured by the ethical framework of the covenant. It reinforces the fact that, despite the fall into noetic apostasy, all humans alike seek to learn from experience and to interpret this experience in a way that gives coherence to their lives. The biblical idea of wisdom based on human experience is one of the strongest bulwarks against a docetic interpretation of the Christian life.[17]

The traditions of wisdom in Israel, whether written or oral, were passed on from generation to generation. The sages were teachers and they taught their pupils ultimately that they should know the fear of the Lord. The world of human experience is a real world with which we are in touch. It is a world that

---

15. See Prov. 1:1; 10:12; 25:1; 1 Kings 3 – 4 and 10 form a wisdom *inclusio* for the entire pericope.
16. This is important for the consideration of contextualization. See ch. 18.
17. That is, a view that discredits our human responsibility to think through issues in favour of direct personal guidance.

all people will understand to some degree, but only up to a point. True wisdom and true knowledge of ultimate reality come from the submission of one's mind and actions to the fear of the Lord. This fear is not an undefined religiosity, but is given its shape by the words and actions of Yahweh.[18] The emphasis in Proverbs on the words, thoughts and experiences of people should not obscure the overarching assumption of the interpretative framework of the word of God.

Prophets

The Former Prophets of the Hebrew canon of Scripture contain the bulk of the historical narratives of the Old Testament.[19] The Former Prophets overlap with the Torah in that the narratives of Moses deal with him as the definitive prophet.[20] The development of the prophetic office from Moses through to Samuel, Nathan and Gad contains a consistent pattern.[21] When God has a word to his people, either to chosen individuals or to the nation, he speaks through his prophets. It is also a consistent feature that the prophetic word, after the time of Moses, is a word that never moves outside the interpretative framework of the covenant and law revealed by Moses. New

---

18. Joachim Becker, *Gottesfurcht im Alten Testament* (Rome: Papal Biblical Institute, 1965).
19. These are Joshua, Judges, Samuel and Kings. The fact that narratives such as Ruth, Esther, 1 and 2 Chronicles, and Ezra-Nehemiah are placed in the *kĕtûbîm* (the Writings) does perhaps raise some hermeneutical questions, particularly those about the intended effects of these accounts on the post-exilic community. Each of the books in this third section of the Hebrew canon has to be dealt with on its own terms. There is no clear specific theological umbrella that qualifies the Writings for that grouping other than the big picture of Israel before her God.
20. Some Old Testament theologians, such as Gerhard von Rad, have suggested that the Pentateuch, or Torah, ought really to be redefined as the Hexateuch by including Joshua. There is also the well-received theory that the Former Prophets belong with Deuteronomy and have been crafted into a 'Deuteronomistic History' by some editorial hand or hands. These two groupings (Tetrateuch vs Hexateuch), which both differ from the canonical arrangement, indicate the difficulty in defining the boundaries between Pentateuch and Former Prophets.
21. There are some minor figures, unnamed 'men of God' and undefined schools of prophets, whose status and function is not always clear. But the major figures all function as guardians of the covenant.

messages may be given, but these are always within that framework. Thus Nathan's message of God's covenant with David and his descendants (2 Sam. 7) simply gives specific shape to the wider and more general earlier promises to Israel.

A sequel to the narrative of the Former Prophets is found in the narratives of restoration and reconstruction in the post-exilic period.[22] When Ezra read the law to the assembly of the returned exiles, it was necessary for someone to provide 'the sense, so that the people understood the reading' (Neh. 8:1–3, 7–8). Some suggest this was due to the need for teaching about the significance of the law because of the spiritual condition of the remnant. Others see it as purely a function of language, in that Aramaic had become the language of the people during their sojourn in Babylon. The Hebrew of the Torah was thus strange to them. Certainly, the later productions of Aramaic and Greek versions of the Old Testament were driven by the loss of Hebrew as the ordinary language of the Jews.

The Latter Prophets introduce a more definite eschatological perspective as God's way of dealing with the ethical and hermeneutical problem. Eschatology is the major biblical denial of all forms of relativism. The *eschaton* (the last thing) is the goal towards which the sovereign Lord is moving human history. It is portrayed in the Prophets as something totally under the control of God. It is the ultimate goal of creation and redemption. The prophets understand that people do not know the Lord as they should because of sin. Also, they can know truly that they do not now know God as they ought. The Latter Prophets reinforce a couple of hermeneutical factors that have already occurred in the narrative accounts. These are the effects of sin and the need for a radical remedy. For example, Isaiah emphasizes the sinfulness of lack of understanding:

> The ox knows its owner,
>   and the donkey its master's crib,
> but Israel does not know,
>   my people do not understand.
> (Isa. 1:3)

---

22. Some suggest that the inclusion of Ezra and Nehemiah in the *kĕtûbîm* is due simply to the lateness of their composition, presumably after the *nĕbî'îm* (the Latter Prophets) were identified as a group. There were, of course, the three post-exilic prophets in the prophetic canon, so it is possible that these narrative books were excluded from the prophets for other reasons.

This lack of understanding can be the result of a judicial act of God, somewhat like the hardening of Pharaoh's heart (Exod. 4:21; 9:12).

> And he said, 'Go, and say to this people:
>
> '"Keep on hearing, but do not understand;
> keep on seeing, but do not perceive."
> Make the heart of this people dull,
> and their ears heavy,
> and blind their eyes;
> lest they see with their eyes,
> and hear with their ears,
> and understand with their hearts,
> and turn and be healed.'
> (Isa. 6:9–10)

The metaphors of blindness and deafness are apt descriptions of the unregenerate heart and mind. These defects will be dealt with in the eschatological grace of salvation, when the eyes of the blind are opened and deaf ears made to hear (Isa. 35:4–5). Furthermore, the future events of the Day of the Lord will be accompanied by the perfection of understanding. The darkness of rebellion against God (e.g. Isa. 1:3; 6:9–10; 44:18) will turn to light with the coming salvation (e.g. Isa. 9:2–7; 35:4–5). This is a result of grace, and the epistemology of the prophets includes the promise that the grace of God will restore knowledge and understanding through a rational act of repentance and faith. Yet these are based upon divine thoughts and ways that are above human understanding:

> Seek the LORD while he may be found;
> call upon him while he is near;
> let the wicked forsake his way,
> and the unrighteous man his thoughts;
> let him return to the LORD, that he may have compassion on him,
> and to our God, for he will abundantly pardon.
> For my thoughts are not your thoughts,
> neither are your ways my ways, declares the LORD.
> For as the heavens are higher than the earth,
> so are my ways higher than your ways
> and my thoughts than your thoughts.
> (Isa. 55:6–9)

It is no problem for Isaiah to say that human language conveys divine truth while pointing out the limits of human understanding. Jeremiah places the restoration of true understanding squarely with the renewal of the covenant, not by replacing its content, but by forgiveness of sins and renewing of hearts:

> Behold, the days are coming, declares the LORD, when I will make a new covenant with the house of Israel and the house of Judah, not like the covenant that I made with their fathers on the day when I took them by the hand to bring them out of the land of Egypt, my covenant that they broke, though I was their husband, declares the LORD. But this is the covenant that I will make with the house of Israel after those days, declares the LORD: I will put my law within them, and I will write it on their hearts. And I will be their God, and they shall be my people. And no longer shall each one teach his neighbour and each his brother, saying, 'Know the LORD,' for they shall all know me, from the least of them to the greatest, declares the LORD. For I will forgive their iniquity, and I will remember their sin no more. (Jer. 31:31–34)

Forgiveness, renewal and the knowledge of God are the ultimate goals of redemption. Ezekiel likewise sees renewal of the human spirit as the restoration of the covenant relationship that in turn provides the key to understanding reality (Ezek. 36:22–28).

The apocalyptic literature introduces a new language of symbolism, but this is not left to speculative interpretation.[23] If the symbolism is not transparent within the cultural background of the original recipients, it is usually given an interpretation through supernatural intervention (Dan. 7:15–16; 8:15–27; 9:21–27; 10:1, 10–21). The main difference between Daniel's prophetic passages and the eschatology of the Latter Prophets lies in the literary idiom and the perspective on the world and its future. The premise of Daniel, both in the narrative and the visions, is that 'there is a God in heaven who reveals mysteries' (Dan. 2:28).

---

23. The one undisputed source of apocalyptic in the Old Testament is the book of Daniel. It does not belong with the canon of the *nĕbî'îm*, the Latter Prophets, but is found in the Writings. The definition of the genre of apocalyptic is not without problems, and however it is defined, the book of Daniel as a whole does not fit the usually accepted criteria. Some features of Jewish apocalyptic, however, do provide pointers to the way similar features in both Daniel and Revelation should be understood.

The Gospels

A detailed biblical theological study of interpretation would include much of the Christological material that I have referred to in chapter 3 and which I shall not repeat here. I shall refer only to a few further considerations. The four Gospels not only stand as our primary testimony to the Christ, but they also clearly express the conviction that God, the Father of our Lord Jesus Christ, establishes the existence and meaning of objective reality by his word. The Synoptics begin with the historical events surrounding the advent of Jesus of Nazareth. John takes us back briefly to the foundational fact that God, the Word, created all things. The same Word comes among us 'full of grace and truth'. The meaning of truth and reality is thus asserted to reside in the Christ. Biblical realism is given its final and definitive expression in the person of Jesus of Nazareth.[24] The sovereignty of God, the nature of reality and the effective communication of these to receivers are all clearly indicated in the prologue to John's Gospel. The epistemological problem is alluded to in that many who were addressed by the incarnate Word did not receive him. Those who were born of God did receive him (John 1:12–13).

The Gospels also present Jesus as the definitive interpretation of the Old Testament. This is summed up in Luke 24:27, 44–45.[25] These are key passages because they highlight the dynamic of hermeneutics that carries meaning beyond the original and literal meaning to the person and work of Jesus the fulfiller. There is also a hermeneutical spiral involved in the use of the Old Testament. As Thiselton comments:

> Although the primary emphasis concerns the use of the Old Testament as a context of understanding, it is also the case that the New Testament writers see Christ as an interpretative key for the interpretation and understanding of the Old Testament. Luke 24:27 and 45 uses [*sic*] the Old Testament as a frame of reference for understanding Christ, and Christ as an interpretative key for understanding the Old Testament.[26]

There are two dimensions involved here: the objective organic relationship of Jesus to the expectations of the Old Testament, and the subjective ability of

---

24. Royce Gruenler, *Meaning and Understanding* (Grand Rapids: Zondervan, 1991), pp. 168–175.
25. Luke 24:27 applies a compound of the Greek word *hermeneuō* to the process.
26. Thiselton, *New Horizons in Hermeneutics*, p. 150. The question of the relationship of the two Testaments will be taken up in more detail in ch. 16.

people to grasp this truth (hence the need to be born from above, as stated in John 3:3). The many references to prophecy being fulfilled in the person and work of Jesus reinforce the fact that Jesus is the hermeneutical norm. Because, contrary to neo-orthodoxy, we cannot allow the salvation history that climaxes with Jesus to be removed from the context of general world history, we recognize the relatedness of all historical events, including the history which we specifically understand as salvation history.

The definitive role of Jesus shows that the fulfilment of the Old Testament is never mere literal correspondence (there is always unity/distinction). Jesus' role as the Word of God incarnate is to be the final and definitive revelation from God. The Gospels' application of the Old Testament texts to Jesus and his work indicates that the progressive revelation of the Old Testament has its meaning determined by Jesus. Thus, while the Old Testament provides the salvation-historical context for the person and work of Jesus, he determines the true meaning of that context. In providing the theological-prophetic categories by which Jesus is identified, the Old Testament shows itself in need of completion through the one who fulfils it. All other hermeneutic criteria must bow to the centrality of Christ the fulfiller. Only thus can we deal with the interpretative tensions that Jesus creates over key Israelite themes such as the law, prophetic fulfilment and the temple. On the one hand, Jesus affirms the Old Testament and the nation of Israel as the context within which he is to be understood. On the other hand, he provides the only definitive meaning of these antecedents to his coming in the Israel-focused world history from creation onwards.

Acts

Acts provides an important hermeneutical bridge between the period of Jesus' presence on earth and the situation of the church today: the Lord being absent in the flesh but present by his apostolic word and his Holy Spirit. Jesus' reply to the question about the kingdom (Acts 1:8) indicates how he interprets the meaning of the Old Testament in the light of himself. The ascension of Jesus and the subsequent coming of the Spirit establish the nature of the coming of the kingdom that radically alters the apparently literalistic expectations of the disciples. A period of gospel-activity throughout the world would take the place of the immediate consummation for which the Jews hoped. After the ascension and Pentecost, Jesus continues this interpretative role by his Holy Spirit. The apostolic preaching emphasizes the gospel event, with its climax in the resurrection, as the ultimate interpretation of all things, including the Old Testament (e.g., Acts 2:16–36; 13:26–41).

The Pentecost event is unrepeatable, because it marks the transition from the period of Jesus being present in the flesh to that of his absence in the flesh and presence by his Spirit. A biblical theology of the Holy Spirit would thus take account of the fact that the Spirit has been present and active in the world since creation, but his presence now is new in that it relates to the completed gospel event and its proclamation. Pentecost marks the reversal of the two hermeneutical disasters of Genesis: the fall and Babel.

Three things at least in the Acts show that the last days, the days of the *eschaton*, have arrived.

- These are the days of the proclamation in all the world of the good news of salvation.
- These are the days of the new giving of the Spirit.
- These are the days of the entry of God's Christ into his kingdom.

Thus we can know with confidence that the people of God have a place to stand, a reference point for interpretation: the finished work of God in Christ.

The Epistles

The Epistles show the same perspective and deal more directly with the epistemological matters. Some of the key points that emerge include the following.

- All reality has its meaning in Jesus Christ: he is the purpose and the goal of creation (Col. 1:15–16).
- Wisdom, knowledge and understanding are found in Christ (Col. 2:3).
- Christ is the true wisdom and the reason for avoiding human philosophies (1 Cor. 1:18–31; Col. 2:8–10).
- The human condition is one of a fatal suppression of the truth that is available to all in the creation (Rom. 1:18–23; 1 Cor. 2:6, 8, 14; Eph. 2:5).
- The Spirit of God regenerates people so that they exercise saving faith in Christ, and so that they have renewed minds to understand the truth of reality (1 Cor. 2:7, 10–13, 15–16).

Revelation

The book of Revelation emphasizes the sovereign control of God over all reality. Not only does God, through the person and work of Jesus Christ, govern all human history, but he also gathers up all the apparently loose threads of reality in the glorious consummation of his purposes. The focus of Revelation is the gospel of the Lamb of God.[27] The key to reality is the 'Lamb standing, as though it had been slain' (Rev. 5:6). He alone is able to open the scroll and reveal the truth of God's kingdom. Here indeed is the magisterial hermeneutic. The almost oppressive emphasis on judgment in this book reminds us of the accountability of the human race before God. Accountability means that truth is there to be understood and received. Accountability also means that the final reference point for understanding and interpretation is the one before whom all are accountable. The beatific vision of the new heaven and the new earth belongs to those who have washed their robes in the blood of the Lamb (Rev. 5:9–14; 7:13–17; 12:11).

Conclusions

Those acquainted with something of the modern hermeneutical debate and literature will recognize that many of the questions that have arisen do not come in for direct treatment in Scripture. There are a number of reasons for this. One possible reason to be considered is that many of the current issues have been generated by non-biblical philosophical assumptions about the nature of reality. I have endeavoured here to indicate some of the relevant biblical assumptions. This has been merely a preliminary sketch of a biblical theology of interpretation. Among the issues to arise from the study of Scripture itself, we might mention the following by way of summary:

- the nature of God;
- the nature of mankind;
- the noetic effects of human sin;

---

27. I have dealt with this theme in more detail in my book *The Gospel in Revelation* (Exeter: Paternoster, 1984), now published as part of *The Goldsworthy Trilogy* (Carlisle: Paternoster, 2000). It is, perhaps, ironic that the book of the Bible that has generated much discord and diversity over its own interpretation should be so clear about where the key to all interpretation lies.

- the manner and goal of redemption;
- the word as God's chosen medium of communication;
- the Holy Spirit's role in noetic regeneration;
- the centrality of Jesus Christ in the gospel as hermeneutic norm.

This brief survey of the progression of biblical revelation from creation, through fall and redemptive history, to the new creation reveals a consistent approach to the basics of hermeneutics. In essence it shows that hermeneutic failure is due to human sin. The fact that we struggle for meaning and understanding as fallen creatures in a fallen world is ultimately problematic only if God has not acted to redeem the situation. But, because we believe he has acted redemptively in Christ, it is to this Christ that we must turn for hermeneutic salvation.

PART II

CHALLENGES TO EVANGELICAL HERMENEUTICS

Introduction

The purpose of Part II is to survey the nature of some of the main alien influences that have affected biblical interpretation from sub-apostolic times to the present. These constitute challenges to authentic evangelical hermeneutics. I want to emphasize that I have not set out to give a summary of the history of hermeneutics. My reliance on secondary sources serves to show some of the reactions and evaluations occurring in recent scholarly comment, particularly by evangelicals. This helps us to see how the various trends in hermeneutical theory have troubled and exercised the critical judgment of evangelicals.

Paul exhorted the Christians in Colossae thus:

> See to it that no one takes you captive by philosophy and empty deceit, according to human tradition, according to the elemental spirits of the world, and not according to Christ. For in him the whole fullness of deity dwells bodily, and you have been filled in him, who is the head of all rule and authority. (Col. 2:8–10)

He clearly contrasts the traditions of the world and the authority of Christ. As he does in 1 Corinthians 1, he again warns of a point of view or intellectual framework that seeks to establish truth apart from Christ. In writing to Christians, it is unlikely that Paul thinks they are in danger of completely rejecting their Christian faith. But he does understand how error can creep in under the guise of being Christian. This has always been the nature of heresy, in contrast with complete apostasy and unbelief. A false premise, a distorted starting point, a truth emphasized out of proportion so that it is unchecked by other equally important truths: these are the ways heresies arise. Furthermore, none of us is immune to the seductions of points of view that are consistent with non-Christian world-views but poison to the truth as it is in Jesus.

The subtitle of a recent book on hermeneutics by Garrett Green refers to 'The crisis of interpretation at the end of modernity'.[1] An older book by Brevard Childs bears the title *Biblical Theology in Crisis*.[2] But if there were, or are, such crises we may well ask, 'Crises for whom?' One group's crisis is another group's opportunity. More neutrally, one group's crisis may go unnoticed by another group that experiences no such crisis. One of my teachers, referring to a book in vogue when I was a student, H. H. Rowley's *The Re-Discovery of the Old Testament*,[3] remarked that many of us had never mislaid it! Which leads me to ask, is there a crisis in hermeneutics? One could certainly understand why many evangelical Christians would answer with a resounding 'no'. Others would say that there is a crisis, but it is of our own making. For two thousand years the Bible has been read and understood well enough for people to be convicted, converted and nurtured in the faith their whole lives. None would deny that there are difficulties and differences of opinion about even important biblical doctrines. Nor would any deny that there are times in the life of the church when the light of Scripture has been largely obscured. But, even though there is presently a wide acceptance of humanistic beliefs in the churches, evangelical Christianity is perhaps stronger now than it has ever been since the Enlightenment.

The crisis for biblical theology to which Childs refers was little more than the realization that one approach to the discipline had painted itself into a corner. But at the same time that the so-called American biblical theology movement was in crisis, biblical theology was not only alive and well, but was finding new vitality among Reformed and evangelical theologians around the world. We rejoiced that Rowley and others had rediscovered the Old Testament, but at the same time we could not help feeling that its loss as a

1. Garrett Green, *Theology, Hermeneutics and Imagination* (Cambridge: Cambridge University Press, 2000).
2. Brevard Childs, *Biblical Theology in Crisis* (Philadelphia: Westminster, 1970).
3. H. H. Rowley, *The Re-Discovery of the Old Testament* (Philadelphia: Westminster, 1946).

source of Christian sustenance for so many should never have happened. So what do we make of the crisis of interpretation? What kind of crisis afflicts hermeneutics?

In this section we will examine some of the many changes of direction that have occurred in biblical interpretation throughout the centuries. Whether or not they constitute crises is really not important. My aim is simply to highlight the ease with which either potential or actual crises can occur in the way the Bible is read and understood. These divergences usually occur within the nurturing fellowship of the church, and thus represent more serious situations than those that occur outside this context in the realm of the secularist. This latter is, of course, a matter of concern for us, and especially for the evangelist and the Christian apologist. Any historical survey of biblical interpretation anticipates the postmodern concern for the readers and their responses to the text. I consider the readers of different periods as those who cannot be dismissed, and whose interpretative grids can both instruct us and warn us. As Christopher Wright says, 'We need to recognize that the meaning of the texts does relate to, and cannot ignore, who is doing the reading and what they bring to their reading from their own cultural background, presuppositions, assumptions and so on.'[4]

Green's book includes an historical section dealing with Enlightenment thinkers and those who came after. The purpose he expresses is 'to better understand our situation by grasping how we got into it in the first place'.[5] He also uses it to reopen questions closed to us by the dominance of modernism. Both of these are laudable aims and, in many respects, coincide with my own aims in this section. If we take a larger view of the universal church so that it includes all those who confess faith in Christ (whatever that means to them), then we recognize a duty of fellowship to contend for the truth as we believe it to be, while at the same time being humble enough to listen to other Christians who dot their theological i's and cross their t's in a different way from us. Even non-Christians and those who challenge our assumptions may give us insights and get us to ask relevant questions that we may never otherwise have asked.

A section that heads each chapter as 'The eclipse of the gospel in . . .' should contain at least one chapter on 'The eclipse of the gospel in evangelicalism'. Certainly, I would never want any of these chapters to be read

---

4. Christopher J. Wright, 'Interpreting the Bible among the World Religions', *Themelios*, 25/3 (2000), p. 49.
5. Green, *Theology, Hermeneutics and Imagination*, p. 16.

as a claim that I have never eclipsed the gospel in my own thinking and living, for I know full well that I have. The metaphor of eclipse, which I borrowed from Adrio König,[6] should be taken with the recognition that eclipses are not always total and can even be partial enough to pass unnoticed by all but those trained to look for them. But as Green pointed out, we need to see not only where we are, but also how we came to be there. A sense of the history of theology, of which the history of hermeneutics is a part, is vital if we are to make any sense of where we are and where we ought to be heading. The titles of the chapters in this part have a uniformly negative tone. This does *not* mean that I see nothing positive in those periods under investigation. As I state above, this section is not intended to be in any sense a complete survey of the history of interpretation in the Christian church. There are plenty of such histories available.[7] My aim in Part II is a relatively modest one. I want to highlight *some*, and only some, examples of major philosophical influences that have impinged negatively on Christian biblical interpretation in certain periods of the church's history. At the same time I want to acknowledge that we evangelicals can learn, and have learned, from those whose view of Scripture is quite different from ours.

---

6. Adrio König, *The Eclipse of Christ in Eschatology* (Grand Rapids: Eerdmans, 1989).
7. For example, most of the introductory texts already referred to, including those by Berkhof, Mickelsen, Kaiser and Silva; Klein, Blomberg and Hubbard all contain sections on the history of interpretation. More comprehensive treatments can be found in Gerald Bray, *Biblical Interpretation Past and Present* (Leicester: Apollos, 1996); and Donald McKim (ed.), *Historical Handbook of Major Biblical Interpreters* (Downers Grove and Leicester: IVP, 1998). See also Alan J. Hauser and Duane F. Watson (eds.), *A History of Biblical Interpretation, Vol. 1, The Ancient Period* (Grand Rapids: Eerdmans, 2003).

5. THE ECLIPSE OF THE GOSPEL IN THE EARLY CHURCH

The context of hermeneutics

A history of biblical interpretation naturally follows from an examination of the hermeneutics in the Bible itself. This historical study, then, may be regarded as a sequel to the biblical-theological study of interpretation. There are, of course, important differences between a biblical theology and a post-biblical historical study. The former will provide the normative material by which the interpretative processes and presuppositions in the extra-biblical literature must be assessed. I have argued for the existence of a consistent, if diversified, expression of theism in the Bible. The diversity is found in the many different emphases and perspectives on the unified truth of God and creation that reaches its climax in the person of Jesus Christ. The perspectives of the biblical writers will highlight both transcendence and immanence. They will include both the sovereignty of God and human responsibility. We need to examine all subsequent interpretation for its connection to biblical theism. For the purposes of this study, we will concentrate on the evidence for the invasion of non-biblical philosophical frameworks into the interpretative process.

The evidence from the New Testament has led us to the conclusion that we may summarize the hermeneutical method of Jesus and the apostles as Christological. The biblical norm is that interpretation of Scripture proceeds from the revelation of God in Christ outward to the humanity of the biblical texts. This could be referred to as a hermeneutics 'from above'. Any attempt at a hermeneutics 'from below', moving in the opposite direction from human reason to an assessment of Christ and revelation, is inconsistent with evangelical interpretation. Understanding the biblical texts may involve an appreciation of their historical-cultural contexts. But the texts themselves claim overall to offer redemption from the godlessness of human history and culture, and to sit in judgment on such godlessness. Among some contemporary scholars there is an emphasis on the Jewish interpretations, including those of the Dead Sea Scrolls, as the background that explains much of the interpretation of the Old Testament in the New.[1] While we may gain from the understanding of this cultural context, we need to remember that the New Testament itself and not its Jewish context is the norm, and that Jesus was not noted for his conformity to standard Jewish interpretation. We further observe that the New Testament shows that a massive hermeneutical cleavage occurred between Jesus and the Jews of his day. Thus, while Judaizing tendencies dogged the churches of Galatia and Colossae, the apostolic norm for combating these errors was the gospel.

The sub-apostolic age

According to David Dockery, the apostolic fathers remained Christological in their hermeneutics, but there was a shift in emphasis onto the moral or functional use of Scripture. Interpretation was grounded in the church's exposition, especially in the sermon, in the context of liturgy.[2] One might query, then, the validity of the Christology that is implied in this shift. The ontological Christology behind the definition of the two natures of Christ is closely related to the work of Christ. It would appear that very early in Christian history there occurred a concentration on the exemplary and ethical Christ, rather than on the substitutionary and redemptive Christ. This slippage

1. See David Dockery, *Biblical Interpretation Then and Now* (Grand Rapids: Baker, 1992), pp. 23–26. I do not deal with the subject of Jewish-Rabbinic interpretation here, which can be referred to in most historical surveys. Some studies have investigated how far it can be said that Jesus and the apostolic writers used the methods of Jewish exegesis. See, for example, Richard Longenecker, *Biblical Exegesis in the Apostolic Period* (Grand Rapids: Eerdmans, 1975).
2. Dockery, *Biblical Interpretation Then and Now*, p. 45.

anticipates the reversal of the roles of justification and sanctification in medieval Catholicism. Thus 1 Clement (c. 96) and the Didache major on ethical instruction.[3] The seven letters of Ignatius (early second century) exhibit an emphasis on moral issues and inexact use of Paul. There is also a transition towards authoritative hermeneutics in his focus on the role of the bishop.[4] The tendency to move away from the centrality of the gospel to a greater emphasis on Christian behaviour was not a new phenomenon. Legalism and moralism were always dangers in the early church, as the New Testament letters so clearly indicate. If this apparently sudden collapse of apostolic gospel-centricity in the sub-apostolic period seems inexplicable, it may help if we remember that the apostolic scriptures were themselves uniquely prophetic. They alert us to the ever-present tendency of the human heart to diverge from the truth. Thus, while the philosophical label of humanism belongs to modern times, the phenomenon is as old as Adam and Eve.

This period of early formation contains a number of important transitions. First, the age of the apostles had passed. The unique and distinctive claims to authority of the apostles were no longer a living reality in the church. The question of the new locus of authority would come to be of great importance from this time on. Until the canon of the New Testament was established and recognized, it was easier for doctrinal and ecclesiastical authorities to have pre-eminence over Scripture. The canon of the New Testament was still in a state of flux and would remain so until the fourth century.[5] Second, with the matter of the canon still fluid, the relationship of the gospel and the apostolic doctrine to the Hebrew Scriptures was problematic. Third, the practice of exegesis and the hermeneutics of a Scripture 'for the church' were embryonic. The more remote in time the church became from the apostolic churches, the more it was necessary to establish how normative authority functioned. Finally, the cultural context of the early church was complex and philosophically alien to the gospel.

The Acts of the Apostles reminds us of the difficulties the first Jewish Christians experienced in recognizing that the grace of God was extended to the Gentiles. Paul constantly battled various forms of Judaizing tendencies in the New Testament churches. The tension was one that would become

---

3. 'Clement's letter reflects the movement away from the Pauline faith to a type of Christianity in which ethical interests and concern for law and order predominate.' Cyril Richardson (ed.), *Early Christian Fathers*, Library of Christian Classics, vol. 1 (London: SCM, 1953), p. 39.
4. Dockery, *Biblical Interpretation Then and Now*, pp. 51–54.
5. R. T. Beckwith, 'The canon of Scripture', *NDBT*.

a permanent part of Christian hermeneutical discussion: the relationship of the law to the gospel, of works to grace. The apologists of the second and early third centuries help us to understand what was going on in the use of the Bible. Justin Martyr (c. 100–165), Irenaeus (c. 130–200) and Tertullian (c. 160–225) had to establish the Christian hermeneutic of the Old Testament in order to deal with the rejection of the Old Testament by Marcion.[6] While thus seeking to preserve the Old Testament, at the same time they had to show how the Christian gospel implied a rejection of any tendencies to legalism.

Allegory and the Alexandrines

Both Greeks and Jews used allegory as a method of interpretation. The Greeks used it to resolve the tension between their religious and philosophical traditions. Hellenized Jews found allegory a way to resolve the tension between their religious traditions and the Hellenistic philosophers, especially Plato.[7] The probable founder of allegorical interpretation was the pre-Socratic Greek Theagenes of Rhegium. The philosophers began to express philosophical ideas with mythological imagery. Amongst the Jews of Alexandria, Philo sought the philosophical meaning of the Bible by means of the allegorical method. He accepted the dualism between the material and non-material, and the Stoic notion of the *logos* as mediator between the transcendent God and the material world. The Bible was regarded as having multiple meanings. Philo was aiming to bring Judaism together with Greek philosophy. The doctrinal rule of faith advanced by Irenaeus and Tertullian was seen to contradict many Greek Gnostic teachings. But the Fathers had sought to deal with the Gnostics by denying them the use of the Scriptures. This did not satisfy the Christians in Alexandria, who were next to adopt the allegorical method. They developed a hermeneutical system that aimed to retain the rule of faith and to meet the challenge of the Gnostics.

Clement and Origen turned to Platonic philosophy and allegorical hermeneutics. Both regarded much of the Platonic philosophy as having its origins in the Old Testament.[8] Clement (c. 150–215) saw the literal meaning as

---

6. Dockery, *Biblical Interpretation Then and Now*, ch. 2.
7. Bernard Ramm, *Protestant Biblical Interpretation*, 3rd rev. edn (Grand Rapids: Baker, 1970), ch. 2.
8. Deirdre Carabine, 'A Dark Cloud: Hellenistic Influences on the Scriptural Exegesis of Clement of Alexandria and the Pseudo-Dionysius', in Thomas Finan and

the starting point for the mass of Christians. But, in Platonic thought, earthly things are inferior to the heavenly forms and only shadows of them. In the same way, the literal sense of the Bible is inferior to the spiritual sense. The deeper, allegorical meaning is the means by which people are led to a better understanding. So every text was thought to have one or more additional and deeper meanings beyond the literal. This method was developed for apologetic and theological reasons. Clement differed from Tertullian in that he had little concern for the authority of the hierarchy of the church, and in that he welcomed the insights of Platonic philosophy as propaedeutic.[9] Paul Tillich comments, 'Clement's thought is a great example of a synthesis of Christian thinking and Greek philosophy.'[10] Thus, Clement said, Platonism was given to the Greeks as a preparation for the coming of Christ. His first hermeneutic principle was that the text had both a literal sense, that could be observed, and an allegorical sense, that must be discovered. Clement also used Platonic thought to establish the unity between the two Testaments. Using three main approaches, he arrived at five interpretative perspectives: an essentially literal approach yielded both historical and doctrinal interpretations; typology gave a prophetic interpretation; and allegory was the mainstay for philosophical and mystical interpretations.

Origen (c. 185–254) studied under Clement. He accepted the literal sense, but not necessarily as the primary sense. Clement had developed a hermeneutical approach in which Scripture has three meanings: (i) literal or physical; (ii) moral or psychical; and (iii) allegorical or intellectual.[11] The foundations of his procedure were: (i) every text has a deeper meaning which requires allegory; (ii) nothing unworthy of him should be said of God; and (iii) nothing should be affirmed against the rule of faith. The need to avoid saying unworthy things about God suggests the anticipation of modern exegesis in which the unacceptable is expunged on the basis of reason. Who determines what is unworthy of God? The rule of faith involved Origen in Scripture and tradition, and thus included the principle of the interpretation of Scripture by Scripture. Some tension arose between Origen's allegorical interpretations and the rule of faith.

Vincent Twomey (eds.), *Scriptural Interpretation in the Fathers* (Dublin: Four Courts Press, 1995), pp. 61–74.

9. i.e., preparatory to Christian theology. Tertullian, on the other hand, asked the famous question, 'What has Athens to do with Jerusalem?'

10. Paul Tillich, *A History of Christian Thought*, ed. Carl Braaten (New York: Simon and Schuster, 1967), p. 56.

11. Ramm, *Protestant Biblical Interpretation*, p. 31.

According to Gillian Evans,[12] Origen established certain foundational principles for the study of the Bible, namely: (i) the Bible is a unity, but it requires the allegorical method to open it up; (ii) nothing in it is redundant; and (iii) it contains progressive revelation. When Arius challenged the teaching of the church, Athanasius responded using a method derived from Origen. He interpreted the whole Bible by the New Testament and the New Testament by the Gospel of John. He was more inclined to use analogy rather than allegory. In Athanasius the rule of faith came to dominate more than in Origen. In assessing Origen, Moisés Silva suggests that he 'anticipated virtually every substantive hermeneutical debate in the history of the church, including some that have persisted to this day'.[13] We might not like Origen's answers, but we cannot avoid his questions. Thus Origen recognizes the tension of the divine nature of the Bible and its humanity.[14] Because he is known for his use of allegory, Origen opens up to us the whole question of the figurative versus the literal, and the nature of typology and allegory. Thiselton notes the concerns of Origen to move beyond the historical text to contemporary pastoral application.[15]

While Origen concentrated on the divine nature of the Bible, his attitude to textual and philological matters showed his concern for the human dimension. The divine-human tension cannot be avoided in Origen's work. There is also the matter of literal and figurative interpretations. Origen regarded the literal meaning as important. It is useful for simple believers (implying that mature believers will go beyond the literal). His allegorical interpretation had theological significance because the Jews had rejected the gospel in line with their literal interpretation of the prophets.[16] He was also convinced that to interpret everything literally would necessarily lead to blasphemy or contradiction. He pointed to the New Testament use of allegory as justification for his approach. Origen thought that God had deliberately veiled the truth so that there is a secret meaning that is hidden from the majority. He also distinguished between immature and mature believers. The latter showed their maturity in allegorical understanding. Silva goes on to comment that 'the

---

12. Gillian Evans, *The Science of Theology* (Basingstoke: Marshall Pickering; Grand Rapids: Eerdmans, 1986), p. 34.
13. Moisés Silva, *Has the Church Misread the Bible?* (Grand Rapids: Academie; Leicester: Apollos, 1987), p. 36.
14. ibid., p. 39.
15. Anthony Thiselton, *New Horizons in Hermeneutics* (Grand Rapids: Zondervan, 1992), pp. 167–173.
16. Silva, *Has the Church Misread the Bible?*, pp. 59–63.

allegorical method was not an isolated quirk among early Christians. They did not adopt it arbitrarily or unthinkingly but viewed it rather as one of the foundation stones in a large theological and intellectual edifice.'[17]

Typology and the Antiochenes

As we turn to the Antiochenes, let us bear in mind the warning of Silva: 'It is simplistic to view Origen and the Antiochenes as representing two opposite approaches more or less exclusive of each other.'[18] Jaroslav Brož indicates a common principle in the two schools: 'For the Fathers, the non-literal meaning of a text was always related to the confession of orthodox faith and to the communion of the church.'[19] Origen used and defended the literal interpretation, while the medieval concern for the literal meaning did not signal an abandonment of the allegorical. The distinctive feature of the Antiochene school was the conviction that the primary sense of Scripture was the historical. Thiselton comments that 'there remains a greater emphasis on history and a related suspicion of polyvalent meaning among the Antiochene Fathers'.[20] For Brož, the two schools may be compared thus:

> In the Antiochene typology, the horizontal plane of the history of salvation prevailed as the principle that enabled a comparison to be made between a type and its fulfilment. Origen's hypothesis regarding the three senses of Scripture made it possible for features common to Christ and various Old Testament figures to be found on every level of the traditional vertical anthropology . . . Thus, we may conclude that typology stresses the universality of salvation in the sphere of time and space, i.e. salvation covers the entire expanse of human existence. Allegory then underlines the universality of salvation with regard to each human being in every stage of his completeness, i.e. salvation encompasses the whole human being as a person.[21]

17. ibid., p. 63.
18. ibid., p. 53.
19. Jaroslav Brož, 'From Allegory to the Four Senses of Scripture: Hermeneutics of the Church Fathers and of the Christian Middle Ages', in Petr Pokorný and Jan Roskovec (eds.), *Philosophical Hermeneutics and Biblical Exegesis* (Tübingen: Mohr Siebeck, 2002), p. 303.
20. Thiselton, *New Horizons in Hermeneutics*, p. 172.
21. Brož, 'From Allegory to the Four Senses of Scripture', p. 307.

Theophilus became bishop of Antioch in about 169, and his early work *To Autolycus* pre-dates Irenaeus and Tertullian. Theophilus saw the Old Testament as an historical book containing the history of God's dealings with his people. The relation of the Testaments was Christological. Antioch thus became the centre of opposition to the allegorical method of Alexandria. Lucian of Antioch (born c. 240) led this reaction, emphasized the literal meaning of the text and developed the method of typology. Diodore of Tarsis (died c. 394) regarded allegorical interpretation as foolishness.

The distinctive of Antiochene interpretation was the *theoria*. By this they meant that spiritual insight could be gained from the literal sense.[22] Thus the predictions of the prophets could be both historical and Christocentric. Unlike allegory, the prophetic or messianic meaning did not tend to downplay the literal, but rather was built upon it. John Breck suggests that the Alexandrines sought two meanings of Scripture, while the Antiochenes looked for a double meaning.[23] The latter underlines the organic relationship between the type and antitype which allegory easily obliterates. Theodore of Mopsuestia (c. 350–428) stressed that *theoria* did not do away with the literal or historical meaning. He saw the Bible as a unified record of the historical development on the divine plan of redemption. John Chrysostom (c. 354–407) was concerned with the critical, literal, grammatical and historical interpretation. The Bible was God's supreme act of condescension to mankind. He focused on the dual authorship, the divine and the human, of the Bible. The Bible was historical and addressed to historical communities. Scripture had to be interpreted by Scripture.

The Antiochene approach, then, differed from Alexandrine allegory in two main ways.

- While typology looked for historical patterns in the Old Testament to which Christ corresponded, allegory was based on the accidental similarities in language and concepts.
- Typology was dependent on the historical interpretation, while allegory was not.

---

22. Roger W. Bernard, 'The Hermeneutics of the Early Church Fathers', in Bruce Corley, Steve Lemke, Grant Lovejoy (eds.), *Biblical Hermeneutics*, 2nd edn (Nashville: Broadman and Holman, 2002), p. 94.
23. John Breck, *Scripture in Tradition* (Crestwood, NY: St Vladimir's Seminary Press, 2001), p. 23.

Roger Bernard suggests that the main alien influences on the Antiochene school were Jewish literalism and Aristotelian empiricism.[24] Both maintained that truth is available directly from the world around us. The emphasis on the human aspect of the Bible encouraged the Christological heresy of Nestorianism, and this brought the Antiochene school into some disrepute. But we must not overlook the fact that Antiochene thought stressed the genuine and complete humanity of Christ along with the literal and historical interpretation of the Bible. In this we may see the implication that proper grammatico-historical exegesis stems from the fact of the incarnation. Typology is oriented to the historical patterns, allegory to the linguistic and notional patterns.

Assessment

The hermeneutical questions raised by an examination of the early history of Christian interpretation include the shift from New Testament and apostolic hermeneutics. This, of course, raises the further question of the principles in the New Testament for the interpretation of the Old Testament, a matter we will examine separately. Christopher Ocker refers to Dilthey's essay of 1900 in which the sixteenth-century Lutheran Flacius is blamed for consigning medieval Christian hermeneutics to oblivion. 'Flacius believed there was a progressive distortion of revelation that began soon after the age of the apostles, effected by a train of non-scriptural influences, beginning with Greek philosophy, including the "theologians" and ending with monastic superstitions.'[25] Flacius may well have underestimated the real concerns of both early and medieval hermeneutics, but our investigations suggest that he was right to recognize the deleterious effects of Greek philosophy.

What, then, is happening in the early Christian hermeneutics when we get the shift away from gospel-centredness to a more moralistic and even legalistic concern? How do we account for the split in hermeneutical practice between the schools of Alexandria and Antioch? What in each of these schools is worth preserving? If there is a shift away from a Christ-centred hermeneutics, we can apply dogmatic structures to help us understand what is happening. The allegorical, notwithstanding Silva's positive comments about

24. Bernard, 'The Hermeneutics of the Early Church Fathers', p. 94.

25. Christopher Ocker, 'Medieval Exegesis and the Origins of Hermeneutics', *SJT* 52/3 (1999), n. 1, p. 328.

it, would seem to involve some measure of surrender to the Gnosticism of Hellenistic thinking. The historical, literal meaning of the text was downgraded so that the focus was on the hidden spiritual meaning. Allegorical interpretation is thus a tendency towards Docetism, and hence involves a Christological problem. On the other hand, the tendency for Antioch to lead to Nestorianism shows how easy it was to move from the recognition of the two natures of Scripture to a separation of the two. Antiochene interpretation was at its best when it recognized the unity of the literal and the spiritual along with the distinctions between them.

James McEvoy puts a more positive slant on the development from the apostolic handling of the relationship of the Old Testament to Christ, through to the Fathers and medieval interpreters. He sees the spiritualizing processes as continuous with those begun in the Old Testament itself. But he seems to ignore the foreign influences that invaded the early church and laid the foundations for the distinctive characteristics of Roman Catholic interpretation.[26]

It is clear that the Reformers, and Calvin in particular, rejected much of the medieval interpretation that stemmed from early Alexandrine hermeneutical method. It is also clear that they were eclectics when it came to the great Fathers of the church. The modern evangelical interpreter should learn from them. Moisés Silva warns against too ready a dismissal of the allegorists,[27] and Graham Keith also tries to put a positive slant on them by showing the questions they sought to deal with.[28] We can certainly be inspired by the integrity of their endeavours, the zeal with which they fought vital apologetic battles, and their concern to preserve the integrity of the Old Testament as Christian Scripture. Nevertheless, they remain a warning to us of the effects of watering down the Christ-centred perspective of the apostles with alien thought forms.

---

26. James McEvoy, 'The Patristic Hermeneutic of Spiritual Freedom and Its Biblical Origins', in Thomas Finan and Vincent Twomey (eds.), *Scriptural Interpretation in the Fathers* (Dublin: Four Courts Press, 1995), pp. 1–25.
27. Silva, *Has the Church Misread the Bible?*, ch. 2.
28. Graham Keith, 'Can Anything Good Come Out of Allegory? The Cases of Origen and Augustine', *EQ* 70/1 (1998), pp. 23–49.

6. THE ECLIPSE OF THE GOSPEL IN THE MEDIEVAL CHURCH

Precursors to medieval interpretation

Jerome (c. 341–420), translator of the Bible into Latin (Vulgate) and champion of monasticism, settled in Antioch in 372. He avoided the study of pagan philosophers and began to study Hebrew. He returned to Rome from 382 to 385 and began the translation of the Bible. He then settled in Bethlehem in 386, where he became convinced that he must use the Hebrew text for the translation of the Old Testament. In theory he developed some sound principles, especially because of the influences of the literal school of Antioch. These influences notwithstanding, in practice he was an allegorist. He was influenced by Didymus the Blind, a follower of Origen. He developed a love for the spiritual sense of Scripture. But as R. M. Grant says, 'No matter how ingenious the allegorization, Jerome had to insist upon the reality of the literal meaning. The deeper meaning of Scripture was built on the literal, not opposed to it.'[1] His later works moved more towards historical and philological exegesis and away from allegory. David Dockery regards him as an eclectic who combined what is best in both the Alexandrine and Antiochene

---

1. R. M. Grant, *A Short History of the Interpretation of the Bible* (New York: Macmillan, 1948), p. 98.

schools.[2] Dennis Brown suggests that the fact that he was apparently more influenced by Origen, at least in his earlier period, can be explained by his being contemporary with the Antiochenes, so that fewer of their works had become available to him.[3] If Jerome was influenced by alien philosophies, it seems to have been simply a result of his eclecticism.

The greatest precursor to medieval interpretation was Augustine. In Carthage, and before his conversion, he studied many different philosophies. He read Cicero and became consumed by a desire for wisdom. He turned to the Bible, but found it disappointing. He then turned to the Manichaeans, a sect of Gnostics who mocked the Old Testament. After nine years he became disillusioned about their ability to provide the answers he wanted. In 383 he went to Rome and then became master of rhetoric in Milan. Here he met a band of philosophers who regarded themselves as leaders of a renaissance of real Platonic philosophy. However, the preaching of Ambrose of Milan appealed to Augustine. 'Ambrose made use of the Greek fathers who had pioneered the work of reconciling Christianity and Neo-Platonism, especially Philo and Origen.'[4] Thus Ambrose provided the newly converted Augustine with a key to the interpretation of the Old Testament by the use of allegorical hermeneutics. With his discovery of Neo-Platonism, Augustine sought to develop a Christian philosophy.

Augustine produced a handbook of hermeneutics and homiletics called *De Doctrina Christiana*, in which he develops a theory of signs. Bernard Ramm summarizes Augustine's largely orthodox hermeneutics under twelve points.[5] These indicate that he valued both the literal-historical sense and the allegorical. Perhaps of most significance is his regard for the rule of faith. It is not hard to see how a concern that exegesis be controlled by already formulated doctrines can develop into a rule that subordinates the meaning of Scripture to the teaching authority of the church. On the other hand, he set sound standards of exegetical practice and of using the analogy of Scripture. He also insisted that a true Christian faith was necessary.

Ramm points out that Augustine frequently violated his own rules of interpretation. In his *City of God* Augustine puts forward his view of the unity of

2. David Dockery, *Biblical Interpretation Then and Now* (Grand Rapids: Baker, 1992), ch. 5.
3. Dennis Brown, 'Jerome', in D. K. McKim (ed.), *Historical Handbook of Major Biblical Interpreters* (Downers Grove and Leicester: IVP, 1998), pp. 42–47.
4. Gillian Evans, *The Science of Theology* (Grand Rapids: Eerdmans, 1986), p. 49.
5. Bernard Ramm, *Protestant Biblical Interpretation*, 3rd rev. edn (Grand Rapids: Baker, 1970), p. 36.

the Bible. Both Testaments simultaneously described both the earthly and the heavenly realms. Thus, says Dockery, 'Augustine presented a unified canonical approach to the Bible that still allowed for the significance of the coming of Jesus Christ, while maintaining the essential unity of the two Testaments.'[6] The Platonic influence on Augustine, says Dockery, can be seen in his epistemological maxim *Credo ut intelligam* ('I believe in order to understand').[7] This philosophical foundation, according to Dockery, came from the Platonic notion of innate first principles, which enabled persons to understand particulars in this world. But, the historical origins or influences notwithstanding, the question to be decided is whether or not Augustine expresses a biblical notion in this dictum. Augustine believed that for the mind to see God it must be illumined by God, and this results in faith, hope and love.[8] It is not a pagan credo, but Christian faith that leads to understanding. Augustine rejected Pelagianism, not because of Plato, but because of the Bible.

Dockery indicates that it was Augustine who proposed the fourfold sense of Scripture adopted by later medieval theologians, the literal, allegorical, tropological (moral) and anagogical (eschatological) senses. That is, beyond the purely literal we have the three meanings that teach faith, love and hope. James Preus, however, claims that this scheme came from John Cassian (died 435).[9] When Augustine proposed that the literal sense of Scripture contains both edifying and unedifying material, he regarded both as being found in both Testaments. But Preus suggests that with Augustine there has appeared the potential for future hermeneutical development in which the whole of the Old Testament will be regarded as unedifying and that the New Testament provides the edifying meaning of the Old. Thus begins the fixing of the wrong kind of hermeneutical divide between the two Testaments.

Preus seeks to underline the key issues at the end of the early medieval period:[10]

> One [issue] is the function of the Bible's literal sense in the formation of Christian religious and theological thought: whether terminology can be kept clear, or whether it will succumb to the potential for confusion already present in Augustine's hermeneutical statement. Second, can the whole canon really function in the

6. Dockery, *Biblical Interpretation Then and Now*, p. 139.
7. ibid., p. 140.
8. ibid., p. 141.
9. J. Preus, *From Shadow to Promise* (Cambridge, Mass.: Belknap, 1969), p. 21.
10. ibid., p. 22f.

> theological enterprise, or will the letter-spirit distinction be transposed into Old Testament/New Testament terms, thus threatening a loss of the theological as well as grammatical-historical meaning of the Old Testament. The third question is the function of the Old Testament promise: whether, as 'promise of Christ' or some other inviolable divine commitment to his people it can contribute to and inform the Christian theological expression of faith and hope; or whether, as mere promise of *temporalia*, it will be relegated to the status of *signum tantum*, mere sign.

Preus further poses the question about whether redemptive history, with authentic word of God and faith, begins in the Old Testament, or only with the coming of Christ. And finally, what effect will the ambiguity of the earliest definition of anagogy have on the function of promise in biblical interpretation? The distinction between edifying and unedifying material raises important hermeneutical questions. If all Scripture is inspired and profitable, as Paul says in 2 Timothy 3:16, how can it be unedifying? That some kind of hermeneutical divide exists between the Testaments is clear. But to develop this in the direction of unedifying/edifying is fundamentally erroneous. It suggests that the apostolic hermeneutic based on Christology was by now well over the horizon.

The later medieval period

Biblical interpretation in the 'middle' period of the Middle Ages is difficult to define. Preus jumps seven hundred years from Augustine to Hugh of Saint Victor (died 1141). Beryl Smalley starts her investigations, apart from a brief introduction, at 1300.[11] R. M. Grant comments:

> And yet there is little in medieval interpretation that is strikingly novel. As far as interpretation in concerned, the Middle Ages are a period of transition from the old patristic exegetical theology to the divorce between biblical interpretation and theology which we find in the work of Thomas Aquinas.[12]

According to Grant, Jewish exegesis in the twelfth century gave fresh emphasis to the literal meaning. But, he says, allegorical interpretation was the most

---

11. B. Smalley, *The Study of the Bible in the Middle Ages* (Notre Dame: University of Notre Dame Press, 1964).
12. Grant, *A Short History of the Interpretation of the Bible*, p. 116.

characteristic among Christian exegetes. Many confined themselves to two meanings while others, Franciscan mystics and then the Dominicans such as Aquinas, insisted on four. The reason, says Grant, is that no adequate theory of the relation of revelation to reason had been worked out. A second reason was the Platonism that had influenced Christian thought through Augustine. Scripture mirrors God. God's words and will are not expressed in Scripture, but hidden in it.[13]

Preus refers to the importance of the Victorine school (Hugh, d. 1141) as lying in its care for the literal-historical meaning of the Old Testament. There developed a view of the double significance of the text. The literal sense was important for establishing the theological sense (allegorical). But he rebukes the allegorizers of his day for not attending to the literal meaning which has been put there by the Spirit to lead us to the spiritual. 'Do not therefore despise the humility of the word of God, for through humility you will be enlightened to divinity.'[14] Thus the word signifies a thing, which in turn signifies another (third) thing. Only by a proper understanding of the literal word and its signification can we move on to understand the theological meaning. Hugh thus rather tantalizingly suggests some convergence between the emphases of Alexandria and Antioch.

When it came to the Old Testament, however, Hugh admitted that the literal meaning is sometimes unclear. 'The Old Testament period is, then, one of figure and promise. When the promise is fulfilled, the Old Testament figures can be identified and filled with New Testament content, real *doctrina*.'[15] Thus Hugh fixes the hermeneutical divide firmly between the Testaments. The Old is important because it is the sign and figure of what lies in the New. We must applaud his instincts that require the fulfilment in the New Testament to enable us to understand the Old. This is what a Christological hermeneutic relies on.

The scholastic theologians

Peter Lombard (d. 1160) saw the literal meaning of the New Testament providing the spiritual meaning of the unedifying Old Testament. The promises in the two Testaments also differ in that those of the Old Testament are earthly and those of the New Testament are heavenly. Bonaventura (d. 1274) said,

---

13. ibid., p. 120.

14. Preus, *From Shadow to Promise*, p. 29.

15. ibid., p. 32.

'The whole of Scripture teaches these three things, namely, the eternal generation and incarnation of Christ (allegory), the order of living (moral), and the union of God and the soul (anagogy).'[16] But his view of anagogy was more in the direction of mystical union than eschatology. He obscures the fact that biblical eschatology is an extension of the pathway of the literal-historical redemptive acts of God. Anagogy changes the way the gospel leads to salvation away from faith in the historic Christ and towards mystical union and fulfilment. Thus the Old Testament was effectively cut off from having historical and theological interest. The idea of the Old Testament as *signum* and *figura* of the New Testament does not allow a promise-fulfilment relationship. Preus comments, 'This classic medieval exposition of the relationship between law and gospel considerably narrows the scope of Old Testament exegesis – in fact, it all but eliminates that book from the sphere of theological interpretation and construction.'[17]

Concerning Thomas Aquinas, Preus makes the following points.[18]

- There is a shift of emphasis from promise to grace. The law was not intended to kill, but when it is accompanied by grace through the sacraments of the church (infused grace), it leads to justification.
- The need for sacramentally infused grace removes any theological value from the people of the Old Testament.
- The time before grace is a time of not-having. The promise is extrinsic and inferior to inner grace.
- In hermeneutical theory Thomas stressed that biblical words have one meaning. Thus spiritual senses cannot be discerned by unveiling multiple meanings. The words (*voces*) do not signify many things, but the things which are signified by the words are able to signify other things.
- The meaning of the historical sense is retained in the Old Testament, but the theological meaning is lost. The real meaning of the Old Testament is revealed in the New.

Thomas, then, has taken the question of the relationship of the Old Testament to the New down a slippery slope. The dogmatic formulation of infused grace has changed the notion of grace from the biblical perspective of the attitude of a gracious God towards undeserving sinners. Grace is no longer demonstrated

---

16. ibid., p. 41.
17. ibid., p. 45.
18. ibid., pp. 46–60.

in the historical redemptive acts of God and has become a mystical infusion into the soul of the believer. Since the mediator of such grace is the sacraments of the Catholic Church, such grace does not exist for the people of the Old Testament. The spiritual senses correspond to the unfolding of redemptive history. The literal sense of the New Testament is the spiritual sense of the Old Testament, while the church is the thing signified by the New Testament. The hermeneutical function of promise is transferred out of the sphere of biblical interpretation into ecclesiology. The *res ultima* is God himself, whose literal meaning interprets the others.

The philosophical question of Thomas's hermeneutics relates to his use of Aristotelian categories and its effect on his use of the Bible. As Schaeffer points out, the Thomist view of Nature and Grace had some good effects in giving the creation a better place in medieval thought.[19] But it also had great destructive effects. Thomas's liking for Aristotle meant that he moved in the direction of a natural theology (as distinct from common grace). Empiricist philosophy led him to a position of autonomous reason, and the conviction of the legitimate use of pagan philosophy as a handmaid to theology. Philosophy was thus separated from revelation. Schaeffer's point is that human nature is such that, as soon as nature is made autonomous from grace, it begins to eat up grace.

Thomas develops a theological tendency that goes back to Irenaeus, who distinguished the *image* and the *likeness* of God in Genesis 1:26. The image referred to the original natural disposition (endowment with reason, etc.), while likeness represented supernatural destiny.[20] For Aquinas the fall does not alter nature. It only undoes what God had done in adding the supernatural gifts.[21] This weakening of the effects of sin implies that a valid philosophy and natural theology are still possible apart from grace. And it means a redefinition of grace as that with which we can cooperate and which works within us to restore the likeness of God.

Assessment

My heavy reliance on secondary sources in this chapter does not, I believe, undermine the possibility of assessing some of the key areas of concern. As

---

19. Francis Schaeffer, *Escape from Reason* (Downers Grove: IVP, 1968), pp. 9ff.
20. Helmut Thielicke, *Theological Ethics* (Grand Rapids: Eerdmans, 1966), vol. 1, p. 202.
21. ibid., p. 207.

with the hermeneutics of the early church, we need to ask in what way medieval hermeneutics has diverged from the apostolic patterns. The question of philosophical intrusions cannot be far away. If we can observe the influences of Aristotle, Plato, the nominalists and others on medieval hermeneutics, the question of the legitimate role of philosophy is raised. Can we use philosophy, or, indeed, must we use it, in the hermeneutical process? Can we engage the categories of philosophy without compromising our stand on the Bible? Perhaps more important is the question of the possibility of a genuinely biblical philosophy. While Anthony Thiselton's studies are focused more on the philosophical issues of later (post-Enlightenment) hermeneutics, he has proposed that philosophy has a role in pointing up the issues which we might otherwise overlook, and in giving us the categories for their analysis.[22] Others have proposed that the quest for a truly biblical philosophy is a realistic one (e.g. Herman Dooyeweerd, Gordon Clark and Cornelius Van Til). Thomas shows that medieval theological thought had become so intertwined with unbiblical philosophical categories that the resulting hermeneutics was seriously compromised. His shift in the notion of grace to infused, sacramental grace in the context of the church was to have enormous theological and hermeneutical implications, particularly for the understanding of the Old Testament. The process that would lead to the Enlightenment's downgrading, and eventual dismissal, of the transcendent and its primacy over the immanent was already well and truly advanced.

---

22. Anthony Thiselton, 'The Use of Philosophical Categories in New Testament Hermeneutics', *The Churchman* 82/2 (1973).

7. THE ECLIPSE OF THE GOSPEL IN ROMAN CATHOLICISM

The theological antecedents

The Roman Catholic perspective, given its most enduring expression by Thomas Aquinas (1224–74), builds upon the theological distinction made by Irenaeus (late second century). Irenaeus gave exegetical support to his distinction between the natural endowment of man and his supernatural destiny by arguing that the terms 'image' and 'likeness' in Genesis 1:26 are not synonymous. The image is the natural endowment of man, while the likeness is the supernatural addition that can be won or lost. Helmut Thielicke remarks on the result of this analysis:

> [T]here has arisen that distinction so basic for later Roman Catholicism between nature and supernature, between nature and grace, the distinction which allows for the *imago's* having an explicitly ontological character (as against relational) which continues intact through its impairment by sin and its restoration by grace.[1]

Thielicke further comments on the position of Catholicism:

---

1. Helmut Thielicke, *Theological Ethics* (Grand Rapids: Eerdmans, 1966), vol. 1, p. 203.

> What takes place, then, at the fall? Negatively, it may first be said that the fall does not alter nature. It cannot affect the *imago* qualities of man in any radical way. It can only undo what God had done in adding the supernatural gifts. Only in respect of these gifts do we move in that variable sphere which can be affected and altered by sin and redemption.[2]

This theological distinction that is based on a faulty exegesis affects the whole course of Catholicism, including its hermeneutics.[3] It produces a dualism of nature and grace that affects ultimately the way supernatural saving grace, and thus Scripture, is understood in relation to human nature. The dualism stemming from the dichotomy of nature and grace was most prominently expressed by Thomas Aquinas, but it was also to be found in other medieval theologians. Thus, although Thomism was not really established as normative Catholicism until the Counter-Reformation, the nature-grace dualism was common long before that.

According to Vittorio Subilia, a number of influences in Catholicism go back to the end of the first century.[4] These include the syncretizing of Gnosticism, popular philosophy, mystery religions and other influences. 'It is a phenomenon of *complexio oppositorum*, into which totality is gathered.'[5] The result is that:

> Catholicism is a grandiose synthesis of syncretism and authority. It has become a *complexio oppositorum*, in which gospel elements exist alongside non-gospel elements in a confusion that at times prevents their recognition . . . Catholicism has made the norm of the Church the Church itself, without there being over the Church any authoritative point of reference to determine in the ultimate instance what is truth.[6]

This, if it is an accurate assessment, has far-reaching implications for Roman Catholic biblical interpretation.

---

2. ibid., p. 207.
3. ibid., p. 202: 'Although more recent Roman Catholic theology has long since abandoned this exegesis, the substance of the distinction has remained.'
4. Vittorio Subilia, *The Problem of Catholicism* (London: SCM, 1964), p. 101. In the English Translator's Note (p. 11), the statement is made of the original Italian edition: 'It was hailed by Catholic reviewers as being one of the most realistic studies of the subject from a Protestant pen, and a much needed counterweight to over-facile and sentimental Protestant ecumenism.'
5. ibid., p. 101. *Complexio oppositorum* means a combination of opposites.
6. ibid., pp. 103–104.

Subilia also names Ignatius (early second century) as another early formative influence on later Catholicism. Although an enemy of Gnosticism, Ignatius seems to have allowed certain of its ideas to influence him.[7] For Ignatius the unity and authority of the church, rather than being aspects of its relation to Christ, become mystical and ontological properties.[8] The bishop incarnates Christ, and submission to him is submission to Christ. Here are the seeds for the authority of the Pope and the magisterium to which all biblical interpretation must submit.

Finally, we note the influence of Augustine (354–430) and his view of the *totus Christus* (the total Christ). Subilia regards this as one of the vestiges of Augustine's adherence to Manichaean Gnosticism.[9] Although Augustine sought to preserve the distinction between Christ as the head and the church as the body, he seems to have allowed their unity to overshadow the distinctions. He makes many statements in which the identity of Christ and the church is asserted.[10] Thus, says Subilia, 'Gnosticism is infiltrating into Christianity and producing damage so deep-seated that the very life-centres of the Christian organism are affected, and it is being changed into quite a different organism.'[11]

These significant concerns are only pertinent to this study in so far as they affect Roman Catholic hermeneutics. We need to recognize that hermeneutical concerns are not only exegetical but also presuppositional. Even if Roman Catholic scholars agree with Protestant scholars on the exegesis of texts, their authoritative hermeneutics and the use to which texts are put is of concern. The effect of those influences leading to the Romanist ecclesiology is to change the whole understanding of the way the Bible functions in the church. As Subilia says, 'The grand New Testament phrases, "through Christ", "in Christ", "with Christ", "in the sight of Christ" undergo a change from a Christological to an ecclesiological reference, and take the meaning "through the Church", "in the Church", "with the Church", "in the sight of the Church".'[12] The church no longer sits under the authority of the Bible, but

7. ibid., p. 104.
8. Subilia, ibid., p. 111, refers to the study of Ignatius by T. Preiss in which it is said that Ignatius's view of unity and authority 'derives directly from this mystic theory of unity'.
9. ibid., pp. 114–120.
10. ibid., pp. 116–117.
11. ibid., p. 119.
12. ibid., p. 121.

assumes authority over it. Its hermeneutic is no longer gospel-based, but ecclesial. The rule of faith, Catholic dogma, has become absolute.

Thomas Aquinas and Tridentine Catholicism

Jacques de Senarclens observes:

> Neo-Protestantism[13] is pleased to find in man powers which render the work of the Holy Spirit almost completely superfluous. Roman Catholicism attributes similar capacities to the Church. In these systems the Holy Spirit is little more than a mysterious influence. But the Reformation, standing on biblical ground, has to confess man's total blindness to God and opposition to his work. If he is to find God in Jesus Christ, a new miracle is needed, not in Christ now, but in man himself.[14]

De Senarclens continues:

> In both Roman Catholicism and Neo-Protestantism the analogy of being (*analogia entis*), the natural proportion between the fallen creature and a holy God, is an attack on the doctrine of the Holy Spirit . . . The Reformation doctrine of the Holy Spirit is basic since it attributes to God under the form of the third person of the Trinity all that Neo-Protestantism ascribes to the moral consciousness, religious feeling and history . . . Similarly, [the Spirit] contains all the powers which Roman Catholicism allots to nature and the Church and which find their classic expression in Mariology . . . The Reformation doctrine implies that God alone responds to his own address to us, so that faith is not an achievement of our own nature but a miracle of the living God.[15]

Aquinas recognized that salvation was dependent on revelation, but he also fixed the relationship of theology to natural philosophy. This was because he understood that God reveals himself naturally and supernaturally. His view of nature and grace is in stark contrast with the Reformation principle of *grace alone*. Human reason will demonstrate the existence of God *a posteriori* – that is, by moving back from the effect to the cause. Reason is primary because it

---

13. Neo-Protestantism is this author's way of referring to what we would generally designate 'liberal Protestantism'.
14. Jacques de Senarclens, *Heirs of the Reformation* (London: SCM, 1963), p. 101.
15. ibid., p. 102f.

establishes preliminary proofs and also shows the self-consistency of revealed truth. The *analogy of being* goes beyond the relational understanding of the image of God in man, and extends towards an ontological relationship of the created to the Creator. Thus there is between the creature and God a certain continuity that enables us to know God without revelation or the Holy Spirit. Grace supplements nature that, even though corrupted by sin, remains related to God.

On this basis Catholicism establishes its fundamental theology that sets out its presuppositions to faith by rational argument. A rational philosophy and apologetics become the necessary condition of theology:

> The starting point of the Roman Catholic position, especially since the time of Trent, is thus the knowledge of God received by the twofold way of grace and nature in virtue of revelation on the one side and of a 'profound structural similarity between nature and supernature' on the other, i.e., through the operation of a twofold alliance, the one set up by the participation of the creature in being and the other by the restitution effected in the reconciliation in Jesus Christ. This arrangement between two elements of unequal importance ascribes to man and the Church a certain power which is expressed in the doctrines of free will, of tradition, of merits, of the authority of the teaching office and Mariology, and which constitutes the chief characteristic of this whole attitude.[16]

It is the participation 'in being' that is the ontological link between humanity and God. It remains essentially intact despite the fall.

Jaroslav Pelikan comments that the nature-grace relationship in Thomism enables its adherents to be both modern and devout:

> There is no orthodox Christian tradition in the modern world that demands less of an intellectual surrender than Rome! Roman Catholicism is . . . a halfway house between the church and the world, where the secular mind may get just enough religion to satisfy its needs but not enough to question its natural propensities. In spite of its violent opposition to Roman Catholicism, the liberal Protestant theology of the past century has actually been an attempt to construct a similar halfway house under Protestant auspices. Protestantism lacked the overarching and undergirding of the church and the tradition, within which Roman Catholicism is gradually learning to be quite relaxed about modern thought.[17]

---

16. ibid., p. 32.
17. Jaroslav Pelikan, *The Riddle of Roman Catholicism* (New York: Abingdon, 1959), p. 153.

Modern Catholicism

In the Counter-Reformation, particularly its expression in the Council of Trent (1545–63), the central position of Thomism was established. Pelikan comments:

> In canonizing not merely Thomas, and not merely his theology, but his philosophy as well, the church has committed itself to a particular theory of knowledge, according to which intellect and reason are superior to will . . . Roman Catholic philosophers live in a world of their own, with their own vocabulary, their own terms of reference, and their own unexamined presuppositions.[18]

In 1950 Pope Pius XII issued his encyclical *Humani Generis*, in which the role of natural reason was reasserted and the importance of scholastic philosophy affirmed.[19] The task of the theologian is to 'show how the teachings of the living magisterium are to be found either explicitly or implicitly in holy scripture or in divine tradition'. One must expound Scripture 'according to the mind of the church, which has been made by Christ the Lord, guardian and interpreter of the whole deposit of revealed truth'.[20]

While there are undoubted changes and developments in post-Vatican II Catholicism, the essentially Thomistic structures seem to persist. The Roman Catholic theologian Aidan Nichols, in a section on the role of philosophy in theology, provides a good example.[21] He states:

> Our understanding of this transformation [of human nature] by grace comes from revelation and when formally expressed is theology. But this still leaves open the possibility, indeed it posits the necessity, of a more limited but still valuable understanding of an independent kind: an understanding of the nature that is thus transformed by grace. This understanding derives from ordinary human experience and when formally expressed is called philosophy. So the distinction between nature and grace in Catholic teaching has a mirror effect in a distinction of two kinds of

---

18. ibid., p. 65.
19. Josef Neuner and Heinrich Roos, *The Teaching of the Catholic Church*, ed. Karl Rahner (New York: Alba House, 1967), pp. 45–49.
20. Subilia, *The Problem of Catholicism*, pp. 128–129.
21. Aidan Nichols, *The Shape of Catholic Theology* (Edinburgh: T. & T. Clark, 1991), section 2.

Bible in the Church'.[31] He shows how the Commission is open to, almost demanding of, the use of the historical-critical method. However, it issues some caveats. It rejects historicism and positivism in historical research. While Williamson describes hermeneutics as the hinge that joins faith and reason in the exegetical enterprise, he refers to the Commission's warning that 'some hermeneutical theories are inadequate because of presuppositions that are incompatible with the message of the Bible'.[32] Principle 6 of the Commission describes 'A Hermeneutic of Faith'. Williamson explains, 'The pre-understanding that properly accompanies Catholic interpretation is not merely unthematized belief, but rather the fullness of Catholic faith.'[33] As to the function of the magisterium, he says, '[It] is not to set itself between Scripture and the people of God, but rather to render authoritative judgments as the need arises.'[34]

The point has been made that modern Catholicism is founded on presuppositions that closely relate to those of liberalism. Clearly Catholicism laid its humanistic foundations long before Protestantism did. The outcome has been markedly different in the two streams. At one level, however, that of exegesis and biblical studies in general, there is not a lot of difference, if any. One can see how it may appear to Protestant eyes that Catholicism seems to walk in two opposite directions at once. But, in the final analysis, the magisterium is supreme. The Fourth Session of the Council of Trent (1546) declared the church to be the interpreter of Holy Scripture.

> Further it determines, in order to restrain irresponsible minds, that no one shall presume in matters of faith or morals pertaining to the edification for Christian doctrine to rely on his own conceptions to turn Scripture to his own meaning, contrary to the meaning that Holy Mother Church has held and holds – for it belongs to her to judge the true sense and interpretation of Holy Scripture – or to interpret the Scripture in a way contrary to the unanimous consensus of the Fathers, even though such interpretations not be intended for publication.[35]

---

31. Peter Williamson, *Catholic Principles for Interpreting Scripture: A Study of the Pontifical Biblical Commission's 'The Interpretation of the Bible in the Church'*, Subsidia Biblica 22 (Rome: Pontifical Biblical Institute, 2001). A summary article is Williamson's 'Catholic Principles for Interpreting Scripture', *CBQ* 65/3 (2003).
32. Williamson, 'Catholic Principles for Interpreting Scripture', p. 335.
33. ibid., p. 337.
34. ibid., p. 338.
35. Quoted in Neuner and Roos, *The Teaching of the Catholic Church*, p. 61.

The Third Session of the First Vatican Council (1870) reinforced this declaration with a similar one. '[I]n other points the analogy of the faith (*analogia fidei*) must be followed, and Catholic doctrine as it has been received from the authority of the Church must be employed as the supreme criterion.'[36] The analogy of faith is thus not, as Protestants receive it, the analogy of Scripture, but the analogy of Catholic dogma.

In 1893 Pope Leo XIII issued his famous encyclical *Providentissimus Deus*, which addressed the questions raised by modern biblical criticism. On the one hand, it gives qualified support to the new 'scientific' study of the Bible, but on the other hand, it seeks to check it by means of the *analogia fidei* – the analogy of faith.[37] Protestants may find it curious that the Roman Church, with all its mystery and supernaturalism, can so heartily endorse modern biblical criticism provided that it does not lead to the eroding of church dogma. It is because of the nature-grace dialectic that the body of dogma has received much, if not all, of its aberrant content that the Reformers rejected. This dialectic allows for the synergism of cooperating grace that in turn leads to the whole structure of merits, invocation of saints, Mariology, purgatory and the upside-down relationship of justification and sanctification.

The apparent inconsistencies, to the evangelical mind, of Catholicism's ability to embrace the historical-critical method so wholeheartedly, while at the same time defending the inspiration and authority of Scripture, are indeed *only* apparent. The decrees of the Trent and Vatican councils, along with the various relevant papal decrees and encyclicals, are consistent with Thomist philosophy. But one must conclude, nevertheless, that some inconsistencies do occur. If the hermeneutical principle in Catholicism leans heavily on the dogmatics of the *analogia fidei* or, as the early Fathers called it, the rule of faith, on what does the formation of dogma rest? Francis Sullivan SJ looks at the hermeneutics involved in understanding the meaning of conciliar dogmas especially as they fall under the aegis of papal infallibility. He refers to Avery Dulles' exposition of 'moderate infallibilism' in a paper to the Lutheran-Catholic dialogue in the USA.[38] Dulles gives a number of conditions that limit the notion of papal infallibility. The first is that 'a papal definition must be in agreement with scripture and tradition'. The second is that it 'must be in

36. ibid., p. 62.
37. ibid., p. 64.
38. Francis A. Sullivan, 'The Meaning of Conciliar Dogmas', in Daniel Kendall and Stephen Davis (eds.), *The Convergence of Theology* (New York: Paulist Press, 2001), pp. 73–86.

agreement with the present faith of the church'.[39] Is this a true hermeneutic circle, or is it a proscribing of Scripture to fit the already existing dogmatic framework? I suspect it is the latter. The Lutheran-Catholic dialogue has led some to assert that in all essentials the Lutheran doctrine of justification by faith is the same as Rome's.[40] It still remains a point of contention for evangelicals that, if Catholic interpretation of the relevant biblical texts is the same as ours on such a central doctrine, why do we find the whole Roman system of the papacy, the mass, penances, indulgences, purgatory, Mariolatry, merits, invocation of the saints, prayers for the dead, and the rest, to be utterly in contradiction to justification by faith alone, and totally inimical to the gospel? Clearly there is a great difference in the way the Bible is being understood and applied.

---

39. ibid., p. 81.
40. Anthony N. S. Lane, *Justification by Faith in Catholic-Protestant Dialogue* (London: T. & T. Clark, 2002), provides a useful summary of the various dialogues over these essentials.

8. THE ECLIPSE OF THE GOSPEL IN LIBERALISM

The Enlightenment

The study of theology, according to Grenz and Olson, shows the way two parallel truths are handled.[1] These are the divine transcendence and the divine immanence. Modern theology is marked by the revolt against an emphasis on transcendence, a revolt that began at the Enlightenment. 'In the seventeenth and eighteenth centuries, the balance developed by the theologians of the Middle Ages and honed by the Reformation was permanently and radically disrupted.'[2] It is not difficult to see the implications of this claim for gospel-centred hermeneutics. The relationship of transcendence and immanence is directly involved in the relationship of the divinity and humanity of Christ. This, in turn, is directly involved in the doctrine of the Trinity. The common factor is the relationship of the *one* and the *many*, of unity and distinction. Any system that fails to handle this relationship biblically will obscure the true nature of the gospel.

---

1. S. J. Grenz and R. E. Olson, *20th Century Theology* (Downers Grove: IVP, 1992), pp. 11–13. See also Kenneth Hamilton, *Revolt Against Heaven* (Grand Rapids: Eerdmans, 1965).
2. Grenz and Olson, ibid., p. 16.

The Enlightenment is said to have begun with Francis Bacon (1561–1626). Although as a movement it ran through to the end of the eighteenth century, its influences are still with us today. It placed human reason, not God, at the centre. The *credo ut intelligam* ('I believe in order to understand') of Anselm and Augustine became 'I believe what I can understand'.[3] The principles of the Enlightenment stem largely from the philosophy of Descartes, in which the reasoning subject and not the revelation of God is the starting point for rational thinking. Diogenes Allen suggests that the process of transition from the medieval dominance of Aristotle to the Enlightenment began with nominalism. Nominalism emerged because of the attack on Aristotle by the theologians of the *via moderna* (modern way), which moved away from the duality involving normative Christian dogma and autonomous philosophy.[4] The *via antiqua* (old way) of Aquinas, Scotus and others represented various attempts to harmonize Aristotle and theology. By rejecting Aristotle's generalized knowledge of *genera* (the way species are alike) and *species*, these new theologians laid the foundations for a more directly empirical approach. Aristotle had rejected Plato's universals as actual heavenly forms, but this was not enough for the nominalists, who allowed no reality at all to universals, since only particulars are open to us. Causality, especially divine causality, cannot be observed and is relegated to the realm of faith. The natural theology of Thomas is thus ruled out.

The undermining of Aristotle and Thomas by the nominalists and their successors led eventually to Copernicus and Galileo. That a quantum shift in the theory of motion should have such repercussions in philosophy and theology may seem strange. But the *via antiqua* held to the view that motion must have a mover, namely God, as long as there is motion. Thus, as Allen notes:

> Descartes' conceptual analyses (in contrast to experiments) of matter and motion led him to the concept of inertia. (Galileo himself never quite reached it in his work.) It utterly subverts Aristotle's principle that whatever moves has a mover continuous with the motion (or has something always in the state of act). For the principle of inertia (which became Newton's first law of motion) is that a body at rest or in motion (in a vacuum) continues to be at rest or to move uniformly in a straight line *indefinitely*.[5]

---

3. ibid., ch. 1.
4. Diogenes Allen, *Philosophy for Understanding Theology* (London: SCM, 1985), pp. 151–169.
5. ibid., p. 164.

Thus, 'Nature as a great self-sustaining machine, is not related to God in its operations; this appears to support atheism.'[6] The principles which Descartes espoused include reason, nature, autonomy, harmony and progress. Divine transcendence is dissolved in the immanence of the divine in the orderly realm of creation and reason. Descartes' dictum *cogito ergo sum* ('I think, therefore I am') expressed a starting point of complete subjectivity and autonomy. He thus turned on its head the dictum of Augustine, *cogito ergo Deus est* ('I think, therefore God exists').

Liberal Protestantism of the Enlightenment

Jacques de Senarclens notes Kant's definition of the Enlightenment: 'It is the movement by which man emerges from the state of inferiority which made it impossible for him to use his reason without submission to the direction of others.'[7] As well as Leibniz, the eighteenth century contributed such men as Rousseau, Voltaire, Lessing and Kant who, in spite of every difference, were agreed on the priority of life over theory, of conscience over all external domination, of subject over object. 'The 18th C. never claimed to reject Christianity. It sought rather to appropriate it, first making it acceptable to the reason and conscience of the new man in order that it, too, might contribute to the development of life.'[8]

According to de Senarclens, there were four stages in the transformation of theology to accommodate humanism.[9] First, the appeal to reason was not to refute faith, but rather to show that there was no serious reason to reject faith. Second, reason was placed on the same level as revelation. But once the gate is opened to natural theology one cannot prevent it from taking over. As it had done with Aquinas, nature overcomes grace again. Third, nature's predominance means that reason becomes superior to revelation. Revelation is accepted only in so far as it conforms to natural religion. Thus dogmas involving the supernatural realm are found to be incompatible with the natural realm of reason and the senses. Fourth, Christianity is reduced to the expression of virtues with no great profundity.

6. ibid., p. 165.
7. Jacques de Senarclens, *Heirs of the Reformation* (London: SCM, 1963), p. 35.
8. ibid., p. 36.
9. ibid., pp. 36–38.

In order to understand the starting point of liberalism, we need to observe three parallel aspects that lead to the Protestant liberalism of the nineteenth century. The first of these is Schleiermacher's (1768–1834) view of religious consciousness.[10] Colin Brown comments that there had been two basic approaches to the knowledge of God.[11] The Reformers proceeded from biblical revelation, while the philosophers tried to work out a natural theology through logical deductions about the nature of the world. From Aquinas onwards there were those who tried to combine the two simply by adding nature to grace, but Kant argued that the two approaches cancelled each other out. Schleiermacher tried to get the best of both worlds. He regarded the Bible not as divine word, but as a record of human religious experience. From religious experience he sought the essence of religion. This is neither activity nor knowledge, but an element common to both. 'The common element in all howsoever diverse expressions of piety . . . is this: the consciousness of being absolutely dependent, or, which is the same thing, of being in relation with God.'[12] This led him to say, 'All attributes which we ascribe to God are to be taken as denoting not something special in God, but only something special in the manner in which the feeling of absolute dependence is to be related to him.'[13] According to Schleiermacher, then, Jesus Christ is thus not the God/Man of orthodoxy, but the one above all whose sense of dependence upon God was, and is, unparalleled. Subjectivity has all but totally replaced any true objectivity.

Second, there is the moral consciousness of Kant (1724–1804).[14] In his *Religion within the Limits of Reason Alone*, Kant attempted a moral reconstruction of religion. The religious *a priori* is to be found in the categorical imperative, the moral law within. On this, and on this alone, is religion – a religion of practical reason – built. He regarded the essence of religion as the restoration to its power of the original predisposition of good. While giving some dignity to Scripture, he asserts the superiority of reason over doctrinal exposition. Moral improvement is the goal of scriptural exegesis. There is no place for knowledge of God from outside. In the place of purely rational investigation the philosopher substitutes not the knowledge of grace by revelation, but that which proceeds from moral obligation. Kant moralizes the Christian faith in

10. ibid., pp. 39–52.
11. Colin Brown, *Philosophy and the Christian Faith* (Downers Grove: IVP, 1968), p. 110.
12. ibid., p. 111.
13. ibid.
14. De Senarclens, *Heirs of the Reformation*, pp. 53–68.

a way that makes biblical religion hardly more than an instrument to serve morality.[15] This moral religion is the striving of man after the good whereby we save ourselves. 'Salvation is simply our moral transformation, and expiation is the sanctification that we can acquire by imitating Jesus.'[16]

Third, there is the historical method.[17] Here de Senarclens recognizes the nature-grace synthesis at work in new ways of finding support for knowledge of revelation in nature or humanity. Historicism is one of these.

> Together with the rise of a sense of history and the great development of philosophies of history which sought to assimilate truth to the movement of the spirit manifested in historical evolution, this new synthesis dragged theology along with it with a force almost as irresistible as that of feeling or practical reason.[18]

Revelation now becomes assimilated to the movements of history. Universal history replaces biblical history and redemption takes place, not at one point, but over the whole. Thus, says de Senarclens, '[T]he first result of the historical method as regards religion is to make its starting point – the personal revelation of God – less extraordinary and unique and more relative.'[19] 'The chief effect of this method, which is philosophical rather than scientific, is thus to abase the divine by making it more human and to elevate the human by making it more divine.'[20]

De Senarclens continues:

> The starting point of modern Protestantism is an immediate association between God and man, based on the hypothesis of a direct relation, and first established in the alliance miraculously achieved, according to the Gospel, in the person of Jesus Christ, true God and true man . . . The result is a Christianity deeply embedded in the culture of the age and bearing its main features . . . This Protestant scheme differs in many respects from the Roman Catholic system . . . Nevertheless, the essentials are the same – the principle of a spontaneous relationship between God and man, the incorporation of faith into culture and history, the movement from nature to grace,

---

15. ibid., p. 55.
16. ibid., p. 66, quoting Charles Secrétan.
17. ibid., pp. 69–81. The historical-critical method will be considered in more detail in ch. 10.
18. ibid., p. 69.
19. ibid., p. 73.
20. ibid., p. 74.

a mitigated immanentism, and inevitable semi-Pelagianism and a more or less pronounced secularization, whether in a religious context or against a wider background . . . Neo-Protestantism as a whole is a particular interpretation of the Christian faith which is sharply divided from its Reformation origins and which links up in essentials with the basic intuition of the Roman Catholic heresy.[21]

Schleiermacher's hermeneutics of understanding

I cannot comment on Friedrich Schleiermacher and his significance for hermeneutics without being mindful of Karl Barth's warning:

H. Scholz wrote with perfect truth of the *Doctrine of Faith*: 'Schleiermacher did not succeed in everything; but his achievement as a whole is so great, that the only threat to it would be a corresponding counter-achievement, not a cavilling criticism of detail.' This counter-achievement, and indeed the man who could not only criticize Schleiermacher but measure himself against him, have not yet appeared. Let it be said in warning that with every step which exceeds careful listening and the careful asking of questions one may, not inevitably but very easily, make oneself look ridiculous.[22]

Though mindful of his greatness, we must nevertheless criticize him. Schleiermacher is regarded as both the father of liberalism and the father of modern philosophical hermeneutics. He broadened the scope of hermeneutics beyond questions about the biblical text to that of understanding and meaning in general. We must ask whether, given the philosophical starting point of liberalism, evangelical hermeneutics could ever have progressed without the insights of men like Schleiermacher. His outlook was only in the broadest sense that of the Enlightenment, for he pointed the way to a wider application of hermeneutics from that of earlier thinkers. He was, in fact, part of what Paul Tillich refers to as the Classic-Romantic reaction against the Enlightenment.[23] Tillich sees this as stemming from Kant's *Critique of*

21. ibid., pp. 81–83.
22. Karl Barth, *Protestant Thought from Rousseau to Ritschl* (New York: Harper & Row, 1959). Barth's quote is from H. Scholz, *Christentum und Wissenschaft in Schleiermachers Glaubenslehre.*
23. Paul Tillich, *A History of Christian Thought*, ed. Carl Braaten (New York: Simon and Schuster, 1967), p. 367.

Judgment rather than the *Critique of Pure Reason*: 'This means that romantic philosophy replaced religion by aesthetic intuition. Whenever you find the statement made by artists or in works on art that art is religion itself, you are in the sphere of the romantic tradition.'[24] The tendency of liberalism is to move the whole concern of the Bible and its interpretation into the common arena. That is, the Bible comes eventually to be regarded as merely a human book to be treated and interpreted like any other book. Commonality cannot be denied, for notwithstanding its divine nature and origins, the Bible is still a human book exhibiting human language, thought forms and culture.

> [Schleiermacher] was careful to criticize dogmatic maxims that have crept over into the field of biblical interpretation without proper scrutiny, and he shared the Enlightenment view that the Bible must be read as any other book insofar as it asserts that dogmatic appeals to divine authorship can never ultimately settle questions of meaning.[25]

Barth contrasts Schleiermacher's perspective with that of the Reformers:

> A pure teaching of the Word will take into account the Holy Spirit as the divine reality in which the Word is heard, just as a pure teaching of the Spirit of the Son will take into account the Word of God as the divine reality in which the Word is given to us. It was with this thought in mind that the Reformers propagated the teaching of the Word of God in its correlation with faith as the work of the Holy Spirit in man. Schleiermacher reversed the order of this thought. What interests him is the question of man's action in regard to God.[26]

Anthony Thiselton provides a comprehensive summary of Schleiermacher's hermeneutics, and first makes several preliminary observations about his method.[27] First, he moved hermeneutics into the concern for human understanding in general. Second, he asked how understanding and human

---

24. ibid., p. 379.
25. D. DeVries, 'Schleiermacher, Friedrich Daniel Ernst', in Donald McKim (ed.), *Historical Handbook of Major Biblical Interpreters* (Downers Grove and Leicester: IVP, 1998), p. 352.
26. Barth, *Protestant Thought*, p. 340.
27. Anthony Thiselton, *New Horizons in Hermeneutics* (Grand Rapids: Zondervan, 1992), ch. 6.

knowledge were possible. Third, he maintained that understanding of people requires a certain amount of creativity. Fourth, he distinguished two aspects of interpretation: the grammatical concern for the language, and the psychological concern for the author.

> Schleiermacher therefore explicitly raised for the first time a question which remains of permanent importance for hermeneutics: can we interpret the meaning of texts purely with reference to their language, or purely with reference to their authors' intention, *or does textual meaning reside somehow in the inter-relation or inter-action between both*?[28]

Thiselton raises the concern that the 'divining' of the relationship between text and author may reduce the process to the personal perceptions of the interpreter. But he credits Schleiermacher with being 'one of the first to formulate the *comprehensive* significance of several different factors in consideration of a text and the text's author'.[29] In fact he grasped, in a way that is often lost from sight, that interpretation is not to be achieved by a focus on only one dimension, be it author, text or reader:

> [t]he hermeneutical task . . . involves the author's thought, experience, and situation; the content, context, language, and effects of the text; the first readers of the text, including their linguistic and other capacities and competences; and the consciousness and experience of later interpretation.[30]

This comprehensiveness, which was lost in the later hermeneutic theories of the nineteenth and twentieth centuries, seems to have arisen from an amalgam of Romanticism and the Enlightenment. Yet Schleiermacher's concern for all aspects of the text did not reflect the true subjectivity-objectivity of Christian theism. Nor did it deal satisfactorily with the relationship of transcendence to immanence. His indebtedness to Romanticism was limited and accounts mainly for the creative and intuitive side of his approach. He did not reject the Enlightenment and its dependence on rational thought, but rather he went beyond it to include imagination and feeling. Thiselton identifies his background in Moravian Pietism as contributing to his notion of 'the consciousness of being absolutely dependent', which is to be conscious of a relationship

---

28. ibid., p. 206 (italics his).
29. ibid., p. 207.
30. ibid., p. 208.

with God.[31] Thiselton goes on to refer to major themes in Schleiermacher's system of hermeneutics:

> (a) [U]nderstanding consists in re-experiencing the mental processes of the author of a text; (b) it is grasping the meaning of the parts through divining the whole, and understanding the whole through grasping the parts; (c) it involves perceiving the individuality of the author as a human user of shared language; (d) it seeks to understand more than a text may have explicitly expressed, and hence to achieve a fuller grasp of the author's thoughts or purpose than the author articulated or perhaps understood.[32]

Schleiermacher's contemporary Friedrich Ast (1778–1841) had already formulated the notion of the hermeneutical circle. Schleiermacher ran with this notion as meaning that each part of the interpretative process belongs within the whole. His distinction between the grammatical and psychological aspects requires that they both be regarded as parts of this circle, and as affecting the relationship of the parts of a text to its whole. This, one might think, had great potential for a successful approach to hermeneutics. But the relationship of the transcendent to the immanent was taken by Schleiermacher, notwithstanding his Romanticist challenge to the Enlightenment, as solvable in terms of subjectivity. By reducing biblical hermeneutics to general hermeneutics, and by refusing to allow that Scripture had a privileged status due to divine inspiration, he expressed a position of immanence that is incongruous with the doctrine of the incarnation of the Word. Jesus is no longer regarded as the true and unique union of full deity and full humanity. He simply exhibits a more complete humanity in that he reaches a unique and unsurpassed level of the feeling of absolute dependence. Jesus has a greater consciousness of God than we have.

Thiselton refers to H. R. Mackintosh's assessment that 'for him theology is less concerned with God than with man's consciousness of God'.[33] He then notes three theological areas that give cause for concern. First, the uniqueness of Christ is merely one of degree of God-consciousness, not one of his human sinlessness and true union with the Godhead. Second, on the basis that the gospel shows us the problem it is intended to deal with, Schleiermacher's Christ has all but eliminated the moral dimensions of sin. Third, he has no place for the supernatural in the formation of the Scriptures.

31. ibid., p. 211.
32. ibid., p. 216.
33. ibid., p. 229.

Notwithstanding his warning, Barth concludes his chapter on Schleiermacher with a comment that points us back to the Christological implications of his position. If Christ is distinguished by having a greater degree of that which we all have in some measure, then: 'The two foci of the ellipse [the divine, objective, transcendence and the human, subjective, immanence] draw relentlessly closer to one another, and how is the dissolution and disappearance of the objective moment in the subjective to be prevented?'[34] In other words, the Romantic in Schleiermacher is completely immanentist. The truly divine in Christ and in the Bible is absorbed into a god who is only within.

Assessment

Modern liberal Protestantism, then, takes its start from a philosophically oriented perspective similar to that of all the major hermeneutical aberrations from the early Gnostic interpreters onwards. It may appear that Enlightenment liberalism is the direct opposite of Gnostic Docetism, in that it seems to exhibit an Ebionite emphasis in settling on the humanity of Christ and revelation at the expense of the divine elements of both. However, it is a short step from a position which reduces the divine to a property of human being and imagination, to a position which turns the historic individuality of Jesus into a mere ideal to be imitated. The Jesus of the Enlightenment, along with his word, is at the same time merely human and merely an ideal. Romanticism was not able to retrieve hermeneutics from what Thielicke refers to as a Cartesian perspective. The relationship of subjectivity to objectivity is so distorted that the term 'scientific', as applied to biblical criticism and interpretation, is lost in a vicious circle of subjectivity that now determines the criteria for defining objectivity. The viciousness of the circle has arisen because the only true basis for understanding the relationship of subjectivity and objectivity – the God who speaks 'Thou' to his creatures – has been effectively eliminated from the equation. Revelation, at best, can only be reflected on as what humans are pleased to name their religious ideas. It can never be equated with an objective and authoritative prophetic word. Consistently, liberalism has to domesticate God or eliminate him.

---

34. Barth, *Protestant Thought*, p. 352.

9. THE ECLIPSE OF THE GOSPEL IN PHILOSOPHICAL HERMENEUTICS

On being eclectic

The history of biblical interpretation has shown us that the adaptation of non-Christian philosophies has been a constant factor in the development of theology and hermeneutics. Hellenistic Gnosticism, Platonism, Neo-Platonism and Aristotelianism, along with the philosophies of the Enlightenment, have all played a part in the way Christians have thought about the Bible. We will need to maintain a distinction between the use of philosophical categories in thinking about the dimensions of biblical communication, and the actual adoption of non-Christian noetic and epistemological frameworks. It is not only possible, but is indeed probable, that non-Christian thinkers will ask questions and engage in analyses that at times complement theistic dogmatics. This admission is not to sell out to secularism, but simply to recognize that a degree of eclecticism is valid if controlled by biblical theism. If, for example, non-Christians can show me something of how human language works, I regret that we cannot agree on the ultimate significance of language, but I believe I can still learn something useful from them.

As Christian thinkers we can easily settle into a framework of thought that reflects the particular dogmatic structure with which we have become comfortable. To engage minds that think outside our framework can challenge us to at least consider ideas and structures that we would otherwise never have contemplated. Anthony Thiselton approves of James Barr 'in his claim that categories which come from outside the Bible are not necessarily wrong or inappropriate'.[1] He also agrees with Wittgenstein that philosophy affects our perspectives on things that have gone unexamined simply because they have always been there before our eyes.[2]

The Enlightenment was driven by non-Christian philosophical notions and resulted in the redefinition of theology and hermeneutics in terms of these alien intellectual frameworks. Part of our task is to understand what happened, what is still happening, what an authentic Christian response is, and to what extent we need to learn from the insights of Enlightenment-modernism and postmodernism. If this is not to be a purely historical exercise, we must try to determine what effects such insights might have in our attempts to secure an authentic evangelical hermeneutics.

The devolution of hermeneutics

We have seen that almost from the beginning of Christian history there seems to have been a failure to understand the comprehensive nature of biblical revelation. Perhaps it was almost inevitable that in periods of transition the characteristics of the changes involved were difficult to plot until they had become the subject of retrospective historical investigation. These failures have contributed to the corruption of Christian theism by leaving unrecognized gaps in the areas of revelation and authority. Unacknowledged vacuums were easily filled by alien thought forms.

According to Richard Palmer, the history of hermeneutics has involved at least six distinct approaches to the definition of hermeneutics.[3] These are more than purely chronological stages in the development of the discipline, since they each represent a distinct 'moment' or approach to the matter, a standpoint from which hermeneutics is viewed, and each brings to light different but legitimate sides of the act of interpretation. Palmer has sketched the transitions from the classical hermeneutics of the Middle Ages to the present. What one notes in his analysis is that the development of modern hermeneutics begins where modern evangelical hermeneutics has its major

1. Anthony Thiselton, *The Two Horizons* (Exeter: Paternoster, 1980), p. 9.
2. ibid., p. 7.
3. Richard E. Palmer, *Hermeneutics* (Evanston: North Western University Press, 1969), ch. 3.

practical concern – the biblical text. Notwithstanding the gains of Schleiermacher and his successors, we have become mostly, perhaps exclusively, concerned with biblical exegesis and application. The insights of those who have widened the scope of investigation are valuable to us mainly in so far as they assist our primary aim.

The first approach that Palmer describes, then, is the concern for hermeneutics as a theory of biblical exegesis. The first textbooks on hermeneutics as a distinct discipline were texts of *hermeneutica sacra* and served the needs of Christian ministry in the seventeenth and eighteenth centuries. Our concern is to understand something of the developments from that point to the present, primarily to see if we can learn ways to sharpen our exegetical skills.

Second, according to Palmer, there was the perspective of hermeneutics as philological methodology. This was a major shift brought about by some of the fathers of the Enlightenment such as Spinoza and Lessing. Grammatical analysis was not new. It had been engaged by early Christian commentators, energized by the Renaissance, and applied with great care by the Reformers. But the subsequent shifts often took place at the expense of the notion of the privilege of an inspired text.

Third, we have the gains made by Schleiermacher's hermeneutics of understanding, which was still mainly concerned with biblical exegesis and theology. Schleiermacher's theory of general hermeneutics was not taken up in earnest until one of his successors, Wilhelm Dilthey, developed the fourth perspective: hermeneutics as the methodological foundation for the humanities in general.

Dilthey left Schleiermacher's theologically centred hermeneutics behind and took up the challenge of philosophical hermeneutics in its own right. The growth of the natural and empirical sciences was beginning to endanger the credibility of the *Geisteswissenschaften*: the arts, literature and all those studies we usually refer to as the humanities. In a real sense, Dilthey carried on the insights of Schleiermacher and applied them to fields far beyond the theological and biblical interests that had occupied Schleiermacher. He pressed on with the concern for the personhood of both author and interpreter and once again directed attention to the subjective-objective relationships. Kevin Vanhoozer puts it this way:

> Wilhelm Dilthey's (1833–1911) fateful distinction between the natural and the human sciences prepared the way for what we might call the 'second coming' of hermeneutics. The natural sciences aim to explain what happens in the natural world by formulating universal causal laws . . . The human sciences, on the other hand, aim

> at understanding human behaviour. Dilthey argues that what we seek to grasp in the human order is not matter in motion but 'mind,' 'spirit,' or 'lived experience'.[4]

Dilthey's concern for lived experience is, as Diogenes Allen describes it, 'the notion that human experience is embedded in the stream of life, and we can view and understand the human sciences only through participation in that stream'.[5] The emerging natural sciences, in addition to the Enlightenment rethinking of the relationship of God and humankind, meant that the subject-object relationship was also under scrutiny. Allen describes it as a dilemma:

> This dilemma can be characterized as follows. On the one hand, there are three options. We may treat the self (subject) as known but the existence of its objects as doubtful, as in Descartes. We may have objects constituted by the self so that the existence of objects independent of the subject is denied, as in Berkeley. Or we may reduce what we are aware of to mere appearances and have objects as 'things-in-themselves' and utterly unknowable, as in Kant. On the other hand, we may begin with objects as bundles of sense qualities as real, as in Hume, and reduce the self to a bundle of sense qualities.[6]

Neither Schleiermacher nor Dilthey resolved the dilemma in a Christian theistic way. In this matter, de Senarclens is right in finding the *analogia entis* of Rome in liberal Protestantism. It leads to varying degrees of the divinizing of humanity of which Eastern Orthodoxy and Catholicism are at one end of the spectrum and liberalism at the other. The problematic feature is that God and Man are seen to share a common general being. The real distinction between God and Man is thus muted or even lost. The subject-object relationship will always be a dilemma until it is re-established on the basis of this distinction, of Chalcedon and the incarnation, and is thus grounded in the Trinity.

Richard Palmer's fifth perspective is hermeneutics as the phenomenology of *Dasein* (existence) and of existential understanding.[7] Although Palmer has

---

4. Kevin Vanhoozer, *Is There a Meaning in This Text?* (Grand Rapids: Zondervan; Leicester: Apollos, 1998), p. 219.
5. Diogenes Allen, *Philosophy for Understanding Theology* (London: SCM, 1985), p. 271.
6. ibid.
7. Palmer, *Hermeneutics*, pp. 41–43. A comprehensive treatment of the existentialist developments in hermeneutics is given in Thiselton, *The Two Horizons*. See also Werner Jeanrond, *Theological Hermeneutics* (New York: Crossroad, 1991), pp. 57–70 and ch. 6.

warned against simply seeing these perspectives as chronological developments, a degree of such a continuum is clearly to be found. Dilthey drew on Schleiermacher and Heidegger drew on Dilthey. The sense of personal involvement in all of them, along with the immanentist perspective that has long since retreated from the transcendence-immanence of Christian theism, prepares the way for the existential hermeneutics of Kierkergaard and Bultmann. Martin Heidegger (1889–1976), who brings us into the age of modern hermeneutical theory, was influenced by Dilthey's concern for a foundational theory for the humanities. Palmer notes that Heidegger marks a transition from philosophical hermeneutics to hermeneutical philosophy. Thus we move from philosophy as an aid to unravelling hermeneutical questions, to hermeneutics as the very essence of philosophy.

Heidegger was influenced by Edmund Husserl (1859–1938), who was the founder of the phenomenological movement, to the extent that he paid attention to the basic phenomena of human existence. His *Sein und Zeit* (being and time) was presented as a hermeneutical philosophy, a hermeneutic of *Dasein* (existence). Palmer notes that hermeneutics in this context refers neither to the science of rules of text interpretation, nor to a methodology for the *Geisteswissenschaften*, but to Heidegger's phenomenological explication of human existence itself. Understanding and interpretation are foundational modes of human existence. Now hermeneutics is concerned with the ontological dimensions of understanding.

Sixth, Palmer refers to hermeneutics as a system of interpretation: recovery of meaning versus iconoclasm.[8] Paul Ricoeur, in *De l'interpretation* (1965), adopts a definition of hermeneutics, says Palmer, which goes back to a focus on textual exegesis as the distinctive and centrally defining element in hermeneutics. 'We mean by hermeneutics the theory of rules that govern an exegesis, that is to say, an interpretation of a particular text or collection of signs susceptible of being considered as a text.'[9] Ricoeur provides something of a corrective to the subjectivism of reader-oriented hermeneutics. He seeks a way of reconciling the two opposing perspectives of authorial intent and reader response.[10] This appears to be an attempt to rescue some semblance of objectivity that has been drowned in existential subjectivity. He distinguishes between univocal and equivocal symbols; the former are signs with one

8. Palmer, *Hermeneutics*, pp. 43–45.
9. ibid.
10. Ronald H. McKinney, 'Ricoeur's Hermeneutic and the Messianic Problem', *CSR* 14/3 (1985), p. 215.

designated meaning (symbols in symbolic logic), while the latter are the true focus of hermeneutics. Hermeneutics is the system by which the deeper significance is revealed beneath the surface meaning. Here Ricoeur is concerned with the structures of text as text in order to reach an *explanation*. 'It is in the second phase, called *understanding*, that one arrives at the existential appropriation of the text.'[11]

While Gadamer regards the distance between the reader and the text as something that inhibits understanding, Ricoeur, on the other hand, sees this distance as essential to the process of reaching understanding. The distanciation of the text removes the need for the reader to try to understand the intentions of the author. But it is this that provides, for Ricoeur, the needed objectivity. He fails, of course, to find objectivity in the biblical author or in the speaking God of the Bible, and instead finds it in the text. The text, freed from its author, is always open to new applications. He wants to understand the meaning and the reference of the text itself without being bound by authorial intent or the original context of the text. It is clear that he has failed to escape a crippling subjectivity.[12] Whatever the advances, in a relative sense, made by scholars like Ricoeur, we have to conclude that only a return to Christ-centredness can save hermeneutics.

Postmodernism: total eclipse?

The history of hermeneutics shows that the subject-object dilemma is always present. It is the contention of Christian theism that the doctrine of the Trinity is the foundational standpoint for the understanding of the interrelationship between the objectivity of the text and its world, and the subjectivity of the reader. In modern hermeneutics we see a continual tug for supremacy between the various foci. The whole Christian notion of a divine discourse given through human agents, committed to a text, transmitted through the ages, read by a recipient who seeks understanding and endeavours to relay the message

11. ibid., p. 216.
12. See the detailed treatment of Ricoeur in Anthony Thiselton, *New Horizons in Hermeneutics* (Grand Rapids: Zondervan, 1992), pp. 344–378. Gregory Laughery gives some positive assessment of Ricoeur in 'Ricoeur on History, Fiction, and Biblical Hermeneutics', in Craig Bartholomew, C. Green and K. Möller (eds.), *'Behind' the Text: History and Biblical Interpretation*, SHS, vol. 4 (Carlisle: Paternoster; Grand Rapids: Zondervan, 2003), pp. 339–362.

to others, has been under constant attack. The question being asked is where meaning is to be found. Does it reside in the author's intention to communicate something, in the text (grammar, syntax, semantics), or in the reader? Whereas the scholars of the Enlightenment moved towards what they thought was an unshakeable objectivity of historical investigation, men like Schleiermacher recognized that the interpreter needed to try to penetrate something of the subjectivity of the author. His problem was that for him, the ultimately objective author, God, was really only to be found in the subjectivity of the interpreter. The existentialists simply pressed this to its conclusion of ultimate subjectivity. Thus the focus of hermeneutics moved from the divine author to the human author, who was regarded as really no different from any other human author. No privilege of inspiration could be entertained. Subsequently the focus moved to the text, and finally to the reader.

Defining postmodernism is, as the saying goes, as easy as nailing jelly to a post! Don Carson confronts its relativism and pluralism as its major problems.[13] Stanley Grenz describes it as the attack on modernity.[14] David Dockery comments, 'Postmodernism is a new set of assumptions about reality, which goes far beyond mere relativism . . . Postmodernism tends to view human experience as incoherent, lacking absolutes in the area of truth and meaning.'[15] Andrew Adam refers to remarks by Cornel West in lectures at Yale in which he identifies three aspects of postmodernism:

> Postmodernism is antifoundational in that it resolutely refuses to posit any one premise as the privileged and unassailable starting point for establishing claims to truth. It is antitotalizing because postmodern discourse suspects that any theory that claims to account for everything is suppressing counterexamples, or is applying warped criteria so that it can include recalcitrant cases. Postmodernism is also demystifying: it attends to claims that certain assumptions are 'natural' and tries to show that these are in fact ideological projections.[16]

We can only be somewhat bemused by such claims if, indeed, they fairly represent what postmodernism is about. In refusing to 'posit any one premise as

---

13. D. A. Carson, *The Gagging of God* (Grand Rapids: Zondervan, 1996).
14. Stanley J. Grenz, *A Primer on Postmodernism* (Grand Rapids: Eerdmans, 1996).
15. David Dockery (ed.), *The Challenge of Postmodernism* (Wheaton: Bridgepoint, 1995), p. 14.
16. A. K. M. Adam, *What is Postmodern Biblical Criticism?* (Minneapolis: Fortress, 1995), p. 5.

the privileged and unassailable starting point', one is in fact simply positing one's own privileged premise. In being 'antitotalizing', one is simply 'totalizing' the absolute negative. Why, we might ask, does the postmodern protagonist deny the role of authorial intent, and put the argument in books written quite clearly with the assumption that the reader will, or at least should, understand what the (postmodern) author intends? These concerns perhaps account for Thomas Oden's assertion that postmodernism is in fact ultramodern.[17] It is that which comes about because of 'terminal modernity'. The idols of modernity are autonomous individualism, narcissistic hedonism, reductive naturalism and absolute moral relativism.[18] Oden continues:

> These old modernities are impotent, unfit to transmit values intergenerationally. Their intellectual center is gone. It no longer has the capacity to reproduce itself. The capacity to regenerate is essential to any living organism. None of these four ideologies have the wit or energy to produce and fruitfully nurture another generation.[19]

One might argue that postmodernism has arrived to fill the vacuum created by disenchantment with modernism. But perhaps it is closer to the truth to say that postmodernism *is* the ultimate vacuum. Richard Lints sees postmodernism as the demise of modernism's triumphalism.[20] Orthodoxy took the Bible's authority as extending to a critique of culture. Modernism reversed this, so that culture provides the critique of the Bible. Postmodernism says that both the Bible and culture need critique.[21] Similarly, orthodoxy's epistemology was based on revelation, modernism's on human reason, but in postmodernism even reason is discounted as a dogmatic act of faith.[22] Other ways of viewing these three key hermeneutic stances include the movement from a hermeneutics of trust, to that of doubt, to that of suspicion.[23]

---

17. Thomas C. Oden, 'The Death of Modernity and Postmodern Evangelical Spirituality', in Dockery (ed.), *The Challenge of Postmodernism*, pp. 19–33.
18. ibid., pp. 28–29.
19. ibid., p. 30.
20. Richard Lints, *The Fabric of Theology* (Grand Rapids: Eerdmans, 1993), p. 216.
21. ibid., p. 213.
22. ibid., pp. 218ff. It is difficult to see why saying that reason is a dogmatic act of faith is not itself a dogmatic act of faith.
23. Thiselton, *New Horizons in Hermeneutics*, p. 143.

Assessment

Modern hermeneutics begins with an Enlightenment agenda and with the presuppositions of alien philosophies. Alongside these developments there has been a parallel movement of conservatism. Evangelical scholarship has always sought to modernize itself without compromise. A study of conservative hermeneutics since the Reformation will show us to what extent it has been successful. Our problem is always one of the extent to which we can plunder the Egyptians without returning to the leeks and the garlic (Num. 11:5). In other words, what do the modern and postmodern developments have to teach us, if anything? In the field of exegetical method, few evangelicals would maintain that we should, or even can, return to the so-called pre-critical period. Perhaps this is one difference between fundamentalism and evangelicalism.

It would appear that modern hermeneutical theory has raised all kinds of questions that needed to be raised. The otherwise perverse myopic attention to only one dimension of communication at a time has undoubtedly resulted in detailed analyses of these that are at the same time creative and distorted. Can we work for a genuine evangelical approach to interpretation, taking account of these philosophical developments, but without compromising biblical principles? There is little doubt that the Enlightenment involved an eclipse of the gospel in theology, biblical studies and hermeneutics, which was to lead to an eventual elimination of all the elements that make the gospel the message from a sovereign and gracious God of his saving action in the God/Man, Jesus Christ. It is not only a movement away from any sense of objectivity in relation to our subjectivity, but a movement to complete subjectivity. It is the elimination of transcendent reality. The final hermeneutical atheism of extreme modernism and postmodernism means that the foundation of truth and knowledge has shifted from the ontological Trinity, who is revealed in the gospel, to the utter subjectivity of the self. While modernism's realism about objective truth enables us to make some sense of the world of our experience, postmodernism's construction is something that not even the postmodernist can live by. One can only wonder at the inconsistency, perhaps even hubris, of postmodern philosophers and hermeneutic theorists denying the reader of a text any access to objective meaning or the author's intention, while expecting us all to read their works as they intend, and not to misrepresent their meaning.

10. THE ECLIPSE OF THE GOSPEL IN HISTORICAL CRITICISM

The problem of the method

Christianity is an historical faith; it is based upon the belief that God has acted in history for our salvation. Where is this history and how do we evaluate the evidences for the alleged divine events? Carl Braaten poses the radical question about revelation in modern Protestant theology thus: 'Where can revelation be found at all, now that the traditional equation of Scripture with revelation can no longer stand unchallenged in the face of the historical criticism of the Bible?'[1] Braaten is expressing the major problem created by the presuppositions of historical-critical study. From the outset we need to understand that it is not the notion of critical study of history that is at issue. We cannot avoid it and, indeed, we cannot understand the Bible without it.[2] The problem is the humanistic presuppositions that are assumed to be above criticism and are almost universally employed in the historical-critical study of the Bible. Starting with the Enlightenment, and going on with Kant and Schleiermacher, the autonomy and superiority of reason have continued to govern biblical interpretation. Neither neo-orthodoxy nor the biblical theology movement were able to harmonize

---

1. Carl Braaten, *History and Hermeneutics* (Philadelphia: Westminster, 1966), p. 11.
2. I will discuss the critical-historical concerns in evangelical hermeneutics in ch. 15.

such historical criticism with the idea of biblical authority. The authority of the Bible continues to be asserted, but it is not clear how it is authoritative.

Historical criticism is, of course, much broader than that which is technically referred to as the historical-critical method. It includes any attempt to understand and evaluate the historical truth claims of texts. Even when the focus shifted from the historical background of the existing texts to the literary forms of the texts themselves, the historical question continued to be posed. It was no longer a matter of which parts of the texts were historically accurate, but rather one of the relationship of the stories in textual units to what really happened. We will consider various approaches to such criticism, beginning with the historical-critical method.

The growth of the historical-critical method

Gerhard Maier describes the historical-critical method as a general acceptance of the assertion of Johann Semler (1725–91) that the Bible must be treated like any other book.

> A critical method of Bible interpretation can produce only Bible-critical propositions . . . For the justification and authority of the outcome are still established by the critical scholar himself and, due to the method, cannot come only out of Scripture.[3]

Maier refers to Käsemann's editing of *The New Testament as Canon* in which the contributions of fifteen scholars, written during the period 1941–70, are collected. He regards this as a demonstration of the procedure and the final result of the higher-critical method.[4] He sees the exegetes as engaged in a futile attempt to establish a canon within the canon (Scripture as a whole cannot be equated with the word of God), while the systematicians have tended to retreat into spiritual experience in order to try to define what is the binding word of God.[5] He concludes that the method had to fail because it was unsuited to the subject:

> If there should really be a canon in the canon, then not only would Scripture have to

3. Gerhard Maier, *The End of the Historical-Critical Method* (St Louis: Concordia, 1977), p. 11.
4. ibid., pp. 26f.
5. ibid., pp. 47f.

> be divorced from the Word of God, but also Christ from the Scriptures, the Holy Ghost from the Scriptures, and the one Christ of Scripture from the other Christ of Scripture. The light of a new docetism would then fall on the event of the Incarnation and on certain parts of Scripture.[6]

Harrisville and Sundberg trace the growth of the historical-critical method.[7] The rise of rationalist biblical criticism in the seventeenth century is perceived to be in the work of Baruch Spinoza (1632–77).

> Spinoza attacks the political power of religion by calling into question the legitimacy of religious authorities in matters of civil government. Since the Bible is central to religious authority, Spinoza undertakes a critical investigation of the claims of scripture in order to subvert its role in European political life. This investigation is grounded in modern historical principles. The first such essay of its kind, the *Tractatus* is clear evidence that historical-critical method originated in politically engendered hostility to the claims of faith.[8]

Spinoza's method involves four basic principles:[9] the Bible is an unprivileged and purely human text; its faith-application by synagogue or church cannot be factored into its interpretation; only unaided human reason can be used to decide the truth value of Scripture; and such reason is the property of the educated elite. Harrisville and Sundberg go on to assert four things about Spinoza that had their effect on the subsequent development of the historical-critical method.[10] First, his hostility to his own (Jewish) people anticipated the development of the 'degenerative model of ancient Israelite history'. Second, Spinoza's political slant on exegesis brings him to conclude that the theology of the Bible is generated by the society from which it comes. Third, his concern to treat the Bible like any other book has had the effect of redirecting biblical scholarship from the study of the spiritual message of the Bible to purely historical concerns of the origins of the text. Fourth, the

---

6. ibid., p. 49.
7. Roy Harrisville and Walter Sundberg, *The Bible in Modern Culture* (Grand Rapids: Eerdmans, 1995).
8. ibid., p. 5. However, even if Spinoza's political motivations had not existed, it is difficult to believe that the whole historical-critical programme would not have emerged much as we have it today.
9. ibid., pp. 44–45.
10. ibid., pp. 46–48.

understanding of the Bible is confined to an intellectual elite. This effectively deprives the 'ordinary' Christian of access to the Scriptures.

The development of historical-critical method, then, proceeds through the rationalist Hermann Reimarus (1694–1768), Schleiermacher, Strauss, and eventually to Ernst Troeltsch (eighteenth to nineteenth centuries). Albert Schweitzer commented that it was Reimarus who forced a breakthrough from the dogmatic to the historic treatment of the Gospels.[11] As to later developments, Harrisville and Sundberg assess the method thus:

> From Spinoza through Troeltsch to much of contemporary scholarship that is tied to the university departments of religion, historical criticism has concentrated its effort to understand scripture by attending to the period of biblical composition and searching for temporal causes to explain the dimensions of biblical faith. The 'belief system' of the people of the Bible has been interpreted as the culture-bound effort, born of contingent events, to comprehend the mystery of existence.[12]

They make this telling criticism of the process:

> What has functioned as truth for those who stand in the Enlightenment tradition has been the cultural assumptions that have dominated their social milieu. These assumptions too often have operated as uncritical criteria of judgment; indeed, they have served as the equivalent of revelation. Whether it was deistic rational religion (Spinoza and Reimarus), romantic devotion to feeling (Schleiermacher), the Hegelian dialectic (Strauss and Baur), or the demands of historicism (Troeltsch), the Enlightenment tradition has been motivated by its need to make apology for its 'faith' in the Enlightenment world view.[13]

And again: 'What we have in the Enlightenment tradition of criticism is nothing less than another religion that supplants biblical faith.'[14] Harrisville's and Sundberg's most damning indictment of the historical-critical method is its inability to explain the religious significance of its work, a fact which makes it not merely ancillary, but parasitic.[15] A comparison of some of the critical

11. ibid., p. 62.
12. ibid., p. 266.
13. ibid., p. 267.
14. ibid., p. 268.
15. ibid., p. 269, quoting from J. D. Levenson, 'The Bible: Unexamined Commitments of Criticism', *First Things*, 30 (1993).

a self-revealing and saving God. So also the New Testament writers, then Augustine and the Reformers broke with historical ideas of classical paganism. Hermeneutically this meant that the literal sense was identical with the historical sense.

Various attempts have been made to deal with the problem of history without getting bogged down in the naturalism of Troeltsch. These include resorting to the idea of *Heilsgeschichte* (salvation history), beginning with J. C. K. von Hofmann in the nineteenth century and continuing with the American biblical theology movement and neo-orthodoxy. But these were concerned with a redefining of history involving the distinctions between *Geschichte* (the telling) and *Historie* (the events), which meant a distinction between the Jesus of faith and the Jesus of history. Existentialist history, espoused by Collingwood and Bultmann, reduces the significance of history to our own self-knowledge. Eschatology is not the history of the future, but, for Bultmann, it is Jesus Christ addressing us in the here and now through preaching. Pannenberg rejects what he sees as a fleeing from history in these solutions and maintains that history, not word, is the locus of revelation. What God does in history is not done in 'some *Heilsgeschichtliche* ghetto' visible only to the eye of faith. He rightly insists that *Heilsgeschichte* is part of real history.[20]

Patrick D. Miller states the problem of history as, first, the question of historical knowledge – how do we know the past? – and, second, the question of the relationship of faith and history – is faith dependent on historical research?[21] In response we might suggest that faith does not depend on historical research, but nor are we reduced to a *Heilsgeschichte* 'eye of faith' approach. Presuppositionalism's recognition of the self-authenticating word of God does not drive us to fideism.

Challenges to the historical nature of the gospel

Challenges to the historical gospel came not only from the historical-critical method, but had very ancient sources. The cyclical history of the Canaanites challenged the linear salvation history of Israel. In a not dissimilar way, the dualism and cyclic history of the Hellenists challenged Christianity. Marcion the Gnostic found the history of the Old Testament incompatible with his

---

20. Braaten, *History and Hermeneutics*, p. 44.
21. Unpublished lecture, Union Theological Seminary in Virginia.

Hellenism. The dualism of pure spirit and inherently evil material world meant that the history of Yahweh's acts for the salvation of Israel could not be the work of true divinity. Docetism in its various forms attempted to give a consistent formulation of Christianity without the necessity of a God who acts in the material world and assumes a material, and therefore evil, form in an historical incarnation. That this was perceived very quickly as a threat to the authentic gospel is clear from the condemnation of a 'fleshless' Christ in 1 John 4:2–3. So serious is this heresy that John brands it as the Antichrist. As C. F. Allison says, 'Gnostic versions of Christianity saw both flesh and time as prisons for our allegedly pure and innocent souls.'[22] Gnosticism may thus be seen as an overemphasis on the transcendence of truth and knowledge, so that the union of the transcendent and the immanent in the incarnation makes no sense. Once the history of God's dealings with his people is written off in favour of transcendent knowledge-based salvation, the nature of the gospel is radically changed. In denying the biblical doctrine of creation, Gnosticism effectively removed the whole biblical notion of history as that which exists between the two poles of creation and new creation. As Harold O. J. Brown has stated:

> On Christian soil, the gnostic impulse sought to preserve several Christian ideas and terms while giving up the specific dependence of Christianity on the history of the Jews and, in the New Testament, of Jesus and his disciples. The facts of biblical history were replaced with an elaborate gnosis about the origin and development of divine, spiritual beings – the so-called aeons – and ultimately of the material world.[23]

And again:

> The concepts of a Mediator, of the Logos, of fullness of the Spirit, or incarnation, regeneration, and salvation could all be detached from their historical roots in events in the life of Jesus and the first Christians and interpreted as universally valid philosophical and religious ideas.[24]

We have seen in chapter 7 that a key problem in Catholicism is the dehistoricizing of the gospel that accompanies many of its distinctive doctrines. As J. S. Preus has indicated in his study of the medieval interpretation of the Bible,

---

22. C. F. Allison, *The Cruelty of Heresy* (London: SPCK, 1994), p. 59.
23. Harold O. J. Brown, *Heresies* (New York: Doubleday, 1984), p. 47.
24. ibid.

there was a constant struggle in the Catholic Church to understand the literal and historical significance of the Bible, and in particular of the Old Testament. Nevertheless, the allegorical method gained the ascendancy. The valiant attempts of Augustine and Aquinas to find a more literal and historical significance to the Old Testament were to some degree frustrated by the doctrinal developments in the church. As Preus notes:

> For Thomas, then, the time before grace is a time of unequivocal not-having; having the promise is not theologically meaningful, because promise and threats are 'extrinsic' and therefore inferior to inner grace.[25]

Since the sacraments of the church with their infused grace do not exist in the Old Testament, the historical events leading to the gospel are separated from the gospel. In like manner, the locus of saving grace becomes removed from the historical events surrounding Calvary. The mass and the notion of infused grace have stood the gospel on its head. This infused grace and the internalized gospel of Catholicism made the general subjective focus of the neo-Pentecostal understanding of experience of the Holy Spirit quite acceptable to the Catholic hierarchy.[26]

In Catholicism, then, Pentecost becomes the point around which all that belongs to the historic events of Jesus of Nazareth is turned about-face to become what now belongs to the church and the believer. Thus the Spirit no longer establishes the direction of faith away from the believer to the Christ of history, who is now seated at the right hand of the Father. Instead the Spirit brings Christ down to earth in a ceaseless re-presentation of what was a once-for-all event. By inverting the biblical dependence of the present existential sanctification of the believer on the past, historic, justifying life, death and resurrection of Jesus of Nazareth, justification is torn from its historic anchorage and becomes effected on the basis of the inner existential change.

Bultmann's existentialism left him dissatisfied with the rationalistic approach of liberalism that simply expunged those portions of the New Testament that did not measure up to the Enlightenment way of thinking. Bultmann was convinced that Jesus was a person in history in whom God had

25. J. S. Preus, *From Shadow to Promise* (Cambridge, MA: Belknap Press, 1969), p. 50.

26. Rene Laurentin, *Catholic Pentecostalism* (London: Darton, Longman and Todd, 1977), pp. 22ff.; Edward O'Connor, *The Pentecostal Movement in the Catholic Church* (Notre Dame: Ave Maria Press, 1975), p. 183.

done something for us. To understand what he has done, however, requires us to interpret the mythological elements. As Ian Henderson comments:

> The demythologising of the New Testament does not consist in eliminating its mythology, but in interpreting it anthropologically, or, as Bultmann prefers to say, existentially. That is to say, in dealing with a myth, we must always ask what the narrator is saying about his own existence.[27]

Thus for Bultmann, 'the basic intention of the New Testament is not to tell tales, but to provide its reader-hearer with self-understanding'.[28] If, then, Jesus was an historical figure in whom God did a unique work for us, what exactly did he do? Henderson comments:

> In spite of the assurance that Christianity is gospel and that God has done something for us in Jesus Christ, it is easy for the Christian to be a little disappointed with what it actually is, according to Bultmann, that God has done for us in Christ. He has made it possible, we are told, for the Christian to understand his existence in a new way.[29]

For Bultmann, '*the meaning of history lies always in the present*, and when the present is conceived as the eschatological present by Christian faith the meaning in history is realized.'[30] Helmut Thielicke penetrates to the heart of the issue of history:

> Bultmann, then, is not interested in whether NT facts like Christmas, Easter, or Pentecost are real facts or whether they are myths or perhaps commentaries on facts in mythological form, like the Easter stories. The thought-content of historical events and also that of myth can equally affect the understanding of my existence.[31]

---

27. Ian Henderson, *Myth in the New Testament*, Studies in Biblical Theology, no. 7 (London: SCM, 1952), p. 14.
28. Harrisville and Sundberg, *The Bible in Modern Culture*, p. 215.
29. Henderson, *Myth in the New Testament*, p. 28.
30. R. Bultmann, *History and Eschatology: The Presence of Eternity* (Edinburgh, 1957), pp. 154ff., quoted in Hendrikus Berkhof, *Christ the Meaning of History* (Grand Rapids: Baker, 1966), p. 31. Italics original.
31. Helmut Thielicke, *The Evangelical Faith, Vol. 1, Prolegomena* (Grand Rapids: Eerdmans, 1974), p. 58.

There were many reactions to Bultmann's view that history is not essential to faith. Chief among the critics of this non-linear notion of history are Jürgen Moltmann and Wolfhart Pannenberg. The subjective theology of Bultmann is here reversed in favour of a view of history which is linear and which has its meaning in the eschatological goal. In the words of Carl Braaten, 'The battle cry is that the kerygma without history is a meaningless noise.'[32]

The new hermeneutic and historical criticism

The so-called new hermeneutic, while having its roots in existentialism, nevertheless raises important issues for evangelical hermeneutics. At its back is the philosophy of Martin Heidegger, and its key exponents are Hans-Georg Gadamer, Ernst Fuchs and Gerhard Ebeling. According to Gerald Bray, Anthony Thiselton is its greatest exponent in the English-speaking world.[33] Since Thiselton speaks as a conservative scholar, his work is significant for our understanding of the issues involved. If he is in any sense an exponent of the new hermeneutic, he is also a stringent critic of it.[34] Bray refers to the new hermeneutic's notion of the relative 'horizons' of both text and reader. This matter came to prominence when the problems of Bible translations for people of vastly different cultures were faced. Thus dynamic equivalence translations lean towards the perspective of the new hermeneutic.[35] The related issue, then, is that of the horizon of culture.[36] The relativizing of cultures has caused a lot of problems that from an evangelical point of view need a theological solution.

The new hermeneutic arose out of the double concerns of existentialism as a philosophical base and the desire for the preached word to speak anew to people. Unfortunately, the existential starting point results in a dehistoricizing

32. Braaten, *History and Hermeneutics*, p. 26.
33. Gerald Bray, *Biblical Interpretation Past and Present* (Leicester: Apollos, 1996), p. 488. Bray suggests that the new hermeneutic, like structuralism, is tied to a philosophy that is going out of fashion and, therefore, not likely to last long. However, the issues raised are still important.
34. Anthony Thiselton, 'The New Hermeneutic', in I. H. Marshall (ed.), *New Testament Interpretation* (Grand Rapids: Eerdmans, 1977), pp. 308–333.
35. Bible translation will be dealt with more fully in ch. 18.
36. William J. Larkin, *Culture and Biblical Hermeneutics* (Grand Rapids: Baker, 1988). The meaning of culture is discussed in ch. 18.

of the text according to certain historical-critical precepts. Thiselton quotes Fuchs thus: 'the text is therefore not just the servant that transmits kerygmatic formulations, but rather a master that directs us into the language-context of our existence.'[37] Thiselton points to the reversal of the traditional relationship of subject and object in hermeneutics. He quotes James Robinson: '[T]he flow of the traditional relation between subject and object, in which the subject interrogates the object . . . has been significantly reversed. For it is now the object – which should henceforth be called the subject-matter – that puts the subject in question.'

Hendrik Krabbendam[38] identifies two features of the new hermeneutic. First, it is part of the wider movement starting with Schleiermacher and including Heidegger, Gadamer, Barth and Bultmann. Thus hermeneutics is seen as a comprehensive theory of understanding. Second, it is part of the later movement which actually transcends (in Barth, the later Heidegger and Gadamer) the thinking of Schleiermacher, the early Heidegger and Bultmann. Words and language are no longer the objects of understanding. For Fuchs the important question was one of how the ancient text will strike home to the modern hearer. Language and understanding are 'beyond objectification and conceptualization'.[39] The proponents of the new hermeneutic constantly refer to understanding and language as events. Thus:

> [The interpreter] no longer interprets the text and is no longer asked to initiate understanding. Language determines the occurrence of language and through the text interprets the interpreter. In assigning the primacy to the language-event the modern hermeneutical movement truly turns the tables.[40]

It is understood that the language-event is not to be identified with the text.

Krabbendam goes on to offer the following appraisal of the new hermeneutic from a transcendental (Christian theistic) point of view. It is rooted in the nature-freedom dialectic of Kant. The nature pole is characterized by the scientific, theoretical, subject-object relationship. The freedom pole transcends this. Nothing that is objectifiable belongs to the realm of

---

37. Thiselton, 'The New Hermeneutic', p. 312, quoting Ernst Fuchs, *Studies of the Historical Jesus*, p. 211.
38. Hendrik Krabbendam, 'The New Hermeneutic', in E. D. Radmacher and R. D. Preus (eds.), *Hermeneutics, Inerrancy, and the Bible* (Grand Rapids: Zondervan, 1984).
39. ibid., p. 536.
40. ibid., p. 537.

freedom. The nature-freedom dialect exists because the two poles 'simultaneously exclude and presuppose each other'. Each can only be understood in terms of each other and in contrast with each other. This means that any attempt at synthesis must fail: it can never become a hermeneutical circle with one focal point. Because none of the language of the Bible goes beyond the level of objectification, it is metaphysically deficient. The dialectic, which made the new hermeneutic possible and necessary, also determines its failure. If its proponents assure us they have bridged the gap between the two poles of nature and freedom, their word of assurance has already been ruled out by their theory. Krabbendam concludes that the nature-freedom dialectic is rooted in an act of rebellion against the God of Scripture. 'If the dialectic were to succeed in its search for the synthesis, its view of reality, including that of the world, life and God, would prove to be correct! In other words, the dialectic is on a direct collision course with Scripture.'[41]

Thiselton draws five main conclusions from the general approach of the new hermeneutic:[42]

> (1) Whilst the new hermeneutic rightly faces the problem of how the interpreter may understand the text of the New Testament more *deeply* and more *creatively*, Fuchs and Ebeling are less concerned about how he may understand it *correctly*.
>
> (2) The new hermeneutic is also one-sided in its use of the New Testament and in its relation to the New Testament message.
>
> (3) . . .[T]he new hermeneutic further embodies a one-sided view of the nature of language: . . .[First] Fuchs and Ebeling fail to grasp that language functions on the basis of convention and is not in fact 'reality' or Being itself . . . Secondly, the new hermeneutic has a one-sided concern with imperatival, conative, directive language as over against the language of description or information.
>
> (4) There is some force in the criticism that the new hermeneutic lets 'what is true for me' become the criterion of 'what is true', and that its orientation towards the interpreter's subjectivity transposes theology too often into a doctrine of man.
>
> (5) The new hermeneutic is concerned above all with the 'rights' of the text, as over against concepts which the interpreter himself may try to bring with him and impose on it.

Perhaps the main problem, then, with this existentially oriented hermeneutic is that the knowledge of God and man are not interdependent in the way Calvin

---

41. ibid., p. 554.
42. Thiselton, 'The New Hermeneutic', pp. 323–329.

expressed it. Rather it seems that there is no objective knowledge of God at all to be had from the text of Scripture. The gospel as historical event is dissolved.

Postmodernism and history

As a prelude to postmodernism's view of history, we should consider the hermeneutical moves towards the literary reading of the Bible. As with the existential approach, the question of historicity tends to be submerged under other considerations, namely those relating to the idea of narrative as story (not history). Iain Provan comments:

> It is one of the interesting ironies of this period of historical-critical domination that although interpreters were thus aware that they were dealing with books which were not simply historical, and indeed sometimes (in many minds) not historical at all, yet the vast majority of the effort in interpretation went into the task, not of interpreting the narratives as narratives, but in extracting from them such data of a historical kind as was thought possible.[43]

The new literary criticism thus raised the issue of history and often tended to deal with it by largely ignoring it. To tell the story was what was required in interpreting the Bible. The further move into subjectivism in postmodern attitudes to history also constitutes a serious challenge to the Christian view of history. As Stanley Grenz says:

> The postmodern era spells the end of the 'universe' – the end of the all-encompassing world view. In a sense, postmoderns have no world view. A denial of the reality of a unified world as the object of our perception is at the heart of postmodernism.[44]

Pertinent to our discussion of the historical nature of Christianity is the postmodern view of knowledge. Grenz comments thus:

> [T]he postmodern understanding of knowledge, therefore, is built on two foundational assumptions: (1) postmoderns view all explanations of reality as

---

43. Iain Provan, 'The Historical Books of the Old Testament', in John Barton (ed.), *The Cambridge Companion to Biblical Interpretation* (Cambridge: Cambridge University Press, 1998), p. 199.
44. Stanley J. Grenz, *A Primer on Postmodernism* (Grand Rapids: Eerdmans, 1996), p. 40.

> constructions that are useful but not objectively true, and (2) postmoderns deny that we have the ability to step outside our constructions of reality.[45]

The demise of the metanarrative, the all-encompassing principle which explains the whole of reality, means the end of history. Francis Fukuyama gave us the postmodern view of the end of history in his book of that name.[46] Keith Windschuttle summarizes Fukuyama's notion thus: 'What has come to an end is not the occurrence of events, even large and grave events, but History; that is history understood as a single, coherent, evolutionary process.'[47] If the postmodernists are right about this, we are driven to say that the end of history means the end of the historical gospel and of any realistic sense of objective truth.

Assessment

Greidanus notes that the overall effect of the historical-critical method is 'the separation of the biblical narrative from its underlying history and such extreme scepticism with respect to the historicity of biblical events that some biblical scholars have fled from history into the safety of a non-historical or supra-historical realm'.[48] Thus, in more recent times, Bultmann applied the method to the New Testament as he 'retreated with his revelation into the area of existential meaning in the historicity of the individual'.[49]

The effect of the historical-critical method is to leave us with two widely different pictures of biblical history. Greidanus points out that the very principles of the method have driven biblical interpreters into a corner. This ought to lead the critics to question the method, its principles and assumptions. The principle of analogy has, of course, a basic element of truth: we learn by comparing the unknown with the known. But as applied in modern criticism, it becomes subjectivistic in that the critic's experience must judge historicity. It is also, says Greidanus, reductionistic. It cannot handle unique or first-time events. Yet the Bible claims to deal with a whole string of such events.

---

45. ibid., p. 43.
46. Francis Fukuyama, *The End of History and the Last Man* (London: Hamish Hamilton, 1992).
47. Keith Windschuttle, *The Killing of History* (Sydney: Macleay, 1994), pp. 159f.
48. Greidanus, *The Modern Preacher and the Ancient Text*, p. 27.
49. Braaten, *History and Hermeneutics*, p. 21.

Troeltsch combined analogy with the similarity of events in a way that effectively blocks out the unique.

The problem, then, is not the historical criticism as such, but the naturalistic presuppositions of most of those who practise the historical-critical method.

> If all agree that the Bible testifies that God acts in history, then all should agree that the naturalistic historical-critical method is out of tune with the Bible and does not seek to understand the Bible on its own terms. The naturalistic historical-critical method seeks to assess the Bible from a standpoint, a world view, grounded outside the Bible – a post-Enlightenment world view rather than the biblical world view.[50]

The principle of correlation must be open to the presence of transcendence in history, including divine action. This does not imply an unscientific world view, but only that God can act and that truth can come in non-empirical ways. The Christian gospel is a saving event because it is an historical event, not merely an idea.

Postmodernism, whether we see it as the ultimate expression of modernism, or as the failed revolt against modernism, has not in any sense redeemed us from modernism's assault on the historical gospel. Both are expressions of a revolt against the Lord of history, who has redeemed history through the incarnation and suffering of the Son. Any hermeneutic that refuses to take seriously the historical Christ and his gospel is not only a hermeneutic of suspicion but one of rebellion. We might also suggest that the reason why the 'quest for the historical Jesus' keeps resurfacing is that none of its manifestations has taken seriously the Bible's own claims to be the record of the saving of history by the Lord of history. Each successive expression of it seems to wander further into a desperate determination to prove the Gospels wrong. Such hermeneutical endeavours are houses of cards.

---

50. Greidanus, *The Modern Preacher and the Ancient Text*, p. 35.

11. THE ECLIPSE OF THE GOSPEL IN LITERARY CRITICISM

The place of literary criticism

Since the Bible *is* literature, the critical study of this literature is simply a given. Literary criticism, like all study of the human element of the Bible, is demanded by the incarnation of the word in the person of Jesus Christ. If we are to get at the message of the Bible, we must be able to handle the various forms in which that message is conveyed. We cannot avoid questions of linguistics, and of the various ways language has been used in the writing of the biblical documents. There are also basic issues of the origin and purpose of language in the God-ordained scheme of things. Our focus in this chapter is the way alien philosophies have influenced the assessment of the use of language in the Bible.[1]

It is also important to remember that the Bible is more than literature. Thus the division of our study into chapters dealing in turn with history, literature and theology is only a matter of convenience. We must always take account of the

1. Craig Bartholomew, 'Babel and Derrida: Postmodernism, Language and Biblical Interpretation', *TB* 49/2 (1998), pp. 305–328, argues 'that Christian scholars need to articulate a Christian view of language'.

mutual interdependence of these three dimensions.[2] It might be argued that what has afflicted the modern study of hermeneutics has been the tendency to regard these as three completely independent concerns. As so often happens, an *either-or* approach has suppressed the legitimate and necessary *both-and* approach. For example, how we evaluate the theological content of a document is related to how we understand the historical truth claims in relation to the literary forms.

A glance at the tables of contents of some of the standard evangelical books on hermeneutics is enough to suggest that certain assumptions were made about the nature of language and literature, and of their ability to convey meaning. For example, though nearly thirty years separate them, there is not a lot of difference between the general approach of A. B. Mickelsen[3] and that of Grant Osborne.[4] Both major on the hermeneutics of literature with reference to how language works and the principles of grammar, syntax, semantics and so on, within their historical and cultural contexts, as they are of concern for interpretation. These are obvious matters of interest in any study of hermeneutics.

Tremper Longman points out that literary criticism goes back to the early Fathers and that they often made the mistake of trying to evaluate biblical literature in terms of the standards of foreign literature.[5] But they did appreciate the literary qualities of biblical stories. Linguistic questions have exercised exegetes at all stages of history. In the eighteenth century Robert Lowth broke new ground in his study of Hebrew poetry, establishing in particular the study of poetic parallelism. The advent of historical criticism, source criticism, form criticism, redaction criticism and rhetorical criticism shows the use made of various aspects of the Enlightenment presuppositions. However, these largely maintained certain traditional concepts of language and literature that had been held from antiquity, namely that truth is discoverable and that language and literature are capable of conveying or communicating truth. How this can happen is the concern of the formal study of language or linguistics. We easily take our language for granted, but there are occasions when we need to be more analytical about how language actually works.[6] The study of linguistics

---

2. See the comments that warn against treating the Bible purely as literature, quoted by Tremper Longman III, *Literary Approaches to Biblical Interpretation* (Grand Rapids: Zondervan; Leicester: Apollos, 1987), p. 8.
3. A. B. Mickelsen, *Interpreting the Bible* (Grand Rapids: Eerdmans, 1963).
4. Grant Osborne, *The Hermeneutical Spiral* (Downers Grove: IVP, 1991).
5. Longman, *Literary Approaches to Biblical Interpretation*, p. 13.
6. Peter Cotterell and Max Turner, *Linguistics and Biblical Interpretation* (London: SPCK, 1989), provide an introduction to some of the main concerns of linguistic study.

goes back at least to Plato's *Cratylus*, but modern linguistic study stems from about the eighteenth century.[7]

Modern literary hermeneutics

Hermeneutics has been largely dominated by literary criticism for understandable reasons. The various critical methods have represented differing views about where the meaning of a text was thought to be located: in the author, in the text itself, or in the reader. Thus the distinction can be made between diachronic and synchronic methods. As Terence Keegan states it: 'Diachronic analysis involves viewing things as having been constituted by or as deriving their meaning from an historical progression, i.e., viewing them through time. Synchronic analysis involves viewing things in and of themselves apart from the historical progression of which they are a part.'[8] Thus source criticism and form criticism are diachronic methods which stem from the assumptions made about the value of getting behind the text to its prehistory. Redaction criticism made a bold move to be more concerned with what the biblical authors did with their sources and began to take the final redactor seriously as an author and theologian. But, as Keegan says, 'Redaction and composition critics, even though they focus on the final product, remain bound to the genetic process and focus on the activity of the author as the final stage in the diachronic process.'[9]

Longman comments:

> One possible approach is chronological and charts the different dominant schools of thought in secular literary study and then gives examples concerning how each school of thought has exerted an influence on biblical studies. To proceed in such a way, one would begin with New Criticism, then consider structuralism and semiotics, and finally conclude with deconstruction. Other influential minority positions could then be discussed, particularly reader-response, archetypal, Marxist, and feminist literary criticism.

See also, Peter Cotterell, 'Hermeneutics: Some Linguistic Considerations', *Evangel*, Autumn 1995, pp. 78–82.

7. David Crystal, *The Cambridge Encyclopedia of Language* (Cambridge: Cambridge University Press, 1987).
8. T. J. Keegan, *Interpreting the Bible* (New York: Paulist Press, 1985), p. 24.
9. ibid., p. 32.

> Biblical studies, however, does not follow the chronological pattern of secular theory. Some researchers in Bible write in a New Critical mode long after New Criticism has passed away as a major school in literary theory. Others adopt more traditional modes of literary criticism, even in this age of deconstruction. In reality, of course, this diversity reflects the situation in literary theory. Deconstruction may be the avant-garde movement today, but many in literary theory either blithely or studiously avoid it in order to continue in traditional, perhaps even pre-New Critical, modes of interpretation.[10]

It is convenient, however, to study the development of modern literary criticism as the movement of emphasis away from the author to the text and, finally, to the reader/interpreter.

Author-centred approaches

Author-centred theories are those, mostly from the pre-modern period (pre-1940), which interpret a piece of literature by concentrating on the author. Here the concern is for the background, activities and thought life of the author as critical for the interpretation. To be thorough, we would need to go back to Schleiermacher and his concern for the thought of the author. We would include in this general area those critical procedures that express the desire to get behind the text to its sources and its history. What used to be referred to as higher or literary criticism is now more accurately dealt with under the idea of historical criticism. I do not intend here to deal with source and form criticism, nor with tradition criticism. These are covered in standard texts, and we have surveyed the historical-critical method in chapter 10. We note that redaction criticism straddles both concerns by moving into the question of the intent behind the final form of the text.

An influential modern and conservative advocate of authorial intent is E. D. Hirsch. '[H]e approaches the author's meaning through a study of the text itself, particularly its genre. In other words, he infers the author's meaning primarily through a careful study of the text in relationship to other closely related texts.'[11] Hirsch made an important distinction between the meaning of the text (author's intention) and its significance (the application to the readers on the basis of their background and interests). He has been criticized for what has

---

10. Longman, *Literary Approaches to Biblical Interpretation*, p. 17.
11. ibid., p. 21.

come to be known as the 'intentional fallacy', on the basis that it is impossible to discern an author's intention from what he has written.[12] Notwithstanding the objections that are made towards Hirsch's approach, it has to be said that the authorial intention is generally assumed by evangelical exegetes to be recoverable. More recently, Kevin Vanhoozer has sought to rehabilitate the author with his trinitarian approach to the relationship of author, text and reader.[13]

Text-centred approaches: the New Criticism and structuralism

Text-centred theories represent a reaction against the tradition-critical approach, which focused on the origin and development of a text and virtually ignored the text in the form in which we now have it. The two main text-centred theories, which emerged in the 1940s and 1950s, are New Criticism and structuralism. Thiselton comments that the New Criticism implied that a text stands 'as an autonomous world of meaning, to which its author and situation relate only in the most minimal way'.[14] 'The so-called New Criticism arose in reaction against perspectives of the nineteenth and early twentieth centuries which had concerned themselves with material extrinsic to the text as an aid to understanding and interpreting it.'[15] Thus the principle was proposed that what is important is the self-sufficient text, while the author, his background and intention are unimportant. Behind this lay a concern for real objectivity without trying to feel into the subjectivity of the author.

The concern for the text as text has led to some useful analyses of the way the written text functions. W. R. Tate makes the distinction between natural languages (the languages of the texts: Hebrew, Aramaic and Greek) and literary languages (which involve the codes used to move beyond what the text says to what the text is about).[16] This distinction between what a text says (natural language) and what the text is about (literary language) involves a distinction between the referential quality and the mimetic quality of the text. The

---

12. ibid., p. 20.
13. Kevin Vanhoozer, *Is There a Meaning in This Text?* (Grand Rapids: Zondervan; Leicester: Apollos, 1998), pp. 201–280.
14. Anthony Thiselton, *New Horizons in Hermeneutics* (Grand Rapids: Zondervan, 1992), p. 49.
15. ibid., p. 58.
16. W. R. Tate, *Biblical Interpretation: An Integrated Approach* (Peabody, MA: Hendrickson, 1991), p. 61.

referential is the relationship between the text and the world projected by that language, and the mimetic is the relationship between the world of the text and the real world.[17] While the textual world may or may not approximate the real world, the mimetic quality is the means by which the author can point us to truth about the real world. Tate points out that traditional hermeneutics, which was basically involved with the historical-critical method, was more concerned with referential function than mimetic function. Attention was diverted away from the text to the world that produced it.

Structuralism was not simply a literary theory, but one that was applied to any kind of enquiry.[18] It began in the realm of linguistics with the Swiss linguist Ferdinand de Saussure and was given great impetus in the anthropological realm by Claude Levi-Strauss. Robert Spivey explains it thus: 'At the heart of structuralism is the assumption that the "uninvited guest" for all cultural phenomena is the human brain. Structuralism claims that . . . we may infer that the brain operates in certain ways, that is structures, by observing the qualities which are recurrent in the products of human brains, especially in language.'[19] He illustrates the structuralist theory with the images of musical scores and performance, geological strata, and traffic lights.[20] Narrative consists in both the horizontal dimension (the linear narrative text) and the vertical (the system of relations that emerge out of the versions of the narrative). While the musical analogy points to both linear *melody* and vertical *harmony*, the geological analogy points to the idea that underneath the surface world (landscape) there is the stratum of meaning (geological stratum). Thus we find that different cultures have produced different texts that somehow seem similar, and this, says the structuralist, is due to more basic and prior processes of thinking.[21]

According to Terence Keegan, the two fundamental presuppositions of structuralism are, first, the existence of fixed sets of abstract rules which govern all forms of social activity and, second, the existence in human beings of an innate, genetically transmitted and determined mechanism that acts as

---

17. ibid., p. 62.
18. A useful summary is found in Longman, *Literary Approaches to Biblical Interpretation*, pp. 27–35. See also Vern Poythress, 'Structuralism and Biblical Studies', *JETS* 21/3 (1978), pp. 221–237.
19. Robert Spivey, 'Structuralism and Biblical Studies', *Interpretation* 28/2 (1974), p. 133. This issue of *Interpretation* contains several articles on structuralism.
20. ibid., pp. 135–141.
21. ibid., p. 138.

a structuring force.[22] 'Structuralism is rooted in the belief in the existence of deep structures, for the most part not consciously recognized, that underlie all social manifestations.'[23] Authors do not produce the meaning of their texts. Rather they use, unconsciously, the deep structures that make communication possible.[24]

The traffic light analogy points to the important structuralist idea of the binary structure of thought involving polar opposites. Levi-Strauss saw human thinking as basically binary. The traffic light illustrates how the continuous colour spectrum is interpreted as discontinuous. Red and green are selected as binary opposites, with amber as a discontinuous intermediate signal. Thus the deep structures of the mind are reflected in language. Meaning is determined by a series of binary contrasts that are fundamental to human experience.[25] Saussure argued that language reflects deep structures of patterns that are universally innate to human experience, but that language itself is based on arbitrary social conventions.

The literary application of structuralism was seen most significantly in the work of Roland Barthes, which had the aim of making literary criticism scientific and objective. We see this structuralism as developing from linguistics, and especially Saussure's theory of semiotics (signs). Saussure made the distinction between *langue* (language as abstract rules) and *parole* (language as actual utterances). The structure of the language controls the availability and values of the words and other linguistic units actually used. 'The aim of structural analysis is to get beyond the surface structure of use, formed by the proper use of language and correct grammar and syntax to the more complex structure of language, the deep structure is encoded in language and must be decoded from the surface structure.'[26]

William Dumbrell comments further:

> In structuralist interpretation a text stands on its own regardless of its origins or past, and it is to be interpreted without regard for an author's assumed original intention. Structuralists are equally concerned with the question of how a text communicates as well as with what is communicated, with how a reader decodes a text and resonates with its deep structures or basic meaning. A text is thus read without reference to

---

22. Keegan, *Interpreting the Bible*, pp. 41ff.
23. ibid., p. 43.
24. ibid., p. 45.
25. Spivey, 'Structuralism and Biblical Studies', p. 140.
26. W. J. Dumbrell, Moore College class notes, 1994.

> time. The only questions to be asked are those about the universal concerns of the text and its underlying assumptions.[27]

Philips Long notes a criticism by Robert Alter:

> Alter observes, for example, that among some structuralist interpretations of biblical narratives one often encounters 'rather simple superimpositions of one or another modern literary theory on ancient texts that in fact have their own dynamics, their own distinctive conventions and characteristic techniques'.[28]

Postmodernism and reader-centred approaches[29]

The development in hermeneutics has been described as involving a couple of paradigm shifts. The first was from the philosophical-theological approach of the medieval scholars to the historical approach of the Reformers. We have seen how this historical approach was again invaded by non-biblical philosophical presuppositions at the Enlightenment. Nevertheless, the historical approach dominated, but was amalgamated with theological and literary understandings. Now there has been a new paradigm shift to the literary approach. With it has come a movement away from author-centred emphases, through text-centred approaches, to reader-centred theories of hermeneutics.

It must be recognized that, even if we can describe these developments as paradigm shifts, all three foci are consistently present even if only to be discounted. It is a matter of emphasis and perspective. Thus the renewed emphasis on the literary dimensions of the text has ranged from authorial intent, to relative textual autonomy, and now to reader response. With the advent of the renewed literary focus, the others are not entirely ignored, at least not by all. Thus the literary approach embraces to varying degrees all approaches and all perspectives. For example, E. D. Hirsch, as the exponent of authorial intent, includes the role of the reader in interpretation by making the distinction between meaning and significance. The intended meaning of the text may have different significances as readers seek to apply the

---

27. ibid.
28. V. Philips Long, 'Toward a Better Theory and Understanding of Old Testament Narrative', *Presbyterion* 13/2 (1987), p. 105.
29. See Longman, *Literary Approaches to Biblical Interpretation*, pp. 38–45.

meaning to their own situation. These foci also relate in various ways to the major dimensions of the biblical text: the literary, the historical and the theological.

The move away from the historical method to the new literary criticism is a relocation of the problem of meaning and understanding away from the Bible to the reader. That is, we, the readers, are the problem. Walter Wink objects to the false objectivism of historical criticism because it is not neutral, its 'assured results' are rubbery, it is rigidly rationalistic, and it stands over rather than under the Bible.[30] On the way through to reader-oriented approaches, various philosophical presuppositions have been employed. The more the literary approach emphasized the nature of the literature that did not equate clarity with truth, the more the role of imagination in both author and reader came in view. Literature that transforms is literature that does more than convey information. The use of symbols, verbal images and metaphors in the Bible can leave meaning rather open-ended. It is quite possible that at times such devices are used to stir the reader's imagination as to the possibility of more than one exact meaning. Certainly, one crucial point in the move from the emphasis on author, on text, and then on the reader, is the question of where the meaning lies. The extreme position is to say that the meaning lies only in the reader who creates it. There are those, however, who see an interaction of text and reader (e.g., Thiselton, McKnight). 'If a text is to be understood there must occur an engagement between two sets of horizons (to use Gadamer's phrase), namely those of the ancient text and those of the modern reader or hearer.'[31] Thiselton questions the assumption that the recognition of pre-understanding in the reader means the shift in the centre of gravity from the past to the present.

N. T. Wright characterizes postmodernism as the rejection of both pre-critical piety and Enlightenment historicism in favour of examining the process of reading in itself.[32] Behind this lies the relativism of nineteenth-century philosophy, which was absorbed into literary theory in the 1960s. It was a challenge to the idea of the existence and discoverability of truth. Everything is relative to the individual's point of view. Roland Barthes reversed the role of author to reader and made the latter paramount. Jacques Derrida comes from a philosophy of nihilism and deliberately sets out to make no sense. Any interpretation of a text is as good as any other. His

---

30. Walter Wink, *The Bible in Human Transformation* (Philadelphia: Fortress Press, 1973).
31. Anthony Thiselton, *The Two Horizons* (Exeter: Paternoster, 1980), p. 15.
32. N. T. Wright, *The New Testament and the People of God* (London: SPCK, 1992), p. 9.

deconstructionism goes to the extreme of reader-response thinking – in fact, it is suggested that it has even gone beyond that focus. Deconstructionism is more concerned with what a writer does not say than with what he or she says. Reading 'against the grain' looks for what is actively suppressed in the text. J. Culler comments of deconstructionism, 'It demonstrates the difficulties of any theory that would define meaning in a univocal way: as what an author intends, what conventions determine, what a reader experiences.'[33] This is a claim that we should not be focused on author, text or reader. Yet, on the one hand, Derrida argued for the superiority of writing over speech and, on the other hand, saw in writing the display of the slippage between sign and thing signified. He thus increased the distance between the two by moving on from structuralism's understanding that signs have no inherent meaning. 'The meaning of a linguistic or literary sign is based on its difference in comparison with other signs and as such is always deferred, or delayed. With deconstruction one enters the "endless labyrinth".'[34]

Longman notes that Michael Edwards, as a Christian, approves Derrida's insight into difficulties of communication. 'There are fissures or breaks between words and their referents. Derrida attributes this slippage to an absence of the "transcendental signified" (i.e., God), Edwards (attributes it) to the Fall.'[35] Longman suggests that deconstruction has had little effect as yet on biblical studies, but time will tell. Millard Erickson, in a short critique of deconstruction, points to the problem of presuppositions, namely that the grounds for criticizing postmodernism presuppose the very things that deconstruction questions.[36] This implies that we have no common ground on which to engage a postmodernist in critical discussion. It seems that we keep coming back to the question of why a deconstructionist expects us to take him seriously if we may deconstruct his text and ignore his authorial intent.[37]

---

33. Longman, *Literary Approaches to Biblical Interpretation*, p. 41.
34. ibid., p. 43.
35. ibid., p. 44.
36. Millard J. Erickson, *Evangelical Interpretation: Perspectives on Hermeneutical Issues* (Grand Rapids: Baker, 1993), pp. 112ff.
37. See D. A. Carson, *The Gagging of God* (Grand Rapids: Zondervan; Leicester: Apollos, 1996), p. 102. Carson cites an experience with a 'postmodern' student who could not avoid using modern (or pre-modern) assumptions in trying to get a point of view across. People simply do communicate with the assumption that it is possible to make their authorial intent known.

Assessment

From the perspective of Christian theism, the problems of modern literary criticism are many. Once the author, and especially a divine Author, is disposed of, the Bible can no longer be treated seriously on its own terms. In the same way, it is difficult for us to deal with postmodern criticism on its own terms. The historical movement of foci from author to text to reader seems almost perverse. Christian theism is inclusive of all three. If evangelicals have sometimes not paid enough attention to the nature of the text or the role of the reader, it may be for a number of reasons, including a lack of reflection on the way language works and a horror of subjectivism. On the other hand, we might note the ease with which some evangelical exegetes appear to have become conservative modernists, in that they adopt assumptions and methods that reflect the Enlightenment presuppositions. Longman enumerates a range of pitfalls in modern literary theories, including contradictions, obscurantism and denial of referential function in literature.[38] He is correct in pointing up the significance of the elimination of the author (including God), for this hermeneutical atheism has allowed the *either-or* approach to introduce a reductionism that focuses on one dimension exclusively.

On the positive side, the move to treat the final form of the text as significant has resulted in a much more productive approach to biblical texts. But, if the new exegetes are now telling us, for example, to look at the finished Gospel or the whole book of Isaiah as skilfully crafted documents, evangelicals might be tempted to respond with a bit of a yawn. Nevertheless, we can certainly learn from the better understanding of literary genres, narrative strategies and ancient methods of history writing. We can also confess that we have needed to treat more seriously the role of the reader's presuppositions and community context in our understanding of ancient texts. When we are so sensitized, we may discover to our amazement that the Bible itself contains ample testimony to the role of all three major elements in communication and understanding; that the gospel demands that we treat seriously the authors, the text and the reader.

Evangelical hermeneutics has always paid attention to the literary dimension of the Bible. It could be argued that evangelicals have been too easily seduced by the Enlightenment emphasis on the Bible as literature, in that the theological and historical questions are often given second place in the hermeneutic discussions. On the positive side, recent evangelical interpreters

38. Longman, *Literary Approaches to Biblical Interpretation*, ch. 2.

have taken note of some of the better aspects of the new literary studies. A comparison of older works (e.g. Mickelsen, Berkhof) with more recent studies (e.g. Osborne, Klein et al) shows the way new insights of literary studies, such as genre and narrative criticism, have been taken on board. The questions that continue to face us as we consider the contributions of critical studies include the following.

- What are the philosophical assumptions that critical methods introduce?
- What are the biblical bases for those aspects of critical theory and practice that we find acceptable?
- To what degree can we be eclectic in choosing to follow critical techniques?
- What can we learn from the insights of structuralism, narrative criticism, etc., and even deconstruction?

All of these are relevant to the task of evangelical reconstruction that we consider in Part III.

12. THE ECLIPSE OF THE GOSPEL IN EVANGELICALISM

Hermeneutical perfectionism

Hermeneutical perfectionism is something that is tempting to all of us who believe that truth is knowable. Those who adopt a thought-out and definite position on any matter will have the conviction that they are right. No one holds to a position that they believe is wrong. But thinking that we are right about key issues does not mean that we think we have all the answers in interpreting the Bible, or that our position is infallible. It should not mean that we think we have arrived at the ultimate truth about all matters biblical. In fact, the hermeneutical spiral is a recognition that we must constantly submit our thinking and doing to the light of Scripture. The Reformers understood this when they acknowledged that the Reformed church is always reforming. In this chapter I do not want to appear to be attacking groups who understand their evangelicalism differently from the way I understand mine. I recognize that I must submit to the scrutiny of Scripture as much as any other. Nevertheless, I want to highlight some 'evangelical' hermeneutical perspectives which I believe are not consistent with the gospel, and which we are all quite capable of adopting.

These inconsistencies in our thinking are often taken on board because they are part of the tradition or subculture in which we have been nurtured. While being fairly tolerant of other evangelicals who follow different traditions, we usually treasure our own position as virtually unassailable – that is, until someone spots our inconsistencies and we are challenged to check out our reasoning against the evidence of Scripture. The hermeneutical perfectionist will not contemplate the need to reassess some treasured approaches to the Bible. But we all need to be critical of our own positions and reform when Scripture demands it. The fact that it is possible to identify aberrations within evangelicalism only serves to emphasize the unsatisfactory nature of naïve approaches to the clarity of Scripture. These differences of perspective are, nevertheless, the result of hermeneutical assumptions and methods. The hermeneutical process is always a part of anyone's reading of a text. It seems to me to be safer for evangelicals to recognize this rather than to pretend the problems are not there or that hermeneutics is completely unnecessary. The following subjects are a few examples that strike me as relevant.

Quietism: evangelical Docetism

Quietism is a term with a history,[1] but I will use it loosely to describe the tendency to overspiritualize and dehumanize Christian existence, including the way we use the Bible. We have seen it in the 'let go and let God' holiness piety. Overall, it is an inclination to downplay the function of our humanity in life, as if our relationship to God is almost entirely passive.[2] It leads to strange aberrations, for example in the matter of guidance. Just as the historic heresy of Docetism either denied or ignored the humanity of Jesus, so quietism tends to leave our true humanity out of the reckoning. The quietist's docetic Christian is one who 'doesn't make any decisions because the Holy Spirit makes them for us'. Such a person is also likely to construct a docetic hermeneutic of Scripture. The human characteristics of the biblical documents are ignored. Historical and biblical-theological contexts are regarded as irrelevant. If a text 'speaks to me' in whatever way, the careful exegesis of it is dismissed as cerebral intellectualism. The gospel is neatly eclipsed by what exists beneath a veneer of spiritual commitment. Such quietists would be offended if it were suggested that they denied the humanity of Christ. But the gospel can only be

---

1. 'Quietism', *New Dictionary of Theology* (Leicester: IVP, 1988).
2. Some Reformed theologians speak of the believer's role as passive towards God and active towards the world. This passivity towards God is submission to his lordship; it is not a quietist surrender of our God-given responsibility to think and reason about our actions.

the gospel if it is the message of the Word-made-flesh. We can effectively deny this vital truth simply by ignoring its implications in the way we use the Bible and in the manner of our lives.

Literalism: evangelical Zionism

It seems to make sense to say that we must interpret the Bible literally. The more the liberals throw at us the terms 'literalist', 'biblicist', or 'fundamentalist', the more we tend to adopt a siege mentality and dig our heels in. But if we believe that literalism is the way to go, just what do we mean by it? Some evangelical literalists use what is sometimes referred to as the 'slippery slope' argument – that is, a claim that failure to adopt this particular approach will lead to certain disaster. Thus we are told that if we do not interpret the Bible literally, the text can be made to mean anything we want it to mean. Hermeneutic chaos is predicted as the inevitable result. Yet literalism has seldom proved to be much protection against such a tendency. Literalism raises all the questions about the hermeneutics of texts, questions about the way words can be used, literary genres, how language operates, the locus of meaning, and so on. It is often assumed that the literal meaning of a text is self-evident. Yet the term dies the death of a thousand qualifications once we address the matter of imagery, poetic forms, metaphor, typology, and all the other non-literal linguistic devices.

For evangelicals, one of the areas of greatest concern is in the interpretation of prophecy in the Old Testament. Thus literalists claim to take the promises concerning the restoration of Israel, Jerusalem and the temple at their literal face value. What can be wrong with that? Well, for a start, determining what the literal meaning is can be problematic. The prophets of Israel had a preference for the use of non-literal language, for poetic imagery, symbolism and metaphor, and it can sometimes be difficult to establish the literal meaning. When we add to this the fact that different prophetic texts may describe the same future event with extremely different and sometimes incompatible imagery, the problem is compounded.[3] Although only a small number of examples occur in the Bible, apocalyptic symbolism presents even greater challenges.

---

3. See Archibald Hughes, *A New Heaven and a New Earth* (London: Marshall, Morgan and Scott, 1958), pp. 155–161; Vern Poythress, *Understanding Dispensationalists* (Grand Rapids: Academie, 1987), pp. 78–96; Philip Mauro, *The Hope of Israel: What Is It?* (Swengel, PA: Reiner, n.d.), pp. 16–25.

It could be argued that, though the details may be hard to pin down because of the prophetic preference for poetic imagery and metaphor, the big picture is abundantly clear. On this basis the literalist asserts that God reveals through the prophets that his kingdom comes with the return of the Jews to Palestine, the rebuilding of Jerusalem, and the restoration of the temple along with all its Old Testament ministries. Evangelical Christians who take this approach share some significant convictions with modern Jewish Zionists regarding the restoration of Jerusalem as the centre of the messianic kingdom. Of course, they differ radically over the identity of the Messiah.

The New Testament clearly does not support such a simplistic hermeneutic as literal fulfilment of prophecy. In this kind of Zionism we face the problem that the New Testament seems to be completely indifferent to the restorations referred to. In fact, one great hermeneutic divide that separated Jesus from the unbelieving Jews concerned this very issue of prophetic fulfilment. The Jews of Jesus' day entertained a certain kind of literalism. They also claimed their pedigree through Abraham and Moses, but Jesus refuted this claim because they did not believe in him. That the Old Testament Scriptures are, as he says, about him (John 5:39–47; 8:39–47, 56–58) must seriously qualify literalism, since Jesus (as Jesus) is not literally in the Old Testament. The disciples of Jesus also needed a lesson in the application of the Old Testament to Christ (Luke 24:25–27, 44–45; Acts 1:6–8). When the message got through under the power of the Holy Spirit, the apostolic preachers never varied from the new conviction that the hermeneutical principle was the gospel, not literalism. This meant that the terminology of the Old Testament could only be understood Christologically. How can John the Baptist be literally Elijah (Matt. 17:12–13)? If the promise to David in 2 Samuel 7:12–16 is fulfilled in the resurrection of Jesus (Acts 2:29–32), then it is not a literal fulfilment according to any normal use of the word 'literal'. If, as Paul says, the resurrection of Jesus is the fulfilment of the promises of God to Israel (Acts 13:29–32), then literalism cannot be sustained. If, according to Hebrews 12:18–24, the Jewish Christians have already come to 'Mount Zion and to the city of the living God' through faith in Jesus, this is the only Zion that matters. Because Jesus is an historical figure, an Israelite who has come in the flesh, he indeed fulfils some prophecies in a rather literal way. Thus the Messiah is born in Bethlehem (Mic. 5:2), and is born of a virgin (Isa. 7:14; Matt. 1:22–23).[4] But this does not establish literalism as the basic

4. Matthew is not interested in the possible ambiguity of the Hebrew word *'almâ* in Isa. 7:14.

hermeneutic. The gospel requires that we allow Christ to be the hermeneutic principle.

Evangelical prophetic literalism is an exercise in interpreting the New Testament by the application of a supposed literal meaning of the Old Testament. If the gospel is our hermeneutic norm, then while it is true that the interpretation of the New needs an understanding of the Old, the principal emphasis is on the way the gospel and the New Testament as a whole interpret everything, including the Old Testament. The literalist must become a futurist, since a literalistic fulfilment of all Old Testament prophecy has not yet taken place. Christian Zionism not only reshapes the New Testament's view of the future, but also affects the present period in which such a future is anticipated. It affects the way many Christians view the respective rights of Palestinians and Israelis to live in 'the promised land'. Yet one does not have to be a Zionist to appreciate Paul's emphasis on God's method of salvation, in that the gospel is 'to the Jew first'. That perspective is maintained in the New Testament, while the notion of the restoration of the temple and Jerusalem in Palestine is uniformly absent.

Legalism: evangelical Judaism

Legalism is something to which we are all prone, because it is one of the key tendencies of the sinful human heart. At its base it is an assertion of our control over our relationship with God. It is a soft-pedalling of the greatness of God's grace to sinners. On the surface it may appear to be an exalting of the law, however the law is understood. Yet when we examine the nature of legalism, we find that the opposite is true. Once we imagine that we can somehow add to God's grace or establish our righteousness by our deeds, we have in fact dragged God's law down to our level of imperfection. If salvation is by faith in Christ plus some form of obedience, the gospel is diminished to the extent that we add to the principle of *Christ alone*. Even the first Christians had great difficulty with the implications of the grace of God. Acts 10 – 11 shows how these Jewish Christians found it difficult at first to contemplate the inclusion of the Gentiles in the salvation of Christ. And the conciliar debate in Acts 15 demonstrates that there were those Judaizers who wanted to attach the law to the gospel as the only legitimate path for Gentiles into the kingdom. This Judaizing heresy, the claim that Gentiles should be circumcised or submit to other aspects of the law in addition to having faith in Christ, was a constant problem for Paul in the early churches. The epistle to the Galatians was mainly concerned with this legalistic tendency. In Colossians Paul had to rebuff those who wanted to lay rules of food and religious observance on Christians (Col. 2:16–17). These laws, he said, are only shadows of the real thing, which is Christ.

Legalism is a subtle thing. Those who do not place the same emphasis on the law will be branded as antinomians, as against law, even lawless. But it needs to be emphasized that recognizing that God requires us to honour his laws and to be lawful is not the same as being legalistic. Sometimes the problem is cultural. Young converts often find themselves in a subculture that is strong in its spoken and unspoken taboos. In becoming more mature in the faith, they may realize that the safety of legalism needs to give way to the more risky business of being responsible to work out in the light of Scripture what is acceptable behaviour. All behavioural norms need to be owned, or disowned, on the basis of their consistency, or inconsistency, with the gospel. Legalism is attractive because it is safe. It is easier to have a set of rules agreed on by the wider group than to have to make responsible decisions for Christian living.

Many things that are right and appropriate for Christians can become legalistic burdens. It is right and proper that we regularly read and study the Bible and pray. Yet the evangelical 'quiet time', a good discipline in itself, can be so binding that to miss it because of oversleeping or an emergency can be interpreted as a recipe for a disastrous day. Evangelicals will differ in their attitudes to how the law of God applies. The controversies over the Sabbath versus the Lord's Day continue into the present. Then there are differences over the transference of Sabbath ideals to Sunday as the Lord's Day.[5] This is not the place to try to settle arguments over exegesis of the biblical texts. The hermeneutic question really is about the role of the gospel in pointing to the legitimate interpretation of those texts that might be misused legalistically. It is clear that Jesus was the true law-keeper, the faithful covenant partner of God, the true and perfect Israel of God. He justifies our failed attempts to be lawful by his infallible lawfulness. It is also clear that he often offended the Jewish legalists of his time by his rejection of the burdens they imposed upon people.

The issue of legalism is a touchy one. Douglas Oss quotes from John Murray:

> Too often the person imbued with meticulous concern for the ordinances of God and conscientious regard for the minutiae of God's commandments is judged as a legalist, while the person who is not bothered by details is judged to be the practical person who exemplifies the liberty of the gospel.[6]

---

5. See Andrew Shead, 'Sabbath', *NDBT*, pp. 745–750.
6. Douglas A. Oss, 'The Influence of Hermeneutical Frameworks in the Theonomy Debate', *WTJ* 51 (1989), p. 246. It might be fair to add that a concern for the liberty

For that reason, I have not wanted to be so provocative as to include serious theological stances on the significance of the Mosaic law for the Christian under the term legalism. Furthermore, theologians like Murray, and those Reformed thinkers after him who developed the idea of theonomy, are usually crystal clear about grace and justification. The legalism I am concerned with here is a more uninformed piety that has not really reflected in any concerted way on the relationship of grace to law, of gospel to works. However, even largely unthought-out positions reflect a hermeneutic, and such unreflective evangelicalism can eclipse the gospel.

Decisionism: evangelical Bultmannism

A key evangelical belief is that people must be called to make a decision concerning the claims of Christ. Thus when people decide that Jesus Christ has indeed lived and died for them, they are often said to have made a decision for Christ.[7] There are plenty of biblical grounds for challenging people to repent and believe the gospel. That is not in dispute. The important thing is that the decision should be a decision to place one's trust alone in the Christ who has done all that is necessary for us to be accepted by God and to inherit eternal life.

So, what is my problem with decisions, and why am I so provocative as to refer to decisionism as 'evangelical Bultmannism'? I do this because I have experienced and witnessed the effects of calls to 'decide for Jesus' that have been made when almost no reason has been given why anyone should so decide. Rudolf Bultmann applied his existential philosophy in such a way that for him the historicity of the events of the person and work of Jesus of Nazareth is not the central issue. What matters is the telling of the story, which may or may not be historically factual, and the way this story helps us in our self-understanding and authentic decisions in life. While not endorsing Bultmann's philosophy and historical scepticism, there are evangelicals who are so earnest in calling for decisions for Jesus that they seem to forget to tell people *why* they should decide for Jesus. I remember listening to a speaker at an evangelistic meeting whose only mention of the death of Jesus was a passing reference in his closing prayer. I was acting as an advisor to follow up

---

of the gospel and the primacy of God's grace all too easily invites the accusation of antinomianism.

7. In some circles a person is said to have 'made a commitment'.

on the after-meeting counselling. I spoke to a young couple who had heard the talk, gone out to the front, been 'counselled' and then brought to me. They obviously had not heard any gospel in either the address or the counselling. They had no idea about being justified by faith in the doing and dying of Christ. It seems that the decision can become everything. People are exhorted to turn to Christ, to receive Christ, to ask Jesus into their hearts, and the like, even when they have been given no substantial idea at all of who Jesus was and what he has done to save us.

It should be obvious how gospel-centred hermeneutics addresses this prevalent evangelical approach. Preaching the gospel does not consist in a few generalities followed by an impassioned plea for a decision.[8] To preach the gospel is to state clearly who Jesus is and what he has done. People must be urged to make a decision in the light of the historical events of Jesus and what God says about these events. They must be urged to repent and believe, to put their whole faith and trust in Jesus as the one who has done what is necessary for us to be saved. The problem is not in the call for a decision. The error of decisionism is to dehistoricize the gospel and to make the decision the saving event. To that extent it expresses an existential hermeneutic.

Subjectivism: evangelical Schleiermacherism

Friedrich Schleiermacher is regarded as the father of liberal Christianity. At the time when Beethoven's music was reflecting a transition from the Classical to the Romantic, Schleiermacher's theology reflected a similar refocusing on the affective side of the human spirit. The music of Bach, Mozart and the early Beethoven can certainly arouse one's emotions, but the later Beethoven and the Romantics used music more to describe emotions.[9] In this period of Romanticism, Schleiermacher recast the nature of Christianity. He was not the first theological child of the Enlightenment, but he did, with great erudition and skill, propound a whole system of theology that centred on the notion of a feeling of absolute dependence on the divine. Some may consider that I push

---

8. It is ironic that in the first Christian evangelistic sermon (Acts 2) the appeal came not from the preacher, but from the audience: 'Brothers, what shall we do?' (v. 37). Only then did Peter tell them to repent and be baptized.
9. For example, the first movement of Beethoven's Sixth Symphony is entitled *Erwachen heiterer Empfindungen bei der Ankunft auf dem Lande* ('Awakening of cheerful feelings upon arrival in the country').

the similarity a little too far in suggesting that Schleiermacher is alive and well in some forms of evangelicalism. Yet from time to time one encounters evangelicals who are convinced of the centrality of Christ and the authority of the Bible, but who nevertheless seem to operate primarily on the basis of feeling. Schleiermacher's 'feeling' is not simply subjective emotion, but rather intuitive feeling.[10] In the same way, evangelical 'feeling' is not necessarily purely emotive, but may be an intuitive conviction that is popularly expressed in terms of what a person feels to be the case.

Thus, while one may assert biblical authority, this authority can be subverted by feeling or emotion. 'I just felt that it was right.' 'I knew this was the Lord's leading because I felt such peace within.' Now, I have no doubt that God has made us affective beings and that our emotions are important. The realization of the love and grace of God shown to us should have a great effect upon our emotions. The word 'rejoice' is used so often in the Bible that it is impossible to ignore the implications. The problem arises when we assume the meaning and significance of words that are translated from Hebrew and Greek as 'happy', 'blessed', 'rejoice', 'peace', etc. We easily read into them meanings that are insufficient or misleading. 'Peace' is a good example. The Hebrew *shalom* is usually translated as 'peace'. Does this mean inner tranquillity, absence of hostilities, absence of noise and confusion, all of the above, or what? For the Hebrews it was far more than merely a feeling of inner tranquillity. As one dictionary describes it, 'In nearly two thirds of its occurrences, *shalom* describes the state of fulfilment which is the result of God's presence.'[11] Thus *shalom* is above all relational. Paul's use of *eirēnē*, the Greek word for 'peace', is Hebraic rather than Hellenistic in meaning.[12] Thus 'the peace of God, which surpasses all understanding' (Phil. 4:7) is much more than a feeling of tranquillity. We may experience such peace and not feel tranquil at all.

Here we have two related problems affecting evangelical hermeneutics. The one is eisegesis, reading into the text an assumed meaning rather than trying to ascertain how the word is used in the biblical text. The other is allowing the

---

10. Paul Tillich, *A History of Christian Thought*, ed. Carl Braaten (New York: Simon and Schuster, 1967), p. 392.

11. R. Laird Harris (ed.), *Theological Wordbook of the Old Testament* (Chicago: Moody, 1980), vol. 2, p. 931.

12. G. Kittel (ed.), *Theological Wordbook of the New Testament* (Grand Rapids: Eerdmans, 1964), vol. 2, pp. 406–417, describes the New Testament uses of *eirēnē* as: the normal state of things; the eschatological salvation of the whole man; peace with God; [peace] of men with one another; peace of soul.

importance of emotions, and an idea of Christian experience, to dull the objectivity of the word. It is in fact a form of reader-response hermeneutics in which the reader, often under the guise of being led by the Spirit, determines the meaning of the text. Gospel-centred hermeneutics sees Christ as the determiner of meaning.

'Jesus-in-my-heart-ism': evangelical Catholicism

Many evangelicals use the evangelistic appeal to 'ask Jesus into your heart'. The positive aspect of this is that the New Testament speaks of 'Christ in you, the hope of glory' (Col. 1:27); of Christ dwelling 'in your hearts through faith' (Eph. 3:17), and the like. It speaks of the Christian as having 'received Christ Jesus the Lord' (Col. 2:6). But it also makes clear that Christ dwells in or among his people by his Spirit, for the bodily risen Jesus is in heaven. Furthermore, there are no examples or principles of evangelism or conversion in the New Testament involving the asking of Jesus into one's heart. In many cases this practice represents a loss of confidence in *faith alone*, for it needs to resort to a Catholic style of infused grace to assure us that something has happened.

Now, when people are genuinely converted by asking Jesus into their hearts, and I have no doubt that there are many, it can only be because they have understood the gospel sufficiently well for this prayer to be a decision to believe that this Jesus is the one who lived and died for their salvation. Why, then, have I called this section 'evangelical Catholicism'? An aspect of Catholicism that Protestants have rejected is the reversal of the relationship of objective justification to its subjective outworking or sanctification. Another way of putting this is that the focus on the grace of God at work in the historic gospel event of Jesus Christ is muted compared to the emphasis on the grace of God as a kind of spiritual infusion into the life of the Christian. The gospel is seen more as what God is doing *in* me now, rather than what God did *for* me then. The focus is on Jesus living his life in and through me now, rather than the past historic event of Jesus of Nazareth living his life for me and dying for me. When the legitimate subjective dimension of our salvation begins to eclipse the historically and spiritually prior objective dimension, we are in trouble. The New Testament calls on the repenting sinner to believe in Christ, to trust him for salvation. To ask Jesus into one's heart is simply not a New Testament way of speaking. It is superfluous to call on Christ to dwell in us, for to be a believer is to have the Spirit of Christ dwelling in us. In the same way, it is not the

New Testament perspective that we should call on God to give us the gift of new birth.[13]

Once again, we see that it is not always an outright error that we are dealing with. Rather, it is allowing something that is good and necessary (Christ present by his Spirit) to eclipse something that is of prior importance (faith in the doing and dying of Christ) and upon which the good thing we emphasize actually depends. The result can be disastrous. I believe that many people have made their decision for Jesus and asked him into their heart without really understanding the gospel and its demands for repentance and faith. These are spurious conversions, and the last state is worse than the first if the 'convert' becomes disillusioned and hardened against the real gospel.

A tendency that is encouraged by this evangelical aberration is a kind of Christomonism.[14] This is a theological deviation from the Christian doctrine of the Trinity. If the centre of my concern becomes Jesus living in my heart ('heart' usually being undefined), then Jesus has taken the place of the Holy Spirit and is likely to replace the Father also. It undermines the bodily resurrection and ascension of Christ. It affects prayer, among other things, so that the New Testament perspective on prayer to the Father is lost.[15] Its tendency is to a docetic hermeneutic.

Evangelical pluralism

First, a clarification of the term 'pluralism' is in order. As I see it, there are some different perspectives on the notion that evangelicals can engage in some form of pluralism. One position involves the critique of evangelical monism: seeking to unify the biblical text into a single, tightly unified system of truth.

---

13. I have heard, more than once, this exhortation given on the basis of John 3:7, 'Do not marvel that I said to you, "You must be born again."' But this is not a command to get oneself born again. Jesus tells Nicodemus in the indicative, not the imperative, that it is necessary for one to be born again. When Nicodemus presses the question, 'How . . .?' Jesus finally puts the answer in terms of believing in him (v. 16).
14. See ch. 3.
15. The popular 'Dear Lord Jesus' prayer is conspicuously absent from the New Testament. The biblical norm is prayer to the Father, through the mediation of the Son, enabled by the Holy Spirit. See my book, *Prayer and the Knowledge of God* (Leicester: IVP, 2003), pp. 82–83.

Thus by 'pluralism' Douglas Jacobsen indicates a willingness to listen to other points of view and even be instructed by them.[16] He goes on to say:

> The crucial hermeneutical question that separates evangelical monists and pluralists is this: Does the Bible have one and only one meaning that resides in the text, or is it possible for the Bible to be interpreted validly and responsibly in different ways by different people?[17]

This is not a helpful way of putting it, unless we clarify what 'one and only one meaning' implies. I would suggest that an important hermeneutical question, if not the crucial one, is this: does God say contradictory or incompatible things in Scripture, or is it that some things may appear to us as contradictory or incompatible because we do not fully understand them in relation to the 'big picture' of the Bible? The fact that we can and do err, and that no interpreter of the Bible other than God himself is infallible, does not mean that God did not speak a unified truth in his word. If pluralism means that the Bible does not speak with the one voice of the Holy Spirit, then it is in error. But if it means that the gospel message, or even a specific text, may have different applications in different situations, I can see no problem.

There are two broad approaches to this matter that may or may not produce widely differing results. The first is the Christian theistic presuppositional approach for which I have argued. It involves exegesis of key texts as well as the dogmatic formulation of a doctrine of Scripture. If we apply a gospel-centred hermeneutic to the Bible as a whole, we must conclude that Jesus and the apostles were in no doubt as to the truth, the inner coherence and consistency, and the accessibility of the Scriptures of the Old Testament. The question, then, is whether the New Testament shows a similar consistency and unity. What Vern Poythress refers to as symphonic theology, a multiplicity of perspectives, is not the same as asserting disparate and incompatible perspectives.[18] The second possible approach is one that leans more to empiricist presuppositions. It was this that was favoured by the old liberal historical criticism, or higher criticism as it was called. Evangelicals who use a perfectly valid descriptive approach to the Bible can be, and sometimes have been, wooed by those who claim that difficulties or different perspectives cast doubt

---

16. Douglas Jacobsen, 'The Rise of Evangelical Hermeneutical Pluralism', *CSR* 16/4 (1987), pp. 325–335.
17. ibid., p. 326.
18. Vern Poythress, *Symphonic Theology* (Grand Rapids: Academie, 1987).

on the idea of a single, unified word of God. If the descriptive and synchronic study of the Bible is not checked by the diachronic holistic approach based on the recognition of the unity of the word of God, it can lead to a revision of the sense of the authority of the Bible.

Evangelical pragmatism

Evangelical aberrations are often a dehistoricizing of the gospel. When the gospel is reinterpreted primarily as how God does good and useful things in our lives now, a pragmatic hermeneutic may take over. This can take many forms, but the same basic problem is the constant of these aberrations. Good and important biblical truths are allowed to crowd out the central truths of the historic events of the gospel. Theologically speaking, this usually involves allowing the present experience of the Christian, rather than the finished work of Christ, to become the hermeneutical norm. It means focusing on the continuing work of the Spirit at the expense of the finished work of Christ. It undermines the centrality of our justification in Christ. Such distortions are easy to fall into, and they are also easy to accept when they are confidently taught as biblical truth. The problem lies in the fact that these things are not themselves the gospel, yet the gospel does not take place without them. Dehistoricizing the gospel undermines its reality and puts the believer's assurance in jeopardy. Instead of contemplating the finished and perfect work of Christ, one is tempted to focus on the incomplete work of the Spirit within us. We then easily adopt a pragmatic approach to what we consider to be the Spirit's work.

Evangelical pragmatism takes on many forms and may include any or all of the matters already mentioned. Pragmatism is the view that what works is true. It ignores the issue of how we determine what kind of results we should look for. Thus, if it feels good it is true; if it brings people to church it is valid and right; if we get the numbers and a good cash flow our methods are correct. We conclude from good results that we must be acting biblically. Once again, it need only be said that the gospel hermeneutic does not necessarily support these views. Pragmatism is really a hermeneutical framework that is used to determine not so much the meaning of texts, but the meaning of events. It is usually not a thought-out philosophical position such as the pragmatism that was applied by John Dewey in American education theory, or by Carl Rogers in his non-directive psychotherapy. It is rather expressive of religious enthusiasm, and even reflective of spiritual hedonism. It is at its core a trinitarian error and a form of religious humanism.

Assessment

The irony of modern evangelicalism is that many of its aberrations have occurred because of a siege mentality and an attempt to ward off the effects of the Enlightenment. When evangelicals become reactionary, they can often flee unwittingly into the arms of another enemy waiting in the wings.[19] Most reactionary moves tend to compound the problem. Pietism and quietism were earlier reactions to either doctrinal or critical sterility. Other aberrations were simply attempts to protect the importance of personal faith, conversion and regeneration. It could be argued that they represent a loss of nerve; a failure to trust the power of the gospel and the accompanying ministry of the Spirit. How easy it is for us, while priding ourselves on being people of the Book, to be quite unquestioning about cherished beliefs and practices in the interpretation of the Bible.

In modern evangelicalism we could mention current usage of the words that are quite far removed from their main function in the New Testament. One classic example is the use of the word 'worship' to refer either to what we do in church, or to that part of the weekly congregational meeting given over to the singing, often repetitiously, of popular 'spiritual' choruses and songs.[20] The problem is that lazy exegesis and unreflective usage end up by obscuring the gospel-based significance of worship. Other problems arise when a hermeneutical approach exalts doctrinal categories by muting the dynamics of biblical theology. Those matters raised in this chapter should move us to be more diligent in allowing the gospel to shape our hermeneutics, even if this means appearing to be somewhat tiresome in our questioning of some of the traditions of our evangelical culture.

---

19. Mark A. Noll, *The Scandal of the Evangelical Mind* (Grand Rapids: Eerdmans; Leicester: IVP, 1994), p. 24, notes that certain evangelical movements were all 'strategies of survival in response to the religious crises of the late nineteenth century'.
20. David Peterson, *Engaging With God* (Leicester: Apollos, 1992), shows how far the popular use of the term has strayed from its biblical uses.

PART III

RECONSTRUCTING EVANGELICAL HERMENEUTICS

Introduction

In the first part of the book I set out to define the foundations of hermeneutics in the principles of evangelicalism as consistent Christian theism. In Part II we examined a range of challenges to such Christian theism as they have emerged in biblical interpretation throughout the Christian era, mainly as a result of inconsistent presuppositions and the influences of alien philosophies. We are now in a position to make progress towards the reconstruction of evangelical hermeneutics using the insights, both positive and negative, gained in the first two parts of the book. Most evangelicals would agree, I think, that it is neither possible nor desirable to try to return to so-called pre-critical times. As much as we see ourselves as standing on the shoulders of the Reformers and, through them, on the shoulders of the apostles, living in the modern and postmodern world means that we often need to ask different questions of Scripture from those of our forebears. Just as the Protestant Reformers learned much from the classical Renaissance, so we should be open to the possibility of learning from those around us who do not share our basic convictions.

What, then, can be the shape of contemporary evangelical hermeneutics? There are at least two major concerns in raising this question. One concern involves the apologetics of Christianity: our ability to argue the case for

Christianity rationally in a postmodern world. Any such rational argument involves us in questions of the authority of the Bible. This, in turn, brings us to hermeneutics, for showing how the Bible is authoritative cannot be done if it is misread, misunderstood or misused. Every so often something happens that is seen by many to challenge the integrity of Christian faith. In my lifetime we have gone from Auschwitz and Hiroshima, through constant horrors of warfare and famine, to AIDS, the terrorism of 11 September 2001, the tsunami of 26 December 2004 and more recent disasters too numerous to mention. For many, these refute the notion of the goodness of God. Christian responses must be biblical. The other concern of contemporary evangelical hermeneutics is more self-critical. Negatively, this involves becoming sensitive to the pitfalls and errors in biblical interpretation into which we have fallen, so that we may seek to reform our ways. Positively, we may find that others have done for us what we seemed unable to do for ourselves. They have asked questions and made expert analyses of various dimensions of the Bible that we have failed to ask and make. We may eventually have to part company with them because of their presuppositions and the conclusions they reach. But we can, and should, assess these questions and analyses in the light of the biblical evidence and, where possible, put them to good use. Finally, there is the ongoing task of reassessing, refining and reforming if necessary the hermeneutical principles and practices that we have adopted as evangelicals.

In Part III we consider the role of critical evangelical approaches to the literature, history and theology of the Bible. The role of biblical theology in the hermeneutic process is of major concern. Our missionary mandate also requires that the discussion includes the role of hermeneutics in communicating the gospel into other cultures. What is now referred to as contextualization includes the mode of communication of the message into our own culture, with its myriad subcultures, as well as in cross-cultural mission. Bible translation is thus a consideration. In the final analysis the challenge for evangelical hermeneutics is the struggle to make the 'old, old story' available to a needy postmodern and pluralistic world without compromising the gospel's power to save. Sound practices must be based on sound theoretical foundations. The purpose of theoretical formulations must always be linked with the goal of clear, authoritative proclamation of the word of life. Evangelicals have regained a lot of the confidence that was lost as a result of the Enlightenment's attacks on orthodoxy. We dare not squander this position by zeal without knowledge. If we do, the rising star will soon set. Our aim should be to have a confidence that is well placed in foundations that are carefully thought out and clearly expounded.

13. PRE- AND POST-ENLIGHTENMENT EVANGELICAL INTERPRETATION

The pre-Enlightenment background to evangelical belief

I have previously referred to Carl Henry's suggestion that there are three alternative presuppositional stances open to us in theological and hermeneutical thinking:[1]

- *Fideism*, reflecting Tertullian's exclusion of rational tests for revelation. This characterizes mysticism and aspects of existential theology.
- *Empiricism*, either Thomist (nature plus grace) or Enlightenment (nature alone).[2] This produces unqualified evidentialism and higher-critical scepticism.
- *Presuppositionalism*, as found in Augustine, Anselm and the Reformers.

Henry comments on the significance of the unavoidable presuppositional stance:

---

1. Carl F. H. Henry, *Toward a Recovery of Christian Belief* (Wheaton: Crossway, 1990). See ch. 2.
2. Empiricism was, of course, only one aspect of Enlightenment philosophical positions.

> The decisive issue about the interrelation of revelation and reason is whether we derive the governing content of philosophical reasoning from transcendent revelation, or whether we elevate human reasoning as a supreme or secondary instrument of revelation and therefore view it as a final authority alongside of or in lieu of the Word of God.[3]

It should also be clear by now that I have favoured a form of presuppositionalism as the most consistent evangelical stance. This is required by the Bible's realism in its teaching about the effects of sin, and by the sovereign grace of God in revelation and salvation. In this chapter I want to examine the interaction of the essential evangelical foundations with the movements of the post-Enlightenment. But before that, it is worth spending a moment on some of the ways in which the Reformers laid the foundations for modern evangelical thought.

Up to this point I have attempted to trace the basis for a sound hermeneutic from a consideration of evangelical foundations, and from the way orthodox Christian interpretation has been challenged by alien philosophies. We have considered the presuppositions and starting point of the Reformers and their claim to be returning to the truly catholic position of the Fathers and the apostles. We need now to look more closely at some of the hermeneutical principles of evangelical theology, particularly as expressed by the Reformers. Luther and Calvin did not operate in a hermetically sealed environment any more than Augustine or the apostle Paul did. The Renaissance anticipated the Enlightenment, and it too was challenging the claims of medieval Catholicism at the same time as the Reformers were.

The position of a Renaissance humanist such as Erasmus should be noted. Here is one of the forces for the movement away from the medieval method of interpretation. First, Erasmus accepted the humanist principle of *ad fontes* ('to the source'). From this arises a concern for the original biblical languages and for textual criticism. Luther leaned on this method, although he regarded Erasmus as altogether too broad in his approach. For Luther the only source was Scripture; *ad fontes* for him meant *sola scriptura*. Erasmus's second principle was that the authority of his sources was determined by the *philosophia Christi* ('the philosophy of Christ'), but this was a reductionist notion centred on the ideals of love, simplicity and purity. Thus he could accept classical literature along with the Bible as prime sources. His third principle was erudition through the learning of antiquity. The Reformers consequently identified only

---

3. Henry, *Toward a Recovery of Christian Belief*, p. 106.

in a qualified way with these three principles of Erasmus. Nevertheless, the Renaissance influence may be seen in the Reformers' emphasis on the original languages and sources; on the natural, historical and grammatical sense; and on the application of criticism in study of the texts.

Paul Althaus makes the following points summarizing Luther's Reformation position on Holy Scripture.[4]

- The sole content of Scripture is Christ. All Scripture points to Christ alone. Because Christ is the incarnate Word, the Bible can only be the Word of God if it deals with Christ.
- Scripture authenticates itself. It is the master and judge of all. Thus no one is in a position to validate, or invalidate, Scripture. The church's witness to Scripture is nothing more than obedient recognition of the witness that Scripture bears to itself as God's word. The Scripture validates the church.
- Scripture interprets itself. It is a corollary of Scripture authenticating itself that the standard for its interpretation must come from within itself. This includes the hermeneutical principle that it must be interpreted according to its simple literal sense. It also presupposes that Scripture is clear in itself.
- Christ is Lord of the Scripture. For Luther this meant that a Christocentric interpretation is inherent in Scripture. His understanding of the literal sense is qualified by this principle. The analogy of Scripture is nothing less than the analogy of the gospel, so that all Scripture is interpreted by its relationship to the gospel.

There are, then, important implications for hermeneutics in the four 'alones'. If our only hope is in Christ, in the gospel as it is set out in Scripture, Christ must redeem hermeneutics and every principle of interpretation must be drawn from Scripture. Once we accept the priority of God's revelation, all else follows. This is not to turn our backs on the refinements in biblical study that have emerged even from those who do not share such presuppositions, but it is to say that we must be ever vigilant to resist alien encroachments on biblical truth.

The Reformed or Christian theistic hermeneutic was given a formative – one could say definitive – expression in the opening chapters of Calvin's *Institutes*. This massive achievement, which Calvin finally revised and

4. Paul Althaus, *The Theology of Martin Luther* (Philadelphia: Fortress, 1966), pp. 74–81.

enlarged in 1559, is clearly one of the greatest theological treatises of all time. It could be claimed that in the opening chapters Calvin demolishes the whole Thomist system of nature plus grace without even mentioning it. Rather than starting with the Aristotelian categories used by Thomas Aquinas, Calvin derives his epistemology from Scripture. He also shows his alignment in this with the great Fathers such as Anselm and Augustine. He, more than anyone, provided a systematic Reformation theology that stands on the presuppositions of Scripture. While he often engages in quite strongly worded polemics, the method overall is a model of positive, evangelical formulation of doctrine from Scripture, undertaken as an expression of godly devotion and true piety.

> At the beginning of the Institutes he [Calvin] deals impressively with the theme: How God is known. The whole work is suffused with an awed sense of God's ineffable majesty, sovereign power, and immediate presence with us men . . . God is not known by those who propose to search him out by their proud but feeble reason; rather, he makes himself known to those who in worship, love, and obedience consent to learn his will from his Holy Word.[5]

Calvin begins by stating that without knowledge of self there is no knowledge of God.[6] The two main objects of knowledge are God and humanity. There is no attempt at an abstract ontology here. This approach contrasts with the Reformed tendencies from the seventeenth century onwards, which dwell more fully on the classification of God's attributes. For Calvin our knowledge of ourselves and of God is relational. As Warfield says, 'To know self implies, therefore, the co-knowledge with self of that on which it is dependent, from which it derives, by the standard of which its imperfection is revealed, to which it is responsible.'[7] This recognition of the relational basis of our knowledge of God anticipates all the modern hermeneutical questions about the relationship of subjectivity and objectivity. Thus, says Calvin, we cannot attain knowledge of God without at the same time coming to know something of ourselves and our imperfections.[8] When our thoughts rise to God, we see our own foolishness

---

5. Editor's Introduction to John Calvin, *Institutes of the Christian Religion*, trans. Ford Lewis Battles (Philadelphia: Westminster, 1960), p. li.
6. Calvin, *Institutes*, 1.1.1.
7. B. B. Warfield, *Calvin and Augustine* (Philadelphia: Presbyterian and Reformed, 1956, new edn 1980), p. 31.
8. Calvin, *Institutes*, 1.1.2–3.

and weakness. At the centre of this theological realism is the recognition of the distinction between our subjective understanding and objective reality. But, in stark contrast to the position Kant would take some two centuries later, Calvin allows the gospel to direct his thinking so that distinction does not become separation. The true subjectivity-objectivity of our knowledge is governed by who and what God is, and how he has made us to relate to him. Thus true piety is necessary for a true knowledge of God.[9] Calvin could never have contemplated the hermeneutical developments in modernism that broke the nexus of Author/author, text and reader. Rather he provides for us a reminder of the trinitarian- and gospel-based perspectives in hermeneutics of the relationship between God, the word and the believer.

At the heart of Calvin's understanding is the knowledge of God that is innately within us. This makes it inexcusable to fail to worship him.[10] An ineffaceable sense of deity is engraved upon all people's minds; it is our endowment from birth. This is what distinguishes us from the animals. It would thus seem to be the implication of being made in the image of God. It implies that human beings are created not only with the ability to know what is real, but with the inability to escape successfully the knowledge of what is real. The fact that, as sinners, we constantly try to escape the truth by suppressing it does not alter the fact that we ultimately fail and are left without excuse.

Calvin's theology, and evangelical theology after him, differs from the modern and postmodern views of human understanding in that it takes with utmost seriousness the biblical testimony of our fallenness.[11] Because of our rebellion against the truth, natural or general revelation does not translate into a valid natural theology. The true knowledge of God is smothered and corrupted, either through deliberate revolt from God, or through superstition. The sinner repels all remembrance of God. He denies God by denying his providence and government of the world. Religions are the result of such denial of God while substituting the existence of god or gods. Sinners know that they cannot overthrow God and his judgment so, out of dread, they perform some semblance of religion. This leads to spiritual blindness and the utter corruption of the innate awareness of God.

God shows himself in the workmanship of his creation. The marks of his glory are obvious, and thus all are without excuse. Human science points to the mysteries of divine wisdom. The clearest example of God's wisdom is

9. ibid., 1.2.
10. ibid., 1.3.
11. ibid., 1.4.

humankind itself, yet sinners take the evidence and turn it against God. The evidence for God is there in his lordship over creation and human society. The evidence is even there in human reason and human language. But this revelation of God does not have its effect on us because of superstition and error. Our eyes are blind to the truth unless they are illuminated by the inner revelation of God through faith.

Since we cannot read the truth about God in nature, we need Scripture for the knowledge of God as Creator and Redeemer. Scripture comes to us as the word of God. Without it we can only remain in error. Scripture can communicate to us what revelation in God's works cannot. This, however, is not a simple matter of reading and understanding the words of the Bible. Calvin's view of sin becomes a major qualification in his epistemology. This warping of human subjectivity that blurs the objective requires the regenerative work of the Holy Spirit to overcome it. No hermeneutic that ignores these two factors can claim to be authentically Christian. As Wilhelm Niesel points out:

> [T]he focal point of the Bible to which Calvin wishes to bear witness in his theology is not comprehensible by the unaided reason. It is by the grace of God that Scripture mediates to us the living Christ. The Holy Spirit must unfold to us the treasures of the words of Scripture if our study is to lead to this goal.[12]

The authority of Scripture comes from God, not from the church. In fact, the church is based on, and created by, Scripture.[13] The church does not establish the authenticity of Scripture. Scripture exhibits clear evidence of its own truth and needs no external witness. It is the witness of the Holy Spirit that establishes Scripture's authenticity to us. We cannot establish the authority of Scripture by rational proofs, for it will not find acceptance in men's hearts until it is sealed there by the inner testimony of the Spirit. The authentication of Scripture through the Spirit's testimony is a privilege granted only to the elect. Calvin here anticipates the evangelical understanding of the hermeneutic spiral. The circularity of which modernism now accuses us is admitted. But this is not a vicious circularity, because the all-wise Spirit of God oversees it.

The error of the enthusiasts of Calvin's day, and of some Spirit-focused Christians of our day, is to make the Spirit a substitute for our humanity and

---

12. Wilhelm Niesel, *The Theology of Calvin*, trans. Harold Knight (Grand Rapids: Baker, 1980), p. 30.
13. Calvin, *Institutes*, 1.7.

our responsibility before God to engage in careful exegesis of the text. Such an approach is docetic, while Calvin's approach is informed by the relation of God and man that the gospel expounds. Thus, as Warfield remarks, '[W]hat [Calvin] calls the testimony of the Spirit concerns the accrediting of Scripture, not the assimilation of its revelatory contents.'[14] But this also must be distinguished from mere acknowledgment of the Bible as the word of God. Again Warfield sums it up: '[I]t seemed to him utterly unimportant that a man should be convinced by stress of rational evidence that the Scriptures are the Word of God, unless he practically embraced these Scriptures as the Word of God and stayed his soul upon them.'[15] When Calvin enumerates rational proofs, he declares that 'those arguments – not strong enough before to engraft and fix the certainty of Scripture in our minds – become very useful aids'.[16] In other words, only the elect believers will be convinced and encouraged by them.

The fact that the Reformers had to deal with the enthusiasts (or fanatics, as Calvin refers to them) makes the *Institutes* timely for the present when experience governs many people's interpretation of Scripture. Thus Calvin is clear on the unbreakable bond between the Word and the Spirit. This is an affirmation of the inseparable relationships of the persons of the Trinity.

> For by a kind of mutual bond the Lord has joined together the certainty of his Word and of his Spirit so that the perfect religion of the Word may abide in our minds when the Spirit, who causes us to contemplate God's face, shines; and that we in turn may embrace the Spirit with no fear of being deceived when we recognize him in his own image, namely, in the Word. So indeed it is. God did not bring forth his Word among men for the sake of a momentary display, intending at the coming of his Spirit to abolish it. Rather he sent down the same Spirit by whose power he had dispensed the Word, to complete his work by the efficacious confirmation of the Word.[17]

This trinitarian error of which Calvin warns is a constant danger to hermeneutics. Modernists and postmodernists separate word and Spirit. Many modern evangelicals and enthusiasts fuse the two. De Senarclens summarizes the Reformation starting point, with particular reference to Calvin, thus:

---

14. Warfield, *Calvin and Augustine*, pp. 70f.
15. ibid., p. 75.
16. Calvin, *Institutes*, 1.8.1.
17. ibid., 1.9.3.

> *The starting point of the Reformation* is that God has demonstrated himself in Christ. The Reformed position is not ashamed to be involved in a *petitio principii* [argument in a circle]. For this circle, which is closed from our point of view, is in fact the only means to breach the vicious circle in which we are enclosed by sin. To begin with revelation is to begin with the Jesus of history.[18]

He goes on to indicate the centrality of grace as the only answer to the bondage of the will, and Christology as the substance of the doctrine of grace.

> Christology is both the truth of God and our truth, since the Son recapitulates in himself all that concerns God and affects us. Our theology, worship and service automatically disqualify themselves if they are guilty of even the slightest deviation from this one point of reference in favour of another object which is thought to be more accessible, e.g., the Church, the sacraments, religious feeling, pure or practical reason.[19]

Christology and the doctrine of the co-inherent persons of the Trinity must therefore be at the heart of our doctrine of Scripture and of our whole hermeneutic endeavour. The distinction between Jesus as the Word of God incarnate and the Bible as the word of God inscripturate must not obliterate their unity. As the Holy Spirit is the enabling power for dead and blind sinners to perceive the reality of Christ, so he is also the enabling power for us to recognize the Scriptures as the authoritative word of Christ.

Post-Enlightenment evangelical scholarship

I have deliberately avoided reference in this chapter to pre- and post-critical evangelical interpretation. Two things should be clear by now: first, orthodox and Reformation thinking was always critical, and second, the word 'critical' has now come to signify for many the particular stance of the Enlightenment. I deny emphatically that to be critical is to adopt the presuppositions of the Enlightenment. Most of us will have read works of 'critics' that are blatantly uncritical in their acceptance of the current modernist assumptions. An implication of the arguments of this book is that orthodox, conservative,

---

18. Jacques de Senarclens, *Heirs of the Reformation* (London: SCM, 1963), p. 98.
19. ibid., p. 101.

evangelical Christian theism is critical in the best sense of the word.[20] Of course, some evangelicals are just as much at fault as some liberals in the uncritical approach to the Bible. The use of the term 'pre-critical' to denote orthodoxy before the Enlightenment can be as unhelpful as the term 'fundamentalist'.[21]

Having traversed, albeit briefly, the range of biblical interpretation from the early church to the present, we may now well ask whether it was worth the effort. I would contend that to try to learn the lessons of history is at least one step towards learning to avoid the mistakes of the past. But has anything positive come out of it? Evangelicals, particularly those who adhere to a confessional tradition, usually recognize the value of their particular heritage from the pre-modern period. Anglicans have the Thirty-nine Articles (1563), Presbyterians have the Westminster Confession of Faith (1646), Lutherans have the Augsburg Confession (1530), and the Reformed churches have the Belgic Confession (1561). Evangelicals of both confessional and non-confessional traditions can become nostalgic for the halcyon days of biblical orthodoxy when the inspiration and authority of Scripture was almost universally accepted amongst Christians. Even Rome's Counter-Reformation Canons of the Council of Trent (1546) accepted certain pre-modern notions of inspiration and authority in the Scriptures.

When we come to contemporary evangelical scholarship, there is little doubt that much has changed. The style and exegetical approach of Calvin or the English Puritans in their commentaries on Scripture, for example, are very different from those of the learned evangelical commentaries of the twentieth century and beyond. It is not simply that the modern commentators recognize the need to write in contemporary style, but the approach to exegesis and application often suggests that post-Enlightenment evangelical scholarship is quite unabashed about some of the influences of modern scholarship. The art and science of exegesis do not remain static. The Reformers themselves differed considerably from the early Fathers in their approach to biblical commentary. How can we evaluate these changes? I have already raised the question as to whether or not the whole critical movement of the Enlightenment has had only negative effects from the evangelical point of

20. I have argued this in ch. 10.

21. David Steinmetz, 'The Superiority of Pre-Critical Exegesis', *TT* 37/1 (1980), pp. 27–38, uses the term 'critical' to mark the historical divide between historical-critical exegesis and that which preceded it, especially medieval exegesis. I believe this is misleading terminology.

view. I believe the answer is 'no'. If that answer can be sustained, we need to go on to ask about the positives; what the benefits are, and how evangelicals can sustain them. But even if we were to reject any gains from the Enlightenment, we would still need to ask about the movement in evangelical scholarship beyond the pre-Enlightenment situation.

The fact is that recent evangelical biblical studies do converge with non-evangelical studies in many ways. At the level of close exegesis, especially as found in the more technical exegetical commentaries, is it possible that evangelical exegetes at times do not see the wood for the trees? Do they unwittingly adopt the views of the wider scholarly world, almost certainly dominated by modernist scholarship, because that is the world in which they themselves increasingly move? On the other hand, could the most conservative of modern evangelical scholarship have achieved its level of exegetical expertise without the Enlightenment? Given that the Enlightenment was built on the non-Christian philosophies of Spinoza, Descartes, Kant and the rest, could evangelical scholars have developed new sensitivities to language and its use in the construction of the texts if the Enlightenment had never happened? I realize that hypothetical and 'what if' questions are seldom helpful. My tentative answer to these ponderings is that the Enlightenment represented a turning away from God and his word, but God in his sovereignty has allowed us to capitalize on some aspects of it and to turn them to his glory.

To raise these questions at the hermeneutical level is to move into the consideration of wider issues than exegesis. It is to try to understand the nature of the forest at large and not only the individual trees that constitute it. To shift the metaphor, hermeneutics requires us to look at the philosophical worldview, the metanarrative, and all the theological presuppositions that structure our approach to the task of understanding the meaning of the biblical text as God's enduring word to all ages. Hermeneutics requires us to ask both exegetical questions about the text and theological questions about the exegetical task. Also, the apologetic task is never far from hermeneutical considerations. Without compromising basic principles, evangelical biblical scholarship needs to be able to state its case and do its work without the appearance of being the fossilized remains from prehistoric times.

What, then, are the gains for evangelicals of the last two centuries of biblical and theological scholarship? In the last fifty or sixty years alone there has been much re-evaluation of classical evangelical positions of Scripture and the formulation of doctrine. Some would argue that this represents a slippage towards the abyss. Others would say that it is the advance necessary to meet the needs of the modern world. But we have heard that argument often enough in recent times from radicals such as Bultmann or John Spong.[22] Yet the changes that these men have proposed seem to have had the reverse effect to the revival outcome they have looked for. If the world does not want to play by biblical rules, shifting the goal posts is not the answer.

In the following chapters I will attempt to answer some of the questions relating to how far the modern evangelical interpreter can engage in lateral thinking and move out of traditional evangelical parameters without compromising the authority of the Bible and the task of interpreting it. We will consider matters relating to the literary, historical and theological dimensions of Scripture. Before we do that, we need to ask whether or not the great Reformation principles can stand in our postmodern age.

Contemporary re-evaluation of Reformation principles

The Reformation asserted that salvation is by grace alone, in Christ alone, through faith alone, revealed in the Scriptures alone. These principles also have their outworking in that aspect of our being saved which involves us being able to hear and rightly understand the word of God in the Scriptures. I have argued that these are based on Scripture and follow from the doctrine of the sovereignty of God and the radical fallenness of humanity.

The sole content of Scripture is Christ (unity). The hermeneutical implications of this are enormous, but the application of the principle is not simple, as the history of sub-apostolic and medieval interpretation shows. It does mean that a Christological method of interpretation is developed which recognizes not only that every text in some way testifies of Christ, but that interpretation cannot succeed without reference to the reality of the gospel. Included here is the principle of the analogy of Scripture: Scripture interprets Scripture. That is, the total scriptural context interprets any given text of Scripture. This is also involved in the matter of authority.

Given the presuppositions of Christian theism, the unity of the Bible is not a purely empirical assessment, but rather it is an article of faith. This is not to involve ourselves in fideism against all the contrary evidence. But it does mean that what is often taken as evidence for the theological plurality of the Bible must be carefully assessed in the light of the fact that not all the data are available to us. To put it another way, we assert the unity of the Bible, not because

22. e.g. John Shelby Spong, *Why Christianity Must Change or Die* (San Francisco: Harper, 1998).

it is a matter of empirical observation, but because the teachings of Jesus and the apostles render it unavoidable. Disunity in the Bible is as much a function of the non-theistic presuppositions of Enlightenment thought as unity is the function of theistic presuppositions. Biblical theology is an important discipline in enabling us to discover both the revealed propositions of unity and the empirical shape of it. We also recognize that what are sometimes taken as evidence of disparate and *contradictory* theologies in the Bible are, in fact, expressions of disparate and *complementary* theological foci. The Enlightenment has challenged the notion of unity, and modernist theologians suggest that evangelicals do not treat seriously the diversity of the Scriptures. In so doing they only remind us of a principle of unity and diversity that becomes elusive once the nature of the gospel is compromised.

Scripture is self-authenticating (authority). For the Reformers this meant that other authorities, notably the church and its tradition, must submit to the authority of the Bible. The church can only recognize the canon and the authority of Scripture; it does not donate them. The Roman argument that the church gave us the Bible and thus has the right to interpret it was seen for what it was: a confusion of the source and the effect. It is an idolatrous assertion that allows the church to displace God as the effective author of Scripture. The same Word who called the universe into existence calls the church into existence and rules it. That Word is known to us only through the word of Scripture.

The traditional evangelical approaches to the authority of Scripture have been queried by some contemporary evangelical scholars as to the appropriateness of the terms which have become commonplace. Anthony Thiselton has proposed that the problem stems from the attempt by evangelicals to see the contents of the Bible as entirely propositional.[23] He wants to distinguish between propositional content and propositional force. This is a useful distinction now that the idea of propositional revelation has come under scrutiny. Furthermore, when the questions of authority or Christology are approached exclusively 'from above', then hermeneutics is likely to be seen as 'one fallible link in what may be thought of as an otherwise infallible chain'.[24] Thiselton rightly notes that a limiting factor of one traditional approach

23. Anthony Thiselton, 'Authority and Hermeneutics: Some Proposals for a More Creative Agenda', in P. E. Satterthwaite and David F. Wright (eds.), *A Pathway into the Holy Scripture* (Grand Rapids: Eerdmans, 1994), pp. 108f.

24. ibid., p. 113. To proceed exclusively 'from above' is to ignore the humanity in the process in a docetic manner.

> has been to accord undue privilege, even exclusive monopoly, to the mode of discourse of prophetic oracle, as against hymns, psalms, projected narrative worlds of actual or fictive possibilities, deconstructionist or other exploratory strategies in the wisdom literature, and pledges of promise, liberation and love.[25]

John Goldingay asserts that terms which are applied in a specific way to certain parts of the text came to be applied to the whole without distinction.[26] Thus authority is extended to become a way of speaking about Scripture as a whole. Both Thiselton and Goldingay are raising the question of how the authority of Scripture can be discerned (as against merely being asserted).

Scripture is clear and self-interpreting (meaning). This is at the heart of the hermeneutical questions facing today's evangelicals. It was faced by the Reformers. Zwingli, for example, regarded the word of God as light and as intrinsically clear.[27] God, not the official teachers of the church, must interpret his word. When people do not see the clear meaning, it is because they are confused by the apparatus of the church, which makes it difficult. He recognized the need for humility and the Spirit of God if we are to be taught by the word. As the Reformers practised this principle, we must note that it implied neither that hermeneutic endeavour is superfluous, nor that we are individualistic in refusing to climb on the backs of those who have gone before us (tradition). As Thiselton comments, 'Although the Reformers believed that the Scriptures stood, as it were, on their own feet rather than being dependent for their use and understanding on the *magisterium* of the church of the day, Luther and Calvin deeply respected the early patristic traditions.'[28] Luther formulated his idea of clarity in the context of Erasmus's reticence about the Reformation and his sense of the obscurity of human affairs. Luther's clarity doctrine was not initially a reference to the exegesis of particular passages, but to the way Scripture as a whole provides criteria of knowledge. For Luther it is possible to make truth-claiming assertions on the basis of Scripture. But, says Berkouwer, Luther accepts that there are obscure places in Scripture resulting from the lack of clarity in the words.[29] On the other hand, he speaks of

---

25. ibid., p. 134. Thiselton here refers to the legacy of B. B. Warfield.
26. John Goldingay, *Models for Scripture* (Grand Rapids: Eerdmans, 1994), p. 6. See also Goldingay's *Models for Interpretation of Scripture* (Grand Rapids: Eerdmans, 1996).
27. See J. P. Callahan, *The Clarity of Scripture* (Downers Grove: IVP, 2001), pp. 129–139.
28. Anthony Thiselton, *New Horizons in Hermeneutics* (Grand Rapids: Zondervan, 1992), p. 179.
29. G. Berkouwer, *Holy Scripture* (Grand Rapids: Eerdmans, 1975), p. 276.

a double clarity: an internal clarity in the heart which is decisive for the right knowledge of the faith, and an external clarity in Scripture which does not evaporate because of the problem of internal clarity (subjectivity/objectivity). In addition to the internal clarity (spiritual perception as a grace of the Holy Spirit) and the external clarity (grammatical clarity), the Reformers recognized the thematic clarity of the person and work of Christ.[30]

For the Reformers, the natural or literal meaning of the text is normative. The natural sense is the grammatical sense. This position, it seems, owes something to the impetus of the humanism of the Renaissance and the degeneration of medieval scholasticism. But, more importantly, we note that the Reformers' approach is consistent with both their dogmatic theology and their sense of biblical theology. Historical criticism has abused these insights by limiting historical questions to an immanentist world-view. Post-Enlightenment evangelicalism needs to reclaim what rightfully belongs to it: a truly historical-critical method that acknowledges the Lord of all history.

From a Reformed point of view, grammatico-historical exegesis is in reality expressive of the incarnation understood both as dogmatic construct and as an event in the history of salvation. The humanity of Christ is manifested not as an abstract and timeless ideal. It is a concrete event in time and space, a specific event which we recognize as the coming of the God/Man in the midst of human history. In similar manner, we recognize the Bible as the inscripturation of the word of God, itself a time-related matter. It is the inspired testimony to the saving activity of God in history. Thus the critical study of the biblical text within its historical and cultural context is more an implication of orthodox theistic presuppositions than it is an implication of non-theistic ones. The issue is not whether a Christian theist (evangelical Christian) can engage in critical exegesis, but whether a rationalist-empiricist can truly do so. Evangelical critical study will be concerned with all the issues raised by the Enlightenment, and more. Bernard Ramm comments:

> The Scripture is a long book with a great diversity of literature and themes . . . It is an oriental book with flora, fauna, geography, peoples, customs, and languages foreign to the Western mind. How does the interpreter make sense of this strange and diverse book, and what is the unity in the midst of such great diversity? Is there a theme that

---

30. Kevin Vanhoozer, *Is There a Meaning in This Text?* (Grand Rapids: Zondervan; Leicester: Apollos, 1998), pp. 315–317, makes a similar point: '*The clarity of Scripture is neither an absolute value nor an abstract property, but a specific function relative to its particular aim: to witness to Christ*' (p. 317, italics his).

> binds it all together, or is it in the final analysis a hodgepodge of theologies? This is the problem of the clarity of Scripture.[31]

The search for the solution to all these problems must begin with the centrality of the person of Jesus Christ.

The Roman Catholic understanding of the clarity of Scripture was expressed in the Council of Trent (fourth session, 1546). It reflected the pre-Reformation teaching of the Roman Church when it claimed that the church has the right to 'judge of the true sense and interpretation of the holy Scriptures'. This meant that the magisterium was able to know what Scripture means and thus to make it clear. The Roman understanding of the clarity of Scripture is that the Roman Church makes it clear. By contrast, the Protestant understanding of clarity has been addressed by J. P. Callahan.[32] He points out that Protestants always conceded that perspicuity was never intended to supplant interpretation. Protestant scholastics saw certain principles involved, namely:

(a) no necessary doctrine is obscure;
(b) Scripture alone is the means of saving faith;
(c) Scripture is its own interpreter;
(d) perspicuity is limited only by human sin and ignorance;
(e) God, the author, can only speak clearly and understandably.[33]

For Protestants, then, it was necessary to assert that no ecclesiastical authority was needed. It was also necessary to state that God speaks so as to be understood. Who, then, may understand these clear Scriptures? The Pietists believed that only the obedient believer may understand; thus there is a sense in which Scripture is both clear and obscure. 'A notion of plenary perspicuity – that the entirety of the Bible is clear in itself – was foreign to Protestant hermeneutics.'[34] The modern theories of hermeneutics have turned away from the notion of perspicuity in relation to the confession of faith and now see it in terms of words, grammar and history. Callahan seeks to rescue the authentic sense of perspicuity.[35] Protestants use the doctrine of clarity to

---

31. Bernard Ramm, *The Evangelical Heritage* (Waco: Word, 1973), p. 31.
32. J. P. Callahan, '*Claritas Scripturae*: The Role of Perspicuity in Protestant Hermeneutics', *JETS* 39/3 (1996), pp. 353–372.
33. ibid., p. 356. See also Callahan, *The Clarity of Scripture*, p. 143.
34. ibid., p. 360.
35. ibid., pp. 369ff.

avoid the totalitarianism of Rome. Ironically, the Protestant tradition is now rejected by deconstructionists, who see any quest for the authoritative interpretation as a form of totalitarianism. We now have the extremes of Scripture viewed either as totally perspicuous or as totally indeterminate. Callahan suggests that Protestant hermeneutics needs to be rescued from the either/or choice of a perfectly perspicuous or hopelessly obscure Bible. He concludes, 'Perspicuity is hermeneutically ambiguous: It embodies a larger struggle over authority, epistemology and language, and historical issues such as modernity. But it is confessionally unambiguous: It invites the reader to approach the text with the confidence that Scripture is meant to be understood.'[36] It is with that confidence that we continue our investigation. Post-Enlightenment evangelical hermeneutics, then, seeks to use every means at its disposal, including insights gleaned from the wider world of scholarship, to overcome every obstacle to the understanding of Scripture. Its greatest weapon against obscurity and darkness is the light of the gospel itself.

---

36. ibid., p. 372. See also Mark Thompson, *A Clear and Present Word: The Clarity of Scripture* (Nottingham: Apollos, 2006).

14. THE GOSPEL AND THE LITERARY DIMENSION

Biblical literature

The *Concise Oxford Dictionary* gives one definition of literature as 'writings whose value lies in beauty or form or emotional effect'. But it also gives another definition: 'the books etc. treating of a subject'. And further: 'printed matter'. Thus we have some basis for assuming that the whole Bible is literature. But there are those who use the word more narrowly, suggesting that some parts of the Bible do not qualify as literature. For example, Robert Weathers talks about literary approaches that 'emphasize literary portions of the Bible'.[1] For our purposes it will be necessary to consider the Bible from the broader view that literature is the result of purposeful writing.

The Bible is a collection of books, and each of these must be dealt with on its own terms. This seems to state the obvious, yet the historical-critical method worked on the assumption that we should be more interested in the prehistory of the text than the text itself. Nevertheless, most of the earlier hermeneutical texts gave much attention to the way language works in the different biblical books. Since we do not have any oral tradition to work

1. Robert A. Weathers, 'Leland Ryken's Literary Approach to Biblical Interpretation: An Evangelical Model', *JETS* 37/1 (1994), pp. 115–124.

from directly, we will include a concern for linguistics under the umbrella of literature.[2] Following from our earlier discussions, it seems that a post-Enlightenment evangelical hermeneutic must do at least two things:

- First, it must proceed from sound theistic presuppositions and, in harmony with biblical theology and a biblically based dogmatic system, use all the tools at its disposal for the understanding of the text in the way demanded by the whole text itself.
- Second, it must address the hermeneutical developments of our time and test the validity of their presuppositions and principles, their methods and results, in the light of the presuppositions and principles of Christian theism.

It is on this basis that we should examine matters raised by the renewed interest in literary studies. Once again we shall look out for any developments that may assist us in the task of understanding how language works, particularly in its literary forms.

The biblical-theological context of the literature

The biblical-theological context reminds us that the Bible contains a dynamic, historical process that covers a long period of time. Thus within the biblical process there are changes not only in language (Hebrew to Aramaic to Greek), but also in geographical context (Mesopotamia to Egypt to Palestine) and in historical context (e.g. the successive ascendancies of Egypt, Assyria, Babylon, the Hellenistic empire and Rome). There is also the specific historical context of the biblical action that is closely linked with the biblical-theological context. The historical events being recorded are understood within the dynamic of God acting to bring in his kingdom. Some would restrict biblical theology to the examination of individual texts. This is the application of synchronic methods to attempt to describe historically the religious content of single books or even portions of books. An evangelical biblical theology, however, recognizes the canon of Scripture as the unified work of God through the Spirit-inspired human authors. The ultimate literary context of any given text is the whole canon of Scripture.

---

2. I am not discounting the evidence for oral traditions that may lie behind the formation of written texts.

This canonical biblical-theological context brings us to focus on the person of Jesus of Nazareth. The fact that the prophetic word of the Old Testament leads to the incarnate Word, who is the explicit subject of the New Testament (Heb. 1:1–2), means that we examine and take on board the evidence for the relationship of all Scripture to Christ. The dynamic of biblical theology demands a sound theological exegesis that is the heart of our movement from text to hearer. Concern for the literature of the Bible must never be pursued apart from the recognition that God has spoken through his Son, whom he has made heir of all things.

Another aspect of this context is that biblical theology is linked to the narrative plot of the Bible. This provides the basis for understanding an overarching metanarrative. Furthermore, it is this narrative context that is essential to the interpretation of the individual texts that make up the totality. Narrative criticism is a part of this process and is not to be lightly dismissed by evangelicals, but should be assessed for its explanatory power.[3] Mark Hargreaves suggests that evangelicals need to pay much more attention to the nature of narrative and how it provides the unifying framework of the Bible.[4]

The dogmatic-theological context of the literature

The hermeneutics of grace is built on the presuppositions of redemption from a state of fallenness. The epistemology of grace begins with the fear of the Lord. This implies regeneration by the Spirit of God, and the conforming of knowledge to the world-view of the gospel. The hermeneutics of grace is the biblical hermeneutics. It is what Christians have striven for with varying degrees of self-conscious focus on the biblical presuppositions and on the gospel. Because of creation and the incarnation the gospel does not take us into a docetic hermeneutic. Thus a hermeneutic of grace is as much concerned with the human and natural phenomena of the Bible as is the hermeneutics of nature. The difference is that grace means a *both-and* approach, while nature excludes or subordinates the supernatural in favour of the concern for the natural. When evangelicals become preoccupied with the literary question in hermeneutics, the danger is that the *both-and* focus is likely to be blurred.

---

3. A useful summary of narrative criticism is found in Mark A. Powell, *What is Narrative Criticism?* (Minneapolis: Fortress, 1990).
4. Mark Hargreaves, 'Telling Stories: The Concept of Narrative and Biblical Authority', *Anvil* 13/2 (1996), pp. 127–139.

Nature and grace go together, but not in the focus proposed by Thomas Aquinas. Nature can only be preserved when it submits to grace, since this is the order of reality in which a sovereign God rules his creation and interprets it by an act of grace.

Dogmatic theology enshrines the principles and presuppositions of biblical theology in a formal way. Yet dogmatic theology is also derivative of biblical theology. This is one aspect of the hermeneutic circle (or spiral) at work. Dogmatic theology must also systematize its own presuppositions and data derived from biblical and exegetical theology. It points to the implications for exegesis of the Word incarnate and the relationship between this Word and the word inscripturate. Dogmatic theology provides the formal means of expressing the relationship between the divine and the human natures of Jesus and, in a related way, the relationship between the divine and human natures of the biblical text. Sound exegesis must include recognition of the role of the Holy Spirit in the production of the biblical text and in the spiritual perception of its meaning. But it must also include recognition of the humanity of the text, in that the role of the Holy Spirit does not eradicate the role of the human authors who have been historically, culturally and theologically conditioned. Dogmatic theology also confronts us with matters such as the nature of fallen humanity, general revelation, epistemology, human wisdom, etc., and the interaction of these with redeemed humanity, special revelation, spiritual knowledge and the fear of the Lord as the beginning of wisdom.

To summarize, then, dogmatic theology establishes the validity of linguistic and literary analysis in the process of exegesis. It demands the consideration of the human context of language, geography, history and culture. Grammatico-historical exegesis is not a self-evident or self-authenticating process. It is demanded by the gospel event of the incarnation and must be controlled by it. It is demanded by the overarching truth of God's spoken word into the creation. On these terms, exegesis is a theological discipline.

The nature of exegesis

Exegesis is generally understood as getting to the original meaning of the text. It might therefore be argued that it is the essence of, or is coterminous with, hermeneutics. However, we also recognize that hermeneutics is concerned with more than what the text meant for its original author or readers. We are always concerned to know how it applies to us now. But if exegesis is understood as a close reading of the text in order to understand what it is saying, how do our presuppositions affect it?

Broadly speaking, our presuppositions have the nature of traditions that we bring with us to the task. They need not adversely affect exegesis. A warning is sounded by Gordon Fee, who helpfully differentiates five forms of tradition.[5] Tradition, the *paradosis* or what is handed down, can refer to:

(i) the oral and early written biblical texts;
(ii) what the church came to accept as the teachings of the church;
(iii) church tradition with an authoritative role in the (Roman Catholic) church's life;
(iv) the multiplication of traditions (denominational or theological);
(v) personal traditions of individuals.

Fee is particularly concerned about the way the latter two may adversely affect hermeneutics. His focus is on the way traditions, in these senses, may induce the exegete to deal quite unfairly with the text.

But is exegesis merely doing the obvious according to a common-sense application of our knowledge of the biblical languages and how they work? Evangelicals and liberals, especially when aware of their own traditional prejudices and presuppositions, can, it would seem, arrive at a fair amount of agreement about the meaning of a given text within its immediate context. Exegesis can be defined in a narrow sense, or more broadly. A look at a range of exegetical commentaries on biblical books shows that there has emerged, from the nineteenth century on, a tendency to concentrate on the preliminary linguistic work. On this view, it fits with Krister Stendahl's distinction between what the text meant (exegesis) and what it means (hermeneutics).[6] This view sees exegesis as mainly an historical study that is not concerned with saying how the text speaks to us today.

Exegesis, whatever limits we set on it, is part of a total process. We start with a text within the canon and we work towards understanding the text as that which speaks to us today as the word of God.[7] The tendency of

---

5. Gordon D. Fee, 'Exegesis and the Role of Tradition in Evangelical Hermeneutics', *Crux* 27/1 (1991), reprinted in *ERT* 17/4 (1993). See also Vern Poythress, 'God's Lordship in Interpretation', *WTJ* 50 (1988), pp. 27–64. On pp. 27–29 Poythress deals with the supposed neutrality of exegesis.
6. Krister Stendahl, 'Biblical Theology, Contemporary', *Interpreter's Dictionary of the Bible*, vol. 1 (Nashville: Abingdon, 1962).
7. See Kevin Vanhoozer, 'From Canon to Concept: "Same" and "Other" in the Relation Between Biblical and Systematic Theology', *SBET* 12/2 (1994), pp. 96–124.

Enlightenment-driven exegesis was to assume a particular epistemology that enabled the exegete to think of the task as neutral and objective. Evangelical thinking has always accepted the theological assumptions of a divinely appointed unity to Scripture and its consequent authority as God's word. Theological presuppositions may have minimal self-conscious effect on the initial stage of the exegete's work, which seeks to understand what the words are saying. They will certainly play a more explicit role in what John Bright refers to as theological exegesis. He defines the first stage of exegesis as grammatical-historical, in that 'it seeks to understand the language of the text (grammar) in the light of the situation in which it was first written or spoken (history)'.[8] He goes on to define theological exegesis as 'exegesis of the text in theological depth, an exegesis that is not content merely to bring out the precise verbal meaning of the text but that goes on to lay bare the theology that informs the text'.[9] This process would be regarded by some as hermeneutics.[10]

There is another theological aspect to exegesis that may or may not affect the actual practice of it. This is the question of the theology behind not just a particular text, but the reality of us as readers and interpreters of the text. Grammatico-historical exegesis is required by the incarnation, by the fact that God has spoken to us in a divine-human Word. We have already considered something of the significance of this, in that God is a communicating God within himself (Trinity), and he makes us in his image and communicates with us. Exegesis is a function of our being created in the image of God and of our being recipients of God's word.

Hermeneutics textbooks usually contain extensive sections treating the whole matter of language and how it works.[11] The term 'exegesis' derives from the Greek verb *exegeomai* ('to lead out' and, hence, 'to interpret'). Once we consider the relationship of the exegete to the text, all the questions we have raised about the need for hermeneutics come into play. This involves us, the modern readers, in a process that originally involved a sender, a text and a receiver, all belonging to a far-off time and culture. As we have seen, this is complicated by the question of a double authorship, in that God speaks his word through

8. John Bright, *The Authority of the Old Testament* (London: SCM, 1967), p. 169.
9. ibid., p. 170.
10. Hence the notion that hermeneutics is the bridge between exegesis and application to the present. This is the view that I proposed in my book *Gospel and Kingdom* (Exeter: Paternoster, 1981; now in *The Goldsworthy Trilogy*, Carlisle: Paternoster, 2000), though I realize that it may be seen otherwise.
11. See e.g., the standard texts by Mickelsen, Berkhof, Osborne and Klein et al.

a human mouthpiece. Exegesis is thus regarded as a quest for the meaning of a text as it was originally intended. Some would say there can only be a single meaning, since equivocal or ambiguous texts cannot speak the truth. In fact, it appears that some texts, particularly in the wisdom literature, are deliberately ambiguous in order in induce thought about possible meanings and applications. The same may be said of poetic imagery and the openness of metaphorical language.

A distinction that is frequently made is that between exegesis and exposition. This was the guiding principle of the *Interpreter's Bible*, in which commentary pages were divided between a section on exegesis (what it meant) and one on exposition (what it means).[12] The separation of exegesis from the contemporary interpretation raises certain problems. Not least is the recognition that the contemporary reader is involved in the process of determining what an ancient text meant. However, to distinguish is not necessarily to separate. Don Carson makes a different distinction between exegesis and hermeneutics by including in exegesis most of the matters we have considered in hermeneutics.[13] The distinction lies in exegesis being involved in the actual interpretation of texts, while hermeneutics is the theory of the process.

Modern hermeneutical theory has refocused attention on the fact that interpretation is never done in the cold light of neutral objectivity. Evangelicals have needed this salutary reminder. Bruce Corley, for example, criticizes the old modernist distinction between exegesis and exposition and urges us to return to the recognition of the roles of Author/author, text *and* reader.[14] There is a renewed emphasis on the need to deal with all the dimensions of biblical literature, history and theology. In 1960 James Mays spoke of exegesis as being a theological discipline.[15] In a wide range of views on what precisely this means, we find a common element. This is that we come to the text asking

---

12. A similar distinction is made by A. B. Mickelsen, *Interpreting the Bible* (Grand Rapids: Eerdmans, 1963), ch. 3. By contrast, Moisés Silva equates exegesis with hermeneutics, in Walter Kaiser and Moisés Silva, *An Introduction to Biblical Hermeneutics* (Grand Rapids: Zondervan, 1994), pp. 19ff.
13. D. A. Carson, *Exegetical Fallacies* (Grand Rapids: Baker, 1984), pp. 22–23.
14. Bruce Corley, 'A Student's Primer for Exegesis', in Bruce Corley, Steve Lemke, Grant Lovejoy (eds.), *Biblical Hermeneutics*, 2nd edn (Nashville: Broadman and Holman, 2002), ch. 1.
15. James Luther Mays, 'Exegesis as a Theological Discipline', inaugural address as Professor of Biblical Interpretation, Union Theological Seminary in Virginia, April 1960.

theological questions. The basic issue of how it is possible to do exegesis at all is, among other things, a theological matter. Modernism has led us to suppose that the application of certain linguistic techniques against a critical historical appraisal of the original context of the text leads us to a fair and objective exegesis. As Christians we are going one step further by granting special privilege to the biblical text as divine revelation. But, in view of what we have discussed concerning our theological and epistemological presuppositions, the more consistently evangelical perspective would be that submission to a divine author should be the norm. It is not that we add something to general exegesis, but that secular modernism subtracts the vital element from all its deliberations. That is, as Cornelius Van Til often pointed out, the secularists use 'borrowed capital' when they fail to acknowledge that their very reasoning and speaking is evidence of the Christian theism they reject.

Kevin Vanhoozer highlights the interdependence and interaction of what might be considered discrete activities: doing exegesis, doing biblical theology, applying hermeneutics, and making expository and homiletical application. Helpfully, he prefers to look at exegesis as involving different levels of textual description.[16] He describes this as a series of expanding interpretation frameworks: the semantic range, the historical context, the literary context, and finally the canonical context. Moisés Silva takes a similar approach.[17] He equates exegesis with interpretation and sees it as the search for meaning at a number of levels, starting with the linguistics of the passage and ending with the present significance. This approach is not unlike Peter Cotterell's when he suggests, 'An utterance has both context and co-text, and the meaning of an utterance must be determined in the light of text, co-text and context.'[18]

Linguistics

The subject of linguistics is too broad to do more here than simply mention it, although, indirectly, we have been dealing with it throughout this study. The

16. Kevin Vanhoozer, 'Exegesis and Hermeneutics', *NDBT*, pp. 52–64.
17. Kaiser and Silva, *An Introduction to Biblical Hermeneutics*, pp. 19–20. Silva suggests that exegesis seeks meaning in terms of linguistics, historical setting, teaching of the passage, historicity of the narrative, literary setting, canonical context, history of interpretation, and the present significance.
18. Peter Cotterell, 'Hermeneutics: Some Linguistic Considerations', *Evangel*, Autumn 1995, p. 79.

study of how language works takes us into all the areas related to exegesis of a text. A useful summary of the scope of linguistics in hermeneutics is found in the work by Peter Cotterell and Max Turner. They include chapters on semantics, discourse analysis, word studies, grammar and lexicography, and so on.[19] It is fair to say that no aspect of hermeneutics is unaffected by linguistic study, since both are involved with language. Modern linguistic study has called into question a number of the 'givens' of exegetical practice, for example the significance of tense in both Hebrew and Greek. Verbal aspect is a notion that has shaken a lot of generally accepted rules for the understanding of the way these languages work. Most of the older standard Hebrew grammars recognized that 'tense' is an inappropriate description for the time-relatedness of Hebrew verbs. The terminology, borrowed from Latin grammar, that describes perfect tense as past action and imperfect as future is qualified by the recognition that tenses refer to completed or uncompleted action.[20] Thus a future perfect (e.g. 'by the weekend *I will have read* the book') would demand the use of the perfect verb.[21]

It is now generally agreed that James Barr's definitive work on semantics precipitated a much needed revision of the way word studies are done, and led to a modification of the approach of the later volumes of the Kittel *Theological Wordbook of the New Testament*.[22] Revision of the principles by which lexical studies and lexicons should be organized is another direct result of modern linguistics and particularly the work of Ferdinand de Saussure. Modern linguistic study is challenging to the exegete, but often inconclusive in the extreme. The challenge for the Christian theist is, as always, to try to

---

19. Peter Cotterell and Max Turner, *Linguistics and Biblical Interpretation* (London: SPCK, 1989). See also Max Turner, 'Modern Linguistics and the New Testament', in Joel B. Green (ed.), *Hearing the New Testament* (Grand Rapids: Eerdmans; Carlisle: Paternoster, 1995). A useful general survey of language and linguistics is David Crystal, *The Cambridge Encyclopedia of Language* (London: Guild Publishing, 1988).

20. It is now recognized that a similar kind of analysis is more fitting for Greek verbs. Russian is another language that uses verbal aspect. Modern Hebrew has, it would seem, resolved the matter more in the Latin direction of past (perfect), present (participle) and future (imperfect).

21. This may account for what some commentators refer to as the prophetic perfect – the common situation in which a prophetic oracle predicting a future event is translated as having already happened (thus treating the perfect tense as past).

22. James Barr, *Semantics of Biblical Language* (Oxford: Oxford University Press, 1961).

discern to what extent modern secular studies and philosophical stances actually reflect reality that can be 'baptized' into the sphere of the fear of the Lord. One such area that has been examined and taken on board by some evangelical scholars is speech-act theory. We shall now examine it in more detail.

Speech-act theory

Craig Bartholomew warns against considering the literary dimension in isolation:

> Biblical hermeneutics is a kind of ecological habitat in which all sorts of components interact with each other in a delicate balance, so that it is difficult and necessarily distorting to abstract out of the ecology one single aspect – in our case, language . . . Not only do issues of language inevitably connect with other issues in interpretation, but it is also hard to separate out different aspects of language – such as theology and philosophy, translation and literature.[23]

With Bartholomew's caveat in mind, we turn to an aspect of the literary concerns while remaining aware of the holistic context. Vanhoozer poses the question thus: 'How does the diversity of Scripture's literary forms affect the way we take biblical propositions and understand scriptural truth?'[24]

Associated with this concern is the question of how diverse literary forms can in any sense be 'propositional', particularly as the bearers of revelation.[25] As Vanhoozer points out, part of the problem is in deciding what we mean by 'proposition'. How one understands propositions will have consequences for one's method in theology.[26]

---

23. Craig Bartholomew, C. Green and K. Möller (eds.), *After Pentecost: Language and Biblical Interpretation*, SHS, vol. 2 (Carlisle: Paternoster; Grand Rapids: Zondervan, 2001), p. xxxi.
24. Kevin Vanhoozer, 'The Semantics of Biblical Literature', in D. A. Carson and John D. Woodbridge (eds.), *Hermeneutics, Authority and Canon* (Leicester: IVP, 1986), p. 56.
25. D. B. Knox, 'Propositional Revelation the Only Revelation', *RTR* XIX/1 (1960). Knox's prime target is the view that God reveals by his acts and that the human words of Scripture are merely reflections upon this revelation.
26. Vanhoozer, 'The Semantics of Biblical Literature', p. 63.

> [O]ur concern is to provide a model of biblical revelation that will preserve the substance of 'propositional' revelation (i.e., the emphasis on verbal, cognitive communication) while at the same time allowing for greater appreciation of the 'ordinary' language of Scripture and its diverse literary forms.[27]

After considering the importance of genre for identifying the purpose of any piece of literature, Vanhoozer suggests that we need to take account of the ordinariness of biblical language. This he does without disputing the importance of considering the Bible as God's word. The indisputable fact is that the Bible is written in ordinary language. 'What seems to be needed is a "philosophy" of language and literature that does justice to the "ordinariness" of the biblical texts.'[28] He proposes the model of speech-act theory, which 'tries to explain how ordinary language works rather than seeking to "perfect" it by putting it into some other form'.[29]

Vanhoozer thus joins the ranks of those who have considered some kind of adaptation of the speech-act theory of J. L. Austin and John Searle. In borrowing from a secular philosophical theory, he is simply accepting that this theory attempts to explain how language is actually used in ordinary human discourse. It is an analytical strategy which acknowledges that not every statement can be taken as a proposition, for language is used to do different things. This, in turn, affects the way we understand concepts of truth, falsity, inerrancy, errancy, infallibility and fallibility. It also affects the way we assign meaning to texts. It is undeniable that the Bible presents us with its first quoted words, the divine *fiat* in creation, as a series of spoken acts: God does things by saying.

The focus of this consideration is Austin's analysis that there are three components to speech:

- the *locutionary* act (the verbal content of what is being said);
- the *illocutionary* act (what is being done when something is said);
- the *perlocutionary* act (the effect of saying something).

At the heart of this theory is the significance of the illocution. This goes

---

27. ibid., p. 67.
28. ibid., p. 86.
29. ibid. It should be noted that speech-act theory is examined with great thoroughness by evangelical scholars such as Kevin Vanhoozer, Anthony Thiselton, Nicholas Wolterstorff, and others. Not all evangelical biblical scholars, however, are as convinced of the value of this pursuit.

beyond the bare meaning borne by each element to the force of the statement. As Searle systematized Austin's notions, he stressed that the basic unit of linguistic communication is not the sentence but the speech-act. In asserting that something is done in saying something, Searle and Austin restored the idea that *someone* is doing it – that is, there is a concern for the intention of the author as well as for what is said and the effect it has on the hearer or reader.

Gregg Allison provides a useful treatment of the theory and its application.[30] He begins by putting the discussion into the context of the inerrancy/infallibility question. To what in Scripture do these terms apply? Can inerrancy have implications for any verbal moods other than the indicative (direct propositions)? In what sense is a wish or a poetic image infallible? This is a significant question, because it reminds us that we recognize a variety of modal forms in Scripture, as in ordinary speech (imperatives – commands; interrogatives – questions; subjunctives – suppositions; optatives – wishes; and so on), which cannot be judged either true or false in themselves. Allison contends that 'according to speech-act theory, much more of Scripture than its propositional statements needs to fall within the purview of this important doctrine' (i.e. inerrancy/infallibility).[31]

J. L. Austin took up the distinction between *constatives* (stating something) and *performatives* (doing something other than stating). He thus refuted the notion that all we do in saying something is to make a statement. He also delineated the distinctions between the locution, illocution and perlocution. On top of this, he spoke of what was necessary for a successful speech-act. This, too, is significant, as it raises the possibility of assessing the inerrancy of a speech-act in other ways than true/false. John Searle, who said that the basic unit of communication is the speech-act, developed Austin's ideas. He went on to distinguish between the illocutionary force and the propositional content of speech-acts. The latter he understands as the content of the utterance that could be expressed with different illocutionary force in different sentences (i.e. the mode could be a question, a command, a wish, and so on). Searle uses certain criteria to establish a taxonomy of speech-acts.[32] These are set out below.

(i) Differences in illocutionary point; the purpose for which a speech-act is undertaken. A successful speech-act fulfils its purpose.

30. G. Allison, 'Speech-act theory and its Implications for the Doctrine of the Inerrancy/Infallibility of Scripture', *Philosophia Christi* 18/1 (1995), pp. 1–23.

31. ibid., p. 1.

32. ibid., pp. 5f.

(ii) Differences in the direction of fit between words and the world; the relationship of the propositional content and the world. Thus, for example, assertions want the words to fit the world; promises want the world to fit the words.
(iii) Differences in expressed psychological states. This involves sincerity, in that the speaker must express belief in the propositional content for it to be successful.
(iv) Differences in propositional content (as appropriate to the nature of the various illocutionary aspects).
(v) Differences in the relationship of the speaker and hearer to the speech-act. For example, a successful command requires that the speaker be in a position of authority over the hearer.

Allison follows up this approach with the example of the proposition consisting of the referring expression (e.g. *Jesus Christ*) and the predicating expression (e.g. *come again*). These can be used in a variety of ways with different illocutionary force. Thus we can have a simple statement of fact, a wish, a command, a promise, a declaration that brings about the event, and so on. This distinction between illocution and propositional force was perhaps anticipated by D. B. Knox when he proposed that 'all revelation, insofar as it reveals God to us, is propositional'.[33] If, as Allison proposes, it is possible to resolve the content of wishes or commands into propositional force, the question of inerrancy can apply.

Crucial to the whole discussion is the idea of a successful speech-act. Some speech-acts have intended perlocutions (e.g. obedience to a command). Some result in unintended perlocutions. But it is not the result of an intended response that constitutes a successful speech-act. Rather it is the satisfaction of certain of the illocutionary aspects, leading to the comprehensibility of the propositional content (locutionary aspect) and the force (illocutionary aspect) of the speech-act by the hearer.[34] Searle is quoted thus:

> In the case of illocutionary acts we succeed in doing what we are trying to do by getting our audience to recognize what we are trying to do. But the 'effect' on the

33. Knox, 'Propositional Revelation the Only Revelation', p. 1.
34. Allison, 'Speech-act theory', p. 9. Allison indicates these conditions as 'essential, sincerity, propositional, and preparatory', but does not seem to explain what these mean.

> hearer is not a belief or response, it consists simply in the hearer understanding the utterance of the speaker.[35]

So, Allison says, 'As long as the locutionary and illocutionary aspects are recognized, the speech act is successful.'[36]

In 'The Semantics of Biblical Literature' Vanhoozer refers to Austin's view that speech-acts are subject to 'infelicities', or Searle's that they are subject to 'defects'. They are, in other words, fallible. Allison comments, 'This is not the case, however, when it comes to divine speech acts; Scripture is infallible, because all the conditions are always satisfied so that success may be obtained in every case.'[37] Thus Vanhoozer says:

> Scripture is, therefore, indefatigable in its illocutionary intent. It encourages, warns, asserts, reproves, instructs, commands – all infallibly. Note that this makes inerrancy a subset of infallibility. On those occasions when Scripture does affirm something, the affirmation is true. Thus, we may continue to hold to inerrancy while at the same time acknowledging that Scripture does many other things besides assert. Logically, however, infallibility is prior to inerrancy. God's Word invariably accomplishes its purpose (infallibility); and when this purpose is assertion, the proposition of the speech act is true (inerrancy).[38]

In Vanhoozer's view, then, it is a mistake to try to apply the notion of inerrancy to all Scripture, since it properly applies only to assertions. But Allison is concerned to provide some modification. Every speech-act raises the question of the truth or falsity of the referring expression and of the predicating expression. The force does not affect the referring expression, but it does affect the predication. 'No matter what the illocutionary point may be, the question of the truth or falsity of the predicating expression is raised.'[39] Allison's point is that to consider the propositional content (locution) of a speech-act, which is not changed by its illocutionary force, is to consider the question of its truth or falsity. Allison concludes his argument thus:

---

35. ibid.
36. ibid.
37. ibid., p. 10.
38. ibid., quoting Vanhoozer, 'The Semantics of Biblical Literature', p. 95.
39. ibid., p. 12. F is the illocutionary force, R is the reference (subject), and P is the predication. In the example given above, R is *Jesus Christ*, P is *come again*, while F is different in each case.

> The implication of our discussion for the doctrine of the inerrancy/infallibility of Scripture is clear: As we treat Scriptural assertives, commissives, declarations, expressives, and directives as divine speech acts, we discover that all of Scripture (with appropriate exceptions, as noted above) is assessable as to its truth or falsity . . . This extends the doctrine of inerrancy beyond the traditional boundaries of consideration typical of evangelical formulation of this doctrine. [40]

Double-agency discourse

In his discussion Allison has raised an obvious concern: in what sense can the words of, say, a wise man, a narrator, or a psalmist expressing praise to God be at the same time the words of God? Even the prophet whose oracles begin, 'Thus says the Lord . . .' raises the issue of how his words can also be the words of God. A key contributor to this discussion is Nicholas Wolterstorff.[41] He deals with the biblical notion that God speaks and that this is not inconsistent with the human face of Scripture. His main argument is that we need to engage in authorial-discourse interpretation. Wolterstorff criticizes the *authorial-intention* hermeneutics (e.g. of E. D. Hirsch), which gave way to the *textual-sense* interpretation, and suggests that a better way is *authorial-discourse* interpretation.[42]

> I hold that the full promise for biblical interpretation of authorial-discourse interpretation, and of its corollary, speech-act theory, is opened up for us only if we think in terms of what I call double-agency discourse . . . What I have in mind is those cases in which one person performs some illocutionary act by way of another person performing either some locutionary or some illocutionary act.[43]

He goes on to apply speech-act theory to double-agency discourse, so that it 'enables us to understand Scripture as the manifestation of God speaking by way of human beings speaking, and then of interpreting them accordingly'.[44] This provides the advantage of being able to regard the whole Bible (in its unity) as God's single work. It also enables us to 'acknowledge the infallibility

---

40. ibid., p. 16.
41. Nicholas Wolterstorff, *Divine Discourse* (Cambridge: Cambridge University Press, 1995); 'The Promise of Speech-act Theory for Biblical Interpretation', in Bartholomew, Green and Möller (eds.), *After Pentecost*, pp. 73–90.
42. Wolterstorff, 'The Promise of Speech-act Theory', p. 82.
43. ibid., p. 83.
44. ibid.

of God's word without ascribing a similar infallibility to the human words'.[45] Wolterstorff summarizes his approach thus:

> Interpreting Scripture for divine discourse requires a double hermeneutic: first one interprets these writings so as to discern the human discourse of which they are the trace; then, and only then, does one move on to interpret for what God said by way of this human discourse.[46]

In his 'second hermeneutic', the dogma of Scripture (that it is God's book) comes into play.

Vanhoozer has developed some of his ideas from previous works, and especially his trinitarian conclusions in his major work.[47] In his 'From Speech Acts to Scripture Acts', he develops ten theses. He maintains that the Bible treats human speech as speech-acts and that this understanding avoids reducing meaning to reference or proposition. While theorists differ over details, there is general agreement over four things.

- Language is used to do more than picture states of affairs.
- The postmodern assertion of the irrelevance of the author is rejected.
- The operative concept is action rather than representation.
- Readers are not free to manipulate text meaning to serve their own ends.[48]

Speech-act, or discourse, deals with 'language-in-communicative-use'. Significantly, Vanhoozer seeks to place this notion of language squarely in a theological context. Thus he sees all language as covenantal, in that simply to address another is to create a relationship. The word of God points to the fact that the paradigm of all communication is the communicating triune God.[49]

---

45. ibid., pp. 84–85. Human authors may express certain false beliefs without preventing God from infallibly speaking by way of what they say.
46. ibid., p. 87.
47. Kevin Vanhoozer, *Is There a Meaning in this Text?* (Grand Rapids: Zondervan; Leicester: Apollos, 1998). In his later essay, 'From Speech Acts to Scripture Acts', in Bartholomew, Green and Möller (eds.), *After Pentecost*, pp. 1–49, Vanhoozer enumerates some of the advances beyond this earlier work (p. 5, n. 11).
48. Vanhoozer, 'From Speech Acts to Scripture Acts', pp. 6–7.
49. This seems to share in Poythress's view of the trinitarian archetype of communication. See Vern Poythress, *God Centered Biblical Interpretation* (Phillipsburg: Presbyterian and Reformed, 1999).

The trinitarian basis is that the communicative agent is Father/author; the communicative action is Son/word; and the communicative result is Spirit/reception.[50] Vanhoozer goes on to tie meaning to the responsible communicative action of the agent or speaker/writer. The literal sense is the sum of the author's intentional illocutions. The hermeneutic process is to understand these intentional illocutions. The role of the Holy Spirit in Scripture is to make illocutions effective at the perlocutionary level. Vanhoozer has thus adapted a secular linguistic theory to accommodate the biblical understanding of communication that stems from the Trinity. Such communication is propagated both as divine speech and human speech, which, of necessity, mirrors divine speech because of the image of God in man. We would have to say that the canonical perspective is that God's illocutions are his testimony to Christ.

Some conclusions[51]

Speech-act theory has thus found some enthusiastic proponents among evangelicals. We must continue to examine its credentials and presuppositions. The above discussions suggest that we are dealing with some genuine insights into the way language functions. The following tentative conclusions on the hermeneutical value of the Christian adaptation of speech-act theory are suggested.

- As it can be applied to the inerrancy debate, so also it addresses the matter of the authority of the Bible and its interpretation.
- It addresses the perceived dichotomy of personal and propositional revelation by proposing that it is a matter of *both-and*. This dichotomy is misused sometimes to suggest that personal revelation, our encounter with God, does not require inerrancy. The suggestion that we can identify the propositional force, the truth or falsity, of non-propositional statements may help to break the stalemate in the debate over propositional revelation.
- It provides a way of evaluating the truth claims of Scripture that avoids a slavish literalism. It allows a more flexible approach to the various

50. This restores the place of author, text and reader, instead of reducing hermeneutic concerns to one or other of them.

51. I am grateful to Anthony Petterson for some of the issues raised in his fourth-year Moore College Hermeneutics essay (1998).

ways of speaking and to the various literary genres. It shows that the context of a statement and, thus, the illocutionary force are vital for the determination of the truth claim.

- The Bible indicates the speech-act aspect of language by its reference to the ultimate speech-act: how God speaks and, in speaking, acts. The climactic form of this is the incarnation of the Word. The word of God is always an act of God. When God said, 'Let there be light', there was light. When Jesus said, 'Your sins are forgiven', the man was forgiven. In the same way, what the Bible says as the word of God written is linked with what it does. It saves the believer and judges the unbeliever.
- The incarnation of Christ suggests that we have a paradigm of human speech that does not imply the necessity of error.
- Speech-act theory treats seriously all three dimensions that had become separated in the modern hermeneutical debates: author, text and reader/hearer. The focus on discourse provides a way to include double-agency discourse and so link the human words of the biblical text with the divine word.
- The fulfilment of prophecy and the nature of typology are areas that can be investigated from the point of view that the same locution has different illocutionary forces at different points in salvation history.

Such assessments of new literary theories can be, and are being, used to help evangelical hermeneutics regain lost ground. In doing so, it is vital that we are vigilant that attempts at making old formulas acceptable do not open the door to new ways of undermining the centrality of Christ in hermeneutics. The kinds of studies referred to above give us grounds for some optimism.

15. THE GOSPEL AND THE HISTORICAL DIMENSION

A Christian theological philosophy of history

Two questions mainly concern us in this chapter. First, what does it mean to say that Christianity is an historical faith? Second, how does the Bible give testimony to the historical events upon which the Christian faith rests? The word 'history' is used in at least two distinct ways. It can mean what actually happened in the past, or it can mean how people have attempted to reconstruct the past (usually in writing).[1] Any reconstruction inevitably involves some kind of interpretation of the significance of the events, both then and now. The universal sense of history, that we have a past and a future, as much as anything can be, is a fact of history. History writing also shows us that there has been an ongoing struggle to define the nature and meaning of history. We may pose the question: is there hope for the future, or is history at an end in the way the postmodernists proclaim? From the Christian point of view, the nature and meaning of all history are defined by the historical, redemptive revelation of God in his Son, Jesus Christ. He defines the past, the present and the future. But how are we to understand that redemptive event in relationship

---

1. This not to discount the role of oral tradition in many societies. In Western cultures, however, the written tradition undoubtedly predominates.

to us and to our time, and how can we most effectively proclaim that event to a culture that is increasingly sceptical about the possibility of discovering the meaning of history? The assumptions that we make about history and its meaning form the basis of our philosophy of history, which may or may not be thought out and formally presented.

An evangelical philosophy of history is a theology of history. This is, perhaps, one of the more significant differences between a Christian and a secular view of history. Since by history we usually mean human history, we stand with Augustine and Calvin in saying that we can only truly know ourselves as living within history in so far as we know God. Creation and the sovereignty of God are crucial doctrines for history. Thus R. J. Rushdoony stresses the doctrine of creation in the formation of a biblical philosophy of history.[2] He asserts nine implications of creation.

- The universe, time and history are the work of a sovereign, triune God.
- The meaning of history is established in terms of that God.
- Creation is divine act, not a continuing process.
- Creation is totally under the government of God.
- The mainspring of history is God and his eternal decrees.
- God speaks through infallible Scriptures.
- The origin of time is not in chaos but in eternity.
- God created humankind, which is passive towards God and active towards nature.[3]
- All factuality is made personal because it is made by a personal God.

A truly evangelical view of history will involve these, or similar doctrinal foundations.

Earl Cairns offers a contrast between an authentic evangelical philosophy of history and secular notions.[4] Secular philosophies have been either pessimistic (e.g. the cyclic views of classical paganism and Eastern thought) or optimistic (e.g. the linear views of Marxism or Toynbee's syncretistic theism). Against this is the pessimistic-optimistic philosophy of history as found in the

---

2. R. J. Rushdoony, *The Biblical Philosophy of History* (Phillipsburg: Presbyterian and Reformed, 1979), pp. 3ff.
3. That is, God rules humanity while humanity is given the task to have dominion over nature.
4. Earl Cairns, 'Philosophy of History', in Carl F. H. Henry (ed.), *Contemporary Evangelical Thought* (Grand Rapids: Baker, 1968), ch. 7.

Bible, and in Augustine's *City of God.* Augustine acknowledges the importance of special creation and of original sin. Human sinfulness necessitates the distinction between the city of God and the city of earth. Linear history is the obvious corollary of redemption. Cairns criticizes the neo-orthodox approach to history because of its virtual absolute dualism of redemptive history and secular history. An evangelical philosophy of history sees the dualism as temporal and not a total separation of the transcendent and the immanent. God is Lord over history in creation, in providence and, finally, in the incarnation. God's lordship over history includes his lordship over the historical processes in the communication of his word.

The nature of the gospel is such that it involves us in the quest for a biblical theology of history. It raises the question of how the biblical authors viewed and understood history within the framework of their understanding of God. It is significant that Israel's attention to history probably pre-dates all others, and it stems from the sense of God acting in the life of the nation and in the world. The covenant implies both ultimate divine authority in creation and God's sovereign working towards the eschatological *telos*, the purposeful outcome towards which history is moving.[5] A biblical theology of history, then, must enquire into the sense of history that emerges from the various biblical documents. From such an enquiry we may hope to arrive at both a biblical history and a biblical philosophy of history. The former is the storyline, which biblical scholars have reconstructed in various ways.[6] The latter is a way of explaining the story. This is consistent with the presupposition of Christian theism that revelation must inform reason. G. C. Singer asserts a similar view:

> No philosophy, whether it be humanistic or naturalistic in its presuppositions, can offer any true interpretation of history, for history cannot supply the key to its own meaning, and the human mind cannot impose its subjective interpretation upon objective factual data.[7]

---

5. Oliver O'Donovan, *Resurrection and Moral Order*, 2nd edn (Leicester: Apollos; Grand Rapids: Eerdmans, 1994), p. 64, argues that, while various forms of historicism see an immanently present *telos* for history, a Christian view of history understands history's *telos* as the *eschaton* in which God does something new.
6. See the discussion of historical method in Iain Provan, V. Philips Long and Tremper Longman III, *A Biblical History of Israel* (Louisville: Wesminster John Knox Press, 2003).
7. C. G. Singer, 'A Philosophy of History', in E. R. Geehan (ed.), *Jerusalem and Athens* (Phillipsburg: Presbyterian and Reformed, 1980).

It cannot be argued that a gospel-centred hermeneutic relies on the mere events of Jesus of Nazareth as self-interpreting, and that consequently history does provide its own meaning. The Word incarnate is not to be separated from the verbal revelation that interprets the event. The teachings of Jesus, far from being mere moral guidance, are the definitive interpretation of history, including his own being and doing.

If we take the gospel as our motive and starting point for biblical theology, then we have some basis for assessing the historical content of the biblical narrative as a whole. On this basis, a biblical theology of history turns out to be a form of salvation history. It is a coherent sequence of events that is interpreted as having saving significance. Moreover, a part of that interpretation is that God is Lord over space and time, and that he has made us capable of receiving his word of revelation. This is implied by the fact that God makes covenant with people and speaks to them. The biblical story is a story of events in space and time involving the saving activity of God in a specific and chosen part of the history of the created order.

Salvation history as an approach to theology has different expressions according to the different fundamental assumptions behind them.[8] However, there is a general acceptance that the Bible contains a metanarrative, or big picture of narrated events. Differences lie in the assessments of the relation of the biblical view of events to the actual historical events. Thus one of the effects of the historical-critical method has been to assess the historical truth claims of the texts with varying degrees of negativity. This was due to the humanistic assumption that God could not, or would not, be an element in the equation. Biblical claims involving miracles or predictive prophecy are simply ruled out. The existential modification of the alleged discrepancy between the asserted or proclaimed events and the historical reality was just as negative. No longer was it regarded as important to be able to reconstruct the history of the events that lay behind the kerygma of the biblical texts and, in time, the kerygma became the only real consideration. Any connection between the real events (*Historie*) and proclaimed events with existential significance (*Geschichte*) is unimportant.

In his treatment of the genesis of the salvation history approach, Oscar Cullmann sees the basis of the message of the New Testament in the narration of interpreted events.[9] He does not accept Bultmann's radical separation of history and the kerygma. He points out that the New Testament writers presuppose the recorded events of the Old Testament. We see this in Paul's

8. See Carl Braaten, *History and Hermeneutics* (Philadelphia: Westminster, 1966), ch. 5.

9. Oscar Cullmann, *Salvation as History* (London: SCM, 1967), pp. 88–97.

confession in 1 Corinthians 15:3–11. Here the events of Christ's death and resurrection are interpreted in terms of the Old Testament scriptures. Cullmann notes that 'in the genesis of New Testament salvation history, all events, the past, the present, and the ones expected in the future, are summed up in one event as their high-point and mid-point: the crucifixion of Christ and the subsequent resurrection'.[10] The interpretation is to be seen as part of the salvation history process – that is, '[the] inclusion of the saving message in the saving events is quite essential for the New Testament'.[11] However, we must go further to emphasize that the biblical story is about real events. I can tell a story, but if I do not tell the story *of the events*, I have not told *the* story.

The gospel and God's perspective on history

If, as Calvin says, we can only know ourselves as we know God, then we can only know our history and its meaning as we know God's mind on it. The gospel sets forth the action of God in history in such a way as to show its meaning and its true goal. The context of the gospel event of Jesus of Nazareth is the culture of a people with an overwhelming sense of the linear movement in history towards the goal which God has set and which is revealed in his prophetic word. Furthermore, the gospel is presented as the event in time and space towards which all history has been moving from the beginning. Cullmann's designation of Jesus' death and resurrection as the mid-point in history is convenient but misleading.[12] It is certainly a high-point, but the biblical eschatology makes it clearly the end-point rather than the mid-point of history. How this is so when the consummation is also an end-point is a matter for biblical theology to unravel.[13]

---

10. ibid., p. 86.
11. ibid., p. 89.
12. Oscar Cullmann, *Christ and Time* (London: SCM, 1951), ch. 5.
13. I have dealt with this in outline in my books *The Gospel in Revelation* (Exeter: Paternoster, 1984) and *According to Plan* (Leicester: IVP, 1991). The New Testament distinguishes between the end as it has come in the incarnation, the end as it now comes to the church as the ongoing manifestation of the body of Christ, and the end as it will come in the consummative return of Christ. In other words, the whole end comes in three distinct but related ways. Another way of expressing it is that we have been saved, we are being saved, and we will be saved. This perspective is dealt with by Adrio König, *The Eclipse of Christ in Eschatology* (Grand Rapids: Eerdmans, 1989).

Integral to this perspective is the sense of God's sovereignty in history. While predestination is not the essence of the gospel, without the divine decrees and predestination the gospel and our salvation would be a matter of pure chance. The fact that the decrees of God are expressed as stemming from before the foundation of the world indicates that God's acts in history are never an afterthought in response to the contingent. The notion that what God did in Jesus is the fulfilment of the time (Mark 1:14–15) and the fulfilment of prophecy implies the sovereignty of God over all history. The gospel shows that the movement from creation to new creation is inevitable. The incarnation as historical event is the focus of God's rule in world history. Furthermore, all world history is defined by salvation history, so that all the peoples of the world are implicated one way or another in the saving events. Again, from a biblical point of view, history begins with the word of God calling all things into being and setting humanity on its historical course (Gen. 1). The incarnate Word of God then brings history to its goal and interprets it (Eph. 1:8–10; Col. 2:2–3). The word of God will end the history of this present order and herald the consummation (2 Pet. 3:5–7). History cannot be understood without God's word to interpret it.[14]

The gospel presents the incarnate God as the Word become flesh. This historic Word-event is God's fullest and final word to humankind. It is the climax of the biblical witness to the fact that an event cannot be revelation without the word of God interpreting it. The biblical pattern is consistently that God speaks about what he will do; then he does it; and finally he speaks about what he has done. There are no wordless events in revelation. The word-event nexus preserves revelation from being a mystical and purely existential moment. It is always an objective word from God. Conceiving of wordless events as revelation is a form of natural theology that breaks the connection between God's word and events.[15] Because of the interaction of God's grace and human sinfulness, the word that accompanies the event, and the event that is interpreted by the word, must be more than mere information giving. It must be

14. Vern Poythress, *God Centered Biblical Interpretation* (Phillipsburg: Presbyterian and Reformed, 1999), ch. 5, provides a view of history that is tied to the self-revelation of the trinitarian God of Scripture. He makes the important point that God's speaking and God's acting go together, a point denied by the 'event as revelation' theologians.

15. This was the emphasis made popular by such biblical theologians as G. E. Wright, in *God Who Acts*, Studies in Biblical Theology, no. 8 (London: SCM, 1952).

a redemptive word-event that has the power to break through our self-imposed, sinful darkness. It is not the story *as* story that does this. Redemption is in the event by which God reconstructs an acceptable human history while judging the unacceptable. The doctrine of justification by faith involves the substitution of God's righteous history in Christ for our fallen and condemned histories of rebellion.

The gospel defines history in terms of its goal in the *eschaton*, the last things. All secular attempts to define history purely in terms of the past or a secular goal (as in Marxism) are inadequate. Thus the cliché that history will eventually judge the lives and actions of people is also inadequate. The gospel reminds us that God will judge history by the man he has appointed, in demonstration of which he has raised him from the dead (Acts 17:31). The corollary of the gospel-based *eschaton* is that all people should repent of their own part in the dysfunctional nature of human history (Acts 17:30). God has put our rebellious history to death in the death of Christ. In the resurrection of Jesus he has brought the *eschaton* into our history. The resurrected Jesus is the new man of the new age. That single past event guarantees that, through our faith union with Christ, our past and our present will find consummation in the future.

Time, Rushdoony has reminded us, does not emerge from primeval chaos, but from the eternity of God. The creative-redemptive acts of God were in his mind from all eternity. The witness of Paul in Colossians is to the Christ of history, but he is the one in whom, through whom and for whom all things were created (Col. 1:16). History is not the story of God's trial of something good that failed, thus requiring him to come up with an emergency package as an afterthought. God's ultimate creation plan was not Adam and Eve in Eden, but Christ in his gospel. It may be impossible for us to comprehend, but we can grasp it as a proposition nevertheless: God's plan from all eternity was the new creation and a people created and redeemed in Christ. The blueprint of creation and of all history is the gospel.

Some, by diluting the biblical sense of God's sovereignty over history, reduce the gospel to a first-aid measure. This view simply cannot account for the biblical sense of history ruled by God.[16] It cannot account for the perfect number of redeemed and the mighty multitude gathered around the throne of God and the Lamb in the consummation (Rev. 7). It cannot account for the inevitability of the fullness of time and the fixed time of the *parousia*. The words of Jesus in Mark 1:15 indicate fulfilment of God's purposes in time.

16. Pelagianism and all forms of semi-Pelagianism may be said to err in this way.

Furthermore, 'the time is fulfilled' (*peplērōtai ho kairos*) is too consequential a statement to be weakened to 'the time has come', as it is in the NIV. Rather it implies that the whole process of promise and redemptive revelation in the Old Testament finds its fulfilment in Christ.

The resurrection is linked by Jesus and the apostles with, among other things, the Davidic covenant (Acts 2:30–1), the renewal of the temple (John 2:19–21), the fulfilment of all prophecy (Acts 13:32–33), the justification of believers (Rom. 4:25) and our regeneration (1 Pet. 1:3). The resurrection demonstrates that Jesus is the Son of God – that is, he is the acceptable human covenant partner with God, the last Adam and the new Israel (Rom. 1:4). That Jesus was raised for our justification (Rom. 4:25) is highly significant. The human life of Jesus is restored to him in space and time as the grounds of our acceptance with God. God the Father, by this act, gives a resounding 'Amen' to everything Jesus achieved in his life and death for us.

Acts 1 indicates that Jesus' discourse in Luke 24 is only partly understood by the disciples. Gloom turns to joy as they now grasp that the death of Jesus was indeed part of God's plan. But their view of history still needs some work to bring it into line with God's view. They ask, 'Lord, will you at this time restore the kingdom to Israel?' (Acts 1:6). It appears that they expect the resurrection to be the signal for the full glory of the eschatological kingdom to be revealed. But instead Jesus begins to redirect their view of history in terms of the giving of the Holy Spirit and the proclamation of the gospel in the entire world. Instead of the expected glorious reign of the Christ in a renewed Jerusalem, we learn that the sceptre of the risen Christ is the preached word that will be the focus of the worldwide missionary endeavour of the church.

The pivotal point in time is the ascension as the completion of the exultation of Jesus begun in the resurrection. Through his ascension Jesus takes his humanity into the very presence of the Father, where he remains as the Man for us. It is this event of the ascension, not some condition fulfilled by the apostles, which brings about the gift of the Spirit at Pentecost. As T. F. Torrance says, the ascension highlights the gap between our new humanity as it is in Christ and the corruptible humanity that we still possess.[17] The ascension establishes the historic gospel, which is now to be proclaimed in the whole world, as the only way to God. It acts as a kind of eschatological pause that establishes the nature of Christian existence during this overlap of the ages. Integral to this is the missionary task of the church as the instrument of

---

17. T. F. Torrance, *Space Time and Resurrection* (Grand Rapids: Eerdmans, 1976), p. 133.

Christ's rule in the world. The ascension also points to the nature of the *eschaton*. This is a perspective that is not obvious from the emphasis in the Old Testament, where the *eschaton* is seen as the single coming of the Day of the Lord. The ascension clinches the answer given to the disciples' question in Acts 1:6. There will be no immediate universal revelation of the consummation. The ascension restructures the *eschaton*, so that the church now has to understand the history of this age of the Spirit in terms of the new age overlapping the old. The ascension of Jesus shows the tension between the 'now' and the 'not yet'. Empirical historical study can only observe, record and reflect upon the events of our era. By contrast, the church now gives its testimony to the meaning of history by being the eschatological community of faith.

The ascension proclaims Jesus to be Lord and Christ, the ruler of history and the Saviour of his people. The ascension is the fulfilment of the vision of Daniel 7 as the Son of Man comes in the clouds to God to receive from him all dominion. This is the basis of the missionary charge in Matthew 28:18–20. It is in accord with the fact that Jesus indicates that his contemporaries will witness the coming of the Son of Man. This event cannot be isolated in some remote future.

> There are some standing here who will not taste death until they see the Son of Man coming in his kingdom. (Matt. 16:28)
>
> From now on you will see the Son of Man seated at the right hand of Power and coming on the clouds of heaven. (Matt. 26:64)
>
> You will see the Son of Man seated at the right hand of Power, and coming with the clouds of heaven. (Mark 14:62)

The Son of Man's coming *again* will be in like manner (Acts 1:11), and the full revealing of his coming in his kingdom must wait for that event. The ascension has not only created this eschatological hiatus, but it has also established the means of the rule of Christ in history until the consummation. The pouring out of the Spirit at Pentecost is not a unique event as such, for the Spirit has been active in the world since creation. Its uniqueness lies in the fact that for the first time the Spirit comes to minister with respect to the finished gospel event. He will convince the world of righteousness 'because I go to the Father' (John 16:10). He will also convince the world of judgment 'because the ruler of this world is judged' (John 16:11). Pentecost is the demonstration that the millennium has begun, Satan is bound, and Christ reigns through his gospel.

The gospel and the believer's perspective on history

That God has acted in history to save indicates that the problem is within human history. The nature of the problem is seen in what God had to do in order to rectify it. For the believer, then, coming to understand that he or she is a sinner is integral to coming to faith in the doing and dying of the historical Christ. The gospel thus determines the nature of the believer's view of history. The cross is God's judgment on the failure of world history and on our own personal failed histories. God judges the history of the world according to his sovereign status as Creator and upholder of the universe. History as such does not judge individual people's lives in any ultimate sense. Rather one Man's life and his death on the cross judge all human history. The other side to this pivotal event is that the resurrection of the same Man provides a new and acceptable history before God for all who believe. The resurrection is the Father's acceptance of the perfectly lived human history of Jesus. To be clothed in the righteousness of Christ is to be redefined, not by our own failed histories, but by his perfect history. Thus the Christian mind, shaped by the gospel, is realistic in its view of the present brokenness of human history. As George Buttrick puts it:

> The Bible is blunt: history has a fatal flaw. Compare this honesty with the Marxist dialectic ending in a stainless steel paradise. Compare it with Hegelian optimism supposed to come to climax in the perfect Prussian state. Compare it with American faith in the natural goodness of man and the endlessness of material progress. Then be grateful for the honesty of the Bible story.[18]

The other side to this brutal honesty is the promise of history that features the redeeming love of God.

The incarnation demonstrates that the human problem involves both God and our humanity. The secular notion of the problem, even when the word 'sin' is used, is of a purely human problem and the God of the Bible does not come into it. The 'gospel of God', as Paul refers to it in Romans 1:1, is a gospel which is revealed to deal with God's problem of how the Holy One can justify people in godless rebellion against his person and word. To those who say that we need the law first – that is, we need to perceive our problem before we will flee to God for grace, we must reply that such an assertion assumes the ability without grace to understand the law as natural law. The gospel is the clearest

18. G. A. Buttrick, *Christ and History* (New York: Abingdon, 1963), pp. 22f.

explication of the law, both in its perfect fulfilment and in the effects of its being broken.

The covenant provides a unifying thread running the length of biblical revelation in salvation history. The covenant expressed the gracious commitment of God to his creation, a creation at the head of which he established mankind as the ruler in space and time. Salvation history in the Old Testament focuses on a people who are elect, redeemed and blessed with the gift of the Promised Land. The problem being dealt with is that of the relationship of God to his creation. This is the only problem that exists for us; all other problems are simply reflections of that one problem. The solution to the problem is directed at the fallen 'kings of the earth' who are being raised up again through goodness and mercy, the covenant faithfulness of God. At every stage in the salvation history of the Old Testament the saving events, known to be such only because of the prophetic word that interprets them, keep pointing relentlessly to a permanent and glorious solution. Yet the problem seems constantly to frustrate the solution. The events of covenant, exodus, possession of the Promised Land and, ultimately, the Davidic rule in Zion all appear to come to naught as every tangible evidence of God's presence seems to evaporate in the destruction of Jerusalem and the exile into Babylon. Into that hopeless situation the prophetic word brings renewed promise of a Day of the Lord in which all shall be put right.

The coming of Jesus is hailed as the fulfilling event. He is the *eschatos*, the last one who constitutes the *eschaton*, the last event. In the light of the prophetic word of the Old Testament, along with the teaching of Jesus and the proclamation of his apostles, the first Christians struggled with the question of who and what manner of person Jesus was. It became clear to them that Jesus was the solution to the human problem. But understanding the problem and understanding the solution went hand in hand. What God had to do in Jesus is revealed as the solution that perfectly dealt with the problem and thus definitively sets out both the problem and the solution.

Prophetic and apocalyptic eschatology in the Old Testament prepare the way for the gospel event as that which reveals and establishes the goal of history. Humanistic critical presuppositions applied in the historical-critical method reject the notion that history was under the lordship of God. Both predictive prophecy and miracle thus remain a constant problem to this type of criticism. Salvation history, on the other hand, recognizes that God created all things good and set the history of the universe in motion. God judged the failed history of our first parents and subjected the whole of creation to judgment because of human sin. God also entered into the history of fallen Adam's race in order to restore that race, and the whole creation with it, to a right relationship with himself. In the midst of the ongoing failures of Israel, a message of hope is proclaimed which sees both the end to the history of fallenness and the new beginning of a history that merges with eternity.

Thus the eternal purpose of God was to rule history in such a way as to achieve infallibly the goal determined before the foundation of the world. The eschatology of the Old Testament is expressed in terms of time and space in such a way that it involves the restoration, not the eradication, of the physical universe along with the salvation of people. The New Testament reveals this restoration to be involved in the bodily and very human agony and death of Jesus, and in his bodily resurrection from the dead. The end of history is the cross. The cross is also the beginning of a new history. The failure of history is nailed to the cross so that the new may emerge from the tomb on the third day. Thus through the resurrection of Jesus we are born again to new life, to a new history (1 Pet. 1:3).

History and biblical hermeneutics

To what end, then, is this concentration on the nature of history and its relationship to the gospel? In the final analysis, the concern of the biblical exegete and preacher is not only to understand how revelation and history are related, but also to understand how we should proclaim the story of the Bible. Narrative and narrative frameworks characterize by far the largest amount of the biblical text. It is not history as history that we have first of all to deal with, but text that in various ways tells stories or implies stories. These stories make historical truth claims. The historical dimension of the Bible, then, cannot be dealt with apart from a concern for the literary vehicle of narrative. The narrative does not have to be a sustained telling of story, but may also be implied or merely alluded to.[19]

It is wrong to set up dichotomies between the Bible as history and as literature or theology. It is, of course, a book that engages in all three. V. P. Long points out that how we view the Bible as *macro-genre* is important for how we assess its truth value. Then again, it is one thing to believe it to be true and

---

19. Thus non-narrative texts such as Paul's epistles may in various ways indicate a dependence on the narrative. See the discussion of Bruce Longenecker (ed.), *Narrative Dynamics in Paul*, in Richard B. Hays, 'Is Paul's Gospel Narratable?', *JSNT* 27/2 (2004), pp. 217–239.

another to understand it. The truth value will be largely determined by our assessment of the *macro-genre*. If it is the inspired word of God, its truth value promises to be greater than if it is merely human. But understanding the truth claims is another matter involving genre recognition.[20]

The interpreter must strive for ancient literary competence in order to discover 'the intrinsic meaning of the source, not from some of his own scale of values, but that of the original writer or speaker'.[21] Some regard this as unattainable, but realistically there is a degree of commonality between ancient genres and modern writing. Biblical interpretation, then, involves genre criticism. But genre itself is not an easy concept to pin down. One reason for this is that discourse occurs at various levels. Thus we need a tiered system. Greidanus[22] suggests the term 'mode' to cover the whole Bible as proclamation. Then we have the canonical genres such as narrative, prophecy, wisdom, etc. Finally we have specific forms within the other larger genres.

Long suggests some important qualifications to genre criticism.[23]

- It is primarily descriptive, so that we cannot expect authors to stick to the rules.
- Early and late do not necessarily correspond to simple and elaborate.
- Commonality does not mean that unique texts cannot exist.
- We cannot insist that only those genres exist which are found outside the Bible.
- The genre of the larger discourse affects the smaller units within it.

Long also argues that the concept of fiction, if it can be properly defined and guarded against misunderstanding, may be fruitfully employed in discussions of biblical historiography.[24] Craig Blomberg disagrees and says that an

20. Genre recognition is surely affected by the claim to be inspired. That is, as Meir Sterberg says, 'With God postulated as double author, the biblical narrator can enjoy the privileges of art without renouncing his historical titles.' Quoted from V. Philips Long, 'Toward a Better Theory and Understanding of Old Testament Narrative', *Presbyterion* 13/2 (1987), pp. 102–109.
21. S. W. Baron, quoted in V. Philips Long, *The Art of Biblical History* (Grand Rapids: Zondervan, 1994), p. 33.
22. Sidney Greidanus, *The Modern Preacher and the Ancient Text* (Grand Rapids: Eerdmans; Leicester: IVP, 1988), pp. 20–23.
23. Long, *The Art of Biblical History*, pp. 43–46.
24. ibid., p. 58.

historical narrative is the opposite of fiction.[25] But Robert Alter says that fictionality and historicity are not antithetical.[26] Does he differ from Blomberg in his view of fiction or of history? Now, of course history can mean what happened in the past, or what people write about the past. Alter argues that in biblical history 'we are repeatedly confronted . . . with shrewdly defined characters, artfully staged scenes, subtle arrangements of dialogue, artifices of significant analogy . . .'[27] Thus the literary shaping and artistry play a role in biblical history no less than in fiction.

A distinction needs to be made between narratives that are essentially representational (historiographical) and those that are not. Form alone is not sufficient as a criterion for the distinction. Long suggests that only the overall sense of purpose can help us here. Only context can show us the purpose of the narrative. That the historian is constrained by the facts of the past does not mean there is no creative input in writing history. 'The past does not present itself in such a way that historians need make no creative choices in the construction of a historical account of some aspect of it. But if the past does have some inherent structure (as I believe it does), then the first task of historians is to seek to discern that structure.'[28] And again, 'Literary artistry and reliable historiography should not be set in opposition.'[29] Long also points out that literary narrative has a greater explanatory capacity than bare chronicle. Historical reporting is more akin to painting than to photography. He emphatically rejects the assertion that to allow artistry into historiography is to compromise the truth value of the narrative.

Long proposes a method for discovering the historical import of biblical narrative. It involves the three stages of preparation, procedure and presentation. Preparation involves a model of reality (fundamental assumptions) and then the steps by which interpretation is arrived at. The assumptions will include the conviction of where final authority lies (the Bible as the word of God, or some other). The procedure has two steps: first, listening to the text in an effort to discover what, if any, historical truth claims it makes, and second, testing the truth value of these claims by internal and external

---

25. Craig Blomberg, *The Historical Reliability of the Gospels* (Leicester: IVP, 1987), referred to by Long, ibid., p. 59.
26. Robert Alter, *The Art of Biblical Narrative* (New York: Basic Books, 1981), p. 32, quoted in Long, ibid., p. 59.
27. Alter, ibid., quoted in Long, ibid., p. 61.
28. Long, ibid., p. 71.
29. ibid., p. 74.

checks.[30] As to the first, he says that good listening means an open attitude and attention to context. Testing by internal consistency includes trying to make sense of the story. External checks may be made on the basis of other biblical literature, extra-biblical literature and material remains.

What, then, can the exegete do with the narrative material that makes historical truth claims while at the same time manifesting what appear to be the marks of creative and artistic composition? It is clear that we do not depend on so-called scientific historical evidence, as useful as it may be when it is available. In commenting on Alvin Plantinga's 'warranted' approach, Craig Bartholomew makes this significant comment: '[B]y far the most interesting question in my opinion is how the historical question of the Bible looks in the context of faith seeking understanding rather than in the context of unbelief seeking understanding.'[31]

I propose the following guidelines for the evangelical preacher who is aware of the problem of the disjuncture between biblical history writing and modern scientific historiography. First, the overall historical timeline and metanarrative of the Bible are not in question. The details of them may be disputed, but the sense of history is too pervasive to be written off. At the climax of this history is the person and work of Jesus of Nazareth, who is presented as a unique figure in the history of mankind. He is the God/Man and the Saviour of the world. He is presented as the *telos*, the goal, of all history. All biblical texts stand in identifiable relationship to Jesus. The biblical interpretation of Jesus is the gospel. All texts take their ultimate meaning from the gospel. This means that narrative detail must be understood in this canonical context. To forget that the Bible gives the account of God's words and deeds is to end up wrongly focusing on a purely human story.

Second, the danger in preaching the narrative details as fact lies not in misrepresenting as 'fact' some detail that is possibly a feature of narrative art, but in misrepresenting its connection to the wider biblical narrative which biblical theology uncovers. Thus a frequent failing of preaching programmes or study curricula is the fragmentation of the biblical story, so that events and characters become isolated from the big picture and the goal of the gospel. While Jesus emphasized that the Old Testament was about him, a pietistic approach

30. ibid., pp. 176ff.

31. Craig Bartholomew, 'Warranted Biblical Interpretation: Alvin Plantinga's "Two (or More) Kinds of Scripture Scholarship"', in Craig Bartholomew, C. Green and K. Möller (eds.), *'Behind' the Text: History and Biblical Interpretation*, SHS, vol. 4 (Carlisle: Paternoster; Grand Rapids: Zondervan, 2003, p. 75).

so often misses the obvious and treats narrative as exemplary in a way that applies primarily to us. Of course, it is about us in various ways, but only because it is about Jesus first and foremost. Our lives are defined by Jesus the fulfiller, not by isolated narratives and the characters in them.

Third, the exegete can safely interpret the narrative as fact, since it is the theology conveyed in the narrative that is our main concern. Narratives may rearrange or craft the accounts of events, but we cannot accept that they do so in order to deceive or to convey a spurious theological message. Thus, while there is a certain obvious sequence of events in the Gospels' accounts of the life of Jesus (birth, boyhood, adult ministry, suffering, death, resurrection), the arrangements within that scheme may well bow to theological purpose (e.g. John's account of the temple-cleansing early in Jesus' ministry, while the Synoptics place it late), or serve to emphasize aspects of Jesus' ministry (e.g. Matthew's collection of kingdom parables). Attempts at harmonizing the Gospels, it seems to me, have usually ignored the way history has been narrativized. John Goldingay points to the narrativizing as serving the theological interpretation. It is important to recognize both aspects.[32]

> Real historical events can seem so important that the literary creativity that features in biblical narratives can be ignored, or we can become so aware of this creativity that we cease to recognize the fact and/or the importance of the fundamental historicity of the biblical story.

Fourth, in dealing with the bulk of biblical narrative as it occurs in the Old Testament, the exegete must keep in mind the connection of the Old Testament to the gospel. Just as the historicity of the four Gospels is essential to the authentic gospel, so these four testimonies to the historical Jesus depend for their interpretation on two facts: the self-authenticating person and word of Jesus, and the relationship of his being and doing to the story of the Old Testament. The whole New Testament testifies to its understanding of Jesus as the Christ, the Messiah promised in the Old Testament. Jesus is seen to be the fulfiller of the Old Testament *in toto*. He does not simply develop or embody ideals. The theological connection of the Old Testament to the historical Jesus establishes the historical reality of its witness.

Fifth, while there are grey areas in which evangelical opinions over the historical truth claims may differ (e.g. 'Is Job historical or parabolic?' 'Is Jonah a factual missionary story?'), the preaching of such as historical fact is only

---

32. John Goldingay, *Models for Scripture* (Grand Rapids: Eerdmans, 1994), p. 29.

problematic when the concern for historicity overshadows the concern for the theological message. Some of Jesus' parables may well be drawn from real life, but their significance does not depend on their being 'historical'.[33] The same may be said (cautiously) of Job.[34] The issue, then, is not whether we can accept only what can be tested by scientific historical means, but what relationship the narrated events bear to the gospel. In one sense the history/fiction debate is important to remind us that history writing in ancient times was creative in a way that was not calculated to be deceptive. The crafting of accounts that some may call fiction is not designed to reduce the historical value, but to emphasize it.

---

33. I have never heard a preacher dealing with, say, the good Samaritan qualify it by 'of course this didn't really happen'. It simply is not an issue. What did happen was that Jesus told the story for a reason.

34. It is clear that, even if we regard the book of Job as based on historical fact, it remains a skilfully crafted work that in its literary form of poetic cycles goes well beyond prosaic chronicle.

16. THE GOSPEL AND THE THEOLOGICAL DIMENSION (I): THE TWO TESTAMENTS AND TYPOLOGY

The relationship of Old Testament and New Testament

> Long ago, at many times and in many ways, God spoke to our fathers by the prophets, but in these last days he has spoken to us by his Son. (Heb. 1:1–2)

Thus the biblical author poses the question for us of the relationship of the Testaments: how does the word of Christ relate to that of the prophets and, in broader terms, is the New Testament continuous or discontinuous with the Old? The history of biblical theology as a modern discipline, not to mention the history of its antecedents, shows that the question of the relationship between the two Testaments is of enduring importance and concern. H. G. Reventlow saw it as one of the key problems in twentieth-century biblical theology.[1] I believe it remains a problem to this day. I am also convinced that the nature of the unity of the Bible is the key to biblical theology and vital to biblical interpretation.

Christian theism, biblical theology and evangelical hermeneutics all presuppose that the Bible, notwithstanding its great diversity, displays a

1. H. G. Reventlow, *Problems of Biblical Theology in the Twentieth Century* (Philadelphia: Fortress, 1986), p. 11.

perceptible unity. However, the majority of biblical theologies written in the last century and a half have been theologies of either the Old Testament or the New Testament. There has been a tendency to treat the two Testaments as if they were independent of each other. This is more true of Old Testament theologies than of New, since the latter have to take into account the conviction common to all the New Testament authors that their message has its roots in the Old Testament. All the books of the New Testament, with the possible exception of 2 John and 3 John, contain direct references and allusions to the Old Testament that presuppose some kind of continuity between the Testaments. Yet the tendency in post-Enlightenment times has been to stress the disunity of the Testaments and to discount any meaningful and organic unity.

A number of Old Testament theologians have attempted to address the matter in a theoretical way. For example, G. von Rad has a considerable section at the end of volume 2 of his *Old Testament Theology* that deals with the Old Testament and the New.[2] He gives a detailed exposition of a typological understanding of the unity of the Bible in a way that is strangely remote from the main work. T. C. Vriezen devotes the first two chapters of his work to his concern for the Old Testament as Christian Scripture, but it is not altogether obvious how this presupposition has affected his treatment of the Old Testament itself.[3] W. Eichrodt states in the opening chapter of his *Theology of the Old Testament* that Old Testament religion must be seen as completed in Christ.[4] But in the two volumes of this work there is little that overtly follows this principle through. G. A. F. Knight states that his purpose is to discover what the Old Testament has to say to the twentieth century in the light of the Christian revelation as a whole.[5] Despite the title of his work, one of the crucial questions of continuity, that of Israel and the church, is relegated to a short appendix.

Some see the Old Testament as providing authentic revelation and theology independently of the New Testament. The resistance to a Christological and thus New Testament-based interpretation of the Old Testament can be seen in the more extreme approaches to the diversity of Scripture. Postmodernist trends not only follow modernism in denying transcendence, but refuse to

---

2. G. von Rad, *Old Testament Theology*, vol. 2 (Edinburgh: Oliver and Boyd, 1965), pp. 319–429.
3. T. C. Vriezen, *An Outline of Old Testament Theology* (Oxford: Blackwells, 1958).
4. W. Eichrodt, *Theology of the Old Testament* (London: SCM, 1961), p. 27.
5. G. A. F. Knight, *A Christian Theology of the Old Testament* (London: SCM, 1957), p. 10.

allow any concept of a metanarrative, a comprehensive story and picture of reality in a word from God, which can unite the two Testaments into one meaningful canon of revelation. The notion that there is no transcendent authority or objective truth challenges the very basis upon which a comprehensive biblical theology has been built from biblical times.

We can see, then, something of a continuum of approaches to the relationship of the Testaments that plays a significant role in the history of biblical interpretation. This continuum remains today because of the tenacity of the orthodox adherence to historic Christianity that finds itself in substantial conflict with both modernism and postmodernism. First, in the early church we see attempts to understand the essential unity of the Bible from the epicentre of the person and work of Jesus Christ. These early Christological interpretations of the Old Testament were driven partly by the apologetic needs to counter Judaism by asserting that the Old Testament belonged first and foremost to the church, and partly by the need to understand the Old Testament presuppositions of the apostolic doctrine. Early Christian apologetics also needed to oppose Gnosticism by showing the unity of the Testaments, and at the same time to refute the Judaizers in the church by stressing the distinctions between the Testaments. Medieval Catholicism and Reformation Protestantism were both heirs to the Christological approach.

Second, with the Enlightenment and the advent of humanistic presuppositions in biblical and historical studies, there was a loosening of the theological ties between the Old and New Testaments. As theological concerns gave way to the study of the history of religion, the religion of Israel became a matter for historical investigation virtually independent of the religion of Jesus and the early church. The nineteenth and twentieth centuries saw the development of the parallel disciplines of Old Testament theology and New Testament theology. Some Old Testament theologies were produced from within the framework of certain Christian assumptions about the relationship of the Testaments, but with the clear aim of understanding what the Old Testament is saying in its own right. This is not necessarily a bad thing, but it must never be seen as the whole story.

Third, the postmodern age of religious pluralism encourages not so much the rejection of any connection between the Testaments, but a sense that one can either pursue or ignore the relationship. However, the task of writing Old Testament theologies continues to be undertaken by those who have some allegiance to the New Testament as well. It seems to us Christians remarkable that Jewish writers show little interest in writing theologies of the Hebrew Scriptures, a fact which reinforces the conviction that the very nature of the Christian gospel, in the context of the theology of the New Testament, provides the major impetus for pursuing Old Testament theology.[6]

Unity and diversity in the history of interpretation

Long before the dogmatic theology of the early church had formulated ways of talking about the reality of the incarnation and the God/Man, these issues were surfacing in the handling of Scripture. The relationship of the one and the many is integral to the theology within the Old Testament. The apostolic understanding of Jesus and the incarnational mystery involved an assessment that required a *both-and* rather than an *either-or* approach. Later the church cemented this perspective in the doctrine of the incarnation, and particularly in the formula of Chalcedon in AD 451.[7] The doctrine of the Trinity provides the paradigm of *both-and* in the question of the one and the many. Amongst more orthodox Christians the Hellenistic Gnostic heritage was to be found in the recourse to allegory as a means of relating the Old to the New Testament. Whereas Marcion had rejected the Old Testament as irrelevant, the allegorists treated it as a kind of Judaic overlay that hid from view the true spiritual meaning drawn from the New Testament and, subsequently, from ecclesiastical dogma. While Marcion completely separated the Old from the New, the allegorists used a Hellenistic sleight of hand that effectively removed all differences and fused the two. Either way, the solution was in the direction of

---

6. J. D. Levenson, *The Hebrew Bible, the Old Testament, and Historical Criticism* (Louisville: Westminster John Knox Press, 1993), ch. 2, 'Why Jews Are Not Interested in Biblical Theology'. Levenson cannot find the kind of unity in the Old Testament that the New Testament presupposes.
7. Chalcedon produced a formula for expressing the relationship of the divine and human natures of Christ. In effect it said that Jesus was *both* fully God *and* fully man; there is unity between the two natures, but no fusion; there is distinction, but no separation. This formula has been under attack from a number of quarters, but has staunch defenders in the conservative camp: Klaas Runia, *The Present-day Christological Debate* (Leicester: IVP, 1984); Gerald Bray, 'Can We Dispense With Chalcedon?', *Themelios*, Jan. 1978, and *Creeds, Councils and Christ* (Leicester: IVP, 1984); Norman Geisler, 'Current Chalcedonian Christological Challenges', *ERT* 12/4 (1988); R. J. Rushdoony, *The One and the Many* (Fairfax, VA: Thoburn, 1978), pp. 161–164.

an *either-or* approach.[8] By contrast, typology as a method of relating the Testaments underlined the perspective of both their unity and their diversity. Medieval interpretation maintained the struggle to understand the relationship without abandoning the historical meaning of the Old Testament, but the allegorical prevailed as the major way of dealing with the Christian meaning of the Old Testament. This ongoing docetic tendency not only had ramifications for understanding the relationship of the Testaments, but also tended to the dehistoricizing of the gospel event.

One of the gains of the Reformation was the recovery of a more consistently Christological understanding of the relationship between the Testaments. Not only do the Old Testament Scriptures truly testify to Jesus (John 5:39), but this unity exists in tension with the real diversity within and between the Testaments. The *unity-distinction* structure formulated at Chalcedon can be applied to the word of God inscripturate in the same way as to the Word incarnate. Luther saw the question of the two Testaments as that of the relationship of law and grace. He went a long way towards removing the absolute divide between the Old and the New, because he recognized that there was law and promise (i.e. gospel) in both Testaments. However, he continued to stress the predominance of law in the Old and of grace in the New.

John Calvin significantly places the discussion of the relationship of the Testaments in the wider context of the revelation of the Redeemer. Book 2 of the *Institutes* is entitled *The Knowledge of God the Redeemer in Christ, First Disclosed to the Fathers Under the Law, and Then to Us in the Gospel.* In this section, Calvin first deals with the effects of the fall of the human race into sin and the need for divine grace. Chapter 7 is headed 'The Law was Given, not to Restrain the Folk of the Old Covenant under Itself, but to Foster Hope of Salvation in Christ until His Coming'. In this Calvin includes both the moral and the ceremonial law. The law was the means of revealing Christ to Israel, even though it was only as by a shadow. Calvin's emphasis may be said to point to the essential unity of the Testaments, while in no way ignoring the differences. Two chapters (*Institutes* 2.10 and 11) are given over respectively to the unity of the Old and the New Testaments, and the differences between the two. It is here that Calvin expounds his influential view of the unity of the covenants, although he never arrives at the position of the seventeenth-century covenant theologians.

---

8. Allegory effectively eliminated any distinction between the Testaments by recasting the Old completely in terms of the New. It was docetic in that it removed the real humanity and earthiness of the Old Testament.

Unity and diversity in recent biblical theology

The relationship of the Testaments, then, is one specific aspect of the broader question of the unity and diversity of Scripture and overlaps with the matter of the New Testament use of the Old.[9] Against the background of the history of the Christian interpretation of the Old Testament, which is essentially the question of the relationship of the Testaments, we can look at some of the more recent attempts to formulate this focal point in the matter of the nature of the Bible's unity and diversity. Any attempt to categorize the various approaches suggested by modern biblical theologians will need to recognize that different emphases are just that – emphases, not mutually exclusive perspectives.

On the subject of the canon of Scripture, it will suffice here to mention the conclusions reached by Roger Beckwith that Jesus and the primitive Christian church did not dissent from their Jewish contemporaries over what books constituted the authoritative canon of the Hebrew Scriptures.[10] That being the case, and given the eventual acceptance of a body of literature to make up a New Testament canon, the question arises as to how these two were first perceived as comprising one canon of Christian Scripture. That is the historical question of the canon. The biblical-theological question concerns the internal theological evidence for the canonical status of the two Testaments.

The superiority of the Old Testament

D. L. Baker[11] and H. G. Reventlow[12] have both drawn attention to the idea expressed by some scholars that the Old Testament has priority or superiority over the New. It must be recognized that the examples given are not of Jewish theologians who reject altogether the authority of Jesus and the New Testament. Rather they are theologians who acknowledge the importance of the New Testament and claim adherence to the Christian faith. The best example of this position is A. A. van Ruler.[13] He adopts a salvation history

---

9. This is discussed in G. K. Beale (ed.), *The Right Doctrine from the Wrong Texts? Essays on the Use of the Old Testament in the New* (Grand Rapids: Baker, 1994). See also John S. Feinberg (ed.), *Continuity and Discontinuity* (Westchester: Crossway, 1988).
10. Roger Beckwith, *The Old Testament Canon of the New Testament Church* (Grand Rapids: Eerdmans, 1985), ch. 2.
11. D. L. Baker, *Two Testaments, One Bible*, 2nd edn (Leicester: IVP, 1991), ch. 5.
12. Reventlow, *Problems of Biblical Theology in the Twentieth Century*, pp. 54–64.
13. A. A. van Ruler, *The Christian Church and the Old Testament* (Grand Rapids: Eerdmans, 1966), p. 94.

approach which sees the Old Testament not only as the antecedent to the New, but also as maintaining its own integrity, especially in setting out the message of the kingdom of God. In a sense the gospel fulfils the promises of the Old Testament, but at the same time it regresses from the fullness of the Old Testament message. Thus we are apparently left with the position that the Old Testament is *the* canon of Scripture, and the New Testament is explanatory glossary. The reasons for my rejection of this position will become clear when I deal with typology.

The superiority of the New Testament

The most extreme example of this emphasis is, of course, the rejection of the Old Testament by such Gnostics as Marcion. Marcionite tendencies in more recent times are seen in the *deutsche Christen* and the Nazis, whose anti-Semitism was expressed in the rejection of the Judaic Scriptures.[14] There is also an incipient form of Marcionism that occurs by default in the church and in individual Christian piety. Preachers and lay people alike find the Old Testament problematical, and the consequent neglect results in a canon within the canon heavily weighted in favour of the New Testament. In theory, people will maintain that the whole Bible is equally the word of God, but in practice the difficulties of dealing consistently with the Old Testament can lead to its eclipse or to some intuitive approach to Christianizing it.

The Lutheran dialectic of law and gospel failed to remove a medieval tendency to impose a hermeneutical divide between the Testaments. Rudolf Bultmann's existential approach led him to emphasize this hermeneutical gap to the point where he took the significance of the Old Testament to be a negative one. Bultmann rejects the old liberal notion of the development of religion as the basis for understanding the relationship of the Testaments. This was a view that leaves the Old Testament behind as outmoded by the purer development of New Testament religion. But, Bultmann asserts:

> [F]aith requires the backward glance onto Old Testament history as a history of failure, and so of promise, in order to know that the situation of the justified man arises only on the basis of this miscarriage. Thus faith, to be a really justifying faith, must constantly contain within itself the way of the law as something which has been overcome.[15]

---

14. Baker, *Two Testaments, One Bible*, p. 49.
15. Rudolf Bultmann, 'Prophecy and Fulfillment', in Claus Westermann (ed.), *Essays on Old Testament Hermeneutics*, trans. James L. Mays (Richmond: John Knox, 1964), p. 75.

It was necessary to be under the law in order to understand the grace of the gospel. Bultmann preferred to ask the question of how the Old Testament presents an understanding of human existence. He concluded that it shows the demand of God, not in an exclusive way, but really nevertheless. This understanding of the demand, in Old Testament terms of the law, is necessary if we are to understand the New Testament's view of grace in the gospel. So Bultmann emphasizes the discontinuity of the Testaments.

The equality of the Testaments

David Baker gives a number of examples of this position, but concentrates on that of Wilhelm Vischer, who has invited, unfairly in my view, rather strident criticisms of his position.[16] In his unfinished work *The Witness of the Old Testament to Christ*, he assesses the complementarity of the Testaments thus: 'The Old Testament tells us *what* the Christ is; the New, *who* he is.'[17] Or again, 'In their preaching of Jesus the Messiah the apostles in no way desire to declare anything else than that which is written in the Old Testament.'[18] The continuity element is emphasized by Vischer: 'The New Testament asserts that God's deed in Jesus Christ is not merely one but rather *the* decisive event for the history of Israel.'[19] Vischer employs a quite restrained form of typology, and that only after rather rigorous investigation of the Old Testament text.

Thematic polarities between the Testaments

A number of thematic approaches to the question have been proposed which highlight the nature of the problem in defining the extent of both continuity and discontinuity between the Testaments. None can be seen as a total solution, or as exclusive of all other proposals. Each involves a polarity and certain tensions that cannot be resolved by demolishing one or other pole. Once again, the Christological and trinitarian realities are helpful in warning against facile *either-or* solutions. But proposing that we maintain the *both-and* tension

---

16. Baker, *Two Testaments, One Bible*, ch. 4.
17. W. Vischer, *The Witness of the Old Testament to Christ, Volume 1, The Pentateuch*, trans. A. B. Crabtree (London: Lutterworth, 1949), p. 7.
18. ibid., p. 11.
19. W. Vischer, 'Everywhere the Scripture is about Christ Alone', in B. W. Anderson (ed.), *The Old Testament and Christian Faith* (New York: Herder and Herder, 1969), p. 97.

does not solve for us the exact make-up of the tensions. These have to be assessed according to their distinct characteristics.

Salvation history and eschatological consummation

Oscar Cullmann sees salvation history focusing on Jesus, and includes in it the eschatological tension.[20] It could certainly be argued that salvation history, as a Christian approach to the appropriation of the Old Testament, is found in the words of Peter (Acts 2:16–36), Stephen (Acts 7:2–56) and Paul (Acts 13:16–41). Each of these has a sense of the continuity from the redemptive-historical events of the Old Testament to Jesus of Nazareth, so that Jesus is claimed to be the crowning saving act of God. In the nineteenth century J. C. K. von Hofmann was a key proponent of the idea of salvation history. This emphasis was seen as one implication of the Reformation's retrieval of the historical sense of the Old Testament.

Not all salvation history approaches have such a strong sense of continuity. G. von Rad stresses more of the discontinuity within the Old Testament, so that there is a gap between what can be said to have actually happened and what Israel came to confess. The Old Testament consists of a developed tradition of saving history and the record of Israel's response to that saving history. The processes of reinterpretation, which took place in the Old Testament, continue in the New Testament's appropriation of the Old. This approach raises important questions about the actual historicity of the salvation history story. In what sense has God acted in history if the events that are said to evidence this action cannot be taken as historical?

Cullmann examines the polarity of salvation history and eschatology.[21] Implicit in the whole notion of God acting in history is the goal towards which such history moves. History, to be saving history, must involve eschatology. But eschatology is the end of history as well as its goal. The continuity relationship of the Testaments is usually conceived in terms of some kind of eschatological resolution being arrived at in and through Jesus Christ.

Type and antitype

The approach of salvation history is closely related to the revived interest in typology as a way of understanding the inner theological structures of the Bible. The connection was recognized by von Hofmann in his study in

---

20. O. Cullmann, *Salvation in History* (London: SCM, 1967).
21. ibid., pp. 28–64.

Israel and the church

Is the church the new Israel, and if so, in what sense? In one view, the church virtually takes over all the roles of Israel as the saved people of God. This is the predominant view in Reformed theology. By contrast, dispensationalists, because of their prophetic literalism, see only discontinuity in that they expect the future fulfilment of the hopes of Israel for national restoration and salvation. The *eschaton* for Israel is thus quite distinct from that of the church. A third view takes the Old Testament ideas of the ingathering of the Gentiles to the restored Israel as worked out in that the gospel is to the Jew first (Rom. 1:16). The church then consists of the restored or spiritual Israel (Christian Jews) plus the converted Gentiles who are privileged to share in Israel's blessings.[25] This preserves the structure of the covenant promises to Abraham (Gen. 12:3).

The typology debate: the basis and nature of typology

It is clear that the New Testament refuses to abandon the Old Testament. If all the Old Testament references and allusions were removed from the New Testament, it would not make much sense. Counts vary, but one estimate is that there are some 1,600 citations and allusions to the Old Testament in the New Testament. The New Testament may occasionally appear to use Jewish methods of exegesis, such as pesher or midrash, but it has to be said that it uses its own unique approach to the Old Testament. The most significant departure from Jewish exegesis is seen in Jesus' application of the Old Testament to himself and the claims in the New Testament that the events surrounding Jesus are actually fulfilments of the Old Testament.

Jesus views his own authority as having divine origin, yet he never opposes this authority to that of the Old Testament Scriptures. He frequently endorses the latter. He treats the Old Testament narrative as records of fact. His arguments from the Old Testament are authoritatively final: 'Scripture cannot be broken' (John 10:35). He criticizes the Jewish leaders for their neglect of Scripture, while he himself submits to it. The Old Testament was integral to his whole understanding of himself and his mission. Jesus' use of the Old

---

25. Donald Robinson, *Jew and Greek* (Sydney: Inter Varsity Fellowship, 1961); 'Who were "the saints"?', *RTR* 22 (1963), pp. 45–53; *Faith's Framework* (Exeter: Paternoster, 1985), ch. 4. See also Graeme Goldsworthy, 'Biblical Theology and the Shape of Paul's Mission', in Peter Bolt and Mark Thompson (eds.), *The Gospel to the Nations* (Leicester: Apollos; Downers Grove: IVP, 2000), pp. 7–18.

Testament displays an originality that is not always appreciated by his contemporaries. The way he and his apostles use the Old Testament forms the theological substructure of the New Testament canon, and thus points us to the nature of the unity of Scripture. It is this comprehensive use of the Old Testament as referring ultimately to Jesus that constitutes typology.

We cannot overestimate the importance of the question of typology for hermeneutics. Any kind of canonical approach presupposes a unity to the Bible that establishes the primary context from within which every text is interpreted. The relationship of the Testaments is integral to the formulation of biblical theology that, in turn, is fundamental for the establishment of Christian doctrine. A second consideration is that the New Testament provides the only evidence we have for the hermeneutical procedures of Jesus and the apostles. It is not only the attitude of Jesus to the Old Testament as his authoritative Scripture that concerns us, but also the way he employed it as the Scripture that he himself fulfilled. Studies on the use and interpretation of the Old Testament in the New Testament are thus of great importance to us.

The various approaches to typology show an interest in some kind of recurring pattern or patterns within Scripture. There is a wide divergence of opinions as to how this patterning occurs in the Bible and how the principle of typological interpretation can be employed in the practicalities of bringing the text to the modern hearer. Reventlow distinguishes two main approaches to typology.[26] The first focuses on the correspondence of facts, persons and events as they occur in both Testaments.[27] An example is found in E. Jacob, who specifies three ways in which the type may relate to Christ as the antitype: (i) a relation of similarity, (ii) a relation of opposition (Adam-Christ), and (iii) a relation of progress. It should be pointed out that the relation of opposition actually involves similarity. Adam and Christ, in one sense opposites, are both federal heads of the human race. The dissimilarity is that which makes typology a necessary structure, in that the type fails to be the full reality. Leonhard Goppelt focuses on the way the New Testament understands itself in relation to the Old Testament. His aim is to show the importance of the Old Testament for the church.[28]

These discussions often tend to highlight the explicit examples. There are obvious typological interpretations in the New Testament, but are we confined

26. Reventlow, *Problems of Biblical Theology in the Twentieth Century*, pp. 18–31.

27. ibid., pp. 18–24.

28. L. Goppelt, *Typos: The Typological Interpretation of the Old Testament in the New*, German ed. (1939) trans. Donald Madvig (Grand Rapids: Eerdmans, 1982).

to the texts that are specifically raised in the New Testament? John Currid summarizes a number of views of typology by specifying four essentials for its identification: (i) typology must be grounded in history; (ii) there must be notable historical and theological resemblance between the type and antitype; (iii) the antitype must intensify the type – that is, it must be more theologically significant than the type; and (iv) there must be evidence of the divine intention for the type to represent the antitype.[29] David Baker's approach includes an examination of the Greek words (*typos* and its cognates) as they are used in the New Testament.[30] The use of the term has focused on prefiguration and correspondence. Baker recognizes that typology exists within the Old Testament, and thus we are not dependent on those passages in the New Testament that involve *typos* terminology. I suggest that what we need to do, however, is to try to uncover the principles at work which enable the biblical authors to make the identifications we refer to as typological.

The second approach posited by Reventlow is typology as a method of salvation history hermeneutics.[31] Typology seems to be a fairly natural corollary to salvation history. Thus 'typology is a means of discovering structural analogies between the saving events attested by both Testaments which bridge the gap produced by our loss of a direct relationship in faith to the events of the Old Testament.'[32] It is with this approach that the views of Gabriel Hebert and Donald Robinson have been influential in my own thinking about biblical theology.[33] The essence of this position is that the structure of revelation involves three major stages.

- First, God's kingdom is revealed in Israel's history up to David and Solomon.
- Second, God's kingdom is revealed in prophetic eschatology. This recapitulates the first stage as that which shapes the future.

---

29. John Currid, 'Recognition and Use of Typology in Preaching', *RTR* 53/3 (1994), pp. 115–129.
30. Baker, *Two Testaments, One Bible*, pp. 179–202.
31. Reventlow, *Problems of Biblical Theology in the Twentieth Century*, pp. 24–31.
32. ibid., p. 25.
33. Donald Robinson, 'Origins and Unresolved Tensions', in R. J. Gibson (ed.), *Interpreting God's Plan* (Carlisle: Paternoster, 1997); A. G. Hebert, *The Throne of David* (London: Faber and Faber, 1941); G. Goldsworthy, *Gospel and Kingdom* (Exeter: Paternoster, 1981; now in *The Goldsworthy Trilogy*, Carlisle: Paternoster, 2000), and *According to Plan* (Leicester: IVP, 1991).

- Third, God's kingdom is revealed in the fulfilment of the Old Testament expectations in Christ.

If this scheme is valid, it means that the correspondence is not primarily of facts, persons and events, but of the entire epochs or stages within salvation history. It is because of this 'macro-analogy' that the facts, persons and events do correspond. This correspondence is not necessarily explicitly stated in the text, but it can nevertheless be determined on the basis of theological equivalence. Thus we can say that any person, fact, or event in the Old Testament is a type of Christ to the degree that its theological function foreshadows that of Christ.

The question of the principles that enable Paul, for example, to designate certain Old Testament events as *typikōs* needs to be opened up. Many Christians are nervous about the idea of typology, because it is often confused with allegory and other kinds of fanciful spiritualizing interpretation.[34] Some evangelical scholars seem to be wary of attempts to find unifying themes, theological centres and overall structures in Scripture. Maybe the excesses of some other evangelical interpreters have prompted an overly cautious approach.[35]

Jesus and reality

Typology, broadly understood, illustrates the way dogmatic or doctrinal formulations inform the method of biblical theology. It is of first importance to recognize that the biblical story embraces *all* of reality, namely God and the realm of creation. While it focuses on only certain aspects of reality, the whole is represented either directly or indirectly. The created realm is in turn shown to have its pinnacle in the human race. Only human beings are described as

---

34. Some literalists have an aversion to spiritualizing, but it is clear that there is a real sense in which the New Testament spiritualizes the Old.
35. My one concern with the excellent analysis proposed by Sidney Greidanus, *Preaching Christ from the Old Testament* (Grand Rapids: Eerdmans, 1999), is that his proposal of some eight ways of linking the Old and New Testaments can give the impression that these are largely unconnected approaches which must be chosen to suit the particular instances under review. A brief comparison of Greidanus's view and mine is given by David Peterson, *Christ and His People in the Book of Isaiah* (Leicester: IVP, 2003), pp. 13–19.

created in the image of God and as having dominion over creation. The whole biblical story focuses on the way that mankind's relationship to God affects the rest of the created realm. It does not simply refer to sun, moon and stars as created by God, but goes further to say that they are under the control of God and their destiny is tied up with that of humans. When Adam and Eve sinned, the entire universe fell with them (Gen. 3:17–19; Rom. 8:18–23). Redemption has its goal in a new race of humans and a new creation. Sin fractured *all* relationships except those within the Trinity. Redemption in Jesus Christ puts the universe back together again as a new creation. How is this achieved? The gospel shows us that it is done in a way that involves the promise of new things (the bulk of the Old Testament), the representative restored reality in the actual person of Christ, and the summing up of all things in Christ in the consummation.

To put it another way, Jesus is God incarnate – that is, he is fully God and fully human. But to be human is to be made from the created dust of the earth while being given life by the breath of God. In the God/Man we thus have all of reality present in a representative way that involves no dislocation of relationships. Jesus is thus the representative new creation. If reality consists of God-Humanity-Universe,[36] Jesus is the perfect representative of all three dimensions in which all relate perfectly. Christology in the New Testament shows Jesus to be the comprehensive expression of reality in the purpose of God. The notion of the cosmic Christ rightly applies to the incarnate Son because he is representative reality.

The centrality of Christ for understanding the Bible and, for that matter, the whole of reality can be seen in many parts in the New Testament. A few key passages illustrate what I mean:

- Acts 13:32–33: the bodily resurrection of Jesus is the fulfilment of the Old Testament promises, which include those relating to the renewal of all things.
- Romans 8:19–23: the work of Christ affects the redemption of the whole of creation.
- 1 Corinthians 1 – 2: Christ in his gospel is the wisdom of God, which links him to the Old Testament perspective on God's wisdom as the principle of order in creation.
- 2 Corinthians 1:20: all God's promises, which must include those of a new creation, are affirmed in Christ.

---

36. By 'Universe' I mean everything in creation that is not human.

- 2 Corinthians 5:17: Christ is the locus of the new creation.[37]
- Ephesians 1:10: God's plan is, in the fullness of time, to sum up *all* things in Christ, things in heaven and things on earth. As with Galatians 4:4, the fullness of time is the time of the gospel event. Thus the incarnation is the summing-up event.
- Ephesians 2:13–22: Christ as the new temple fulfils all the expectations of the new temple in the Old Testament, which is closely related to the renewal of the earth; the restored temple in Ezekiel 40 – 47 is the centre of the new Eden.
- Colossians 1:15–20: Christ is the reason for the creation and is the firstborn of all creation. All things hold together in him. He reconciles the whole of the created order to God.
- Colossians 2:2–3: Christ contains all the treasures of wisdom and knowledge.
- 1 Peter 3:1–13: Christians wait for the new heavens and the new earth to be revealed at the coming of Christ.
- Revelation 21 – 22: the goal of the biblical story is the new heavens and the new earth; the final rule of God and his Christ.

The dimensions of reality in the biblical revelation

Thus it can be seen that Jesus gathers up in his being all the dimensions of reality, in that he is God, he is humanity and he is created order. Furthermore, he gathers up in his being and doing all the dimensions of redemptive history in the Old Testament, including the negatives of sin and rebellion.[38] Even those areas that biblical theologians have found difficult to incorporate into a theological unity, such as the wisdom literature, are subsumed under the comprehensive role of Jesus as the new creation, the representative restored reality.

---

37. There is an ambiguity in the Greek here, which literally says, 'If anyone is in Christ, a new creation.' It could mean 'he is a new creation', or 'there is a new creation'. The important point is the perspective of being *in Christ*, and in that way being part of the new creation. The locus of the new creation is in Christ, who is in heaven. This does not contradict the subjective aspect of regeneration in the believer, but puts it in perspective. See my article, 'Regeneration', *NDBT*, pp. 720–723.
38. In being made sin for us and dying (2 Cor. 5:21), Jesus is the final reference point for understanding sin and judgment.

It is also clear that Jesus and the apostles regarded the whole of the Old Testament as testimony to the Christ; it is *all* about Jesus. Thus we conclude that there is no dimension of the Old Testament message that does not in some way foreshadow Christ. If any text is not ultimately about Christ, then what is it about? Two important qualifications must be made here. First, by 'text' we signify a meaningful portion of any given book understood as part of that book and its overall message. Simply isolating a few words or a sentence from its real and immediate context does not qualify. A text takes its meaning from its literary context and from how it contributes to the meaning of that wider context.

Second, to say that an Old Testament text is about Christ is to point to the dynamics of the canon of Scripture, not to some literalistic presupposition. There is always the element of discontinuity between the Old Testament and Christ, but there is also the element of unity. It is to the latter we refer. This raises again the issue of the relationship of the two Testaments, and of the bipolar tensions referred to above. It should be understood that, in so far as these are valid expressions of the connection between the Testaments, they are all related and coinhere.[39] I am proposing that we can subsume them all under a concept of macro-typology that goes beyond the usually identified elements of typology explicit in the New Testament application of the Old. This macro-typology is the underlying principle of theological structure and biblical unity that makes possible all the various perspectives on the relationship of the Testaments.

A further observation can be made. Given the focus of all the creative-redemptive elements on Christ, we have to say that he defines the unity of the biblical message. The unity of the canon is a dogmatic construct stemming from Christology. Unity is a theological presupposition, not an empirically based construct. When biblical theologians think they see a real point of unrelieved disunity, or cannot see the overall unity, it is a problem with the theologians, not a problem with the Bible. There will always be difficult texts that we have trouble in integrating into the unity of Scripture, and the massive diversity of the forms and messages of the different texts must never be overlooked. But to say that discerning some aspects of the unity is difficult is not to conclude that it is not there to be perceived. The theological unity will always

---

39. Coinherence is a way of speaking of the inseparability of the various distinguishable dimensions. It expresses unity without fusion; distinction without separation. Another term that theologians use, especially in speaking of the relationship of the three Persons of the Trinity, is *perichoresis*, a Greek term which literally means 'dancing together'.

be muted to some degree, unless we begin with Christ as the unique Word and hermeneutical principle.

At the practical level of interpreting and applying the Scriptures, we are reminded that there are certain key elements easily overlooked in our zeal to arrive at 'a word of God to me now'. These are as follows.

- Jesus says the whole Old Testament, not merely a few selected texts, is about him. Many Christians want to go immediately to consider how the text is about them rather than about Christ.
- Jesus is the one mediator between God and man. He is thus the hermeneutic principle for every word from God.
- Jesus is the reason for the creation and therefore interprets the ultimate significance of every datum of reality. In other words, every datum can be related to its reason in Christ.
- Jesus alone has merited entrance into his Father's kingdom.
- We enter that kingdom by being in union, through faith, with Jesus.
- We grow in our Christian lives by being conformed more and more to the image of Jesus, not to the image of Abraham or Moses. These latter, and all the other heroes of the Bible, only have exemplary meaning for us because of their respective relationships to Christ.
- Thus the prime question to put to every text is about how it testifies to Jesus. Only then can we ask how it makes real his rule over us, and makes real his presence with us so that we are conformed more and more to his image.

These matters can only be fairly dealt with on the basis of there being a macro-typology in Scripture. To think otherwise is to suggest that Jesus got it wrong and failed to see that there are texts that do not connect with him. It is to suggest that the Spirit of God was in the business of inspiring irrelevancies. This is not to suggest some oversimplified and reductionist scheme. It is simply to say that no text in either Testament exists without some connection to Christ. We may not always be able to pin it down. We certainly may never exhaust the exegetical potential of a given text. But that the connection is there is a matter determined by the word of Christ and his apostles. Scholarly reserve and humility is one thing; loss of nerve in the implications of the New Testament's teaching is another. The cosmic dimensions of Christology point to the fact that we cannot go beyond referring to Jesus as the interpreter of every biblical text in his being the prime goal of all texts. It means also that no datum in the universe exists in isolation from Christ and his interpretation of its ultimate meaning.

While it is not necessary that there be an explicit reference to the antitype in the New Testament, nor that there should always be a confirmation of a type in prophetic eschatology, it is possible to show that the major dimensions of biblical revelation are found in all three stages of revelation. However, it is sufficient for the theological link to be made between the Old Testament stage from creation, through Abraham and his descendants to David and Solomon, and the theological significance of the life, death and resurrection of Jesus of Nazareth. In the left-hand column of the table below are listed the major events of salvation history, including creation and the fall, which occur in the Old Testament salvation history. The second column lists the way that the prophets use the categories of the first column to describe the future coming of judgment, salvation and the kingdom. The third column lists some of the ways in which Christ fulfils these categories.[40]

The macro-typology of the Bible

Old Testament Salvation History	*Prophetic Eschatology*	**Fulfilment in Christ**
God and his creation.	*God will bring in a new creation*	**Jesus is God the Creator. He is the firstborn of all creation. All things were created by him, through him, in him, and for him. He is the new creation, and brings the new creation as the goal of all God's redemptive purpose.**
Human beings are made from the earth; the breath of God is breathed into them.	*God will raise a renewed people for himself and give them his Spirit.*	**Jesus is fully human, and in that sense is part of the created order. He is the perfectly Spirit-endowed human.**
Eden is the focus of man's dominion over the beasts and the rest of creation.	*The kingdom will be a new Eden. The people of God will have dominion over*	**Jesus is the place where God and man meet. He has dominion as the last**

40. I have not included biblical references here, as they are numerous and the themes are sufficiently prominent to stand without further proof.

The macro-typology of the Bible (continued)

Old Testament Salvation History	*Prophetic Eschatology*	**Fulfilment in Christ**
	creation and the beasts.	**Adam: nature miracles, being with the wild beasts.**
Fall and judgment.	*Final judgment will come on those who do not receive the grace of God.*	**Jesus was made to be sin for us. He suffered the wrath of God and the curse of the covenant for us on the cross.**
Redemption; which includes the following dimensions:	*God will redeem Israel and restore creation.*	**Jesus redeems the whole of creation, not merely the souls of people.**
Covenant and calling.	*A new covenant will take the place of the old.*	**Jesus is the true partner of God; the faithful Son of God, the Seed of Abraham, Son of David.**
Promises of land, people, great name, blessing to the nations.	*The people of God will return to the promised land and be great. The nations will come to share in the kingdom of Zion.*	**The land is to be the new Eden, the dwelling of the people with God. Jesus is that place as well as being God and the people. He is the light to the nations.**
Captivity and release in the exodus.	*The captivity will lead to a redemptive release that amounts to a second exodus.*	**Jesus comes to a race captive to sin, Satan and death. He concludes the true exodus by his death and resurrection.**
Prophetic word.	*God will raise up a new prophet.*	**Jesus is the true prophet who speaks the word of God. He is the embodiment of that word. He gives true and faithful obedience to that word.**

The macro-typology of the Bible (continued)

Old Testament Salvation History	*Prophetic Eschatology*	**Fulfilment in Christ**
Law structures the life of the redeemed.	*The law will be written on the hearts of God's people.*	**Jesus fulfils the law and establishes the structure of the life of the community of the redeemed.**
Redemptive worship, priests and tabernacle.	*A new temple will be the focus of worship and fellowship with God.*	**Jesus fulfils the worship of Israel, above all by being the new temple, and the true priest who offers himself as the one true sacrifice for sin.**
Entry, and possession of the land.	*The people of God will return from the nations to the land of promise.*	**Jesus gains entry through his resurrection and ascension into the inheritance of the people of God. He conquers all the powers that resist the coming of the kingdom of God. By being the place where God meets his people, he fulfils the meaning of the land.**
Nationhood involving judges, prophets, kings, wise men.	*A new nation will emerge with all the offices of rule and worship of God.*	**A new nation of the people of God is established in Christ. He is the true prophet, priest, king and wise man.**
Kingship and temple; Davidic throne.	*There will be a new David and a new temple.*	**Jesus, the King and true Son of David, is also the new temple where God and mankind meet.**
Solomon and national decline.	*The Davidic line that failed under Solomon will be reinstated.*	**Jesus takes the consequences of all the**

The macro-typology of the Bible (continued)

Old Testament Salvation History	*Prophetic Eschatology*	**Fulfilment in Christ**
		failures of his people by fulfilling in himself all that God requires of them.
Destruction of Israel and exile.	*The exile into Babylon will lead to a redemptive act.*	**Jesus goes into exile for his people so that he can lead them out of captivity.**
Prophetic ministries: Indictment, Judgment, Promises of restoration.	*Prophetic ministries: Indictment, Judgment, Promises of restoration.*	**Jesus is the true prophet who judges the world, yet at the same time he brings the words of grace and redemption for all who put their trust in him. He defines the fulfilment of the prophetic promises.**
Return and continued rebellion.	*Post-exilic prophets interpret the continued rebellion of Israel*	**The failures of Israel's return from exile are all dealt with in the true return of the true Israel. The consummation shows that all rebellion is finally to be dealt with.**

Thus we can say that all the texts of the Bible speak about either God, human beings, or the created order, or they speak about some combination of these. Since the fullest revelation of *all* these elements is to be found in Christ, we can say that all Old Testament texts in some way foreshadow or typify the solid reality revealed in Christ. The key to this comprehensive typological interpretation is not ingenuity or wild imagination, but the controlled analysis of the theological significance of the texts in the Old Testament, and the clarifying of their significance in the light of the corresponding theological function of Christ and his gospel. One important implication of this perspective is that it emphasizes that the primary application of all texts is in Christ, not in us or something else. This is in keeping with the New Testament's teaching that our salvation involves our being conformed to the image of Christ. Homiletic applications to us and our contemporaries must be arrived at via the person and work of Christ. If the properties of the antitypes belong to us, it is only by virtue of our faith union with Christ. The pietistic tendency of many preachers and Bible readers to go straight from text to personal application is thus curtailed. Typology and, in broader terms, biblical theology are thus integral to preaching and teaching the Bible in a way that fulfils the purposes for which the Bible was inspired by the Holy Spirit. Biblical theology, with its typology, provides the context for textual exegesis and the grounds for the hermeneutic application of any biblical text to the contemporary believer.

17. THE GOSPEL AND THE THEOLOGICAL DIMENSION (II): BIBLICAL AND SYSTEMATIC THEOLOGY

Foundations of evangelical biblical theology

Biblical theology is one of the most important dimensions to any hermeneutical practice, yet it is probably the most neglected in all the literature on hermeneutics.[1] This neglect is reflected in the way that biblical theology is mostly out of mind amongst Bible teachers and preachers, including evangelicals. It is difficult to explain this neglect, except to propose that common practices of devotional Bible reading and the lack of expository preaching have contributed to this malaise. In my view, hermeneutic theory and the use of the Bible in church or in private devotions that fail to understand the big picture of the biblical narrative are seriously lacking. It is also my constant experience that when Christians are introduced to this method of gaining an overview of the one great redemptive story, they respond with both enthusiasm and surprise that no one ever showed it to them before.

---

1. It is gratifying to note that an entire volume of the Scripture and Hermeneutics Series has been devoted to biblical theology. See Craig Bartholomew, C. Green and K. Möller (eds.), *Out of Egypt: Biblical Theology and Biblical Interpretation*, SHS, vol. 5 (Milton Keynes: Paternoster; Grand Rapids: Zondervan, 2004).

Biblical theology is a formal way of determining and describing the theological plan and significance of the whole Bible. How we pursue the discipline of biblical theology as evangelicals should be consistent with our doctrinal preconceptions of the nature of the Bible as the inspired and authoritative word of God. The hermeneutical spiral comes into play, in that we may find our study of the biblical text demands some modifications in the way we conceive of the characteristics of the Bible. It is not possible to do biblical theology without first having some pre-understanding of the Bible which amounts to a doctrine of Scripture, however embryonic it might be. The idea that there is a logical straight line from exegesis, through biblical theology, to systematic theology or doctrine thus needs some qualification. The impetus for both exegesis and biblical theology is our doctrinal pre-understanding. We would have no reason to pursue a biblical theology if we did not have some notion of the Bible as a book containing theology. For the evangelical, this theology is divine revelation. Enlightenment perspectives tend to reduce the theology to culturally conditioned religious ideas without any necessary correlation with the truth. Thus pre-understandings may be consistent with Christian theism, or they may be utterly opposed to it. But, from an evangelical point of view, we start with the self-authenticating Christ as he is revealed in the self-authenticating Scriptures. Consequently, biblical theology can never be merely descriptive. It is descriptive, but not merely so.

An evangelical theory of knowledge recognizes that spiritual conversion involves a radical reorientation of one's world-view. What Paul refers to in Romans 1:18 as the wicked suppression of the truth of God is reversed and the converting sinner ideally comes to re-evaluate every datum of reality in the light of the newly found orientation to the Creator and the Saviour. This, in turn, is what Paul refers to as transformation 'by the renewal of your mind' (Rom. 12:2), and is an ongoing aspect of sanctification. The same contrast between the unrenewed and the renewed is expressed in the words of Jesus recorded in John 10:26–27: '[Y]ou do not believe because you are not part of my flock. My sheep hear my voice, and I know them, and they follow me.'

This is a key aspect of the church's recognition of the canon of Scripture as the word of God. We consequently conclude from the evidence that the word of Christ, which is the true and reliable word of God, establishes the dogmatic basis for the apostolic and New Testament interpretation of the Old Testament.[2] This recognition that Christ clothed in his gospel is the exegetical

2. See Graeme Goldsworthy, '"Thus says the Lord!" – The Dogmatic Basis of Biblical Theology', in P. T. O'Brien and D. G. Peterson (eds.), *God Who Is Rich in*

and hermeneutical norm of Scripture informs the way we do our biblical theology and formulate doctrine. Our presuppositions, then, are those we have examined earlier in this book. They include the authority of the Bible as the inspired word of God, and its consequent unity.

With these presuppositions to guide us, we can propose several complementary ways of doing biblical theology. For example, we may concentrate on the analytical aspects of a synchronic approach. The focus will be on some fairly narrow range of the text, or on a particular book or corpus. Some evangelical works classified as biblical theologies consist of such book-by-book studies.[3] Others follow a narrative-based model.[4] Some New Testament theologies examine the various corpora.[5] Brevard Childs strives after the best of all worlds by following the narrative structure as well as dealing with literary corpora. He concludes with a series of thematic studies that straddle the entire canon of Old and New Testaments.[6] Relatively few biblical theologies have been written to deal with the whole canon as Childs does. The recent offering by Charles H. H. Scobie is a welcome contribution to this genre.[7]

The evangelical interpreter cannot be satisfied with treatments of the Bible merely as literature, or as history. These usually display Ebionite tendencies that ignore the divine element of revelation and theological meaning. Of course, we do not want a docetic approach to the Bible either; one which ignores its humanity in its literature and history. While the task of biblical theology is to uncover the big picture of biblical revelation, it cannot deal with the theological message without coming to terms with the literary and historical dimensions. The question before us, then, is this: what approaches to biblical theology are consistent with evangelical presuppositions? In applying biblical theology as a hermeneutical tool, we need both synchronic analysis

---

Mercy (Homebush West: Lancer, 1986); and 'The Ontological and Systematic Roots of Biblical Theology', *RTR* 62/3 (December 2003).

3. e.g. Paul House, *Old Testament Theology* (Downers Grove: IVP, 1998).
4. e.g. John Goldingay, *Old Testament Theology*, vol. 1 (Downers Grove: IVP, 2003).
5. e.g. G. E. Ladd, *A Theology of the New Testament* (Grand Rapids: Eerdmans, 1974).
6. B. S. Childs, *Biblical Theology of the Old and New Testaments* (London: SCM, 1992). Although Childs has gone beyond most evangelicals in his acceptance of higher critical presuppositions, his work is on the more conservative end of the spectrum.
7. Charles H. H. Scobie, *The Ways of Our God* (Grand Rapids: Eerdmans, 2003). My own introductory study, *According to Plan* (Leicester: IVP, 1991), is based on a course I taught for several years to local church members.

and diachronic synthesis. The former implies a careful or close reading of the text at the most fundamental level; the close exegesis of the text beginning with its most basic units. The unit should then be understood in the context of its wider unit, usually the book. The ultimate context is the canon of Scripture. The canonical perspective implies diachronic synthesis, and the integration of the parts into the whole. As with any concerns for the relationship of parts to the whole, the two aspects form a kind of dialectic process. With the Scriptures this is not a vicious cycle that has no resolution, for we are always made to return to the person and work of Christ and the ministry of the Holy Spirit as the anchors of the process. Biblical theology is an exercise in understanding how the diversity relates to the unity of Scripture. Central to this is the relationship of the Testaments. Unity/diversity continues to be the concern of the evangelical interpreter. This is a dogmatic construct that informs the way we think about all relationships, including those of the parts to the whole within the canon of Scripture. It is a dogmatic construct drawn from the gospel itself, in that the paradigm of unity and diversity is found in the union of God and man in Christ, a union which points beyond itself to the union of three persons in the one God.[8]

The hermeneutical role of biblical theology

Kevin Vanhoozer states, 'The rift that divides biblical studies from theology will be bridged only if we develop a theological hermeneutic – a theory of interpretation informed by Christian doctrine – and if we simultaneously recover the distinctive contribution of biblical theology to the project of biblical interpretation.'[9] Richard Muller comments, 'If [biblical theology] is the most difficult step in the process of biblical interpretation, it is also the most important one for the determination of the theological implications of the biblical message.'[10] This is not the place to take up a detailed discussion of

---

8. The Trinity is thus the basis for the Christian formation of a general ontology or metaphysics. This is well argued by R. J. Rushdoony, *The One and the Many* (Fairfax, VA: Thoburn, 1978). It was the genius of the Chalcedonian formula of unity and distinction that it provided a Christian way of speaking about the relationship of particularity to generality in all spheres of reality.
9. K. Vanhoozer, 'Exegesis and Hermeneutics', *NDBT*, pp. 52–64.
10. Richard A. Muller, *The Study of Theology*, Foundations of Contemporary Interpretation, vol. 7 (Grand Rapids: Zondervan, 1991), p. 85.

the nature of biblical theology.[11] At the heart of it is the macro-typology that I discussed in the previous chapter. It is to be regretted that biblical theology is so little acknowledged in standard texts on hermeneutics. Yet for preachers and teachers it is probably the most significant part of the practical hermeneutical task after textual exegesis. Biblical theology is most obviously a part of the process in moving from Old Testament texts to us, but is not unimportant for dealing with the New Testament. Not all New Testament texts have the same relationship within salvation history to the modern reader. This is often ignored in preaching and teaching from the Gospels. The words of Jesus are automatically taken as words to the contemporary church and it is simply assumed that they can be applied to the contemporary church without qualification of any kind. Thus, for example, the Sermon on the Mount is treated as a Christian manifesto for all time. It is also a similar failure of those theologies that tend to ignore the unrepeatable and transitional nature of the events in Acts by regarding them as normative for all time.

Biblical theology is central to the interpretative process because, as Richard Lints so succinctly expresses it, 'Our interpretative matrix should be the interpretative matrix of the Scriptures.'[12] It is this matrix with which biblical theology is concerned. The major hermeneutic role of biblical theology is to determine the theological meaning of the parts and the whole. It cannot do this without determining the structural matrix of revelation. It thus helps prevent the short-circuiting of texts and reminds us of the centrality of the gospel as the interpretative norm. Readers short-circuit texts when they ignore the structure of biblical revelation and treat all texts as being essentially on the same level and in the same relationship to the contemporary reader. Exemplary preaching encourages this fault. When, for example, a text about a character in 1 Samuel is immediately milked for 'what it tells us about ourselves', it ceases to be part of a structured, time-related story, the unity of which is found in the revelation of Christ. Instead, it becomes one of

---

11. See Graeme Goldsworthy, 'Is Biblical Theology Viable?', in R. J. Gibson (ed.), *Interpreting God's Word, Explorations*, vol. 11 (Carlisle: Paternoster, 1998). Key areas of the discussion are taken up in C. H. H. Scobie, 'The Challenge of Biblical Theology', *TB* 42/1 (1991), pp. 31–61, and 'The Structure of Biblical Theology', *TB* 42/1 (1991), pp. 162–194. See also D. A. Carson, 'Current Issues in Biblical Theology: A New Perspective', in *BBR* 5 (1995), pp. 17–41.

12. Richard Lints, *The Fabric of Theology* (Grand Rapids: Eerdmans, 1993), p. 269. Lints is concerned that systematic theology should reflect the structure of biblical theology.

a multitude of timeless moralizings or spiritual ideas, the unity of which is found in us.

It is important to see that the analytical (synchronic) tasks should be continually related to the synthetic (diachronic) perspective. Biblical theology is truly diachronic when it looks at the way God has progressively revealed how the kingdom of Christ comes. The synthetic task can only be done by moving in both directions. We have started in the New Testament with the gospel and moved from there back into the Old Testament and forward again into the New Testament. But then we must continue to allow the various parts to interact, so that our understanding grows on all fronts. First and foremost, however, this must be an understanding of God and his Christ.

The biblical theological dimension in hermeneutics is thus the major way of addressing the question of the gap between the text and the reader. It allows the reader to find where he or she actually fits into the totality of biblical revelation. If done with care, it will then provide the valid links between the meaning of a text in its own context and its application to the modern reader.[13] The offending gap is the theological distance of texts from the modern reader. But, if the gap is uniformly closed by the reader to give an undifferentiated immediacy to all texts, the result is hermeneutical chaos. Some forms of pietism and 'Spirit-driven' subjective theology result in such an approach, which lacks any differentiation of texts. The kind of piety that primarily focuses on questions concerned with what the text says about us and our Christian living lacks Christological depth. This premature desire for immediate guidance ignores the relationship of the text to Christ. If there is one mediator between God and man, the man Christ Jesus (1 Tim. 2:5), then to seek understanding of either God or man without recourse to the mediator is a procedure that is Christologically flawed. If we are truly to understand what a text says about ourselves, we must follow the biblical path that leads first to Christ, for he defines who and what we are in him.

The hermeneutical role of systematic theology

Systematic theology, or doctrine, provides the framework of conceptualized faith and belief within which each of us stands in order to come to the Bible with faith seeking understanding. Christian doctrine is the application of the

---

13. This is dealt with in Craig G. Bartholomew and Michael W. Goheen, *The Drama of Scripture* (Grand Rapids: Baker, 2004).

biblical text to the contemporary life of the Christian in the community of the church and in the world. Although it does not have to be formally expressed as systematic theology, biblical truth is doctrinal and is the basis of such systematic formulations. Kevin Vanhoozer emphasizes the need for us to be clear about what we mean by doctrine. His own view is that 'doctrine is direction for the church's fitting participation in the ongoing drama of redemption'.[14] Any expression of the way the Bible impinges upon our understanding of God, salvation, human existence and behaviour is doctrinal. Doctrine states in explicit terms what is often implicit in the Bible. It is the crystallizing of biblical teaching about life as God's people in the church and in the world. The contemporary church is steadily becoming post-denominational. Old denominational loyalties do not figure as largely as they once did. One advantage of this is that evangelicals feel freer now to look for a congregation where they can find good biblical teaching. One disadvantage is that it seems to correlate with a neglect of doctrine. People tend not to ask now why one should be Baptist, or Presbyterian, or Anglican, expecting answers in doctrinal terms. I believe this can be a bad thing, even though it may help to avoid senseless bickering. I am convinced that a healthy attitude to doctrine, to systematic theology, is essential to a healthy attitude to the Bible and its interpretation.[15]

From history we know that the formulation of dogma was largely stimulated by the need to combat perceived error. It was recognized that this was not simply a matter of dotting the theological i's and crossing the t's, but was really a matter of life and death for the gospel. In much popular evangelicalism, the gospel has been submerged in a sea of subjectivism. In many churches, doctrine has a bad press and is written off as cerebral and irrelevant.[16] However, we must maintain that at the simplest level systematic theology is the topical formulation of what, on the basis of the biblical data, Christians should believe as the teaching of God's revelation. It is systematic in that it relates the individual

---

14. I. Howard Marshall, *Beyond the Bible* (Grand Rapids: Baker; Milton Keynes: Paternoster, 2004), ch. 4 (which is a response to Marshall by Kevin Vanhoozer), p. 87.
15. Kevin Vanhoozer, *The Drama of Doctrine* (Louisville: Westminster John Knox, 2005), p. xii, argues that 'Doctrine is a vital ingredient in the well-being of the church, a vital aid to the public witness.'
16. Vanhoozer, ibid., quotes Alan Wolf thus: 'Evangelical churches lack doctrine because they want to attract new members. Mainline churches lack doctrine because they want to hold on to those declining numbers of members they have.'

topics to a perceived unity of truth. It involves a process of abstraction from the individual data of exegesis so that the unity underlying the diversity of texts is perceptible. Historically it has coined and appropriated technical terms which require rigorous control and clear distinctions, but which enable the theologian to discuss the abstractions with the assumption that the meaning of technical language is agreed upon. Every thinking human being engages in such activity of abstraction and coining of technical terms, even in childhood. It is the content, not the intellectual process, which makes theology distinct. For some seemingly perverse reason, Christians resist the task when it comes to biblical truth, many writing it off as arid intellectualism, while at the same time becoming experts in many other areas of concern which are just as abstract and technical but far less rewarding.

The relationship of biblical and systematic theology

What, then, is the process of proceeding from the text to doctrine? The answer to that question is really what biblical hermeneutics is all about. At its heart is the way we understand the theological meaning of the Bible. Most evangelicals would agree that biblical theology looks for the structure of biblical revelation so that we might enquire into the existence of a central theme or themes in the Bible, and so that we might trace the development of particular themes within the Bible. Thus biblical theology is, as Osborne suggests, 'the first step away from the exegesis of individual passages and toward the delineation of their significance for the church today'.[17] Under the impulses of the Enlightenment, biblical studies and theology have tended to grow apart. When considering the distinctions between biblical theology and systematics, and in trying to find their proper connection, there has been a tendency in evangelical scholarship to perceive a logical order in relationship.[18] Thus a typical evangelical approach sees the groundwork done in exegesis of the text as a first step in

17. G. R. Osborne, *The Hermeneutical Spiral* (Downers Grove: IVP, 1991), p. 263. Osborne here uses 'exegesis' in its narrow sense.

18. For the purpose of this study I will be content to regard systematic theology and dogmatics as close enough to consider as identical. One distinction that could be made is that dogmatics specifically belongs to the doctrinal formulation of a particular Christian tradition (denominational). But, since systematics will usually be produced by theologians operating within a given Christian tradition, the distinction can be rather blurred.

biblical theology. Then biblical theology provides the data for the derivation of systematic or dogmatic formulations. Geerhardus Vos regarded biblical theology as a part of exegetical theology, and the order then would be thought of as exegesis of the text, leading to biblical theology, from which systematics are derived.[19] Practically speaking, there is sound logic in this and, in general, it is the way we proceed.

The discussions among evangelical scholars concerning the relationship of biblical and systematic theology seem to have followed fairly constantly this order of *exegesis* → *biblical theology* → *systematic theology*. John Murray, in the second of his two articles on systematic theology, makes certain distinctions between the two disciplines: biblical theology deals with the history of the data of special revelation; systematic theology deals with the data of both general and special revelation, 'in its totality as a finished product'.[20] In criticizing the non-evangelical biblical theologies of the twentieth century, Murray rightly rejects the preoccupation of G. E. Wright and others with the notion that revelation is constituted by God's acts as distinct from God's word. Murray, however, does not really take the discussion beyond this polemic against non-evangelical biblical theology and systematics, and he asserts that systematics is wholly dependent upon a proper attention to biblical exegesis. He maintains that systematic theology should be rooted in biblical theology, because special revelation comes to us in historical form that cannot be neglected if we are to appreciate the unity of special revelation. One role of this unified perspective of biblical theology is to prevent the wrong use of texts in supporting doctrine. So far, so good!

Richard Gaffin refers to the fatal divorce of biblical theology from dogmatics,[21] a matter that, more recently, also concerns Francis Watson.[22] But a divorce fatal for whom? Like Murray, Gaffin majors on the undeniable point that good systematics needs good biblical exegesis. Good biblical theology is 'the basis and source of Systematics'.[23] He also refers to the views of Vos, and

---

19. G. Vos, *Biblical Theology, Old and New Testaments* (Grand Rapids: Eerdmans, 1948), p. 13.
20. John Murray, 'Systematic Theology', *WTJ* 26 (1963), p. 33.
21. Richard Gaffin, 'Systematic Theology and Biblical Theology', in John H. Skilton (ed.), *The New Testament Student and Theology* (Nutley, NJ: Presbyterian and Reformed, 1976).
22. Francis Watson, *Text and Truth* (Grand Rapids: Eerdmans, 1997), pp. 1–8.
23. Gaffin, 'Systematic Theology and Biblical Theology', p. 36; a quote from B. B. Warfield.

concludes that both Vos and Murray are concerned in particular with 'the importance of biblical theology for systematics'.[24] Biblical theology, then, impresses the systematician with the historical character of revelation (not to be confused with Wright's idea of history *as* revelation). It is indispensable to systematics because it is 'regulative of exegesis'.[25] Gaffin, then, sees that it is the task of biblical theology to minister to systematics. The fatality mentioned above seems to afflict the systematician in so far as he attempts to theologize without good exegesis and biblical theology informing him. But we should also consider the task of systematics to minister to biblical theology.

A more recent article in this debate comes from Gerhard Hasel.[26] This is a largely historical survey of the changing roles attributed to biblical theology in relation to systematics once the idea of the former as a distinct discipline was accepted. Krister Stendahl's now famous distinction between 'what it meant' (biblical theology) and 'what it means' (systematics), along with some of Stendahl's critics, comes under scrutiny. The debate has now shifted largely due to the influence of existential theologians such as Bultmann and Tillich. Whatever we may think of these radical thinkers, they point to another dimension hitherto largely ignored – the role of presuppositions or prejudice in understanding.[27] Once again, in his evangelical concern that theology should be biblical, Hasel concludes with a series of propositions about the nature of biblical theology, the last four of which are instructive of his perspective on the relationship of the two disciplines. Biblical theology, he maintains, must not accept a structure imposed from systematics or external philosophical systems.[28] For Hasel biblical theology is foundational for systematics. Again the order is clearly asserted: systematics is dependent on biblical theology and therefore derivative of it.

One exception to this general perspective is seen in Grant Osborne's treatment. He first states that biblical theology 'collates the partial theologies of individual passages and books into an archetypal "theology" of Israel and the

---

24. ibid., p. 41.
25. ibid., p. 44.
26. Gerhard Hasel, 'The Relationship Between Biblical Theology and Systematic Theology', *TJ*, NS vol. 5, no. 2 (1984), pp. 113–127.
27. Prejudice, as Hans-Georg Gadamer pointed out, is not to be avoided but recognized. For him, prejudice and presupposition are the same thing, and it can be altered through the processes of the hermeneutical spiral.
28. Some earlier so-called biblical theologies were organized according to doctrinal categories.

early church'. Then, 'Systematic theology re-contextualises biblical theology to address current problems and to summarise theological truth for the current generation.'[29] Again, 'Biblical theology constitutes the first step away from the exegesis of individual passages and toward the delineation of their significance for the Church today.'[30] In his discussion of the relationship of the various kinds of theology, Osborne gives the main controlling function to historical theology. Although he describes exegesis, biblical theology and systematics in trialogue, it is historical theology that does the talking back to the others.[31] But he moves on from there to show how he thinks biblical theology and systematics are interdependent. Osborne asserts that the order, *exegesis* → *biblical theology* → *systematics*, is too simple. The key point, which is rather muted, is this: 'The dogmatic pre-understanding of the biblical theologian interacts in a type of "hermeneutical circle" as each discipline informs and checks the other.'[32] It is a pity that Osborne has not developed this important point, for it takes us beyond the simplistic position expressed by Murray and others in which *exegesis* → *biblical theology* → *systematics* is maintained.

A more recent discussion of the matter is found in contributions by Kevin Vanhoozer and Howard Marshall.[33] Vanhoozer, in company with Gaffin and Watson, laments the divorce between theology and biblical studies. He begins by informing us, 'I will argue that the gulf currently separating biblical from systematic theology can be bridged by better appreciating the contribution of the diverse biblical genres, and that a focus on literary genre could do much to relieve the ills currently plaguing both their houses.'[34] His concerns are important, for they warn against ignoring the function of literary genres as instruments of world-views. But his major concern is the construction of systematics. More needs to be said about the role of systematics in the construction of biblical theology.

---

29. Osborne, *The Hermeneutical Spiral*, p. 14.
30. ibid., p. 263.
31. ibid., p. 264.
32. ibid., p. 269.
33. Kevin Vanhoozer, 'From Canon to Concept: "Same" and "Other" in the Relation Between Biblical and Systematic Theology', *SBET* 12/2 (1994), pp. 96–124; I. H. Marshall, 'Climbing Ropes, Ellipses and Symphonies: the Relation Between Biblical and Systematic Theology', in Philip E. Satterthwaite and David F. Wright (eds.), *A Pathway into the Holy Scripture* (Grand Rapids: Eerdmans, 1994), pp. 199–219.
34. Vanhoozer, 'From Canon to Concept', p. 96.

Howard Marshall's concerns are similar to Vanhoozer's in seeking to understand the way from the biblical data to the formulation of theology and doctrine. He suggests, among other things, that there is a parallel or an analogy between the relationship of the Old Testament to the New and the relationship of the canonical texts to the formulation of systematics. While the analogy cannot be pressed beyond the process of theologizing, this is a useful point, for it can, I believe, be demonstrated that within the totality of biblical revelation the process of conceptualizing is taking place during the course of salvation history. The Old Testament does not simply tell the story of Israel, but in the telling the story is interpreted in a way that lays the foundation for post-biblical systematic conceptualizing. This is nowhere clearer than in the reapplication by the prophets of the story to make it the basis of their eschatology. This insight, however, could have been pushed further. For, just as the relationship of Old Testament to the New invites an emphasis on the process and progressiveness from Old to New, there is also a vital dimension of the New providing the hermeneutical key to the Old. Thus, to follow the parallel again, while there is an undoubted methodological progression from biblical theology to systematics, there is also a vital input of systematics that makes biblical theology viable. The hermeneutical spiral of systematics and biblical theology bears some parallels with the hermeneutical spiral of New Testament and Old Testament.

In like manner, we might suggest that we need to encourage Christians to understand the biblical basis for doing biblical dogmatics. Maybe we need to start with a biblical theology of doctrine. The first words of God to Adam and Eve are foundational in establishing the relationship of mankind to God and to the world. The various covenantal statements are integral to doctrine as truth for life. In the same way, the law is a doctrinal formulation. The prophetic revelation in all its forms is doctrinal, as is the reflection on truth and life in the Psalms and the wisdom literature. If Jesus and the apostles were biblical theologians (which would also make them historical theologians), were they also dogmaticians? The fact that neither Jesus nor the apostles produced systematic theologies is hardly the point. They were in the ongoing business of applying theology to life. The situation of a progressive revelation eventually gives way to the deposit of truth which must be guarded (1 Tim. 6:20), and to the truth once for all delivered to the saints (Jude 3). In criticizing the linear hermeneutics of Scripture, through biblical theology to doctrine, as a failed experiment, Joel Green comments:

> Rather than restricting scripture's role in theology to that of 'foundation' or 'source', it is important to recognize that the Bible is not raw material waiting for theology to

> happen. It is already theology. 'Faith seeking understanding' is already going on in its pages. Here one finds 'theology' both in its critical task of reflection on the practices and affirmations of the people of God, to determine their credibility and faithfulness, and in its constructive task of reiteration, restatement, and interpretation of the good news in response to ever-developing horizons and challenges.[35]

Theology within the Bible is surely one of the impulses that led to the later discipline of dogmatics. Since dogmatics is concerned with norms in Christian truth, we might suggest that what we now call dogmatics gains its impetus from the recognition of the closure of the canon and the corollary that all the data for a biblical theology are now in, until the consummation brings the clarifying revelation of universal regeneration.

Careful and accurate exegesis is absolutely vital to the integrity of Christian thought and action. But textual exegesis is but one part of the process. While we can find in many non-evangelical scholars much valuable exegetical insight, we often have reason to lack confidence in their overall understanding of what truth is revealed in the Bible. This is due to the philosophical prisms through which the exegetical material is refracted in order to arrive at doctrinal formulations. I have already suggested possible reasons for the evangelical preoccupation with exegesis. It is possible to maintain an evangelical view of the authority of the Bible in theory, but to allow this to become subservient to incipient liberalism in the way the Bible is used. Thus Gerald Bray suggests that some expressions of neo-Pentecostal theology lean to liberalism, because in the end experience interprets the objective word.[36]

To summarize this discussion, I repeat what I have proposed elsewhere about the relationship of biblical and dogmatic theology:

> From one point of view, biblical theology is what makes dogmatics necessary. If it were not for the progressive nature of revelation, then all texts would stand in the same general relationship to the believer. Dogmatics is the discipline of saying what the total redemptive and revealing activity of God means for us now. It recognizes that all texts do not stand in the same relationship to us now, but that in view of the unity of revelation they do stand in some identifiable relationship to all other texts

35. Joel B. Green, 'Scripture and Theology: Failed Experiments, Fresh Perspectives', *Interpretation* 56/1 (2002), p. 18.
36. Gerald Bray, 'Theology in the Church: Unity and Diversity in Christian Theology', in N. M. de S. Cameron (ed.), *The Challenge of Evangelical Theology* (Edinburgh: Rutherford House, 1987), p. 78.

> and therefore to us. Biblical theology examines the diversity within the unity . . . The dogmatic basis of biblical theology lies in the fact that no empirical datum of exegesis has independent meaning, and no datum of theology or interpretation has independent meaning.[37]

Exegetical and theological data are interdependent. The Bible itself must determine for us what the Bible is. We add to this perception the fact that our evangelical presuppositions about the Bible are part of our dogmatic formulations of the doctrine of God and revelation. This is only to say that 'the fear of the Lord is the beginning of wisdom', and that a biblical philosophy and a biblical epistemology undergird the evangelical theological process. Thus the movement from exegesis to systematics involves biblical theology and hermeneutics. The importance of dogmatics, then, is that it is in a sense the finished task. It depends on good exegesis, but it also depends on a sound application of biblical theology and hermeneutics. In turn, it provides the unifying framework for understanding the ramifications of the exegetical conclusions. The exegete who is not thinking dogmatics is probably also not thinking biblical theology and hermeneutics. This exegete is not thinking about the dogmatic formulation of biblical unity and so his distinctions, the data of individual texts, become separation of data. He is already on the road to liberalism.

The theological application of the hermeneutical spiral, then, may be summarized as follows.[38]

- Because the gospel of Jesus Christ has laid hold of us, we start with certain gospel-driven presuppositions and doctrinal pre-understandings about the nature of the Bible. The biblical theologian begins with dogma that is formed through conversion and faith and that grants permission to proceed.
- We deal with individual texts by exegetical study of particular expressions of God's revelation in terms of their cultural setting, semantic organization and philological message.
- Biblical theology looks for the unity behind the individual passages by examining the development of ideas in the progressive revelation. In this way, more expansive themes which underlie the individual themes may come to light.
- Systematic theology is a distinctly Christian activity, in that it assumes

37. Goldsworthy, 'Thus says the Lord!', p. 37.
38. Osborne, *The Hermeneutical Spiral*, pp. 264ff.

the completion of revelation. It is in a position to ask the question about what is finally to be believed about the themes of biblical truth. It seeks to formulate Christian doctrine for the present. Thus it synthesizes the findings of exegesis and biblical theology into dogma or doctrine.

- Meanwhile, because theologians usually belong to the ongoing confessional community of the church, they do not theologize in isolation from their contemporaries or their predecessors. Historical theology will influence the way we do exegesis, biblical theology and systematics. We do not 'reinvent the wheel' doctrinally, though we may regularly test its integrity.
- These processes may cause us to adjust some of our presuppositions or pre-understandings. This in turn will affect our outcomes and conclusions about the meaning of the Bible for us today, and so on.

The inter-relatedness of these aspects of theologizing means that a book focusing on one approach to theology will usually make reference to the others from time to time. This is particularly true of systematics, which in one sense is at the end of the process and will to a greater or lesser degree indicate its dependence on the earlier stages. Some writers have attempted a truly integrated approach with varying degrees of success.[39] Richard Lints makes an important point that a theological framework should remain constant, while a theological vision changes as culture changes.[40] He goes on to propose a theological framework based on redemptive history. He does not elaborate on this, but it is another perspective on the relationship of systematics and biblical theology. The hermeneutical spiral is a constant reminder that the various theological disciplines are inter-related and coinhere in the sense that each implies the others.

---

39. An evangelical approach which is only moderately successful in its integration is the three-volume work by G. R. Lewis and B. A. Demarest, *Integrative Theology* (Grand Rapids: Zondervan, 1994). Another kind of integration is found in the Roman Catholic six-volume work of Michael Schmaus, *Dogma* (London and Kansas City: Sheed and Ward, 1968–77), especially in vol. 1.
40. Lints, *The Fabric of Theology*, p. 26.

18. THE GOSPEL AND CONTEXTUALIZATION

Culture and understanding

The cultural gap between the writer and the reader remains an important consideration in interpretation. The person of Jesus Christ makes two things inescapable. On the one hand, we acknowledge that the Bible is divine communication; a word from God given with the express purpose of making himself known to us. On the other hand, that word is communicated through human beings in human words within a specific set of cultural contexts. However, it is a mistake to think of this cultural contexting as an impenetrable barrier, since the origin of the divine word lies outside such contexts and is not itself an expression of them.[1] Within human cultures, the divinely driven process of redemptive history and the goal towards which it moves are not themselves expressions of any culture of this fallen world. God's word is not subject to any human cultural contexts, but rather judges all of them. But human cultures exist because humans reflect in their communities

1. Craig Bartholomew, 'Babel and Derrida: Postmodernism, Language and Biblical Interpretation', *TB* 49/2 (1998), p. 327, refers to the importance of the Word who was from the beginning. Postmodernism allows no such presupposition for the way language works.

the community of the Trinity. We do it sinfully, but really nevertheless. All human culture reflects or images the 'culture' of the divine community of the Trinity.

William Larkin proposes that '[T]o understand the Bible's metacultural framework and authoritative message with regard to culture, it will be necessary to discover its attitude toward the human cultures to which it speaks and above which it stands.'[2] The essential question we face here has been well framed by Larkin:

> Can evangelicals put forward a comprehensive hermeneutical framework of biblical realism which will bring order out of the chaos by presenting a 'balcony view', a metacultural grid, through which to view and assess the various competing hermeneutical proposals?[3]

Postmodernism, with its critique of certainties and norms, has forced us, who believe that both of these exist, to re-examine the grounds for such belief. While we readily accept the need to recognize our own cultural conditioning and the cultural gaps that exist between us and the biblical worlds, we cannot leave behind us the biblical position of a world over which God exercises his sovereign rule. In such a world the word of God is God's activity by which norms are established. Furthermore, such normative features exist in all cultures, even if unrecognized. The confusion comes because they are corrupted into idolatrous world-views.

Given the normative role of the Bible, one of my purposes in this chapter is to attempt to discern some essentials of the biblical theology of interpretation and culture. In what way does the Bible itself provide the rules for dealing with its own phenomenon of being a word expressed through human words in cultural context? Does the Bible indicate that there is, within the world's cultural diversity, a human cultural unity which is sufficiently strong to enable us to bridge the gaps and to allow for the differences in the cultures of the biblical authors, and for those between the reader/communicator and the audience/recipient?

---

2. William Larkin, *Culture and Biblical Hermeneutics* (Grand Rapids: Baker, 1988) p. 192. See also Grant Osborne, *The Hermeneutical Spiral* (Downers Grove: IVP, 1991), ch. 15; David Hesselgrave and Edward Rommen, *Contextualization, Meanings, Methods, and Models* (Grand Rapids: Baker, 1989).
3. William Larkin, 'Culture, Scripture's Meaning, and Biblical Authority', *BBR* 2 (1992), p. 174.

The modern emergence of contextualization

From one point of view, contextualization is just another name for the outcome of hermeneutics.[4] It involves certain transformations of a text from one context to another in a way that aims at enabling its meaning to be understood in the receiving culture. But since the meaning is given in cultural terms, how can we preserve the meaning while transforming the cultural expression of it? The first context might be the original one of the biblical text, or it might be the language, history and culture of a modern missionary. As soon as we attempt any transformation, we are faced with the need to make judgments about the nature of reality in so far as this affects meaning. Contextualization implies that the reality of the message is clothed in something that is relative to a particular culture. This includes the linguistic context of a foreign (biblical) culture. Bible translation is thus an important aspect of contextualization. The problems of translation, along with the account of Babel, may suggest that language is the most incorrigible of all cultural barriers. Humanly speaking, it is by far the most difficult of all the cultural relativities to bridge. But Babel also indicates that the real cultural stumbling block is spiritual.

Paul Hiebert, writing as a missiologist, looks at the subject of contextualization as the outcome of the history of cross-cultural missions, specifically of Protestant missions in India.[5] David Hesselgrave rightly comments that it is a mistake to see contextualization as beginning with the coining of the term in the 1970s. It is as old as missionary activity itself.[6] He also comments that missiologists sometimes define the word so as to prescribe the desired outcome rather than describing what is actually happening in the contextualizing process. Furthermore, some treat the matter as if it were solely a Christian concern, when in fact it is the concern of all communicators. We need to try to pin down a workable definition of contextualization. It is clearly

4. The word 'contextualization' must surely rank among the less happy additions to the English language, involving as it does successive transformations from a simple noun to an adjective to a verb and back to a noun. I would prefer the simple denominative verbal noun 'contexting', but the cumbersome 'contextualization' has become generally accepted.

5. Paul Hiebert, 'Critical Contextualization', in J .I. Packer (ed.), *The Best in Theology* (Carol Stream: Christianity Today, 1987), pp. 387–400.

6. David Hesselgrave, 'Contextualization and Revelational Epistemology', in Earl D. Radmacher and Robert D. Preus (eds.), *Hermeneutics, Inerrancy, and the Bible* (Grand Rapids: Zondervan, 1984), p. 693.

something that has gone on from the beginning and was thus a process that existed long before it was regarded as a distinct concern. The heart of the problem for evangelicals, notes Hesselgrave, is that 'there is not yet a commonly accepted definition of the word *contextualization*, but only a series of proposals vying for acceptance'.[7] Osborne defines contextualization as 'that dynamic process which interprets the significance of a religion or cultural norm for a group with a different (or developed) cultural heritage'.[8] The significance of the term 'dynamic' needs to be kept in mind, particularly in relation to the translation of the Scriptures. A study group of the Lausanne Congress (1974) defined contextualization as 'meaningful communication in forms that are real to the person, and his full response to the Lord in repentance and obedience of faith that affects his whole life-style, his attitude, and his values, etc.'[9] In this definition there appears to be a strangely postmodern and quite unwarranted shift of focus from the text and its meaning to the readers and their responses.

Hesselgrave gives an inclusive working definition:

> Contextualization is the process whereby representatives of a religious faith adapt the forms and content of that faith in such a way as to communicate and (usually) commend it to the minds and hearts of a new generation within their own changing culture or to people with other cultural backgrounds.

It is primarily undertaken in six areas of missiological activity: translation of the Bible, the interpretation of Scripture, communication of the gospel, instruction of believers, incarnation of truth in the lives of believers, and the systematization of the Christian faith.[10]

Problems in contextualizing

Any process of bridging cultural gaps requires the recognition of the problems involved as well as the implementation of a way forward. Hiebert warns against a number of problems that easily arise. These include the denial of

---

7. David Hesselgrave, *Contextualization: Meanings, Methods, and Models* (Grand Rapids: Baker, 1989), p. 35.
8. Osborne, *The Hermeneutical Spiral*, p. 318.
9. Quoted in Larkin, *Culture and Biblical Hermeneutics*, p. 153.
10. Hesselgrave, 'Contextualization and Revelational Epistemology', p. 694.

absolutes in a way that detracts from the uniqueness of Christ; the assumption that form and meaning can be easily separated; dehistoricizing of the biblical message; and an uncritical appraisal of the sinfulness of human cultures.[11] We face the difficulty of avoiding, on the one hand, the old attitudes of cultural imperialism and, on the other hand, modern relativism and syncretism. Hiebert proposes a critical contextualizing which involves the understanding of pertinent aspects of the receiver culture, the understanding of the scriptural position on these aspects, and finally giving the indigenous people the task of evaluating their customs in the light of Scripture.[12]

Hiebert's plan offers only a very broad set of guidelines to the issue of contextualization. If, as he suggests, there is some kind of metacultural framework that provides stability, we need to be sure that it is biblical. The idea of the two horizons or, in the opinion of some evangelical missiologists, the three horizons, is relevant.[13] Thiselton describes the horizon thus: 'Every reader brings a horizon of expectation to the text. This is a mindset, or system of references, which characterizes the reader's finite viewpoint amidst his or her situatedness in time and history.'[14] The Christian communicator, it is said, must attempt to fuse his own horizon of understanding with that of the text, and then he must attempt to bridge the gap between his own horizon, as it has been informed by the text, and that of his hearer. This third horizon exists whether or not there is an obvious cross-cultural gap. The term 'fusion' is fraught with danger, as the Chalcedonian model would remind us. Unity without fusion, and distinction without separation, must surely apply in this matter. In making the biblical horizon understandable to another culture, both must remain distinct. The biblical culture is not the same as our own, and should not be transformed to seem to be so. Richard Howell explains it as 'the interpreter's encounter and response with both the Word of God and with his own culture and that of the receptor'.[15] Carson is right to warn against the possibility that the receptor

---

11. Hiebert, 'Critical Contextualization', pp. 393f.
12. ibid., pp. 395–398.
13. D. A. Carson, 'A Sketch of the Factors Determining Current Hermeneutical Debate in Cross-Cultural Contexts', in D. A. Carson (ed.), *Biblical Interpretation and the Church* (Carlisle: Paternoster, 1984), p. 17. The notion of the fusion of horizons owes much to the new hermeneutic of Fuchs and Ebeling.
14. Anthony Thiselton, *New Horizons in Hermeneutics* (Grand Rapids: Zondervan, 1992), p. 34.
15. Richard Howell, 'Transcultural Theology and Contextualisation', *ERT* 25/1 (2001), p. 33.

horizon may be allowed to impose alien conceptual structures onto the Bible. Nevertheless, as Thiselton points out, both text and interpreter are conditioned by their place in history and tradition. 'For understanding to take place, two sets of variables must be brought into relation with each other.'[16] The comments of Miroslav Volf are relevant as he urges us not to lose sight of our differences. 'To become a Christian means to divert without leaving: to live as a Christian means to insert a "difference" into a given culture without ever stepping completely outside to do so.'[17]

There is another development in recent missiological theory that Carson regards as fundamentally dangerous. He is right in pointing out that all biblical truth comes to us in cultural guise. Simply to use human language is to culturalize. Yet it is possible for a culturally conditioned discourse to point beyond itself to another culture, and to do so with some accuracy. The problem before us is to try to understand what aspects of the cultural milieu of revelation can be adapted without undermining the truth of revelation. The task is to establish what is supracultural in the Scriptures or in one's personal religion, and to communicate that. There is, nevertheless, a problem in the ambiguity of the term 'supracultural'. Carson comments:

> If it refers to the fact that God has revealed certain truth that is objectively true in every culture, it is not offensive; but if there is an attempt to distinguish among parts of the Bible, for instance, according to whether this snippet or that is supracultural or culture-bound, then the attempt is fundamentally misguided and the pursuit of the supracultural an impossible undertaking . . . every truth from God comes to us in cultural guise: even the language used and the symbols adopted are cultural expressions.[18]

Carson proposes a more realistic approach: 'What we must do is so fuse our horizon of understanding with that of the text that we sympathetically and reflectively grasp the principles and arguments and coherence of the subject matter, and do our best to apply such matter in our own lives and cultural contexts.'[19] Compare this with Osborne, who writes, 'A plenary verbal, inerrantist

16. Anthony Thiselton, *The Two Horizons* (Exeter: Paternoster, 1980), p. 16.
17. Miroslav Volf, 'When Gospel and Culture Intersect: Notes on the Nature of Christian Difference', *ERT* 22/3 (1998), p. 204.
18. Carson, 'A Sketch of the Factors Determining Current Hermeneutical Debate', p. 19.
19. ibid., p. 20.

approach to contextualization accepts the supracultural nature of all biblical truth and thereby the unchanging nature of these scriptural principles.'[20] He goes on to say that evangelical contextualization is aware of the transformational character of the current receptor context. While the *content* of biblical revelation is unchanging, the *form* in which it is presented is ever changing. An obvious difficulty in Osborne's approach is that content and form are not always easy to separate.

Is there a biblical theology of contextualization?

The various attempts at definition and the talk of horizons merging or fusing all indicate that we are talking about the need to adapt the way the biblical message is presented in order that someone whose culture is different from the original one (or ones) of the biblical writers can understand the essentials of what it is about. Certain biblical examples immediately spring to mind. For example, in Nehemiah 8:8 the law was read to the returned exiles, and a group of Levites gave the sense so that the people could understand the reading. Whether it was a linguistic necessity due to the Hebrew of the Scriptures having been superseded by Aramaic as the spoken language, or a religious one due to the people's new post-exilic situation, does not alter the fact that a process of interpretation was needed. In Hellenistic times the Hebrew Bible was translated into the Greek Septuagint as a Targum similar in purpose to the Aramaic Targums. All Bible translations share such linguistic functions.

William Larkin has sketched a biblical theology of sorts relating to culture and language.[21] The question raised is that of the existence of some metahistorical and metacultural framework which would enable one to stand above the different historical periods and cultures of later readers and hearers. This would, says Larkin, provide a hermeneutical bridge from which to interpret and apply Scripture's message across time periods and cultures. In this he agrees with Hiebert. He argues that such a framework does exist and 'can be known from a systematic exposition of the Bible's own teaching about

20. Osborne, *The Hermeneutical Spiral*, p. 319.

21. Larkin, *Culture and Biblical Hermeneutics*, pp. 193ff. Some of the other contributors to this subject have given fairly half-hearted surveys of biblical material. A concerted attempt to survey the subject comprehensively by the method of biblical theology seems to be lacking.

hermeneutics and culture'.[22] The reason for this confidence is that the Bible has its origins in God outside any human culture. 'The message proclaimed in Scripture is by its very nature intended to be universally and eternally valid.'[23]

Since contextualization involves some form of cultural adaptation, we should try to pin down what we understand by 'culture'. Larkin gives his definition thus: 'Culture is that integrated pattern of socially acquired knowledge, particularly ideas, beliefs, and values (ideology) mediated through language, which a people uses to interpret experience and generate patterns of behaviour . . . so that it can survive by adapting to relentlessly changing circumstances.'[24] He regards the ideology as primary, while behaviour is secondary. The primary medium for acquiring, using and transmitting culture is language.

Let us, then, attempt to survey cultural (including linguistic) adaptations in the process of progressive revelation and, therefore, in mission. To be true to our biblical-theological method, we should begin by noting that the pre-eminent act of contextualization is God's adaptation to our humanness in the incarnation. Our Christological perspective reminds us that, in this adaptation from the heavenly 'culture' of the Trinity, the second Person of the Godhead did not in any way cease to be God. The incarnational adaptation was into the sinfully corrupted human sphere that nevertheless continues to bear the image of God. The *both-and* perspective is helpful in our consideration of cultural adaptation. The purpose of the incarnation was to bring about change in human beings and, ultimately, in human culture so that both will be restored to the divine image. The divine culture is not lost in adaptation to the human. We cannot overlook the effects of sin and the fact that the receptor culture is in revolt against the truth of God. The divine communication is understandable, but is wilfully resisted unless the Holy Spirit works to overcome that corrupt resistance by his regenerating power.

Now let us go back to the beginning to trace some of the cultural adaptations in the unfolding of redemptive revelation. In the beginning God speaks to Adam and Eve in human language and establishes his word as the medium of divine-human communication. In doing so God is not invading some alien culture, but rather is establishing the first human culture by his word. This word, in a way that is analogous to the person of Christ, is both divine and human: God's word in human language. This is its point of contact as

22. ibid., p. 191.
23. ibid., p. 192.
24. ibid.

God addresses human beings made in his image and likeness. The word is always in this sense incarnate and never a voiceless or wordless mystical communication.[25] This beginning to the biblical story establishes the significance of all human language as the echo of God's word to man. This word from God structures the reality within which the human pair is given the cultural mandate of dominion over creation. Its first expression is Adam's naming of the animals. Culture is a part of God's ordained pattern for human existence, but it is meant to be subject to God's word. All human culture reflects, albeit corruptly, this divinely ordained culture. Communication in Eden was direct and without prophetic mediation. This situation will be recovered in the *eschaton* when, as Jeremiah says, 'No longer shall each one teach his neighbour and each his brother, saying, "Know the LORD," for they shall all know me' (Jer. 31:34).

The human rebellion against God results in a marring of the image of God and the distortion of all human cultural expression.[26] The demonizing of culture results in a diabolical, human-centred response to God. Culture is never neutral. It can only be godly or godless. Theologically speaking, then, culture is the expression of our communal humanity in relation to God (whether people perceive it or not). Just as there are only covenant-keepers or covenant-breakers in the human race, so there are only two types of culture: those that express a right relationship to God and reflect his image, and those that express a rejection of God and rebellion against him. In a fallen world there is no perfection, so godly cultural expressions are always compromised to some degree by sinfulness.

It is against this background that we might raise the question of a metaculture. While I reject the idea of human experience that is acultural, I must accept that our being created in the image of God and the universal sense of deity are points of contact with God.[27] It may be stretching things a little to say that the intra-trinitarian reality is the metaculture, yet the Trinity *is* the basis of all valid human expressions of culture. We simply cannot escape our

25. This is a point that is overlooked in the practice of so-called Christian mysticism. Mysticism seeks a unity without distinction to be achieved without a mediator.

26. Volf makes the pertinent point ('When Gospel and Culture Intersect', p. 202) that 'the environment in which Christians live is not a foreign country, but rather their own proper homeland, property of their God. If they are alien in it, it is because and in so far as their own land has been occupied by a foreign power.'

27. That is, they belong to our essential being even though they are sinfully repressed. They exist as relational realities that suffer when the relation is soured by rebellion.

imageness, but this is far removed from some Platonic ideal of form which transcends all culture.[28]

After the fall, developments in the godless line of Cain (Gen. 4) show the potential for culture to be an expression of rebellion against God. The city, which has its beginnings with Cain and Nimrod, will continue to be a prime expression of cultural godlessness throughout Scripture, for example Babel, Sodom and Gomorrah, Pharaoh's city, Jericho and Babylon.[29] The latter becomes the symbol of all urban godlessness which must be overthrown before the city of God replaces it. The motif of Babylon versus Jerusalem warns against cultural adaptation that amounts to assimilation. We need to consider in what way a concrete reality such as Jerusalem is transformed in the process of revelation. The hermeneutic methods of literalism impose a very rigid no-go zone on the whole process of contextualization. Form and content are perceived to be static in the biblical story. This is a fundamental error.[30] Transformations do occur in form and meaning, but they are always towards the gospel-based redeemed culture of the *eschaton*. Jerusalem renewed, as in Revelation 21 – 22, is the norm of the redeemed culture for humankind.

Abraham's call in Mesopotamia is a call to leave a culture expressive of pagan rejection of God for one based on the covenant promises of God. Though the nations are to receive a blessing through the covenant people, the forms and content of God's revelation to Israel are never to be adapted to the cultures of these other nations. We have, however, some examples of the opposite process of foreigners being joined to the covenant people to share in Israel's blessings. The inclusion of Moses' wife, Rahab, Ruth and others involves their adaptation to the culture of Yahweh's people. This is ideally the culture created by the covenant relationship of this people to God, even though it is in fact confused by sin. Strangers or foreigners who were resident among the Israelites were thus subjected to the law of Moses.

---

28. Science, politics and ethics are all aspects of human culture. The relevance of the Christian doctrine of the Trinity to such things is discussed at length by R. J. Rushdoony, *The One and the Many* (Fairfax, VA: Thoburn, 1978). The trinitarian perspective on culture is also emphasized by Howell, 'Transcultural Theology', p. 32.
29. See Jacques Ellul, *The Meaning of the City* (Grand Rapids: Eerdmans, 1970).
30. Literalism follows a sound instinct in resisting the separation of form and meaning, but it fails in not allowing for the actual transformations that occur in Scripture.

Israel's culture under the law involves a freedom within clear parameters which are intended to reveal and reflect God's character and the nature of the covenant relationship. The law lays on Israel, as God's redeemed people, the necessity of avoiding the idolatrous culture of the Canaanites. They spoke a similar language and wrote with the same *aleph-bet*, but they were nevertheless to stay separate. The holiness code in Leviticus is a potent rejection of non-theistic culture. Israel's failure to remain culturally and theologically separate leads to all kinds of syncretism and idolatry. Solomon's cultural adaptations to his foreign wives bring about his apostasy and the destruction of Israel. The history of Samuel, with the institution of the monarchy, continues the theme of the cultural incompatibility between Israel and her neighbours. The problem with the highly cultured Philistines was not, as is popularly thought, due to some kind of barbarism, but to the fact that they were 'uncircumcised': they were outside the covenant and worshippers of other gods.

Apostasy in the time of Elijah and Elisha involved a radical cultural adaptation which was in the process of eradicating the covenant-based culture of Israel. About this time Jonah went to Nineveh, and there is little in the narrative to suggest intentional contextualization. It is doubtful that the Ninevites' response was a mass conversion to faith in the God of Israel.[31] Also, the account of the healing of Naaman the Syrian (2 Kgs 5) contains a reverse contextualization in that Naaman recognizes the connection between the forms and the content of Israel's faith to the point where he requests a cartload of Israelite soil to take home with him.

Linguistic contextualization is an area that hardly rates a mention in the Old Testament. Linguistic pluralism is portrayed as beginning with Babel and the confounding of languages in judgment. Language barriers rate little mention in the Old Testament, though they obviously existed. In later prophecy and narrative there seems to be a greater concern for the linguistic and cultural differences

---

31. Covenant worship was centred on the temple in Jerusalem. Not until the new temple, whose presence by his word and Spirit becomes universal, does the role of Israel as light to the nations find fulfilment. The Ninevites were to show themselves as the arch-enemies of Israel and Yahweh not long after Jonah. The historical context of Jonah at a time of almost complete Israelite apostasy, as well as the narrative itself, suggests that the purpose of the book is to remind Israel that God can raise up a people for himself even in Nineveh, and is not dependent on Israel to fill that role. I do not think it likely that it was intended to be a missionary kick-starter.

among the other nations.[32] Pentecost signals a reversal of Babel, in that the gospel is heard by each in his own language. The question of form and content is difficult, especially with regard to language. Form is a great deal more complicated than simply identifying the individual words and syntax of a particular language, as we shall see in the consideration of Bible translation. The Hebrew language underwent changes as all languages do. Hebrew, as a spoken language among God's people, was superseded by Aramaic and then by Greek. But a translation of early Hebrew into *koinē* Greek may require only superficially a change in form. Stability in meaning requires a stable frame of reference.

For such stability, we come again to the gospel event as God's established point of reference for all reality. In Christ, God accommodates himself to the human context without in any way adapting to the sinfulness of humanity. Furthermore, his act of contextualization was supremely the event of redemption which was designed not to save individual's souls, but to save whole people to be part of the culture of his kingdom. This came through the breaking in of the *eschaton* in the person of Jesus. The 'servant' passage in Philippians 2:5–11 is relevant. Without falling into the kenotic error,[33] we still recognize that God the Son emptied himself of heavenly glory while remaining fully God. The adaptation, then, did not involve ontological change. This 'cultural' contextualization involved identifying as a recognizable first-century Jew while standing out against all distortions of human nature and culture, and against the present corruption of the revealed will of God for first-century Jews.[34] In fact, it meant conforming to the Israelite prophetic norm in a way no other Jew was able to do. The contextualization of meaning must be governed by the question, 'What do you think of Christ? Whose son is he?' The relationship of the message of the Bible to Jesus has to remain one of the relationship to the Jesus who really came to us in time and space, not to some abstraction of a Jesus-ideal. Everything else in the legitimate process of contextualization stems from that principle.

---

32. See, e.g. references to 'language(s)' in Gen. 11:1, 7, 9; Deut. 28:49; 2 Kgs 18:26, 28; 2 Chr. 32:18; Neh. 13:24; Esth. 1:22; 3:12; 8:9; Ps. 114:1; Isa. 19:18; 33:19; 36:11, 13; Jer. 5:15; Ezek. 3:5, 6; Dan. 1:4; 3:29; 6:25; Zech. 8:23; Acts 2:6, 8; Rev. 5:9; 7:9; 13:7; 14:6.
33. (Gk) *Kenosis*: emptying; the error probably unintentionally suggested by Charles Wesley's famous hymn line, 'Emptied himself of all but love.'
34. When some commentators identify Jesus as a revolutionary, they focus on this 'against the stream' aspect of his life and ministry. They may fail to identify in what way Jesus conformed to the covenant norms still perceptible in Jewish culture.

The gospel, then, is the ultimate paradigm shift that must define the relationship of form and content. The use of the Old Testament by New Testament writers must be considered as a form of contextualization. It involves a reinterpretation of events and promises of the Old Testament into the new context revealed by the advent of the Christ. The first stage in this after the fact of the incarnation itself is the interpretation of Jesus that he himself gives in terms of the Old Testament Scriptures. The process of contextualization reaches its climax in the post-resurrection appearances and discourses, notably Luke 24. The lesser transformations involve the writing of the New Testament in Greek, and the indication at Pentecost that language differences can be overcome. A major theological transformation is from the essentially promissory form of the Old Testament message to that of fulfilment in Christ. In order to achieve this, the promissory form is left intact as the preface to the fulfilment. The New Testament's transformations from the Hebrew Scriptures never change the Israelite-Jewish context of the message. The world of the Old Testament remains intact.

We can thus regard the entire New Testament as a contextualizing literary and theological activity.[35] New Testament contextualization follows that of the Old Testament in maintaining a consistent perspective on the world. We can summarize the biblical perspective in the following way.

(a) There is one world and one human race.
(b) The whole human race is fallen and under the judgment of God.
(c) God's plan of salvation involves his activity which will benefit all nations.
(d) Israel is distinct as the elect nation and the representative of the human race through whom salvation will come for all nations. Out of this representative nation comes the one true Representative Israelite (and therefore human being), Jesus of Nazareth.
(e) The cultural norm is the new man in Christ and the church as Christ's body. The division between Jew and Gentile, which for most Jews had become an absolute, is healed so that the relationship reflects the divine intention to include all nations under the Abrahamic covenant. The people of God consists of converted Jews and converted Gentiles who share their blessings. The New Testament does not suggest that this essential relationship of Jew and Gentile, nor of the Christian church to its antecedents in historical Israel, can ever be

35. See Dean Flemming, *Contextualization in the New Testament* (Leicester: Apollos, 2005).

relativized or contextualized away. The consummation vision in Revelation 7 is of the perfect nation of Israel, the 144,000, along with the numberless multitude from every nation, tribe and language group, gathered in worship around the throne of God and of the Lamb.

(f) The proclamation of the gospel to those of foreign cultures is never done apart from the cultural context of the saving activity of God in history, for example:
- Jesus always maintains the Israelite context of his message (John 4; Mark 7:24ff.).
- Apart from the theological transformation due to the gospel event, Pentecost allows only for language differences. The gospel is preached to Jews from many nations in exactly the same terms.
- Proclaiming the historic Jesus implies his cultural background as a first-century Jew.
- Philip introduces the Ethiopian to the Jewish gospel (Acts 8).
- Peter's vision in Acts 10 cleanses the Gentiles but does not change the message. Such barriers between Jew and Gentile that need to be removed are due to a corruption of Jewish culture and are not authentic.
- Paul and Barnabas at Lystra (Acts 14) fail at first to deal with the pagan context with almost disastrous results. When the problem becomes apparent, they make the adjustment by actually distancing themselves from the cultural perspective of their hearers. Their point of contact is the witness of God in nature (implying the universal sense of deity).
- Paul at Athens (Acts 17) insists on the oneness of God's world and the centrality of the resurrection of Jesus. To identify the 'unkown god' is, as in Lystra, to proclaim him first as the Creator.[36] The fixed point of reference for knowing this god is to know him as God who raised Jesus. This, for the Greeks, is a culturally absurd move.

The big picture provided by a biblical theological survey leaves us with a number of non-negotiable aspects to the question of contextualization. First, the centrality of the gospel as the meaning of all Scripture and the

36. In both Lystra and Athens Paul's proclamation reflects the theology of Romans 1, i.e. God is evident in all of creation, but the truth concerning him is universally suppressed and corrupted.

the original biblical languages, but are translated from simple English versions. These and other variations in translation philosophy really urge the necessity of trying to answer the question, 'When is a translation not a translation?'

The modern theory of translation has focused mainly on two different emphases. The one, sometimes called formal equivalence, is also described as 'more literal' or 'transparent'. It involves a conscious effort to retain, as far as the receptor language allows, the structure and equivalent *wording* of the original source language. There are those who defend this general approach as that which best preserves the meaning of the text. The other theory, which is an emphasis of the Summer Institute of Linguistics and United Bible Societies, is called dynamic equivalence or, more recently, functional equivalence. This, it is claimed, aims at the equivalent *sense* rather than the equivalent wording.

Let us try to put this in perspective by modifying an example proposed by Raymond Van Leeuwen using Psalm 1:1.[40] We will assume that the various translations are meant to reflect the meaning of the accepted Hebrew Masoretic text. A woodenly literal translation that preserves the Hebrew word order and uses the same metaphors would be something like this:

Happy the man
that has not walked in the counsel of the wicked ones,
and in the path of sinners has not stood,
and in the dwelling place[41] of mockers has not sat.

The NKJV, a formal equivalence translation, is word for word the same as the KJV, except that the English is modernized, and the RSV and ESV are almost exactly the same:[42]

Blessed is the man
who walks not in the counsel of the wicked,

---

40. Raymond Van Leeuwen, 'On Bible Translation and Hermeneutics', in C. Bartholomew, C. Green and K. Möller (eds.), *After Pentecost: Language and Biblical Interpretation*, SHS, vol. 2 (Carlisle: Paternoster; Grand Rapids: Zondervan, 2001), pp. 289–290, compares Ps. 1:1 in the RSV with the more dynamic equivalent translation in the NRSV.

41. The Hebrew noun *môšāb* is derived from the root *yšb*, the verbal form of which can mean either 'sit' or 'dwell'.

42. Modern versions that eliminate archaisms such as 'thee' and 'thou', and the present tense endings in 'th', etc., involve the simplest form of linguistic contextualizing.

nor stands in the way of sinners,
nor sits in the seat of scoffers.

These demonstrate the more 'literal' or 'transparent' formal equivalence approach. But the NRSV has moved heavily in the dynamic equivalence direction and also into inclusive gender language. An extreme dynamic equivalence translation is found in The Living Bible:

Oh, the joys of those
who do not follow evil men's advice,
who do not hang around with sinners,
scoffing at the things of God.

One tendency of the more dynamic translations is to iron out metaphors. Thus 'to walk in the counsel' is reduced to the idea of following advice. But, as Van Leeuwen points out, there is a progression in the original from *walk* to *stand* to *sit*. This anticipates the final stage in the last part of the psalm: the wicked *perish*.[43] The dynamicists have translated so as to interpret the metaphors. They have also filled in certain perceived gaps that the original has left open, such as the object of the scoffers' scorn. Their opponents argue, rightly I believe, that the more this approach is used, the more the translation moves away from the culture and world-view of the Bible. But, as I have already argued, cultures are not equally valid in that the biblical culture is chosen and steered by God's word. It is one thing to aim at a linguistic translation, but this should not become a cultural translation.[44]

---

43. Van Leeuwen, 'On Bible Translation and Hermeneutics', p. 289: '[So] that the verbs (walk, stand, sit) instantiate a gradual move towards the immovable stasis of sin.'

44. Two recent books have been added to the already considerable literature on the theory and practice of Bible translation. These are Leland Ryken, *The Word of God in English* (Wheaton: Crossway, 2002); and Glen Scorgie, Mark Strauss and Steven Voth (eds.), *The Challenge of Bible Translation* (Grand Rapids: Zondervan, 2003). Ryken, a professor of English at Wheaton College, served as literary stylist for the translation team of the ESV. The other volume, which generally favours the NIV, contains contributions from a range of notable scholars including Moisés Silva, Don Carson, Dick France, Bruce Waltke, Douglas Moo and Andreas Köstenberger. See my review article of these two books, 'He's a Jam Doughnut? When is a Translation not a Translation?', *The Briefing*, issue 306, March 2004.

Leland Ryken rightly questions the attempt to separate form from meaning. But it becomes clear that it is not simply a matter of one or the other, of literal or dynamic, but of how far along a continuum between the two any translation is positioned. Ryken identifies some commonly held fallacies that are actively promoted by dynamic equivalence theory and practice. These are fallacies about the nature of the Bible, about translation and about Bible readers. For example, the move to produce a colloquial Bible with a simple vocabulary and syntax assumes that it is a uniformly simple book.[45] Another fallacy is that the Bible is primarily a book of ideas rather than of concrete particulars. This leads to the frequent changing of concrete metaphors into abstractions. Further, dynamic equivalence seems to assume that the Bible is a modern book, and that it is devoid of mystery or ambiguity. This, says Ryken, is the reverse of what is actually true.[46]

In dealing with fallacies about translation, Ryken identifies the first as the dichotomy between meaning and words. He refers to Anthony Nichols' view that Eugene Nida's[47] assertion that 'words are merely vehicles for ideas' is docetic, in that it ignores the concreteness of human language. We might also add that it ignores the reality of God acting in space and time. The biblical world-view and the gospel cannot be reduced to ideas that are separated from their concrete forms. Nichols says dynamic equivalence underestimates the relationship of form and meaning, blurs the distinction between translation and communication, and jeopardizes the 'otherness' of the biblical text.[48] Other fallacies include readability as the ultimate goal of translation. What good, asks Ryken, is readability if a translation does not accurately render what the Bible actually says? Perhaps one of his most important points is to refute the idea that translation should make the Bible approximate our contemporary idiom. This, he rightly argues, is to remove the world of the biblical text from view.[49] One extreme example of this is Clarence Jordan's 'translation' of the Gospels into the vernacular of the southern

45. Ryken, *The Word of God in English*, p. 67.

46. ibid., p. 78.

47. Eugene Nida, more that anyone, established the notion of dynamic or functional equivalence.

48. Nichols has criticized the dynamic equivalence approach in 'Explicitness in Translation and the Westernization of Scripture', *RTR* 47/3 (1988); and in 'Translating the Bible', *TB* 50/1 (1999).

49. Ryken, *The Word of God in English*, p. 91.

United States.[50] To reinforce the Southern idiom, he has the events of Jesus' life taking place in the State of Georgia. We must then ask the question, 'Where did the exodus happen?' or, 'Should Paul, in Romans 1:16, have told us that the gospel is "to the American first"?' The biblical world and historical period are simply non-negotiable under the guise of translation. A less extreme dynamic equivalent is found in Kel Richards' Australian vernacular rendition.[51] Richards rightly preserves the biblical time and place so that Jesus is a first-century Jew born in a Roman province in the time of Caesar Augustus.[52]

Ryken questions the assumptions that modern unchurched readers cannot handle any theological or technical terminology; that figurative language is beyond them; that they require short sentences; and that the Bible is more difficult for modern readers than for the original readers. He quotes Robert Martin:

> It is better to teach each new generation the meaning of the Bible's technical terms than to eliminate them and produce a generation [of people who] are biblically and theologically illiterate from having suffered long-term exposure to inaccurate and imprecise versions of the Bible.[53]

Ryken argues not only as a literary scholar, but also as an evangelical Christian who believes that a theology of the Word bears on translation. In particular,

---

50. Clarence Jordan, *The Cotton Patch Version of Matthew and John* (New York: Association, 1973), quoted in Hesselgrave and Rommen, *Contextualization: Meanings, Methods, and Models*, pp. 168–169.
51. Kel Richards, *The Aussie Bible (Well, bits of it anyway!)* (Sydney: Bible Society NSW, 2000). In the Introduction, Peter Jensen suggests that this is not a translation but a retelling. This comment only serves to highlight the question of what a translation is.
52. Unfortunately the illustrator has largely failed in this regard. For example, he depicts Joseph and Mary hiking into Bethlehem (apparently in Australia) dressed as modern Australian country-folk, and passing the town's War Memorial which features a statue of a World War I Australian 'digger' (soldier) with his Lee Enfield .303 rifle! The illustrator does not understand the danger of forsaking the biblical world, nor does he appreciate that the modern vernacular of any language is quite capable of telling a story about events long ago and far away. Illustrations should reflect the actual story.
53. Ryken, *The Word of God in English*, p. 115, quoting Robert Martin, *Accuracy of Translation and the New International Version* (Carlisle, PA: Banner of Truth, 1989), pp. 37–38.

the authority of the Bible, the inspiration of the biblical authors and the plenary inspiration of the Bible lead logically to a 'translation that is essentially literal'. Thus, 'We can rest assured that the Bible as it was written is in the form that God wants us to have.'[54]

In my opinion, one of the most important points that Ryken makes is this:

> A good translation preserves the full exegetical or interpretive potential of the original biblical text. Conversely, a translation is inadequate to the extent to which it diminishes the interpretive potential of the original text.[55]

This is the experience of any expository preacher, and is the reason why we teach the biblical languages to our future pastors and preachers. We are well aware of the problems that individual translations can present when the translator allows his or her theological prejudices to dictate some outcomes. The quest for simplicity or readability is similarly misplaced. Ryken is concerned about the pre-emptive interpretative decisions made in some dynamic equivalent versions. Multiple meanings and deliberate ambiguities in a text are ironed out, while the rich imagery and figurative language of the Bible are often ignored. There is a tendency to reductionism in some dynamic equivalent translations. We might call it a dumbing down of the text and its meaning. Instead of seeing the text as capable of elevating people by redeeming them and their culture, extreme dynamic equivalence implies a readership with no such potential, so that the text must be made to fit them *where they are*.

Ryken's book concludes with an appendix by John Collins, a professor of biblical studies, entitled 'Without Form, You Lose Meaning'. Collins says:

> There are four specific ways that I, as a Bible specialist, find dynamic equivalence to be opposed to accuracy: (1) such translations make interpretive decisions for the readers, and run the risk of deciding wrongly; (2) such a philosophy requires the translator to resolve ambiguities for the reader; (3) this philosophy urges the translator to interpret images and figures for the reader; and (4) this philosophy generally leads to the loss of important repetitions. The feature these defects have in common is that *the reader is limited to what the translator allows him to see*.[56]

---

54. Ryken, ibid., p. 129.
55. ibid., p. 140.
56. ibid., p. 301 (italics mine).

How, then, do the preacher and teacher decide such basic issues as 'What is a good translation?' 'What version should we read in church?' 'What text should I preach and teach from?'[57] I would offer the following suggestions.

- While in practice formal and dynamic equivalence are towards opposite ends of a continuum (no translation is completely one or the other), there are nevertheless major differences in theoretical approach. Dynamic equivalence errs in the direction of reader-response hermeneutics.
- Dynamic equivalence translations tend to make the original text and its meaning more opaque when they remove its form or its particularities.
- While all translation involves a measure of interpretation, translation should not try to pre-empt exegesis and hermeneutics. Translations should not try to take the place of commentaries.
- Translation should be linguistic, not cultural. It is the role of the teacher to assist people to understand the biblical culture.
- Translation should make the language contemporary, but leave the story ancient.
- Translation should be done in the context of the whole canon of Scripture and allow the biblical world to be what it really is. The canon provides a universal grid of the action of God in salvation, which can only be departed from by creating a parallel universe of ideas that is inimical to the biblical gospel.
- Above all, translation should, as far as possible, preserve the full theological significance and exegetical potential of the original. If you cannot have a Bible study from a translation without constantly having to refer to, for example, 'what Paul literally says', or 'what the Greek actually says', then that translation should be discarded.
- There is a difference between translation using the vernacular and the 'vernacularization' of the message. The vernacular is quite capable of telling the story about ancient times in far-away places. To make it sound as if the events take place in the present and in our culture is a gross distortion of the biblical message.

Perhaps it is time for formal equivalence protagonists, of which I confess to be one, to acknowledge that all translations involve some degree of interpret-

57. See David Dewey, *Which Bible? A Guide to English Translations* (Leicester: IVP, 2004).

ation, of subjective judgment and of dynamic equivalence.[58] Nevertheless, there are, I believe, profound philosophical and theological differences involved, especially in the meaning of *meaning*. Dynamic equivalence enthusiasts should ask themselves if the role of translation is primarily to bring the text down to the level of the world and culture of the modern, often unbelieving, reader. Or is it to help the reader, whoever and wherever he or she may be, to enter into and to be transformed by the gospel culture and world of the Bible? Finally, I would suggest that the protagonists on both sides need to acknowledge that it is one thing to try to enunciate a philosophy of translation, but it is much more difficult to put it to work consistently in the taxing and complex task of translating the Bible.

---

58. Allan Chapple, 'The English Standard Version: A Review Article', *RTR* 62/2 (August 2003), pp. 61–96, convincingly argues that the ESV is not consistently successful in its formal equivalence aims. Chapple concludes that all translations are hybrid and the difference between formal and dynamic equivalence is one of degree.

19. THE HERMENEUTICS OF CHRIST

Summary

We have now surveyed the subject of hermeneutics from several points of view. We began by seeking to understand the need for a distinct discipline of evangelical hermeneutics and what it sets out to achieve. Essentially we are concerned with understanding the Bible as the word of God, and we have considered the major factors which distance us from the original Author, his secondary authors and their texts. While it would perhaps be an exaggeration to suggest that hermeneutics takes in the whole of Christian knowledge, it is not too much to say that no Christian knowledge is arrived at apart from the application of the principles of interpretation. Because it is now generally recognized that all investigation or reading is done from a position of pre-understanding or by engaging a range of presuppositions, we have examined the need for a frank recognition of the presuppositions of biblical theism. At the heart of this is the focus of the New Testament on the person and work of Jesus Christ. He is set forth as the Word of God, the truth, and the final interpretation of the Old Testament Scriptures. This has required us to work towards a gospel-centred hermeneutic.

After attempting to delineate our task in hermeneutics, I have looked briefly at selected aspects of the history of biblical interpretation. It was also necessary to investigate the biblical-theological basis for hermeneutics as the background to a critical assessment of the history of interpretation. The aim in this book was to try to understand first of all something of the hermeneutics of the apostolic period, and then the subsequent developments which betray a shift away from biblical norms of hermeneutics. I have traced briefly the course of interpretation through the ages in order to illustrate the increasing influence of various philosophies on hermeneutics, particularly in the handling of the Bible. The unavoidable conclusion is that many non-Christian philosophical influences have contributed to the corruption of the hermeneutic process.

The Reformation represented a largely successful attempt to eradicate the foreign philosophical influences that had shaped Catholicism. Then the Cartesian and Kantian revolutions in philosophy and the subsequent Enlightenment led to theological liberalism which, as we saw, involved the same kind of humanistic starting point or presuppositions as Catholicism. At the same time, the heirs of the Reformation struggled to maintain the presuppositions of Reformed Christian theism, which sought to establish its philosophical position from revelation in the Bible.

As we traced the development of Enlightenment hermeneutics we noted the shift to philosophical hermeneutics, so that what began as a practical issue of understanding difficult biblical texts became a matter of a general philosophy of understanding. The historical-critical method and subsequent developments marked a trend in hermeneutics that would go on reflecting current philosophical trends. A philosophy of understanding is not a bad thing in itself, but our concern is whether or not such developments are focused on the centrality and supremacy of Christ as the Word.

Evangelical interpreters are thus faced with two tasks. First, it is perhaps inevitable that we will never be able to anticipate all the new developments in hermeneutic theory. We will therefore find new and unexpected challenges coming from the academic world. These require us to consider our response to them, while trying to ascertain how much we can take advantage of such scholarship that proceeds from non-biblical presuppositions. Second, we should be constantly seeking to develop contemporary expressions of Christian theism in ways that remain consistent with the truth as it is in Jesus. It is this struggle to formulate a coherent Christian epistemology and metaphysics which will always be a part of an authentic evangelical hermeneutics.

The hermeneutics of the person of Christ

It is common in systematic theology to distinguish between the person of Christ and his work. But to distinguish is not to separate. The person and work of Christ may never be separated, since they are interdependent. We may, however, ask questions about some of the implications of each in turn. To begin with, what are the hermeneutical implications of the person of Jesus Christ, the God/Man? I have considered a number of these in the course of this study, but it would be useful now to try to crystallize them.

The person of Jesus of Nazareth was an immediate hermeneutical challenge to all of his contemporaries, including those who followed him. He showed himself as fully human, and yet made claims of a unique relationship to God the Father. The result was a variety of responses, ranging from charges of blasphemy deserving of death to submission and worship as is due to the one true God. Of course, the formal Christian doctrine of the incarnation, of the God/Man, of the two natures and their relationship, took some time in coming, but the reality of God come in the flesh is what is clearly presented in the New Testament.

I have expressed my conviction that the later formulation of the Council of Chalcedon (451) served to provide a sound doctrinal expression of the implications of the biblical data. I am quite unconvinced by those who relegate the formula of Chalcedon to some kind of Hellenistic intrusion. Its understanding of the relationship of the one to the many is reflective of the thoroughly Hebraic view of unity and distinction. Chalcedon simply gives us a way of speaking about the relationship of the divinity of Jesus to his humanity. This is the basis for a distinctly Christian view of every relationship in all of reality, beginning with the Trinity and the incarnate Son of God.

The formula of Chalcedon does not attempt to solve the mystery of the God/Man, but it sets the bounds for thinking and speaking about the nature of Christ without falling into heresy. In summary, it states that Jesus is true God; Jesus is true human; there is unity without fusion; there is distinction without separation. Thus Jesus is the *God/Man* and the relationship between the two natures is *unity/distinction*. It is important to note that unity/distinction is a relational thing. The ontological question about those things relating in this way must be answered as well. The unity/distinction in Jesus now helps us come to terms with the relationship of Jesus to the One he addressed as Father. The Creed of Athanasius defines the Catholic faith as the worship of one God in Trinity, and Trinity in Unity. As W. H. Griffith Thomas pointed out, the doctrine of the Trinity is required by the gospel.[1] In coming to terms with the fact that Jesus is God, Christians had to learn to speak about God in

1. W. H. Griffith Thomas, *The Principles of Theology: An Introduction to the Thirty-Nine Articles* (London: Church Book Room Press, 1951), p. 22.

a way that could accommodate that truth. That is why the Creed of Athanasius gives the same kind of treatment to the Trinity as it does to the two natures of Christ. God is unity/distinction of Father, Son and Holy Spirit. The difficulty of providing an adequate expression of both doctrines can be seen in the way the creed must constantly alternate between describing the sameness and the difference in these relationships.

The history of Christological thinking shows that a number of representative heretical answers to the question about the person of Christ share a common error. Thus we have the following false solutions to the relationship of Jesus' divinity to his humanity.

- Ebionism assesses Jesus Christ as *humanity without divinity* (special, but still only human).
- Docetism sees Jesus as *divinity without humanity* (he only appeared to be human).
- Apollinarianism asserts that *divinity diminishes humanity* (the divine Spirit replaces the human spirit).
- Nestorianism has *divinity plus humanity* (two persons, two natures, moral unity only).

Heresies show us how people, even Christian people, have misunderstood the truth of God's word. A heresy usually exalts one truth above other aspects of truth, so that the proper perspective is lost and the truth becomes distorted. Because they address the same kind of relationship, heresies about God are usually attempts to solve the mystery of the relationship of Father, Son and Holy Spirit in terms of fusion or separation. These match the heresies concerning Christ: Ebionism, Docetism, Apollinarianism and Modalism all express the primacy of the one over the many. Nestorianism and Tritheism express the primacy of the many over the one. But trinitarian Christianity in its Christology and theology maintains the equal ultimacy of both the one and the many. What, then, are the hermeneutical implications of this unity/distinction of the two natures of Christ? A number of these have already been discussed in this study, and it will suffice to give some examples here.

First, as I have already asserted in several contexts, the relationship of Jesus' humanity to his divinity points to his role of mediator and to his being the representative manifestation of the whole of reality in perfectly ordered relationships. Because I have dealt with this in chapter 16, I will only reiterate that it affects our view of the relationship of the divine word to the human word in Scripture. This has been too often dismissed as irrelevant to the question of the reliability of Scripture. No one is claiming that the human authors of the biblical books were, like Jesus, without sin. Rather it is being claimed that the Holy Spirit oversaw the process, so that what the human authors said is what God says. Since they are human authors, the incarnation also demands that we do not create for ourselves a docetic Bible by ignoring the human dimensions, including the historical and cultural contexts. In chapter 5 I referred to the failure of the allegorists at this point, because they misunderstood the nature of the unity of the Testaments by not allowing for their proper distinction.

Second, the unity/distinction perspective that we derive from the Trinity and the incarnation enables us to deal with the biblical ideas of the one who represents the many. The whole salvation process in the Old Testament anticipates the role of Christ in the key offices or ministries in which one person represents the whole community. This perspective is made explicit in later reflections on the significance of Adam's fall. His role as the federal head representing the whole human race is implied by the history of humanity from Genesis 4 onwards. But passages such as Romans 3:10–18, which quotes a number of Old Testament texts, Romans 3:23, 5:12–19 and 1 Corinthians 15:21–22, 45–49 show that Adam is the representative one for the many who are accounted sinners. In the same way Jesus Christ is the representative one for the many who are accounted righteous. The antecedents to this ministry of Christ include the representative priests, prophets and kings of the Old Testament. The principle of the one representing the many, and the relationships between them as unity/distinction, cannot be removed from the Bible without completely undermining its essential message.

Third, the unity/distinction perspective provides the means of reconciling antinomies or apparent contradictions in emphasis. The obvious example here is the relationship of divine sovereignty and human responsibility.[2] Some speak of human freedom, which is acceptable if all they mean is that we are conscious of making choices and decisions. It is better to speak of responsibility rather than freedom, since true freedom has been lost because of sin. Then the question becomes one of the relationship of such decision-making to our bondage to sin and death on the one hand, and to the sovereign will of God on the other. It seems to me that any Christian who accepts that Jesus is both God and Man, in whom indeed there is both divine sovereignty and true human freedom, and these without any conflict, ought to be able to accept the

2. A good Old Testament example is the hardening of Pharaoh's heart. In the narrative it is said sometimes that he hardened his own heart, and on other occasions that God hardened it.

reality of both divine sovereignty and human responsibility. This is not to understand it, but to accept its mystery.

Fourth, the incarnational unity/distinction perspective requires the reader to allow for his or her real humanity. The new hermeneutic and reader-response criticism have emphasized this, but often at the expense of the reality of God speaking through his word. We avoid both a docetic Bible and a docetic reader. This is not to ignore the divine inspiration of the word and the ministry of the Holy Spirit in authorship, transmission and in the believer's reading, but it is to take full account of the humanity of the Bible and of the reader. To avoid an Ebionite Bible and an Ebionite reader, we recognize the Holy Spirit's gentle and generous ministry at all stages of the word of God coming to us and being received with understanding. The incarnational imperative to account for our own humanity is the basis of the hermeneutical spiral.[3] What a blessing that the original disciples and apostles were not all theologians of the calibre of Paul. The incarnational presence of God was initially to the humble and the 'ordinary' folk. God made himself known through Jesus to the non-erudite. God's hermeneutic was the humble son of Mary and Joseph. Hermeneutical theories which forget that simple fact are in danger of isolating the word of God in the heady, and often unsavoury, ivory towers of those who, like the Athenians, love to spend their time 'in nothing except telling or hearing something new' (Acts 17:21).

Fifth, the unity/distinction perspective is important in doctrinal formulation, so that the truly biblical perspective is maintained in doctrines. In a broad sense it applies to the relationship of signs and symbols to the things they signify. The hermeneutics of the sacraments is a case in point. 'This is my body' has meant different things to different groups. The question to be resolved is the relationship of the symbols of bread and wine to the things signified: the body and blood of Jesus. By the time of the Reformation, Rome had long since hardened its view in which the two became fused: the bread became the actual body; the wine became the blood. This is unity without distinction. At the Reformation some Protestants seemed to have over-reacted to the doctrine of transubstantiation and to have reduced the relationship to one of bare memorial; distinction with very little unity. The Calvinists, whose

3. A point made by Jens Zimmermann, *Recovering Theological Hermeneutics* (Grand Rapids: Baker, 2004). He emphasizes, as I have done, the significance of Calvin's understanding of the relationship of our knowledge of God and our knowledge of ourselves. Calvin's epistemology thus stated is in fact an early assertion of the hermeneutical circle.

sacramental theology is represented now in the Anglican Articles as well as the Westminster formulas, expressed much more of a unity and distinction viewpoint. In taking the bread and wine, we can truly feed on Christ in our hearts by faith.

A more contemporary dispute involves the question of human sexuality. Pro-homosexual arguments often try to discredit the force of biblical texts that specifically target homosexual practices. What they seem to fail to recognize is that these are expressive of a more basic issue of the creation of *'ādām* as male and female. The relationship of the sexes is unity/distinction. When a man cleaves to his wife and they become 'one flesh' (Gen. 2:24), they are still distinct persons of different gender. Both homosexuality and 'unisex' represent unbiblical attempts to fuse so that there is unity without distinction.[4]

Sixth, the unity/distinction perspective underlines the reality of non-literal interpretation and typology. Symbols, images and metaphors need this perspective at one level, but there is also the level where things described, without imagery or metaphor, as historical fact may also function symbolically of some greater reality yet to be revealed. The validity of promise/fulfilment and of typology as ways of understanding the structure of biblical revelation depends upon the unity and the distinction between the various stages of salvation history. Literalism in interpreting prophecy is an exercise in unity without distinction.

Seventh, it is worth pointing out that one of the implications of Jesus as representative reality is that every thing or fact in reality has some point of unity with, and some point of distinction from, every other thing or fact in reality. To put it another way, the doctrines of the Trinity, the incarnation, creation and the distinction between God and the creation establish the unity/distinction of all things.

The hermeneutics of the work of Christ

The hermeneutics of the work of Christ stem from the salvation-historical aspect of the gospel. There is coinherence with the hermeneutics of the person of Christ. But here we enquire into the doings of the God/Man. What was it that Jesus achieved for us in his life, death, resurrection and ascension

---

4. Every relationship of a man to a woman involves some kind of unity and some kind of distinction. The nature of the unity/distinction is determined by the specifics. Thus a man's relationship to his wife, his mother, his daughter and the check-out lady are all unity/distinction, but all different.

that affects the way we understand the biblical text and, by implication, the whole of reality? I have dealt with this in various ways in the course of this study, and it will suffice here simply to draw together some of the main points. We are concerned with what the gospel, seen from the point of view of the actions of God through his Son, implies for the way we understand the Bible.

First, the overall promissory structure of the Old Testament, which anticipates the coming of the Saviour, makes it imperative that we see the whole of the Old Testament as interpreted by the person and work of Christ. The dynamics of salvation history in the Old Testament point towards, and find fulfilment in, the dynamics of the gospel. Because we are dealing here not with mere ideas, but with the actions of God in space and time, it is not only what the God/Man is, but what he does in space and time that provide the ultimate meaning of all that happens in space and time. The ministry of Jesus the fulfiller has immense hermeneutic significance, since it draws together all the variety of themes and events in the Old Testament that foreshadow the fullness of God's purposes.

Second, the fact of the incarnation as God's action has multiple implications. We might mention first of all the pre-existence of Christ, the second Person of the Trinity. He is God from all eternity and the Creator of all things. That this eternal Creator-Word becomes flesh and dwells among us sums up the action of God in Christ. Again it is not an idea, but the real coming of the Christ to his own people. Who better to interpret all things than the One who is the Creator and sustainer of all things? Paul's discourses about the cosmic Christ, the one in whom God is summing up all things, stem from his understanding of the gospel event.[5] Because reality includes humanity as the pinnacle of creation, the restoration of reality must involve the representative human, the last Adam, as a person who lives and acts in space and time.

Third, the incarnation points to the divinity of God's revealing and redeeming Word, coming amongst us to lead us into the truth, as he also redeems us from truth-denying sin and death. What Jesus did in his ministry here on earth is, of course, an expression of his person as the God/Man, and we cannot speak of his action apart from his being. But the redemptive work of Jesus guarantees that the people of God have been put into a positive relationship to the word of God. We have already considered the roles of Christ as the God who speaks, as the spoken Word, and as the true compliant receiver who responds perfectly to God's word. In terms of Christian life and practice, it means that we can read the Bible and know that, in Christ, we have

5. I have referred to this in some detail in ch. 16, in the section on Jesus and reality.

become true sons because his Sonship is attributed to us. Though we go on in some degree corrupting the word and its meaning, our imperfect interpretations of the word are justified by Christ. As Vern Poythress indicates, 'Christ is our redeemer with respect to interpretive sinfulness.'[6] Incarnation and atonement are inseparable. The hermeneutics of the cross are the hermeneutics of repentance and submission to the crucified Lord. Any attempt to reduce the message of the Bible to morality and the mere imitation of Jesus ignores the centrality of the cross. Yet this moralizing is where so much evangelical application of Old Testament texts leads us. The work of Christ should be the magnet that draws our interpretative applications of all texts to the gospel.

Fourth, the doing of Christ demands that the humanity of God's word be treated carefully and understood for what it is. The work of the incarnate Christ includes the living of a perfect human life in relation to God the Father. It shows that God has not finished with humanity, but rather is restoring it. All critical study of the Bible reflects the fact that God has created our humanity in his image. The critic who ignores the creative-redemptive implications of the biblical message demonstrates a perverse willingness to engage in a critical activity that depends for its integrity on the very thing the critic seeks to deny. Using one's critical and intellectual faculties to deny that God has come in the flesh to save us is a corruption of the very processes demanded by the presence of this God in Christ. On the other side, the evangelical who is so wary of critical process that the critical demands of the incarnate Word and his inscripturated word are neglected is suffering a severe loss of gospel-based perspective.

Fifth, the hermeneutics of the doing of Christ the fulfiller demand that we read carefully the Old Testament as a testimony to what he achieves in his life, death and resurrection. The gospel is so dependent on its Old Testament antecedents that we can easily overlook some of its dimensions and texture if we do not examine carefully what it is that he fulfils. The Old Testament perspective on eschatology, with all the rich variety of its expectations of restoration, finds its resolution in the work of Christ. This includes the promises concerning the people, the place of God's kingdom, the temple and redemption from sin. It also includes the promises of a new creation. Thus the hermeneutics of the cross of Christ must go beyond the forgiveness of sin to the new creation. Jesus on the cross was putting the universe back together; he was restoring the true order of creation.

---

6. Vern Poythress, 'Christ the Only Savior of Interpretation', *WTJ* 50 (1988), p. 306.

The hermeneutics of the glorification of Christ

Although I have dealt briefly with the significance of the resurrection in chapter 3, I must now refer to it again in this summary of gospel-centred hermeneutics. The resurrection, ascension and glorification of Christ are summed up in his session and intercession: the fact that he sits with the Father in glory and intercedes for his people. The glorification of Christ is the glorification of the God/Man. Jesus lived bodily, died bodily, rose bodily and ascended to the Father bodily. Any attempt to diminish the bodily resurrection and ascension is docetic. It undermines the whole integrity of God's plan for the created order. It destroys the meaning of the saving life of Christ and of our justification. It produces a diminished gospel of the salvation of the soul without the body. It is the paganizing Gnostic heresy all over again. What, then, are the hermeneutical implications of Christ's exaltation?

First, the bodily resurrection and ascension of Jesus demonstrate the absolute acceptance by the Father of the work of his incarnate Son. The resurrection shows that Jesus is the one true human who has merited life with the Father. The fact that Jesus is God demands the resurrection, but the resurrection is not primarily a demonstration of that fact. The New Testament stresses that the resurrection of Christ is the paradigm for our own resurrection on the day of Christ's return. The unity/distinction between the Christ who died and the Christ who appeared after his resurrection is the demonstration of our destiny in the resurrection of the body.

Second, the resurrection and ascension of Jesus show that the coming of the kingdom is not a literalistic fulfilment of Old Testament promise.[7] The New Testament provides a clarification of the structure of the end times that is not explicit in the Old Testament. The disciples' question in Acts 1:6 evokes an answer that asserts the coming of the kingdom of God in the world through the preaching of the gospel. Whereas the Old Testament predicts one coming of the Day of the Lord, the gospel shows that in fact the Day of the Lord and the coming of the end happens in three ways: in the person and work of Jesus of Nazareth; in the gospel age between Pentecost and the second coming; and in the consummation when Christ returns. This has immense implications for the way we read the Bible, as it indicates that Christ in his gospel is the definitive hermeneutic key to all Scripture and all reality.

---

7. See my discussion of evangelical literalism (Zionism) in ch. 12.

Third, the ascension is the signal that the kingdom of God demands the missionary role of the church. John's vision of the saved of Israel and the nations gathered around the throne of God and the Lamb (Rev. 7) does not imply that these gatherings happen by themselves. This is the result of the gospel going into all the world, a gospel that is to the Jew first but also to the Gentile. Such a mission would be empty of meaning if the Spirit of Christ who sends his people into the world with the word of life does not also guarantee that this same word will be translated and communicated with understanding. The New Testament's exposition of the Christian life, of the nature of the church and its place in the world, is what it is because of the resurrection and ascension.

Fourth, the ascension of the resurrected Christ demands a hermeneutic of the lordship of Christ. It reminds us that Christ rules now in this world through the gospel as it is preached. We should be encouraged greatly by the fact that the power that is restoring the glories of God's kingdom in the entire creation is the word entrusted to us. On the one hand, we should tremble at our responsibility to be faithful. On the other hand, we should remain confident that our weak efforts are justified in Christ, that our hermeneutical stumblings are redeemed and that, in the final analysis, it is the Lord himself who is the evangelistic speaker of his powerful and saving word. The same Lord commissions his servants to relay his gospel as the power of God for salvation to everyone who believes. We use all our hermeneutic skills within the framework of the authority of God and his word in order to 'take every thought captive to obey Christ' (2 Cor. 10:5).

The hermeneutics of the Spirit of Christ

The Enlightenment was anthropocentric and thus lost sight of any role for God, or indeed need for his existence. Christian theism accepts that all three persons of the Trinity are involved in the divine act of communication. If it is the role of God the Father to be the communicator, and the role of God the Son to be the communication, the divine Word, what is the role of God the Holy Spirit?[8] The Spirit was given at Pentecost because of the merits of Christ. He is known as the Spirit of Christ.

First, the Holy Spirit is necessary for the word to be a demonstration of the Spirit and power (1 Cor. 2:4–5). Calvin spoke of the internal witness of the Spirit in bringing us to salvation and enabling us to understand God's Word.[9]

8. Grant Osborne, *The Hermeneutical Spiral* (Downers Grove: IVP, 1991), pp. 340ff.

Fred Klooster points out that 'Paul repeatedly prayed that the believers might grow in understanding and knowledge through the illumination of the Holy Spirit (1 Cor. 2:2; 2 Cor. 4:4–15; Eph. 1:17–19; Phil. 1:9–11; Col. 1:9–13).'[10] The Spirit enables us to overcome the effects of sin on the rational process. He makes it possible for the reader to use every faculty to discern the word of God and apply it. He makes it possible for us to overcome our God-denying pre-understanding in order to discern the meaning of the word, but he does not guarantee that we will do so. There is an aspect of our wills being inclined to receive such guidance. Moreover, the Bible does not say that the unbeliever cannot intellectually interpret it quite accurately. Larkin says that Paul locates the barrier in the area of evaluation rather than cognition.[11] The Holy Spirit deals with the inability of the unbeliever to accept the implications of the text. However, we cannot ignore the fact that submission to the text in faith brings its own rewards of cognition.

Second, the doctrine of inspiration reminds us that it was the role of the Holy Spirit to guarantee that what was written down by human authors was what God intended to be written down. Chalcedon is useful here to remind us that there is unity of Spirit and human word, but no fusion. Another implication of the doctrine of inspiration is that if we can speak of authorial intent, we must take into account the intent of both the divine and the human authors. But we cannot separate these, as some would do, by constructing a divine canon within the total human canon. The distinction between the divine intention and the Spirit-inspired human author's intention is, of course, vital to the recognition of typology or *sensus plenior*. Thus the human authors of the Old Testament spoke of things whose full significance was not revealed until the coming of Christ. Then the promise that the Spirit would lead the apostles into all truth speaks to both the writing of the apostolic witness in the New Testament and to the people of God who are put into contact with Jesus, who is the truth.

Third, it is the Spirit who regenerates and brings the believer to faith in the saving work of Christ. The Spirit's regenerating work is a sovereign act of

---

9. Calvin, *Institutes of the Christian Religion*, trans. Ford Lewis Battles (Philadelphia: Westminster, 1960), 1.7.4–5; 9.1–3.

10. F. H. Klooster, 'The Role of the Holy Spirit in the Hermeneutic Process: the Relationship of the Spirit's Illumination to Biblical Interpretation', in E. D. Radmacher and R. D. Preus (eds.), *Hermeneutics, Inerrancy, and the Bible* (Grand Rapids: Zondervan, 1984), pp. 451–472.

11. William Larkin, *Culture and Biblical Hermeneutics* (Grand Rapids: Baker, 1988), p. 289.

grace, yet it issues in our conscious act of faith and trust. This is the radical hermeneutic realignment whereby we start to view all things in the light of the revelation in Christ. The Spirit's continuing work in the believer is not done apart from our conscious effort; he works through our minds and wills. Hence the function of the many exhortations and commands of Scripture is to be the instruments of the Spirit's working in us. Many aspects of Christian behaviour we learn and perform with little reflection. Others require dedicated effort and the application of will. So with hermeneutics: the Spirit's work in us renews our minds. Conversion results in a reorientation of thinking, so that we see the world as God's world. Facts that once were thought to be watertight arguments against the reality of God and his saving work in Christ now are interpreted as eloquent testimonies of these. Every fact becomes a fact related to the God and Father of our Lord Jesus Christ. One such 'fact' is the Bible. The renewing of our minds means that we begin to view the Bible in a new way. What was once perhaps regarded as a pack of fairy stories and impossible propositions is now gladly accepted as the word of life, the very oracles of God. This represents a massive paradigm shift in interpretation that affects every text of the Bible, and it is a gift of the Spirit.

Christians and their Bible: hands-on hermeneutics

I would certainly not want to imply by a study such as this that only the hermeneutically literate specialist can make a go of reading the Bible with understanding. As the Reformers rejected Erasmus's idea of erudition, so we must reject the notion that only an educated specialist can understand Scripture. The whole Protestant ethos of the Bible for the people, along with the doctrine of the clarity of Scripture, would make nonsense if this were to be so. Yet there is clearly a place for teachers in the biblical view of the communal life of believers, a communal life that has important ramifications for one's private or family life. We acknowledge this by providing quite rigorous training for those who aspire to be teachers, preachers, pastors and evangelists in our churches.

One of the functions of the teaching office is to engender confidence in the Scriptures and to teach the laity to read the Bible intelligently. Of course, the notion of a devotional life that usually involves Bible reading and prayer is not restricted to evangelicals. Evangelicals, however, usually do place great emphasis on personal spiritual exercises in the home, individually and in family groups. Yet sometimes the aids that are employed, and the habits learned, foster techniques and strategies that can be more of a hindrance than a help to understanding the Bible. Bible-reading 'devotional' programmes do not always promote the understanding of the principles inherent in good understanding of the word of God that I have been discussing. For example, less than helpful approaches would include the following.

- Bible-reading programmes consisting of unrelated snippets drawn from all parts of Scripture with no obvious connection other than perhaps some loose thematic relationship.
- Programmes without any perspective on the 'big picture' of the history of redemption (salvation history).
- Strategies that aim at extracting a devotional thought for the day rather than allowing the text to dictate the outcome.
- Lack of any real hermeneutical guide for the application of texts, especially Old Testament passages.
- Asking the wrong questions of the text: usually something like, 'What does this teach me about myself?' before asking, 'How does this passage testify to Christ?'

It should also be clear from this study that there is no one, simple, right strategy for reading and understanding the Bible. This is the implication of the hermeneutical spiral and the fact that the various dimensions we have discussed are inter-related in such a way that it is impossible to say which has absolute priority. Nevertheless, it is possible to distinguish the various elements of the whole process and to suggest a tentative logical order. The Bible reader needs to understand that all of us develop or adopt strategies and practices that become second nature to us. Preachers and teachers will be motivated by different situations and aims in the selection of passages and series of passages in their programmes. The same could be said of the private or family practices of Bible reading. Most evangelicals in these situations would, I believe, favour some kind of planning of reading and preaching programmes. The idea of the worried preacher in his study late on a Saturday evening, pen in hand and a blank sheet of paper in front of him, being asked by his concerned wife, 'Still nothing, dear?' is almost ludicrous.

In the light of the matters I have discussed, and by way of summary, I want now to suggest some basic practical concerns in the application of evangelical, gospel-centred hermeneutics. Some, perhaps most, of these matters become second nature to the maturing Christian and to the experienced teacher or preacher. It is right, however, that we should from time to time examine our practices and consider in what way we can improve them. The hermeneutical spiral implies successive stages of reassessment and adjustment as we improve and move towards maturity and conformity to the gospel. Thus what follows is not a daily or weekly checklist, but a proposed list of some important ingredients in understanding the Bible.

Preparation

1. We should aim at a programme that is meaningfully motivated. This may be a short- or long-term programme. For example, a pastor should, I believe, major on expository preaching which focuses on larger portions, even whole books of the Bible. At regular intervals he may pause to give some variety in topic and focus.[12] One's private Bible reading can follow a similar approach. In my own Bible reading I have recently completed a programme of reading through the ESV from Genesis to Revelation. My usual programme is to read through whole books. One should aim both to understand better the unity of the Bible, and to get close to the distinct parts of the text.
2. We should understand our presuppositions and motives for coming to the text. It takes some self-discipline to address these matters. It may be helpful occasionally to list the assumptions one makes about the Bible that motivate the study of it. An even more arduous exercise would be to try occasionally to understand and to write down the reasons for holding such assumptions and how one could defend them.
3. Christian theistic presuppositions will imply the need to pray as part of the process of reading and understanding the Bible. It is not just another book we are dealing with, but the word of God written under the supervision of the Holy Spirit. We are dependent on the Spirit's help. Humble submission to the word will be prayerful submission.
4. We should aim to improve our understanding of the overall narrative structure, the 'big picture' of salvation history. The better our grasp of this, the better our understanding will become of who and what Jesus is.

Making contact with the text

5. We begin reading by making initial contact with our chosen text, bearing in mind that a text may involve taking in a much larger portion of Scripture than the usually designated few verses of devotional readings. As we get a feel for this text we should prayerfully sit under it, letting it

12. But let the preacher beware. Most congregations would find it intolerably tedious to have to sit through an uninterrupted series of thirty or forty sermons on Leviticus or Judges. Programmes should be intelligently crafted with a mind to the capabilities of the congregation, not to mention their life expectancy!

speak in its own way to us. I have usually found it useful to write my own précis of the passage. Such a tentative summary may need adjusting in the light of further reading.

6. The trained teacher or preacher might make contact with the text in the original languages, and perhaps make a translation which can then be compared with the English text that is being used. Every preacher who has done some study in Hebrew and Greek should at least be able to check up on points of translation as the need arises, even if the ability to make a full translation is lacking. Those who have no Hebrew or Greek can gain by reading the passage in at least two different standard versions.[13]
7. Consider the extent and nature of the literary unit. This is important for a general understanding of the context of the passage. The immediate limits of the unit will be the discourse or prophetic oracle, the narrative or the poetic unit, and so on, of which the chosen text may be a part. The wider context is, of course, the whole book in which the text is found. Finally there is the canonical context of the whole Bible.

Close reading of the text

8. Begin the task of a close and analytical reading of the text. How close one goes depends on one's training and the purpose of the reading. Teachers and preachers in preparation of texts will, of course, need to go into this process in more detail than others. But close reading is not restricted to the linguistically and theologically trained. Even children can begin to understand such issues as:
   - the historical and cultural context of biblical texts;
   - different kinds of literature in the Bible (genre identification);
   - how stories work (narrative analysis, history of redemption);
   - how God is active in the message of the text (biblical theology).

   The teacher or preacher will need to be more attentive to the linguistic, literary, historical and theological matters referred to in this study. It may not need to be said that sermons should not be filled with background information.
9. A close reading will include the placing of the text in its context. The tentative setting of bounds and contexts, as indicated in point 7 above, is an ongoing process that is part of the hermeneutical spiral in close

13. For the reasons given in ch. 18, I stress standard versions rather than simple English versions or one-person translations.

reading. The function of the text in the wider discourse and in the book in which it occurs raises, in turn, questions of how the book functions in the whole canon of Scripture.

10. The main hermeneutical goal is the relating of the text to the person and work of Jesus Christ. This necessitates consideration of all the dimensions of the biblical revelation, and especially biblical theology. I cannot stress too much how important biblical theology is to the process of understanding and applying the Bible. It should be taught to children at home and in Sunday schools. It belongs in adult Bible groups, and it should be intentionally preached from the pulpits. Above all, it should be a required course in every theological seminary and Bible college. Biblical theology provides the link between any part of the Bible and its centre in Christ. This is an essential perspective for valid application of ancient texts to modern readers and hearers. Even those texts, especially in the New Testament, that are written specifically as direction to Christians, are derivative of the place of Jesus Christ in the scheme of things.[14]
11. The last stage in the function of hermeneutics is the determination of what kind of application the text's teaching can have to the Christian. Its application to the original hearers/readers will be relevant, but should not be the final stage. In each situation it is the present hearers' relationship to Christ that is important. The general application to modern Christians must be redirected to the specifics of the actual person or group to whom it is being addressed.

The use of study helps

Any Christian can employ helps in the form of a Bible dictionary, an introductory work on biblical theology and a basic book on doctrine. Teachers exercise their ministry to the wider church in many ways. One method that has a venerable pedigree is the writing of commentaries. While the practice of writing textual notes or glosses goes back into the early church, the Reformation undoubtedly gave a great impetus to the development of the modern genre of Bible commentary. In the light of everything I have said in this book about the eclipse of the gospel, it is clear that commentaries are written from a whole range of presuppositional stances. Not only that, but even if we concentrate on commentaries by evangelical authors, they will have

---

14. I have dealt with this in more detail in my book *Preaching the Whole Bible as Christian Scripture* (Grand Rapids: Eerdmans; Leicester: IVP, 2000).

different aims. The common denominator of all commentaries is the exegesis of the text, but the emphases may differ markedly. Hence there is great need for discernment in the purchase and use of commentaries. It should not be necessary to say that recourse to commentaries and other helps is best left until later rather than sooner in the process of dealing with a text. For the Christian lay person, priority should be given to finding and using a good one-volume commentary on the whole Bible written from an evangelical point of view. Most informed lay people will go beyond this basic minimum and acquire commentaries on individual books. Trained theologians can be expected to use with discernment a wider range of helps from a variety of theological stances.

Other helps that can be used in assisting us in the practicalities of reading and understanding the Bible include works about the background history and culture and a good Bible dictionary. In my opinion, every Bible reader should read a basic book on biblical theology in order to keep the big picture in mind. Furthermore, every Christian parent, again in my view, should aim to help their children to understand the 'big picture' as a preamble to biblical theology.[15] It is sad that so much telling of Bible stories to children ends up as exercises in moralizing and even legalism. The evangelical pastor will find great joy in discovering that there are members of the congregation whose Christian reading has advanced beyond flimsy devotionals or self-help and self-improvement books. Lay people can develop a taste, even a passion, for good theology and doctrine. Although it is true that all expository preaching is doctrinal, the systematic study of doctrine needs to be encouraged.

---

15. There is a revived interest in biblical theology for children although, as yet, good published works are few and far between. One recent addition is the excellent book by David Helm, *The Big Picture Story Bible*, with illustrations by Gail Schoonmaker (Wheaton: Crossway, 2004).

EPILOGUE

Hermeneutics is about reading God's word with understanding so that we might be conformed more and more to the image of Christ. Whatever the role of the intellect in hermeneutics, it is still a spiritual discipline. We can go further and remind ourselves that any spiritual discipline is characterized by spiritual warfare. We are not engaged in Trivial Pursuit or in solving lateral thinking problems in order to feel some sense of satisfaction if we can come up with acceptable answers to various questions and problems. That is why biblical interpretation must be seen as the spiritual struggle that it is. The New Testament describes our warfare in many ways, one of which is in Paul's exhortation, 'Put to death therefore what is earthly in you' (Col. 3:5), followed by the instruction, 'Let the word of Christ dwell in you richly' (Col. 3:16). Furthermore, it is not only the sinfulness within us that is the problem, for the Bible makes clear that the goal of the great deceiver himself is to seduce us to worship the beast (Rev. 13:14). Resistance to this assault requires endurance and confidence in the saving power of him who has written the names of his own people in the Lamb's book of life (Rev. 13:8; 14:12).

Gospel-centred interpretation is eschatological, in that the gospel shows that the meaning of every part of the Bible is given its ultimate expression in terms of the final outcome of the gospel – the *eschaton*. This is nowhere more powerfully expressed than in the final book of the canon of Scripture, the book of Revelation. Throughout this study I have emphasized the overarching nature of God's sovereign rule, his creation and control of all things, and his grand plan which the gospel effects. Gospel-centred hermeneutics is above all the endeavour to understand the meaning of any aspect of reality, including the Bible, in the light of him who is the Light of the World. The book of Revelation testifies to the relationship of the gospel of our Lord Jesus Christ to the grand plan of God which gives significance to all things.[1]

The hermeneutical centre of Revelation is found in the description of the scroll and the Lamb (Rev. 5). As we learn in subsequent chapters, the opening of the scroll with its seven seals leads to revelations about the great spiritual realities that existed at the time John wrote to the persecuted churches in Asia Minor, and the realities that will lead to the consummation of all things. John weeps because no one is found who is worthy to break the seals and open the scroll. Then he is directed to the conquering Lion of the Tribe of Judah as such a one, but he sees in its place a slain Lamb. The hymn that follows sums up our hermeneutical quest:

> Worthy are you to take the scroll
>   and to open its seals,
> for you were slain, and by your blood you ransomed people for God
>   from every tribe and language and people and nation,
> and you have made them a kingdom and priests to our God,
>   and they shall reign on the earth.
> (Rev. 5:9–10)

Through the death of the risen and ever-living Lamb of God, the plan to sum up all things in Christ is achieved. All ultimate meaning is found in this, and in this alone. The hymn extols the kingdom of priests to our God who shall reign on the earth. With this recalling of the promise to Moses (Exod. 19:4–6), the big picture of salvation history is presented as the context within which all human history is played out and interpreted. Hermeneutics is a priestly pursuit for the people of God. We go to God on behalf of the church and seek to bring the word of life to the church on behalf of God. We cannot begin to understand what such a priesthood involves apart from the perfect priesthood of Jesus. The humanity of the priest reminds us that all aspects of biblical interpretation that pertain to the Bible's human face are utterly indispensable. But, in the end, it is God himself who has provided the perfect Priest on our behalf,

---

1. See Graeme Goldsworthy, *The Gospel in Revelation* (Exeter: Paternoster, 1984), now in *The Goldsworthy Trilogy* (Carlisle: Paternoster, 2000).

and through that Priest he has given us the definitive interpretation of reality.

As John describes how the breaking of the seals leads first to the seven angelic heralds with their trumpets, so these in turn lead to the revealing of judgments that must precede the coming kingdom. Yet constantly John reminds us that the ultimate reality is the outworking of the gospel, both in salvation and in judgment. The suffering church in the world is redeemed, and its justified members are seen in white robes. These are 'the ones coming out of the great tribulation. They have washed their robes and made them white in the blood of the Lamb' (Rev. 7:14). In this double process of redemption and judgment, which began at the fall and will end at the consummation, meaning is established, clarified, crystallized and finally made unavoidable.

Christian hermeneutics focuses on the Bible, because through the Bible we gain understanding of the whole of reality. The Bible is God's way of connecting us with redemption and thus of reconnecting us with himself. It is God's way of showing us ourselves and the world. It is God's way of showing us his rule over all creation and thus over all people. It is God's way of establishing and sustaining fellowship with his Son and, through him, with himself. Any hermeneutic exercise that does not have as its focus and aim that we should know the only true God, and Jesus Christ whom he has sent (John 17:3), is finally abortive. That is the prayer of Christ for his people and thus is the goal that we know will be reached.

Christian hermeneutics, then, can never be an end in itself, or even a means of reaching the wrong ends. Everyone needs the place to stand, a reference point for the understanding of anything. The gospel is the one true beacon, but like any beacon it must be directional if it is truly to guide. That is why the definitive hermeneutical key stands in time between the promises of the Old Testament and the consummation promised in the New Testament. We take our bearings on all three together, and thus have a sure path to a safe haven. The end of these endeavours is for us reached in the Saviour and his gospel. But he himself has pointed us to the dimension of eternal life. Just as we need hermeneutic justification and sanctification, so also we look forward to hermeneutic glorification. As Christ infallibly interpreted the word of the Father, so also we, when we are finally transformed into the image of Christ, will know as we are known. We will truly know God as he intends; we will know Christ in his glory, who will nevertheless always be the Lamb who was slain; we will know the fullness of the new creation; and we will know ourselves as we are known. The hermeneutical problems that distance us from the word and its meaning will be no more. In describing the city of God, John says:

> No longer will there be anything accursed, but the throne of God and of the Lamb will be in it, and his servants will worship him. They will see his face, and his name will be on their foreheads. And night will be no more. They will need no light of lamp or sun, for the Lord God will be their light, and they will reign forever and ever. (Rev. 22:3–5)

The purpose of God's word is to bring us to God through the salvation that is in Christ. It does this by revealing his plan and purpose, by conforming us more and more to the image of Christ, and by providing the shape of the presence of God with his people through the Spirit of Christ. When that purpose is perfectly achieved as described in John's vision of the eternal glory of the kingdom of God, our hermeneutical task will have been accomplished, by grace alone, through faith alone, in Christ alone, who has been made known to us by Scripture alone. And all this will resound to the glory of God alone.

BIBLIOGRAPHY

ADAM, A. K. M. (1995), *What is Postmodern Biblical Criticism?*, Minneapolis: Fortress.

ALLEN, DIOGENES (1985), *Philosophy for Understanding Theology*, London: SCM.

ALLERT, CRAIG D. (2004), 'What Are We Trying to Conserve? Evangelicalism and *Sola Scriptura*', *EQ* 76/4.

ALLISON, C. F. (1994), *The Cruelty of Heresy*, London: SPCK.

ALLISON, G. (1995), 'Speech Act Theory and its Implications for the Doctrine of the Inerrancy/Infallibility of Scripture', *Philosophia Christi* 18/1, pp. 1–23.

ALTHAUS, PAUL (1966), *The Theology of Martin Luther*, Philadelphia: Fortress Press.

ALTER, ROBERT (1981), *The Art of Biblical Narrative*, New York: Basic Books.

ANDERSON, B. (ed.) (1969), *The Old Testament and Christian Faith*, New York: Herder & Herder.

AVIS, P. (ed.) (1986), *The Science of Theology*, Basingstoke: Marshall, Morgan and Scott.

BAHNSEN, G. (1995), 'The Concept of Self-deception in Presuppositional Hermeneutics', *WTJ* 57/1.

BAKER, D. L. (1991), *Two Testaments, One Bible*, 2nd edn, Leicester: IVP.

— (1976), 'Typology and the Christian Use of the Old Testament' *SJT* 29.

BARR, JAMES (1961), *Semantics of Biblical Language*, Oxford: Oxford University Press.

— (1999), *The Concept of Biblical Theology: An Old Testament Perspective*, London: SCM.

BARTH, KARL (1959), *Protestant Thought from Rousseau to Ritschl*, New York: Harper & Row.

BARTHOLOMEW, CRAIG (1998), 'Babel and Derrida: Postmodernism, Language and Biblical Interpretation', *TB* 49/2, pp. 305–328.

BARTHOLOMEW, CRAIG and MICHAEL GOHEEN (2004), *The Drama of Scripture: Finding Our Place in the Biblical Story*, Grand Rapids: Baker.

BARTHOLOMEW, CRAIG, C. GREEN and K. MÖLLER (eds.) (2000), *Renewing Biblical Interpretation*, SHS, vol. 1, Carlisle: Paternoster; Grand Rapids: Zondervan.

— (2001), *After Pentecost: Language and Biblical Interpretation*, SHS, vol. 2., Carlisle: Paternoster; Grand Rapids: Zondervan.

— (2003), *'Behind' the Text: History and Biblical Interpretation*, SHS, vol. 4, Carlisle: Paternoster; Grand Rapids: Zondervan.

— (2004), *Out of Egypt: Biblical Theology and Biblical Interpretation*, SHS, vol. 5, Milton Keynes: Paternoster; Grand Rapids: Zondervan.

BATTLES, F. L. (1980), *Analysis of the Institutes of the Christian Religion of John Calvin*, Grand Rapids: Baker.

BEALE, G. K. (ed.) (1994), *The Right Doctrine from the Wrong Texts? Essays on the Use of the Old Testament in the New*, Grand Rapids: Baker.

BECKER, JOACHIM (1965), *Gottesfurcht im Alten Testament*, Rome: Papal Biblical Institute.

BECKWITH, ROGER (1985), *The Old Testament Canon of the New Testament Church*, Grand Rapids: Eerdmans.

BERKHOF, HENDRIKUS (1966), *Christ the Meaning of History*, Grand Rapids: Baker.

BERKHOF, LOUIS (1979), *Introduction to Systematic Theology*, Grand Rapids: Baker (reprinted from 1932 edition).

— (1950), *Principles of Biblical Interpretation*, Grand Rapids: Baker.

BERKOUWER, G. (1954), *The Person of Christ*, Grand Rapids: Eerdmans.

— (1975), *Holy Scripture*, Grand Rapids: Eerdmans.

BIRD, C. L. (2000), 'Typological Interpretation within the Old Testament', *CJ*, January.

BLOMBERG, CRAIG (1987), *The Historical Reliability of the Gospels*, Leicester: IVP.

BRAATEN, CARL (1966), *History and Hermeneutics*, New Directions in Theology Today, vol. 2., Philadelphia: Westminster.

BRATCHER, ROBERT G. (1978), 'One Bible in Many Translations', *Interpretation* 32/2.

BRAY, GERALD (1978), 'Can We Dispense With Chalcedon?', *Themelios*, January.

— (1984), *Creeds, Councils and Christ*, Leicester: IVP.

— (1987), 'Theology in the Church: Unity and Diversity in Christian Theology', in N. M. de S. Cameron (ed.), *The Challenge of Evangelical Theology*, Edinburgh: Rutherford House.

— (1996), *Biblical Interpretation Past and Present*, Leicester: Apollos.

BRECK, JOHN (2001), *Scripture in Tradition: The Bible and its Interpretation in the Orthodox Church*, Crestwood, NY: St Vladimir's Seminary Press.

BRIGHT, JOHN (1967), *The Authority of the Old Testament*, London: SCM.

BROWN, COLIN (1968), *Philosophy and the Christian Faith*, Downers Grove: IVP.

— (1987), *History and Faith*, Leicester: IVP.

BROWN, HAROLD O. J. (1984), *Heresies*, New York: Doubleday.

BROŽ, JAROSLAV (2002), 'From Allegory to the Four Senses of Scripture: Hermeneutics of the Church Fathers and of the Christian Middle Ages', in Petr Pokornỹ and Jan Roskovec (eds.), *Philosophical Hermeneutics and Biblical Exegesis*, Tübingen: Mohr Siebeck.

BRUCE, F. F. (1968), *This is That: The New Testament Development of Some Old Testament Themes*, Exeter: Paternoster.

BUTTRICK, G. A. (1963), *Christ and History*, New York: Abingdon.

CAIRNS, EARL (1968), 'Philosophy of History', in Carl F. H. Henry (ed.), *Contemporary Evangelical Thought*, Grand Rapids: Baker.

CALLAHAN, J. P. (1996), '*Claritas Scripturae*: The Role of Perspicuity in Protestant Hermeneutics', *JETS* 39/3, pp. 353–372.

— (2001), *The Clarity of Scripture: History, Theology and Contemporary Literary Studies*, Downers Grove: IVP.

CALVIN, J. (1960), *Institutes of the Christian Religion*, trans. Ford Lewis Battles, Philadelphia: Westminster.

CARABINE, DEIRDRE (1995), 'A Dark Cloud: Hellenistic Influences on the Scriptural Exegesis of Clement of Alexandria and the Pseudo-Dionysius', in Thomas Finan and Vincent Twomey (eds.), *Scriptural Interpretation in the Fathers: Letter and Spirit*, Dublin: Four Courts Press.

CARSON, D. A. (1984a), 'A Sketch of the Factors Determining Current Hermeneutical Debate in Cross-Cultural Contexts', in D. A. Carson (ed.), *Biblical Interpretation and the Church: Text and Context*, Carlisle: Paternoster.

— (1984b), *Exegetical Fallacies*, Grand Rapids: Baker.

— (1985), 'The Limits of Dynamic Equivalence in Bible Translation', *ERT* 9, pp. 200–213.

— (1995), 'Current Issues in Biblical Theology: A New Perspective', *BBR* 5, pp. 17–41.

— (1996), *The Gagging of God*, Grand Rapids: Zondervan; Leicester: Apollos.

— (2000), 'Systematic Theology and Biblical Theology', in T. D. Alexander and B. S. Rosner (eds.), *New Dictionary of Biblical Theology*, Leicester: IVP.

CHAN, S. (1985), 'Second Thoughts on Contextualisation', *ERT* 9/1.

CHAPPLE, ALLAN (2003), 'The English Standard Version: A Review Article', *RTR* 62/2, August, pp. 61–96.

CHILDS, BREVARD (1970), *Biblical Theology in Crisis*, Philadelphia: Westminster.

— (1992), *Biblical Theology of the Old and New Testaments*, London: SCM.

CLARK, GORDON H. (1977), *Three Types of Religious Philosophy*, Nutley, NJ: Presbyterian and Reformed.

CORLEY, BRUCE, STEVE LEMKE and GRANT LOVEJOY (eds.) (2002), *Biblical Hermeneutics: A Comprehensive Introduction to Interpreting Scripture*, 2nd edn, Nashville: Broadman and Holman.

COTTERELL, PETER (1995), 'Hermeneutics: Some Linguistic Considerations', *Evangel*, Autumn.

COTTERELL, PETER and MAX TURNER (1989), *Linguistics and Biblical Interpretation*, London: SPCK.

CRIM, KEITH R. (1978), 'Old Testament Translations and Interpretation', *Interpretation* 32/2.

CULLMANN, OSCAR (1951), *Christ and Time: The Primitive Christian Conception of Time and History*, London: SCM.

— (1967), *Salvation as History*, London: SCM.

CURRID, J. D. (1994), 'Recognition and Use of Typology in Preaching', *RTR* 53/3.

DAVIES, J. R. (1997), 'Biblical Precedence for Contextualisation', *ERT* 21.

DAVIS, JOHN JEFFERSON (1984), *Foundations of Evangelical Theology*, Grand Rapids: Baker.

DE SENARCLENS, JACQUES (1963), *Heirs of the Reformation*, Library of History and Philosophy, London: SCM.

DEMBSKI, W. A. (1995), 'The Fallacy of Contextualism', *Themelios* 20/3.

DEWEY, DAVID (2004), *Which Bible? A Guide to English Translations*, Leicester: IVP.

DOCKERY, D. S. (1992), *Biblical Interpretation Then and Now*, Grand Rapids: Baker.

— (ed.) (1995), *The Challenge of Postmodernism: An Evangelical Engagement*, Wheaton: Bridgepoint.

DODD, C. H. (1952), *According to the Scriptures: The Substructure of New Testament Theology*, London: Nisbet.

DORMAN, T. (1996), 'The Case against Calvinist Hermeneutics', *Philosophia Christi* 19/1.

DULLES, AVERY (1971), *A History of Apologetics*, New York: Corpus Instrumentorum.

DUMBRELL, WILLIAM (1984), *Covenant and Creation*, Exeter: Paternoster.

DUNNETT, W. M. (1984), *The Interpretation of Scripture*, Nashville: Thomas Nelson.

EBELING, GERHARD (1963), *Word and Faith*, Philadelphia: Fortress Press.

EDGAR, W. (1995), 'Van Til and Schaeffer Compared', *WTJ* 57/1.

— (1996), 'Without Apology: Why I am a Presuppositionalist', *WTJ* 58/1.

EDWARDS, D. L. (1988), with a response from John Stott, *Essentials: A Liberal-Evangelical Dialogue*, London: Hodder and Stoughton.

EICHRODT, W. (1961), *Theology of the Old Testament*, London: SCM.

ELLIS, E. E. (1957), *Paul's Use of the Old Testament*, Edinburgh: Oliver and Boyd.

ELLUL, JACQUES (1970), *The Meaning of the City*, Grand Rapids: Eerdmans.

ERICKSON, M. J. (1993), *Evangelical Interpretation: Perspectives on Hermeneutical Issues*, Grand Rapids: Baker.

ERICSON, NORMAN R. (1978), 'Implications from the New Testament for Contextualization', in D. J. Hesselgrave (ed.). *Theology and Mission*, Grand Rapids: Baker.

EVANS, C. A. (1992), 'Typology', in J. Green and S. McKnight (eds.), *Dictionary of Jesus and the Gospels*, Downers Grove: IVP.

EVANS, G., ALISTER MCGRATH, ALLAN GALLOWAY (1986), *The Science of Theology*, *The History of Christian Theology*, vol. 1, Grand Rapids: Eerdmans.

EVANS, G., ALISTER MCGRATH, ALLAN GALLOWAY (2000), 'New Testament Use of the Old Testament', in T. D. Alexander and B. S. Rosner (eds.), *New Dictionary of Biblical Theology*, Leicester: IVP.
EYRE, E. C. (1979), *Effective Communication*, Made Simple series, London: W. H. Allen.
FEE, GORDON D. (1991), 'Exegesis and the Role of Tradition in Evangelical Hermeneutics', *Crux* 27/1, reprinted in *ERT* 17/4 (1993).
FEINBERG, JOHN S. (ed.) (1988), *Continuity and Discontinuity: Perspectives on the Relationship Between the Old and New Testaments*, Westchester: Crossway.
FLANNERY, AUSTIN P. (ed.) (1975), *Documents of Vatican II*, Grand Rapids: Eerdmans.
FLEMMING, DEAN (2005), *Contextualization in the New Testament: Patterns for Theology and Mission*, Leicester: Apollos.
FRAME, J. M. (1985), 'Van Til and the Ligonier Apologetic', *WTJ* 47/2.
— (1987), *The Doctrine of the Knowledge of God*, Phillipsburg: Presbyterian and Reformed.
— (1994), *Apologetics to the Glory of God*, Phillipsburg: Presbyterian and Reformed.
FRANCE, R. T. (1971), *Jesus and the Old Testament*, London: IVP.
FROELICH, K. (1984), *Biblical Interpretation in the Early Church*, Philadelphia: Fortress.
FRYE, NORTHROP (1983), *The Great Code*, London: Ark.
GAFFIN, RICHARD (1976), 'Systematic Theology and Biblical Theology', in John H. Skilton (ed.), *The New Testament Student and Theology*, Nutley, NJ: Presbyterian and Reformed.
— (1978), *The Centrality of the Resurrection*, Grand Rapids: Baker.
GEISLER, NORMAN (1988), 'Current Chalcedonian Christological Challenges', *ERT* 12/4.
GIBSON, R. J. (ed.) (1997), *Interpreting God's Plan: Biblical Theology and the Pastor*, Carlisle: Paternoster.
GLENNY, W. E. (1997), 'Typology: A Summary of the Present Evangelical Discussion', *JETS* 40/4.
GOLDINGAY, JOHN (1994), *Models for Scripture*, Grand Rapids: Eerdmans.
— (1996), *Models for Interpretation of Scripture*, Grand Rapids: Eerdmans.
— (2003), *Old Testament Theology*, vol. 1., Downers Grove: IVP.
GOLDSWORTHY, GRAEME (1981), *Gospel and Kingdom: A Christian Interpretation of the Old Testament*, Exeter: Paternoster, now in *The Goldsworthy Trilogy*, Carlisle: Paternoster, 2000.
— (1984), *The Gospel in Revelation*, Exeter: Paternoster, now in *The Goldsworthy Trilogy*, Carlisle: Paternoster, 2000.
— (1986), '"Thus says the Lord!" – The Dogmatic Basis of Biblical Theology', in P. T. O'Brien and D. G. Peterson (eds.), *God Who Is Rich in Mercy: Essays Presented to D. B. Knox*, Homebush West: Lancer.
— (1987), *Gospel and Wisdom: Israel's Wisdom Literature in the Christian Life*, Exeter: Paternoster, now in *The Goldsworthy Trilogy*, Carlisle: Paternoster, 2000.
— (1991), *According to Plan*, Leicester: IVP.

— (1998), 'Is Biblical Theology Viable?', in R. J. Gibson (ed.), *Interpreting God's Word, Explorations*, vol. 11, Carlisle: Paternoster, 1998.

— (2000a), *Preaching the Whole Bible as Christian Scripture*, Grand Rapids: Eerdmans; Leicester, IVP.

— (2000b), 'Biblical Theology and the Shape of Paul's Mission', in Peter Bolt and Mark Thompson (eds.), *The Gospel to the Nations: Perspectives on Paul's Mission*, Leicester: Apollos; Downers Grove: IVP.

— (2002), 'Ontology and Biblical Theology – A Response to Carl Trueman's Editorial: "A Revolutionary Balancing Act"', *Themelios* 28/1, pp. 37–45.

— (2003a), *Prayer and the Knowledge of God*, Leicester: IVP.

— (2003b), 'Evangelicalism and Biblical Theology', in Craig Bartholomew, Robin Parry and Andrew West (eds.), *The Futures of Evangelicalism*, Leicester: IVP.

— (2003c), 'The Ontological and Systematic Roots of Biblical Theology', *RTR* 62/3, December.

— (2004), 'He's a Jam Doughnut? When is a Translation not a Translation?', *The Briefing*, issue 306, March.

GOPPELT, LEONHARD (1982), *Typos: The Typological Interpretation of the Old Testament in the New*, German ed. (1939) trans. Donald Madvig, Grand Rapids: Eerdmans.

GRANT, R. M. and D. TRACY (1989), *A Short History of the Interpretation of the Bible*, 2nd edn, Minneapolis: Fortress.

GRATSCH, E. J. (ed.) (1981), *Principles of Catholic Theology*, New York: Alba House.

GREEN, GARRETT (2000), *Theology, Hermeneutics and Imagination*, Cambridge: Cambridge University Press.

GREEN, J. B. (1995), 'Discourse Analysis and New Testament Interpretation', in J. B. Green (ed.), *Hearing the New Testament: Strategies for Interpretation*, Grand Rapids: Eerdmans, pp. 175–196.

— (2002), 'Scripture and Theology: Failed Experiments, Fresh Perspectives', *Interpretation* 56/1, p. 18.

GREIDANUS, SIDNEY (1988), *The Modern Preacher and the Ancient Text*, Grand Rapids: Eerdmans; Leicester: IVP.

— (1999), *Preaching Christ from the Old Testament: A Contemporary Hermeneutical Method*, Grand Rapids: Eerdmans.

GRENZ, STANLEY J. (1995), 'Star Trek and the Next Generation: Postmodernism and the Future of Evangelical Theology', in David Dockery (ed.), *The Challenge of Postmodernism: An Evangelical Engagement*, Wheaton: Bridgepoint.

— (1996), *A Primer on Postmodernism*, Grand Rapids: Eerdmans.

GRENZ, STANLEY J. and R. E. OLSON (1992), *20th Century Theology: God and the World in a Transitional Age*, Downers Grove: IVP.

GRIFFITH THOMAS, W. H. (1951), *The Principles of Theology: An Introduction to the Thirty-Nine Articles*, London: Church Book Room Press.

GROGAN, G. (1986), 'The Relationship Between Prophecy and Typology', *SBET* 4/1.

GRUENLER, R. G. (1991), *Meaning and Understanding: The Philosophical Framework for Biblical Interpretation*, Foundations of Contemporary Interpretation, vol. 2, Grand Rapids: Zondervan.

HAMILTON, K. (1965), *Revolt Against Heaven: An Enquiry Into Anti-Supernaturalism*, Grand Rapids: Eerdmans.

HARGREAVES, MARK (1996), 'Telling Stories: The Concept of Narrative and Biblical Authority', *Anvil* 13/2, pp. 127–139.

HARRELSON, W. (1991), 'Inclusive Language in the NRSV', *ERT* 15/4.

HARRISVILLE, R. and W. SUNDBERG (1995), *The Bible in Modern Culture: Theology and Historical-Critical Method from Spinoza to Käsemann*, Grand Rapids: Eerdmans.

HASEL, G. (1984), 'The Relationship Between Biblical Theology and Systematic Theology', *TJ*, NS vol. 5, no. 2, pp. 113–127.

HAUSER, ALAN J. and DUANE F. WATSON (eds.) (2003), *A History of Biblical Interpretation, Vol. 1, The Ancient Period*, Grand Rapids: Eerdmans.

HEBERT, A. G. (1941), *The Throne of David*, London: Faber and Faber.

HENDERSON, IAN (1952), *Myth in the New Testament*, Studies in Biblical Theology, no. 7, London: SCM.

HENRY, CARL F. H. (1990), *Toward a Recovery of Christian Belief*, Wheaton: Crossway.

HESSELGRAVE, DAVID (1984), 'Contextualization and Revelational Epistemology', in Earl D. Radmacher and Robert D. Preus (eds.), *Hermeneutics, Inerrancy, and the Bible*, Grand Rapids: Zondervan.

HESSELGRAVE, DAVID and EDWARD ROMMEN (1989), *Contextualization, Meanings, Methods, and Models*, Grand Rapids: Baker.

HIEBERT, PAUL (1987), 'Critical Contextualization', in J. I. Packer (ed.), *The Best in Theology*, Carol Stream: Christianity Today.

HOFFECKER, W. A. and G. S. SMITH (eds.) (1986), *Building a Christian World View*, vol. 1, Phillipsburg: Presbyterian and Reformed.

HOFMANN, J. C. K. VON (1959), *Interpreting the Bible*, Minneapolis: Augsburg.

HOUSE, PAUL (1998), *Old Testament Theology*, Downers Grove: IVP.

HOWELL, RICHARD (2001), 'Transcultural Theology and Contextualisation', *ERT* 25/1.

HUGENBURGER, G. P. (1994), 'Introductory Notes on Typology', in G. K. Beale (ed.), *The Right Doctrine from the Wrong Text?*, Grand Rapids: Baker.

HUGHES, ARCHIBALD (1958), *A New Heaven and a New Earth*, London: Marshall, Morgan and Scott.

HUGHES, PHILIP EDGCUMBE (1980), 'Crucial Biblical Passages for Christian Apologetics', in E. R. Geehan (ed.), *Jerusalem and Athens: Critical Discussions on the Philosophy and Apologetics of Cornelius Van Til*, Phillipsburg: Presbyterian and Reformed.

IMASOGIE, O. (1985), 'Contextualisation and Theological Education', *ERT* 9/1.

JACOBSEN, DOUGLAS (1987), 'The Rise of Evangelical Hermeneutical Pluralism', *CSR* 16/4.

JEANROND, WERNER (1991), *Theological Hermeneutics*, New York: Crossroad.

JENSEN, P. F. (2002), *The Revelation of God*, Leicester: IVP.

JESSOP, GORDON (1976), *No Strange God*, London: Olive Press.

JOHNSON, E. E. (1990), *Expository Hermeneutics: An Introduction*, Grand Rapids: Academie.

KAISER, W. C. and M. SILVA (1994), *An Introduction to Biblical Hermeneutics: The Search for Meaning*, Grand Rapids: Zondervan.

KARLBERG, M. W. (1985), 'Legitimate Discontinuities Between the Testaments', *JETS* 28/1.

KEEGAN, T. J. (1985), *Interpreting the Bible: A Popular Introduction to Biblical Hermeneutics*, New York: Paulist Press.

KEITH, GRAHAM (1998), 'Can Anything Good Come Out of Allegory? The Cases of Origen and Augustine', *EQ* 70/1.

KLEIN, W. W., C. BLOMBERG and R. L. HUBBARD (1993), *Introduction to Biblical Interpretation*, Dallas: Word Publishing.

KLOOSTER, F. H. (1984), 'The Role of the Holy Spirit in the Hermeneutic Process: the Relationship of the Spirit's Illumination to Biblical Interpretation', in E. D. Radmacher and R. D. Preus (eds.), *Hermemeutics, Inerrancy, and the Bible*, Grand Rapids: Zondervan.

KNIGHT, G. A. F. (1957), *A Christian Theology of the Old Testament*, London: SCM.

KNOX, D. B. (1960), 'Propositional Revelation the Only Revelation', *RTR*, XIX/1.

KÖNIG, ADRIO (1989), *The Eclipse of Christ in Eschatology: Toward a Christ-Centered Approach*, Grand Rapids: Eerdmans.

KRABBENDAM, H. (1984), 'The New Hermeneutic', with responses by James Packer and Royce Gruenler, in E. D. Radmacher and R. D. Preus (eds.), *Hermeneutics, Inerrancy, and the Bible*, Grand Rapids: Zondervan.

KRENTZ, E. (1975), *The Historical-Critical Method*, Philadelphia: Fortress.

KUGEL, J. L. and R. GREER (1986), *Early Biblical Interpretation*, Philadelphia: Westminster.

LADD, G. E. (1974), *A Theology of the New Testament*, Grand Rapids: Eerdmans.

LAMPE, G. W. H. and K. J. WOOLLCOMBE (1957), *Essays on Typology*, London: SCM.

LANE, ANTHONY N. S. (2002), *Justification by Faith in Catholic-Protestant Dialogue*, London: T. & T. Clark.

LARKIN, WILLIAM (1988), *Culture and Biblical Hermeneutics: Interpreting and Applying the Authoritative Word in a Relativistic Age*, Grand Rapids: Baker.

— (1992), 'Culture, Scripture's Meaning, and Biblical Authority', *BBR* 2, p. 174.

LATOURELLE, R. (1966), *Theology of Revelation*, New York: Alba House.

LAURENTIN, RENE (1977), *Catholic Pentecostalism*, London: Darton, Longman and Todd.

LEVENSON, J. D. (1993), *The Hebrew Bible, the Old Testament, and Historical Criticism*, Louisville: Westminster John Knox Press.

LEWIS G. R. and B. A. DEMAREST (1994), *Integrative Theology*, Grand Rapids: Zondervan.

LINNEMANN, ETA (1990), *Historical Criticism of the Bible: Methodology or Ideology?*, Grand Rapids: Baker.

LINTS, RICHARD (1993), *The Fabric of Theology: A Prolegomenon to Evangelical Theology*, Grand Rapids: Eerdmans.

LONG, V. PHILIPS (1987), 'Toward a Better Theory and Understanding of Old Testament Narrative', *Presbyterion* 13/2.

— (1994), *The Art of Biblical History*, Grand Rapids: Zondervan.

LONGENECKER, RICHARD (1975), *Biblical Exegesis in the Apostolic Period*, Grand Rapids: Eerdmans.

LONGMAN III, TREMPER (1987), *Literary Approaches to Biblical Interpretation*, Foundations of Contemporary Interpretation, vol. 3, Grand Rapids: Zondervan; Leicester: Apollos.

LUNDIN, ROGER, (ed.) (1997), *Disciplining Hermeneutics: Interpretation in Christian Perspective*, Grand Rapids: Eerdmans; Leicester: Apollos.

— (1999), *The Promise of Hermeneutics*, Grand Rapids: Eerdmans.

LUNDIN, ROGER, ANTHONY THISELTON and CLARENCE WALHOUT (1985), *The Responsibility of Hermeneutics*, Grand Rapids: Eerdmans.

MAIER, GERHARD (1977), *The End of the Historical-Critical Method*, St. Louis: Concordia.

— (1994), *Biblical Hermeneutics*, trans. Robert Yarborough, Wheaton: Crossway.

MARSHALL, I. H. (1994), 'Climbing Ropes, Ellipses and Symphonies: the Relation Between Biblical and Systematic Theology', in Philip E. Satterthwaite and David F. Wright (eds.), *A Pathway into the Holy Scripture*, Grand Rapids: Eerdmans, pp. 199–219.

— (2004), *Beyond the Bible: Moving from Scripture to Theology*, Grand Rapids: Baker; Milton Keynes: Paternoster.

MARTIN, ROBERT (1989), *Accuracy of Translation and the New International Version*, Carlisle, PA: Banner of Truth.

MAURO, PHILIP (n.d.), *The Hope of Israel: What Is It?*, Swengel, PA: Reiner.

MCBRIEN, R. P. (1970), *Catholicism*, Minneapolis: Winston Press.

MCCARTNEY, D. G. (1988), 'The New Testament's Use of the Old Testament', in Harvie M. Conn (ed.), *Inerrancy and Hermeneutic*, Grand Rapids: Baker.

MCCARTNEY, D. G. and C. CLAYTON (1994), *Let the Reader Understand: A Guide to Interpreting and Applying the Bible*, Wheaton: Bridgepoint.

MCEVOY, JAMES (1995), 'The Patristic Hermeneutic of Spiritual Freedom and Its Biblical Origins', in Thomas Finan and Vincent Twomey (eds.), *Scriptural Interpretation in the Fathers: Letter and Spirit*, Dublin: Four Courts Press.

MCKIM, D. K. (ed.) (1986), *A Guide to Contemporary Hermeneutics*, Grand Rapids: Eerdmans.

— (1998), *Historical Handbook of Major Biblical Interpreters*, Downers Grove and Leicester: IVP.

MCKINNEY, RONALD H. (1985), 'Ricoeur's Hermeneutic and the Messianic Problem', *CSR* 14/3.

McKnight, E. V. (1990), *Post-modern Use of the Bible: The Emergence of Reader-Oriented Criticism*, Nashville: Abingdon.

McQuilken, J. R. (1980), 'Limits of Cultural Interpretation', *JETS* 23/2.

Mickelsen, A. B. (1963), *Interpreting the Bible*, Grand Rapids: Eerdmans.

Miller, Bruce B. (1995), 'Hans-Georg Gadamer and Evangelical Hermeneutics', in Michael Bauman and David Hall (eds.), *Evangelical Hermeneutics*, Camp Hill, PA: Christian Publications.

Moo, D. J. (1986), 'The Problem of *Sensus Plenior*', in D. A. Carson and John Woodbridge (eds.), *Hermeneutics, Authority and Canon*, Leicester: IVP.

Motyer, Steve (1995), 'Evangel on Hermeneutics', *Evangel* 13/3.

Muller, Richard A. (1991), *The Study of Theology: From Biblical Interpretation to Contemporary Formulation*, Foundations of Contemporary Interpretation, vol. 7, Grand Rapids: Zondervan.

Murray, J. (1963), 'Systematic Theology', *WTJ* 26.

Neuner, J. and H. Roos (1967), *The Teaching of the Catholic Church*, ed. Karl Rahner, New York, Alba House.

Nichols, Aidan (1991), *The Shape of Catholic Theology*, Edinburgh, T. & T. Clark.

Nichols, Anthony H. (1988), 'Explicitness in Translation and the Westernization of Scripture', *RTR* 47/3.

— (1992), 'The Fate of "Israel" in Recent Versions of the Bible', in D. Peterson and J. Pryor (eds.), *In the Fullness of Time: Biblical Studies in Honour of Archbishop Donald Robinson*, Homebush West: Lancer.

— (1999), 'Translating the Bible', *TB* 50/1.

Nida, E. A. (1975), 'Implications of Contemporary Linguistics for Biblical Scholarship', in *Language Structure and Translation: Essays by Eugene A. Nida*, Stanford: Stanford University Press, pp. 248–270.

Niesel, Wilhelm (1980), *The Theology of Calvin*, trans. Harold Knight, Grand Rapids: Baker.

Noll, Mark A. (1994), *The Scandal of the Evangelical Mind*, Grand Rapids: Eerdmans; Leicester: IVP.

Ocker, Christopher (1999), 'Medieval Exegesis and the Origins of Hermeneutics', *SJT* 52/3.

O'Collins, Gerald (1981), *Fundamental Theology*, London: Darton, Longman and Todd.

O'Connor, Edward (1975), *The Pentecostal Movement in the Catholic Church*, Notre Dame: Ave Maria Press.

O'Donovan, Oliver (1994), *Resurrection and Moral Order: An Outline for Evangelical Ethics*, 2nd edn, Leicester: Apollos; Grand Rapids: Eerdmans.

Ollenberger, Ben (ed.) (1991), *So Wide a Sea: Essays on Biblical and Systematic Theology*, Elkhart, Indiana: Institute of Mennonite Studies.

OSBORNE, GRANT (1991), *The Hermeneutical Spiral*, Downers Grove: IVP.

PADILLA, R. (1981), 'The Interpreted Word: Reflections on Contextual Hermeneutics', *Themelios* 7/1.

PALMER, RICHARD E. (1969), *Hermeneutics: Interpretation Theory in Schleiermacher, Dilthey, Heidegger, and Gadamer*, Evanston: North Western University Press.

PAYNE, TONY (2001), 'Is This the English Bible We've Been Waiting For?', *The Briefing*, issue 278, November, pp. 13–15.

— (2004), 'The ESV: Two Years On', *The Briefing*, issue 306, March.

PELIKAN, JAROSLAV (1959), *The Riddle of Roman Catholicism*, New York: Abingdon.

PERDUE, LEO G. (1994), *Wisdom and Creation: The Theology of Wisdom Literature*, Nashville: Abingdon.

PETERSON, DAVID (1992), *Engaging with God: A Biblical Theology of Worship*, Leicester: Apollos.

PINNOCK, C. H. and D. BROWN (1990), *Theological Crossfire: An Evangelical/Liberal Dialogue*, Grand Rapids: Zondervan.

PLANTINGA, ALVIN (2003), 'Two (or More) Kinds of Scripture Scholarship', in Craig Bartholomew, C. Green and K. Möller (eds.), *'Behind' the Text: History and Biblical Interpretation*, SHS, vol. 4, Carlisle: Paternoster; Grand Rapids: Zondervan.

PORTER, S. et al (eds.) (1994), *Crossing the Boundaries: Essays in Biblical Interpretation in Honour of Michael D. Goulder*, Leiden: Brill.

POWELL, MARK A. (1990), *What is Narrative Criticism?*, Minneapolis: Fortress.

POYTHRESS, VERN S. (1978), 'Structuralism and Biblical Studies', *JETS* 21/3.

— (1986), 'Divine Meaning of Scripture', *WTJ* 48, pp. 241–279.

— (1987a), *Symphonic Theology: the Validity of Multiple Perspectives in Theology*, Grand Rapids: Academie.

— (1987b), *Understanding Dispensationalists*, Grand Rapids: Academie.

— (1988a), 'God's Lordship in Interpretation', *WTJ* 50, pp. 27–64.

— (1988b), 'Christ the Only Savior of Interpretation', *WTJ* 50, pp. 305–321.

— (1999), *God Centered Biblical Interpretation*, Phillipsburg: Presbyterian and Reformed.

PREUS, J. S. (1969), *From Shadow to Promise*, Cambridge, MA: Belknap Press of Harvard University Press.

PROVAN, IAIN (1998), 'The Historical Books of the Old Testament', in John Barton (ed.), *The Cambridge Companion to Biblical Interpretation*, Cambridge: Cambridge University Press.

PROVAN, IAIN, V. PHILIPS LONG and TREMPER LONGMAN III (2003), *A Biblical History of Israel*, Louisville: Wesminster John Knox Press.

RAMM, BERNARD L. (1962), *Varieties of Christian Apologetics*, Grand Rapids: Baker.

— (1970), *Protestant Biblical Interpretation*, 3rd rev. edn, Grand Rapids: Baker.

— (1973), *The Evangelical Heritage*, Waco: Word Books.

REVENTLOW, H. G. (1986), *Problems of Biblical Theology in the Twentieth Century*, Philadelphia: Fortress.

RICHARDSON, CYRIL (ed.) (1953), *Early Christian Fathers*, Library of Christian Classics, vol. 1, London: SCM.

ROBINSON, D. W. B. (1961), *Jew and Greek: Unity and Division in the Early Church*, Sydney: Inter Varsity Fellowship.

— (1963), 'Who were "the saints"?', *RTR* 22, pp. 45–53.

— (1985), *Faith's Framework: The Structure of New Testament Theology*, Exeter: Paternoster.

— (1997), 'Origins and Unresolved Tensions', in R. J. Gibson (ed.), *Interpreting God's Plan: Biblical Theology and the Pastor*, Carlisle: Paternoster.

RUNIA, KLAAS (1984), *The Present-day Christological Debate*, Leicester: IVP.

RUSHDOONY, R. J. (1978), *The One and the Many: Studies in the Philosophy of Order and Ultimacy*, Fairfax, VA: Thoburn.

— (1979), *The Biblical Philosophy of History*, Phillipsburg: Presbyterian and Reformed.

RYKEN, LELAND (2002), *The Word of God in English: Criteria for Excellence in Bible Translation*, Wheaton: Crossway.

SANCHEZ, D. (2002), 'Contextualization in the Hermeneutical Process', in Bruce Corley, Steve Lemke and Grant Lovejoy (eds.), *Biblical Hermeneutics: A Comprehensive Introduction to Interpreting Scripture*, 2nd edn, Nashville: Broadman and Holman.

SCHAEFFER, FRANCIS (1968), *Escape from Reason*, Downers Grove: IVP.

— (1970), *The Church at the End of the Twentieth Century*, London: Norfolk Press.

— (1972), *He is There and He is Not Silent*, London: Hodder and Stoughton.

SCHMAUS, M. (1968–77), *Dogma*, London and Kansas City: Sheed and Ward.

SCHMID, HANS HEINRICH (1968), *Gerechtigkeit als Weltordnung*, Tübingen: J. C. B. Mohr.

SCOBIE, C. H. H. (1991a), 'The Challenge of Biblical Theology', *TB* 42/1, pp. 31–61.

— (1991b), 'The Structure of Biblical Theology', *TB* 42/2, pp. 162–194.

— (2003), *The Ways of Our God: An Approach to Biblical Theology*, Grand Rapids: Eerdmans.

SCORGIE, GLEN, MARK L. STRAUSS and STEVEN M. VOTH (eds.) (2003), *The Challenge of Bible Translation: Communicating God's Word to the World*, Grand Rapids: Zondervan.

SELL, A. P. F. (1986), *Theology in Turmoil*, Grand Rapids: Baker.

SHIRES, H. M. (1974), *Finding the Old Testament in the New*, Philadelphia: Westminster.

SILVA, MOISÉS (1983), *Biblical Words and Their Meaning*, Grand Rapids: Zondervan.

— (1987), *Has the Church Misread the Bible?*, Foundations of Contemporary Interpretation, vol. 1, Grand Rapids: Academie; Leicester: Apollos.

— (1990), *God Language and Scripture*, Foundations of Contemporary Interpretation, vol. 4, Grand Rapids: Zondervan.

— (1992), 'The New Testament Use of the Old Testament', in D. A. Carson and John Woodbridge (eds.), *Scripture and Truth*, Grand Rapids: Baker.

SINGER, C. G. (1980), 'A Philosophy of History', in E. R. Geehan (ed.), *Jerusalem and Athens*, Phillipsburg: Presbyterian and Reformed.

SMALLEY, BERYL (1964), *The Study of the Bible in the Middle Ages*, Notre Dame: University of Notre Dame Press.

SMITH, J. K. A. (2000), *The Fall of Interpretation: Philosophical Foundations for a Creational Hermeneutic*, Downers Grove: IVP.

SPIVEY, ROBERT (1974), 'Structuralism and Biblical Studies', *Interpretation* 28/2.

STEINMETZ, DAVID C. (1980), 'The Superiority of Pre-Critical Exegesis', *TT* 37/1.

STENDAHL, KRISTER (1962), 'Biblical Theology, Contemporary', *Interpreter's Dictionary of the Bible*, vol. 1, Nashville: Abingdon.

STUHLMACHER, PETER (1979), 'The Gospel of Reconciliation in Christ – Basic Features and Issues of a Biblical Theology of the New Testament', *Horizons in Biblical Theology* 1.

— (1995), *How To Do Biblical Theology*, Allison Park, PA: Pickwick Publications.

SUBILIA, VITTORIO (1964), *The Problem of Catholicism*, The Library of History and Doctrine, London: SCM.

SULLIVAN, FRANCIS (2001), 'The Meaning of Conciliar Dogmas', in Daniel Kendall and Stephen Davis (eds.), *The Convergence of Theology: A Festschrift Honoring Gerald O'Collins SJ*, New York: Paulist Press.

TABER, CHARLES, R. (1978), 'Translation as Interpretation', *Interpretation* 32/2.

TATE, W. R. (1991), *Biblical Interpretation: An Integrated Approach*, Peabody, MA: Hendrickson.

THIELICKE, HELMUT (1966), *Theological Ethics*, Grand Rapids: Eerdmans.

— (1974), *The Evangelical Faith, Vol. 1, Prolegomena*, Grand Rapids: Eerdmans.

THISELTON, ANTHONY C. (1973), 'The Use of Philosophical Categories in New Testament Hermeneutics', *The Churchman* 82/2.

— (1977), 'The New Hermeneutic', in I. H. Marshall (ed.), *New Testament Interpretation: Essays on Principles and Methods*, Grand Rapids: Eerdmans.

— (1980), *The Two Horizons: New Testament Hermeneutics and Philosophical Description with Special Reference to Heidegger, Bultmann, Gadamer, and Wittgenstein*, Exeter: Paternoster.

— (1992), *New Horizons in Hermeneutics*, Grand Rapids: Zondervan.

— (1994), 'Authority and Hermeneutics: Some Proposals for a More Creative Agenda', in P. E. Satterthwaite and David F. Wright (eds.), *A Pathway into the Holy Scripture*, Grand Rapids: Eerdmans.

— (1997), 'Speech-Act Theory and the Claim that God Speaks: Nicholas Wolterstorff's Divine Discourse', *SJT* 50, pp. 97–110.

THOMPSON, MARK (1998), 'Claritas Scripturae in the Eucharistic Writings of Martin Luther', *WTJ* 60.

— (2006), *A Clear and Present Word: The Clarity of Scripture*, Nottingham: Apollos.

TILLICH, PAUL (1967), *A History of Christian Thought*, ed. Carl Braaten, New York: Simon and Schuster.

TOON, P. (1991), 'Inclusive Language: Right or Wrong?', *ERT* 15/4.

TORRANCE, T. F. (1976), *Space Time and Resurrection*, Grand Rapids: Eerdmans.
TURNER, M. (1995), 'Modern Linguistics and the New Testament', in J. B. Green (ed.), *Hearing the New Testament: Strategies for Interpretation*, Grand Rapids: Eerdmans.
VAN LEEUWEN, RAYMOND C. (2001), 'On Bible Translation and Hermeneutics', in Craig Bartholomew, C. Green and K. Möller (eds.), *After Pentecost: Language and Biblical Interpretation*, SHS, vol. 2, Carlisle: Paternoster; Grand Rapids: Zondervan.
VAN RULER, A. A. (1966), *The Christian Church and the Old Testament*, Grand Rapids: Eerdmans.
VAN TIL, CORNELIUS (1967), *The Doctrine of Scripture*, n.p.: den Dulk Christian Foundation.
— (1969a), *A Christian Theory of Knowledge*, Phillipsburg: Presbyterian and Reformed.
— (1969b), *A Survey of Christian Epistemology*, n.p.: den Dulk Christian Foundation.
— (1971), *The Reformed Pastor and Modern Thought*, Nutley, NJ: Presbyterian and Reformed.
— (1974), *An Introduction to Systematic Theology. In Defense of the Faith, Vol. V*, n.p.: Presbyterian and Reformed.
— (1977), *The New Hermeneutic*, Nutley, NJ: Presbyterian and Reformed.
VANHOOZER, KEVIN (1986), 'The Semantics of Biblical Literature', in D. A. Carson and John D. Woodbridge (eds.), *Hermeneutics, Authority and Canon*, Leicester: IVP.
— (1991), 'Christ and Concept: Doing Theology and the "Ministry" of Philosophy', in John Woodbridge and Thomas McComiskey (eds.), *Doing Theology in Today's World*, Grand Rapids: Zondervan.
— (1994a), 'From Canon to Concept: "Same" and "Other" in the Relation Between Biblical and Systematic Theology', *SBET* 12/2, pp. 96–124.
— (1994b), 'God's Mighty Speech-Acts: The Doctrine of Scripture Today', in P. E. Satterthwaite and D. Wright (eds.), *A Pathway into the Holy Scripture*, Grand Rapids: Eerdmans.
— (1995), 'Exploring the World; Following the Word: The Credibility of Evangelical Theology in an Incredulous Age', *TJ* 16 NS, pp. 3–27.
— (1998), *Is There a Meaning in This Text?*, Grand Rapids: Zondervan; Leicester: Apollos.
— (2000), 'Exegesis and Hermeneutics', in T. D. Alexander and B. S. Rosner (eds.), *New Dictionary of Biblical Theology*, Leicester: IVP.
— (2001), 'From Speech Acts to Scripture Acts: The Covenant of Discourse and the Discourse of Covenant', in Craig Bartholomew, C. Green and K. Möller (eds.), *After Pentecost: Language and Biblical Interpretation*, SHS, vol. 2, Carlisle: Paternoster.
— (2005), *The Drama of Doctrine: A Canonical Linguistic Approach to Christian Theology*, Louisville: Westminster John Knox.
VISCHER, WILHELM (1949), *The Witness of the Old Testament to Christ, Volume 1, The Pentateuch*, trans. A. B. Crabtree, London: Lutterworth.

VISCHER, WILHELM (1969), 'Everywhere the Scripture is about Christ Alone', in B. W. Anderson (ed.), *The Old Testament and Christian Faith*, New York: Herder and Herder.

VOLF, M. (1998), 'When Gospel and Culture Intersect: Notes on the Nature of Christian Difference', *ERT* 22/3.

VON RAD, G. (1965), *Old Testament Theology*, vol. 2, Edinburgh: Oliver and Boyd.

VOS, G. (1948), *Biblical Theology, Old and New Testaments*, Grand Rapids: Eerdmans.

VRIEZEN, T. C. (1958), *An Outline of Old Testament Theology*, Oxford: Blackwells.

WARFIELD, B. B. (1956), *Calvin and Augustine*, Philadelphia: Presbyterian and Reformed, new edn 1980.

WATSON, FRANCIS (1997), *Text and Truth: Redefining Biblical Theology*, Grand Rapids: Eerdmans.

WEATHERS, ROBERT A. (1994), 'Leland Ryken's Literary Approach to Biblical Interpretation: An Evangelical Model', *JETS* 37/1, pp. 115–124.

WESTERMANN, C. (ed.) (1963), *Essays on Old Testament Hermeneutics*, trans. James L. Mays, Richmond: John Knox.

WHITE, H. C. (1988), 'Speech Act Theory and Biblical Criticism', *Semeia*, 41.

WILLIAMSON, LAMAR (1978), 'Translations and Interpretation: New Testament', *Interpretation* 32/2.

WILLIAMSON, PETER (2001), *Catholic Principles for Interpreting Scripture: A Study of the Pontifical Biblical Commission's 'The Interpretation of the Bible in the Church'*, Subsidia Biblica 22, Rome: Pontifical Biblical Institute.

— (2003), 'Catholic Principles for Interpreting Scripture', *CBQ* 65/3, July.

WINK, WALTER (1973), *The Bible in Human Transformation*, Philadelphia: Fortress Press.

WOLTERSTORFF, NICHOLAS (1995), *Divine Discourse: Philosophical Reflections on the Claim that God Speaks*, Cambridge: Cambridge University Press.

— (2001), 'The Promise of Speech-act Theory for Biblical Interpretation', in Craig Bartholomew, C. Green and K. Möller (eds.), *After Pentecost: Language and Biblical Interpretation*, SHS, vol. 2, Carlisle: Paternoster; Grand Rapids: Zondervan.

WRIGHT, CRISTOPHER J. (2000), 'Interpreting the Bible among the World Religions', *Themelios*, March.

WRIGHT, G. E. (1952), *God Who Acts: Biblical Theology as Recital*, Studies in Biblical Theology, no. 8, London: SCM.

— (1969), *The Old Testament and Theology*, New York: Harper & Row.

WRIGHT, N. T. (1992), *The New Testament and the People of God*, London: SPCK.

ZIMMERMANN, JENS (2004), *Recovering Theological Hermeneutics*, Grand Rapids: Baker.

ZUCK, ROY (ed.) (1996), *Rightly Divided*, Grand Rapids: Kregel.

INDEX OF NAMES

INDEX OF SCRIPTURE REFERENCES